14.95

DATE DUE

THE POET AND HIS CRITICS

Robert Frost

THE POET AND HIS CRITICS

DONALD J. GREINER

AMERICAN
LIBRARY
ASSOCIATION
CHICAGO
1974

THE POET AND HIS CRITICS

a series of volumes on the meaning
of the critical writings on selected modern
British and American poets

Edited by CHARLES SANDERS, University of Illinois, Urbana

LIBRARY OF CONGRESS CATALOGING IN PUBLICATION DATA
Greiner, Donald J
  Robert Frost.
  (The Poet and his critics)
  Bibliography: p.
  1. Frost, Robert, 1874-1963. 2. Frost, Robert,
1874-1963—Criticism and interpretation—History.
PS3511.R94Z73   811'.5'2   74-19359
ISBN 0-8389-0191-3

This book is
for Ellen
and for Floyd Stovall

Contents

PREFACE   *ix*

ACKNOWLEDGMENTS   *xv*

CHAPTER 1: *Frost the Man: Letters, Biographies, Memoirs*   *1*

CHAPTER 2: *The Early Criticism of Robert Frost*   *66*

CHAPTER 3: *Frost and His Negative Critics*   *109*

CHAPTER 4: *The Literary Heritage of Robert Frost*   *141*

CHAPTER 5: *Robert Frost as Nature Poet*   *207*

CHAPTER 6: *Frost as "Notable Craftsman"*   *249*

ADDITIONAL STUDY GUIDES   *300*

INDEX   *303*

Preface

Like most creative artists, Robert Frost claimed to be both unaware of and uninterested in the criticism of his work. Part of his public mask was that of a gentle farmer-poet who somehow remained above such pedestrian matters as literary gossip and critical debate. But Frost's professed immunity to commentary about his poetry may have had more meaningful causes than the typical aversion of the artist or the demands of the public pose.

His publicized dismissal of reviews and of critical evaluations may have covered his private determination to succeed as a poet in spite of the discouraging opinions of friends and associates. For Frost was nearly forty years old before he found a publishing house willing to print his first book: in 1913 David Nutt of London published *A Boy's Will*. Before 1913 he experienced more than twenty years of unrecognized creative effort which he feared would go for naught. Between his schoolboy poetry of the early 1890s and the appearance of *A Boy's Will* in 1913, Frost found publication for only a few of his poems. Conservative editors of prestigious journals like *Atlantic Monthly* rejected his work, and an uninformed reading public seemed satisfied with the dormant state of American poetry in the first years of this century. Typical of the discouragement he encountered was the comment by Maurice Thompson that Frost should give up writing because the life of a poet was too hard. In 1939 Frost recalled his frustration when he noted that too often the genuine poet must rely solely upon self-appraisal: "For twenty years the world neglected him; then for twenty years it entreated him kindly. He has to take the responsibility of deciding when the world was wrong" (see "Remarks Accepting the Gold Medal of the National Institute of Arts and Letters," *National Institute News Bulletin*, 1939).

Frost's determination to be a poet despite two decades of

neglect suggests that he knew the world was wrong about him. But his frustration went beyond the fairly common story of the youthful artist seeking a public hearing. In addition to the editors and critics who had to be won over, Frost believed that his family and even his future wife, Elinor White, looked askance at his writing. In 1894 he privately printed two copies of *Twilight*, a booklet of five poems, which he hoped would illustrate his potential achievement with poetry. Giving one to his fiancée Elinor, he soon destroyed his own copy when he decided that she failed to recognize and appreciate his talent. Several years later, following marriage to Elinor, he convinced himself, in spite of facts to the contrary, that his grandfather would rather keep him starving on a poor New England farm than support him while he tried to secure his name as a poet.

The point is that Frost's professed unawareness of the criticism of his work was a stance he had to assume publicly, for in his desire to gain recognition he was forced to decide that the public dismissal of his work was unwarranted. Even during the 1912–15 sojourn in England, those years when he found fame with the publication of *A Boy's Will* and *North of Boston*, Frost broke with Ezra Pound, his first influential supporter, over questions of how he should write. Understandably, then, when he found himself lionized as a major author of the New Poetry, he claimed not to care about reviews and criticism. Since the editors and reviewers, and even his family, had been wrong earlier about his chances of succeeding, they would probably be just as mistaken about his art now that he had proved his worth. Frost's lack of concern was a mask which enabled him to hide his lack of confidence. It may also have helped to endear him to a public ready to believe in the myth of Frost, the farmer-poet, but it did not prevent him from privately expressing disappointment, fear, and rage when he disagreed with published evaluations of his poetry. His letters are full of complaints about conservative editors and ignorant critics, and some of his comments amount to tirades against the supposed injustices of unfavorable reviews. For Robert Frost was a poet who could not tolerate criticism. Louis Untermeyer reports that one negative remark, no matter how insignificant, in an otherwise favorable essay could set off Frost's vindictive temper. Perhaps this is why he cultivated the influential critics of his day: Untermeyer, Lascelles Abercrombie, Edward Thomas, W. S. Braithwaite, Amy Lowell, Sidney Cox, Bernard De Voto, and all of the

others who published consistently appreciative remarks about
his work.

The present study is an evaluation of the criticism Frost professed not to take seriously. When appropriate, I have included
the poet's reactions to those essays and reviews which prompted
him to respond. In general the Frost-Susan Hayes Ward/Wil-
liam Hayes Ward correspondence constitutes the rough beginnings of the criticism of the poet. The Wards were responsible
for the initial publication of a Frost poem in a professional journal. Their acceptance of "My Butterfly" for publication in
the *Independent* (1894) was followed by an exchange of letters in which they offered advice and encouragement to the
fledgling author. Although this correspondence meant a good
deal to Frost, it was not legitimate criticism. As noted earlier,
his poetry did not receive formal analysis until the appearance of
A Boy's Will in 1913. Nearly all of the material commented
upon in the following pages dates from the first reviews and
evaluations of *A Boy's Will* and *North of Boston*.

This book is not an annotated bibliography but rather a selective and evaluative study of the criticism, divided into chapters according to the issues peculiar to a consideration of Robert
Frost. Each chapter is in the form of a running text which in-
corporates the elements of bibliography, criticism, and guides
for a study of the poet. Because Frost has been the subject of an
enormous amount of critical writing, I have had to be selective
about which reviews, essays, and books to include for commentary. If the reader finds a favorite article omitted, I can only
apologize and accept responsibility for the omission. Yet in the
six chapters which follow, I have tried to arrange the massive
amount of Frost criticism into divisions that will facilitate an
overview of the available material published between roughly
1913 and 1974. Following each of the chapters I have listed the
references used therein, organizing them alphabetically by author and chronologically where more than one work by an author is cited. Following most chapters is also a list of additional
essays and books which might be consulted but which are not
commented on in the text. The final chapter is followed by a
list of bibliographies, checklists, and collections of essays on
Frost.

The first chapter considers the letters, biographies, and memoirs, material vital to the study of an elusive subject—Frost the
man. The publication of Frost's letters and, especially, of Law-

rance Thompson's biography points out the incredible differences between the real Robert Frost and the public figure so respected and honored by the nation. I make no attempt in this
chapter to define the true Frost story, but I do comment upon
and evaluate the material at hand. Chapter 2 surveys the early
Frost criticism, an area invaluable to an understanding of the
poet's unexpected and sustained reputation, but nevertheless one
generally unknown today to all but the Frost specialist. The
reader will also find that consideration of this material, dating
from 1913–25, amounts to an indirect commentary upon the poetic renaissance which sparked American literature in the 1910s
and '20s. The third chapter evaluates the negative criticism
Frost's work has received. Given the poet's many decades of
high reputation and his countless awards for outstanding
achievement, it is significant that a substantial number of serious
readers dissent. This chapter specifies the reasons for the negative opinions, the areas of Frost's thought and canon which have
proved controversial, and the specific poems which illustrate
what these critics consider to be the poet's flaws.

In chapter 4 Frost's literary heritage is discussed, particularly
the essays and books touching on his relationships with Wordsworth, Emerson, Thoreau, and New England in general. Frost's
own comments upon the three nineteenth-century authors are
considered, as well as the critical articles which contribute to
the developing controversy over whether or not he deserves
to be remembered as a reliable spokesman for the great literary
tradition of New England. Chapter 5 covers the material relevant to the topic most readers think of when they pick up a
Frost poem—Frost as nature poet. Lively debate exists even
here, for many critics consider the poet to be either a leftover
Emersonian whose poems celebrate a sense of reconciliation between man and nature, or a modern writer whose poems illustrate contemporary man's fears of alienation. The final chapter
takes up Frost's essays and recorded talks which contribute to
an understanding of his theory of poetry. Because most of this
material was published in obscure journals, it remains generally
unknown even to specialists in American literature. More unfortunate, perhaps, is the mistaken belief of many readers that
Frost had no significant new ideas about poetry. This regrettable
opinion is widespread, largely the result of the poet's refusal to
collect his prose or to increase his comments on the art of poetry. I hope that this chapter will provide the reader with an
opportunity to determine the scope of Frost's theory. Relevant

critical articles are also discussed to illustrate how his artistic principles have been interpreted and accepted.

I should point out that this study was written for both educated readers and specialists in literature. For this reason I have tried to unite bibliographical comprehensiveness with a guide to the criticism. In general I have not only selected and arranged but also evaluated and judged because I believe that the interested reader deserves more than just a list of the pertinent material. The risk of encountering objections to some of my evaluations seems to me negligible when the need for an overview of the Frost criticism is considered. For it seems likely that Frost's achievement, like that of all major authors, is bound to undergo reevaluation: he has been dead for more than a decade, and the centennial celebration of his birth is upon us.

Acknowledgments

Acknowledgments are a pleasure to write. This book was supported in part by a grant from the University of South Carolina Research and Productive Scholarship Fund. I also thank the students in my seminar on Robert Frost for stimulating me to rethink some of my opinions of the poet. My greatest debt is to Professor Charles Sanders of the University of Illinois for his enthusiastic support and for his comments when editing the manuscript.

Grateful acknowledgment is made to Holt, Rinehart and Winston, Inc., and to Alfred C. Edwards, Executor of the Estate of Robert Frost, for permission to reprint excerpts from the writings and speeches of Robert Frost.

CHAPTER I

Frost the Man: Letters, Biographies, Memoirs

The primary problem facing a commentator on the biographies and memoirs of Robert Frost results from the length of his life. Born on March 26, 1874, and living until January 29, 1963, he crammed into his near ninety years an extraordinarily diverse number of acquaintances, most of whom he influenced in one way or another. Because Frost earned a worldwide reputation as a major poet, many of these acquaintances preserved in print their impressions of and experiences with him. Thus the task of selecting, from so many, the memoirs to receive comment and evaluation in this chapter is indeed difficult. The problem of evaluation is particularly touchy because Frost was so adept at manipulating his friends. Depending on what he wanted or on the pose he wished to suggest at the time, he presented various personalities and characters to different people. Many of them recorded their personal experiences with Frost, with the result that for a long time objective commentary was lacking.

In addition Frost, despite his protests to the contrary, was a skilled and prolific letter writer. To date there are four separate volumes of letters collected and edited by four different people. While there is necessarily some overlap in these collections, a reading of the four volumes shows that Frost often used his letters to create multiple versions of a single event. All of the variations are important, for they add to the composite view of this complex man. Yet while helping to round out our conception of his personality, these different versions often make it difficult to pinpoint which of Frost's friends and correspondents knew the "real" man.

The purpose of this chapter, then, is not to sort out the true story of Robert Frost from the various anecdotes and biographical discrepancies but to comment on and evaluate the material at hand. The countless impressions—farmer, benign poet, cranky old man, jealous artist—which Frost left with his friends will be noted. But no effort will be made to say which of the impressions is the correct one, for each of these authors clearly expresses his memory of the poet as he knew him. On the other hand, the relative worth of each article and book and its application to the study of Frost will be judged and evaluated. Some of the more serious factual errors will be pointed out as an example of the biographer's carelessness or of the poet's tendency to embroider the facts to suit his private purposes. The authority on Frost's life, and official biographer, was Lawrance Thompson. Because he had access to the materials necessary to establish as reliably as possible the correct biographical facts and chronology of events, his work will be considered the authoritative source when errors in the other biographies and memoirs are noted.

Letters

On October 5, 1937, Robert Frost wrote to Louis Untermeyer, his friend of fifty years, protesting the use of his letters as primary source material for published biographical information. Implying that he probably revealed too much in his private correspondence, he complained: "Say I hate or have come to hate the thought of all the letters I ever wrote. I never intended for them to be kept.... Be easy on me for what I did too emotionally and personally. It spoils letters when it gets so they're undeniably collectors items or biographers material" (Louis Untermeyer, *The Letters of Robert Frost to Louis Untermeyer*, 1963, p. 296). Despite this protest, Frost never forbade the eventual collection and publication of his letters. The only stipulation seems to have been his insistence that they not be published in his lifetime. Yet the hesitancy expressed to Untermeyer was well-founded, for Frost realized how completely he had exposed his personality in the letters.

It is not an exaggeration to say that the "other side" of Frost the man was not generally known until three of the four different volumes of letters appeared shortly after his death. Upon their publication, the public—for years having imagined the artist to be a benign farmer-poet, a genial bard of the nation, and a model to look up to—discovered that Frost was a totally different kind of man. The appearance of the first three volumes particularly all but destroyed the myth of Robert Frost and replaced it with an awareness of his little-known side: the petty jealousies, the rages, the delight in gossip, the vanity and pride, the calculated lies, and the laziness. To understate the reaction, that segment of the public which bothered to read the three editions was shocked.

The myth of Robert Frost, purposely encouraged by the poet and willingly supported by his readers, was an extreme view of him. It was not only false but also misleading and unfair. Yet the reaction in some circles upon awareness of the revelation provided by the letters was in many cases just as extreme. The damage done to the myth was justifiably irrevocable, but the exposé of Frost's less attractive side caused some readers and critics unjustly to reverse the myth's process. Instead of stressing his good points and excluding the bad in order to maintain the public image, as had been the case for fifty years, these readers emphasized the bad qualities and forgot the good. The result, of course, was another distorted picture which oversimplified the many-sided personality of this complex man. Today's readers of Frost now often find themselves being told that a villain wrote the poems. The point is that the reader must keep his perspective and good sense when approaching the letters. No one can now deny that Frost's correspondence reveals him to be jealous, petty, vain, maddening, and spiteful. But the letters also show him to be faithful, generous, concerned, courageous, and wracked by tragedy. The contradictions in the letters reflect the complexities of the man. Once the four volumes are read, the careful reader will find that he has a better understanding of the poet and, most likely, a keener appreciation of the poems.

Margaret Bartlett Anderson's edition of *Robert Frost and John Bartlett: The Record of a Friendship* (1963) is the least comprehensive of the four volumes because its scope is purposely limited. It is nevertheless valuable for its record of Frost as a concerned friend and family man. The daughter of John Bartlett, Mrs. Anderson combines a running commentary with reproductions of the letters to document Frost's relationship with her father, one of Frost's favorite students from 1907 to 1910 when he was teaching at Pinkerton Academy in New Hampshire. After Bartlett graduated and married fellow student Margaret Abbott in 1912, he and Frost kept in touch by letters and visits the rest of their lives. The earliest letter in this collection is Frost's Christmas greeting of 1912; the latest is

dated November 22, 1949. Approximately sixty letters in all
are preserved, of which about thirty-five are also included in
Lawrance Thompson's edition of the *Selected Letters of Robert
Frost* (1964). Eight pages of photographs round out the Anderson volume.

In her preface Mrs. Anderson explains that while the letters
reveal much about Frost the poet, she treasures them more for
what they say about Frost the friend. Evidently her mother
enjoyed reminiscing about those early days with Frost, but Mrs.
Anderson notes that she rarely heard her father talk about the
poet. Bartlett apparently reserved his comments for his fairly
long manuscript "Notes on Conversations," begun in 1932 and
continued after each of Frost's visits. The story of the Frost-
Bartlett friendship is drawn almost exclusively from the letters
and "Notes on Conversations," now housed in the University of
Virginia Library.

Because the letters are not arranged on a page-by-page basis,
but are printed as part of Mrs. Anderson's narrative of the relationship, individual letters in the book are hard to find. The
volume also lacks the marginal notation of dates which is so
useful in a collection of letters. An additional drawback is the
absence of explanatory notes, so that it is often difficult to
determine whether a quoted passage printed as a direct statement by Frost comes from a letter, "Notes on Conversations,"
or Mrs. Anderson's memory of the poet. Happily, however, the
book does have a short index, and the table of contents lists
chronologically dated periods to which specific letters refer.

Except for a few valuable early letters in which Frost sets
down some of his most lucid opinions about his principle of
"sentence sounds," this correspondence does not indulge in the
literary judgments and gossip which enliven the other collections. We see very little of his quick intellect and varied personality. Rather, most of these letters are biographical in nature,
important chiefly for their account of the personal affairs of
the two families. Mrs. Anderson includes a lively record of
Frost's teaching career at Pinkerton when he led the football
cheers, encouraged Bartlett's romance with Margaret Abbott,
and liberated the literature classes from the confinement of prepared assignments. She also prints a light verse by Frost about
John Bartlett in Vancouver, "The Lure of the West," not included in any of Frost's poetry collections.

Perhaps the most enlightening segment of the book focuses
on Bartlett's stay in Vancouver. As a journalist in British

Columbia, he had connections with a number of newspapers and journals. When he wrote to Frost in England and asked for a copy of the poet's first book, *A Boy's Will*, Frost replied with the suggestion that Bartlett purchase fifteen to twenty copies in order to sell them and that he use his newspaper position to secure ads for the book in Canadian papers (June 12, 1913). Frost obviously planned to take advantage of Bartlett's occupation, even to the extent of asking him to buy the books directly from the publisher (David Nutt) in order to convince Mrs. Nutt that he had been "discovered" in the Far West. Mrs. Anderson clearly understands Frost's reliance on her father to help establish a reputation for the newly published poet, for she titles chapter 3 of the volume "Plotting Publicity."

Of particular interest are these various publicity campaigns which Frost planned to launch through his former student. He hoped to convince the public that Bartlett was the author of various opinions about *A Boy's Will* which were appearing in several newspapers, but Mrs. Anderson shows that Frost was supplying her father with already published reviews. The poet even went so far as to dictate in one letter the publicity copy for Bartlett to send to the Derry, New Hampshire, newspaper (July 1913). Either because of embarrassment or because of job and family pressures, Bartlett postponed accepting Frost's plan to use him. The poet's efforts to convince Bartlett make up some of the most revealing letters in the collection. Mrs. Anderson includes the full text of the news article which her father finally wrote for the *Derry News* (Nov. 7, 1913), and, thus, she makes one of the first American notices of *A Boy's Will* easily available to Frost students.

Although this section seems to me the most significant in the book, there are other matters of more than passing interest. For example, the notations and comments about other poets and poems which Frost wrote in Bartlett's copy of an issue of *Poetry and Drama* are revealing, as are Frost's expressions of confidence in both his art and his theory of sentence sounds. Also of interest for what it illustrates of Frost's better nature is his expression of genuine concern for his former students when they were poor and floundering. These letters clearly show that while Frost may have imagined many enemies, he was nevertheless a loyal friend to those he liked, willing to supply needed money and sage advice. For those interested primarily in the Frost side of this friendship, the book very likely contains too much of the Bartlett story and their struggle to conquer poverty

and tuberculosis. It is not that Mrs. Anderson neglects Frost for
long stretches, but that she seems determined to give her parents
an equal share of the attention. Finally, many of the letters suggest Frost's talent for self-criticism. In some he apologizes for
wanting to be vindictive toward those he considers his
"enemies." In others he admits that he worries too much about
the published criticism of his poetry. And in one letter he confesses a bad conscience for accepting a salary from Amherst
when he performed very little work (Apr. 7, 1919). There is
no indication, however, that these self-appraisals resulted in
better control of his idiosyncrasies, but they at least testify to his
awareness of his own shortcomings.

A more comprehensive volume than Mrs. Anderson's is *The
Letters of Robert Frost to Louis Untermeyer* (1963). Along
with *Selected Letters of Robert Frost* (Thompson, 1964) and
Family Letters of Robert and Elinor Frost (Arnold Grade,
1972), Untermeyer's edition is one of three truly important
collections of Frost's correspondence. As Untermeyer writes
in his autobiography, *From Another World*, the letters "supplement Frost's life and work in the same way that Keats' letters
round out the poetry" (1939, p. 209). He has gathered together
approximately 270 letters and telegrams covering a span of nearly
fifty years. Despite the fact that Thompson's *Selected Letters*
reprints some of the most important pieces in Untermeyer's
collection, it cannot illustrate the significance of the Frost-
Untermeyer friendship because it includes only about 40 of
the 270 letters.

Untermeyer's editorial work has been highly praised, especially because of the explanatory notes he supplies before or
after nearly every letter which either clarify Frost's own
statements or establish the context of a particular letter. Ar-
ranging the letters chronologically, Untermeyer also specifies
in the top margin of each page the year of the letter. These
notations are indeed helpful, for the volume lacks a table of
contents. But for all of the excellent organization, the collection
has one regrettable omission—an index. These letters are bound
to be an invaluable reference work for any serious reader of
Frost, for they cover a lengthy segment of the poet's creative
years from March 22, 1915, to April 14, 1962. Yet the lack of at
least a subject and name index hampers those who would use the
collection for research.

This one flaw, however, does not hinder the pleasure of reading the letters. Frost leaves himself open in this correspondence,

for he was probably more honest with Untermeyer than with many other friends. Not only the record of a literary era, these letters reveal personality quirks which most of the adoring public remained unaware of until after the poet's death. As Untermeyer writes in the foreword, his book is more than the record of a friendship; it is a "portrait of a man and his mind" which illuminates "the large theories, the small irritations . . . the extraordinarily playful spirit of a great poet." Frost evidently felt completely at ease with Untermeyer, for his letters are full of irony, little jokes, and acid-edged comments about contemporary "rivals." With this friend he drops the mask of the beloved bard to reveal a serious, sometimes petty, often volatile man. Of particular interest are the many variations of poems later published in considerably different form (for example, "Christmas Trees"), plus the poems and light verse which Frost did not choose to include in his collections (for example, "The Seven Arts"). Readers will also find intriguing Frost's evaluations of his own work, particularly the lists he compiled of his favorite poems (see letter for July 9, 1931).

Here, perhaps better than in any other source, Frost discloses his genuine fear of the slightest derogatory remark. Untermeyer shows how Frost could be literally enraged by an "otherwise laudatory review" because of a single brief criticism. The poet wished to ignore published evaluation of his work as well as to avoid the entanglements of literary gossip, but in his letters he could not help reacting to the criticism or rejoicing in the gossip. On one occasion he offers an iron cross to Untermeyer if he will "kill more than so many of my enemies at once" (July 8, 1915), though, as Untermeyer points out, Frost's "enemies" were usually no more than other poets who might be construed as potential rivals. His jealousy of Edgar Lee Masters, James Oppenheim, Amy Lowell, Wallace Stevens, Carl Sandburg, and others is clearly exposed. Untermeyer does not hide this side of Frost, but Lawrance Thompson has shown that in some cases Untermeyer makes a few silent editorial changes, for example substituting "Braithwaite" for "nigger" when Frost expressed his anger at the influential black critic William Stanley Braithwaite.

More important than the revelation of pettiness and irritation are the many memorable passages in which Frost comments on literature. His attack on poetic diction which ends with a concise definition of literature, "words that have become deeds" (July 8, 1915), or his famous comment that a poem "begins

as a lump in the throat" (Jan. 1, 1916), are only two of the
many delightful and thoughtful statements about his art which
he chose to set down in letters as opposed to formal essays. Because of observations like these, the Frost-Untermeyer correspondence is required reading for anyone interested in Frost's
opinions about poetry and literary technique. Still, Frost provides
such full discussions of literature, and Untermeyer so generously
offers to publish, review, and publicly celebrate Frost, that one
wonders if Frost did not enliven his letters with numerous
quotable passages because he knew that his correspondent might
use them in print. In other words, some letters suggest that Frost
was supplying his influential supporter with readymade materials, just as he did earlier with John Bartlett. Untermeyer
admits that he soon excerpted the comment about "a lump in
the throat" with the result that it became included in standard
textbook material on Frost. Curiously enough, Frost later
claims that he does not know how to "advertise" his own work
(Aug. 7, 1916). He must have meant public advertising, for his
correspondence with Untermeyer is full of advertisements.

This volume also reveals a little known side of Frost's personality—his playfulness. Untermeyer explains that over the years
he took special pleasure in Frost's delight in outrageous puns,
literary nonsense, and joking for its own sake. The letters
show the range of this playfulness, from wordplay like "Sin-
ceriously yours" to the parody of Vachel Lindsay entitled "John
L. Sullivan Enters Heaven." They also show Frost's politics to
be reactionary conservative. In many letters, especially those
written during World War I and the depression, he indulges
his extreme distaste for any kind of social work and, thus, pre-
views the political attitude which characterizes many of his
later poems. Untermeyer's generous notes and comments make
these letters particularly interesting, for he was active in liberal
politics as well as a frequent contributor to journals like the
Seven Arts and the *Masses*. Frost liked some of the individuals
working for these liberal magazines, but he disapproved of
Untermeyer's involvement with the "crowd"—Frost's disparaging term for what he called "gangs of do-gooders." Untermeyer
tells us that Frost could not say "brotherhood" without sneering.
This correspondence remains a primary source for those intrigued by the political stance of a poet who remained conservative while witnessing and worrying about his country's deep-
ening involvement in both world affairs and social problems.

Especially revealing are Frost's comments about his own

family which, to be fair, must be read in context. For example, his outburst that his wife "Elinor has never been of any earthly use to me" (Nov. 7, 1917) surprised the public when Untermeyer finally published it in 1963. But perhaps the statement should be taken with a grain of salt, for it appears in a letter to Untermeyer in which Frost characteristically castigates Amy Lowell, this time for her portrait of him in *Tendencies in Modern American Poetry* (1917) and particularly for her picture of Elinor which Frost interpreted to be "the conventional helpmeet of genius." Frost's comment might be more understandable if we remember the difficulty he had in acknowledging the support of those who helped him during his long struggle to gain recognition. Twenty years later, he reversed himself, and in another letter to Untermeyer, he named Elinor as "the unspoken half of everything I ever wrote. . ." (Oct. 4, 1937). The context is again important, for Elinor had just undergone major surgery. The point is that readers of the Frost-Untermeyer correspondence must carefully weigh the evidence before forming judgments about the poet based solely on comments in the letters. His sad and often irritated concern for his sister Jeanie's insanity and his grief at the deaths of his wife, his daughter Marjorie, and his son Carol testify to the enormous number of personal tragedies which he experienced, and, thus, suggest a clue to the dark tone in many of his poems. He wrote to Untermeyer, "Cast your eye back over my family luck and perhaps you will wonder if I haven't had pretty near enough" (Aug. 9, 1947).

Toward the end of the volume, the number of letters a year is noticeably fewer. Untermeyer explains that as the letters between them decreased, the private conversations became more frequent. Accordingly, he includes several paraphrases of selected conversations which are sprinkled with direct quotations from Frost. The entire book is a delight to read. Full of gossip about other established poets, of opinions about various lectureships and poetry prizes, and of judgments and prejudices, the Frost-Untermeyer correspondence remains an informal history of a great period in American poetry. Untermeyer's tone is always correct in the sense that he never tries to grab the spotlight or crowd his subject. Playing down both the merit of his own achievement in the arts and the significance of his unflagging support of Frost, he directs the reader to concentrate on the poet's words and, in so doing, reveals himself to be a model friend.

The most scholarly collection of the letters is Lawrance Thompson's edition of the *Selected Letters of Robert Frost* (1964). It includes approximately 566 letters to 123 people which Professor Thompson spent more than twenty-five years locating and transcribing. Although this volume received some negative criticism when it first appeared, primarily because of sparse explanatory notes and of the editor's need to respect the privacy of many correspondents, *Selected Letters* is without doubt the authoritative general edition of Frost's correspondence. Inviting the reader to "roll his own" biography of Frost, Thompson apparently considers the book to be an indispensable introduction to the official biography he later published. To this end he has selected letters which span the poet's life and which, more importantly, lucidly expose the many sides of the poet's personality glimpsed at earlier in the Anderson and Untermeyer collections: egotism, arrogant pride, jealousy, and envy, in addition to devoted friendship, concern for family, and fascination with poetic theory and the function of poetry.

The edition includes perhaps too many letters to collectors and people of marginal interest to the Frost story, and certain books and titles are occasionally left unidentified. But on the whole the editor has done an exemplary job—scholarly, intelligent, and careful. Unlike Untermeyer and Mrs. Anderson, he supplies a Table of Letters which pinpoints the physical form, the location, and the date of each letter. Examination of this table informs the reader whether the letters are typewritten, holograph, signed, first draft, and so on. As a special boon, Professor Thompson also provides a detailed, seventeen-page chronology of the poet's life, listing the particulars of names, dates, and places, thus clearing up confusions arising from some obscure references in the letters. One of the most complete chronologies of Frost anywhere, it is an absolute necessity for the student who is interested in more than a surface appreciation. Thompson lists, for example, three extant documents which help to establish 1874 as the correct date of Frost's birth, even though for years the poet specified 1875. Beginning the chronology with the birthdates of Frost's parents, the editor lists such pertinent information as the publication dates of Frost's poems published before *A Boy's Will* and the journals in which they appeared, and the various prizes and honorary degrees which the poet received. There are also eight pages of photographic reproductions of Frost's letters to show the idiosyncrasies and alterations in his handwriting.

Acutely aware of the numerous discrepancies occurring in published accounts of Frost's life, Professor Thompson supplies a selective genealogy designed not so much to be complete but to clarify "certain oblique references" in the letters. Much of the genealogical information remains muddled, and Thompson cautions that the facts included must be taken "provisionally." Nevertheless, his account is the most accurate we have. At the conclusion of the genealogy, he publishes a generally unknown poem by Frost, "Genealogical," which describes the exploits of Frost's Indian fighting ancestor, Charles Frost. Dubbing this poem his "Whitmanism," Frost sent it to his early publisher and supporter Miss Susan Hayes Ward in December, 1911.

To top off this extraordinary source of accurate information, Professor Thompson has compiled an index unusual in concept and biographical in nature, easing the task of readers who would only dip into the edition. Perhaps the most unusual—and most helpful—features of the index are the forty-three topical subheads under the primary entry, Robert Lee Frost. Ranging from such topics as "Cowardice" and "Death" to "Poetic Theory," "Sentence Sounds," and "Style," these subheads include not only letter-entry and page number, but also short, pertinent quotations pinpointing the special nature of each particular indexed reference. The index illustrates both the meticulousness of Professor Thompson's scholarship and the genuineness of his desire that the edition be used as a source for scholarly research. Indeed this is a book whose information can be depended upon.

The introduction hints that one of Thompson's primary concerns is to permit the poet to expose his many masks by publishing the heart of his private correspondence. Although aware that Frost could be reserved and reticent in his letters, and thus warning that revelations resulting from reading them must necessarily be limited, Thompson nevertheless argues that the correspondence remains the most intimate means to a glimpse behind the masks. His hope that the letters will be used initially to "clarify discrepancies between the mythic and actual Robert Frost" is certainly realized, for the disclosure of the poet's less than admirable side which this volume permits has encouraged the reevaluation of Frost's public pose. Such a reassessment was inevitable once the poet died, and Thompson's edition of the letters, when used judiciously, can serve as a source of accurate information as well as a restraining device for those who would rush from one false assumption to another, exchanging the public image of Frost as a beloved bard of the nation for the equally inaccurate portrait of him as a talented but despicable man. The correspondence may shock the unsuspecting reader, but it should not undercut admiration for Frost's strong points. Frost himself was aware of his limitations and more than willing to admit them privately. Instead of seriously undermining his reputation, the letters finally earn for him genuine sympathy in place of blind adoration. Reading of his fears of an eventual breakdown such as his sister suffered, of the doubts magnified by his struggle to continue writing when no one would publish him in book form, and of his guilt resulting from the suspicion that the demands of his artistic needs clashed with family responsibilities, we cannot help but sympathize with his efforts to control these inner torments. Thompson goes so far as to call him a "modern Job." The letters support that judgment.

Turning to the letters themselves, the first thing the reader notices is that nearly one hundred letters written to or about Frost are included. These additional letters act both to clarify the context for Frost's own correspondence and to enrich the volume's narrative value. The drama of give and take—of initial letter and response to it—is thus established, adding to the reader's pleasure. In addition to explanatory notes being scattered throughout, the editor further enhances clarity by dividing the letters into ten general sections based on various periods in Frost's life. Each section is prefaced by a statement which sets the scene, lists relevant biographical data, and specifies significant events which affected the poet during the period of time in question. These comments are indeed helpful, but more explanatory notes within the text itself would be useful.

Of particular interest are five letters written by Frost's parents during courtship and early marriage. The entire Frost-Susan Hayes Ward/William Hayes Ward correspondence is also significant, for it documents Frost's earliest successful efforts to find publication and reveals his evaluation of those writers and books which he believed had influenced him. William Hayes Ward was editor of the *Independent*, the first journal to publish a Frost poem. This particular correspondence is pivotal for those who would know Frost's earliest recorded thoughts on the importance of sound in poetry and his efforts to publish before he sailed for England in 1912.

For those who have not read *Robert Frost and John Bartlett: The Record of a Friendship*, the Frost-Bartlett selections in *Selected Letters* are revealing, particularly those letters written from 1912 to 1914 in which Frost not only sets down some of his most eloquent definitions of sentence sounds, but also conducts his own advertising campaign for *A Boy's Will*. Just as significant are the letters which concern Frost's stormy relationship with Ezra Pound, including those written in 1958 to sesure Pound's release from St. Elizabeth's hospital. Thompson prints a previously unpublished free verse parody of Pound which Frost never showed his rival, apparently following poet F. S. Flint's advice not to be antagonistic. Frost's statements about Pound range from acknowledgment of Pound's help to calling him "an incredible ass" (Oct. 24, 1913).

Readers interested in Frost's relationships with other artists in the English-American poetic renaissance will find especially useful the letters to Edwin Arlington Robinson, Amy Lowell, Louis Untermeyer, Edward Thomas, and Lascelles Abercrombie. In a letter to Sidney Cox, Frost criticizes Robert Bridges who was then poet laureate of England. Attacking Bridges' theory that English-language syllables have a fixed quantity of sound that can never be disregarded when reading poetry, Frost uses his disapproval as a starting point from which to launch one of his best expressions of the "sounds of sense" (Jan. 19, 1914). Finally, the short Frost-John Kennedy correspondence is of special interest, as are several of Elinor Frost's letters and the poet's letter to the Amherst College undergraduate newspaper, the Amherst *Student*. Mrs. Frost's letters often comment on people and events that Frost was writing about in his own correspondence. The editor has carefully placed her letters so that they amount to a point of view additional to Frost's own. In the letter to the Amherst *Student*, Frost defines his thoughts about the balance in life between confusion and form (*c*. Mar. 21, 1935).

Some of Professor Thompson's selections might be challenged, for example the letter to Warren R. Brown concerning the death of Frost's dog, as well as the later correspondence to and from book collectors. But ultimately this is an admirable volume, meticulously edited and a pleasure to read. If asked which section within *Selected Letters* contributes the most to Frost scholarship, I would point to the letters in which Frost discusses, illustrates, and elaborates his ideas about poetry and sentence sounds. It is true that these comments are found largely in the earlier correspondence, but they are of such vital significance to an understanding of Frost's poetics that they justify the entire collection. They assume an even greater importance when we recall that Frost, unlike T. S. Eliot or Wallace Stevens, published relatively few articles of criticism and opinion; thus these particular letters remain the primary source for his definitions of sentence sounds, poetic art, and related subjects. Realizing the importance of these letters, Professor Thompson has included a generous sampling.

Arnold Grade's edition of *Family Letters of Robert and Elinor Frost* (1972) offers 183 letters in all, 182 of which are not included in Thompson's *Selected Letters*. Frost himself wrote 133 of these letters; Elinor the remaining 50. As Professor Grade explains in a prefatory note, nearly all of the available and as yet unpublished Frost family correspondences are gathered here; the few letters excluded are omitted at the request of the family. Some letters have clearly marked deletions, again, apparently, at the family's request. Also included are eight pages of photographs, a family chronology, an index modeled on the general pattern established by Professor Thompson, and an afterword designed to suggest a frame of reference or points of departure for the reader. Lesley Frost's short foreword provides an interesting comment by the person now generally accepted as the family spokesman. Fully aware of what she calls "the powerful complexities of my father's genius," Miss Frost nevertheless stresses her mother's role in the family pattern. She explains that Elinor Frost wrote to each child two or three times a week if they were absent from home, and she advances an opinion which must surprise those familiar with Frost's life: that Mrs. Frost was the shaping element of the family. "After she was gone, the family correspondence was immeasurably reduced and we were to discover that what we had assumed was a patriarchy had actually been matriarchal" (1972, p. x).

The editorial apparatus, the longish, knowledgeable introductions, and the well-stocked indexes which we have become accustomed to when reading Frost's biographical materials are largely absent here. Whether or not these omissions are wise depends upon the individual reader's needs. I am one reader, for example, who has no complaint, though judging from what Professor Grade writes in his editor's note, others do. He aparently encountered some pressure to include what he calls "fuller biographical particulars," but honoring his [and Miss Frost's] belief that the letters speak for themselves, he decided to "minimize material extraneous to the letters themselves."

This does not mean that the letters are presented stripped of editorial commentary and necessary clarification. For example, Grade divides the text into three large groups, 1914–28, 1929–37, and 1938–63, and he includes a short explanatory note before each general section. Each letter is carefully annotated so that names, dates, places, and obscure references are pinpointed. And the chronology supplies an outline of the family history. When and if readers complain of Professor Grade's decision to minimize the biographical particulars, they should perhaps recall that two volumes of the official biography and three other volumes of the letters have already been published. Surely it is unnecessary for him to reprint the information about the poet's life which has been uncovered and evaluated within the past decade. Readers of Lawrance Thompson's biography, for example, who remember the story of Frost's sorry treatment of Raymond Holden will better appreciate the poet's letter of February 8, 1920; yet those who have not read the biography will find the reference to Holden clear enough. Resolution of the contradictions and ambiguities revealed in this volume is not the task of Professor Grade but the duty of future interpreters of Frost's life.

It would be useful to know, however, the reason why family letters written before 1914 are excluded. By 1914, Frost was forty years old; he had been married since 1895; and all of his children had been born. Yet these formative years are not represented. Is it because the letters from that period have not survived? If they are available, have they already been published in one of the other editions of the letters and, thus, are accessible to the reader? Did the Frost estate refuse permission to publish them? No explanation is offered, and the reader is left with an edition of family letters which omits without comment the first forty years of the poet's life. It would also have been helpful if the date of each letter had been printed in the top margin of the book's pages in order to facilitate the task of locating a particular letter.

The letters themselves are a pleasure to read, primarily because of what they reveal about Frost the man. For those interested in the poet's style of teaching, there is a pertinent letter in which he outlines his grading policy: "The only out and out failure will be failing to convince me that they have failed to lead a literary life" (Sept. 26, 1917). More significant, perhaps, is his statement on the student's right to learn. Insisting that any attitude a professor takes toward his subject works an injustice on the students, he writes, "The greatest safeguard then of good teaching is to keep it always before the class that the teachers judgement is ridiculously far from final" (Nov. 13, 1917). His unusually strong competitive nature is apparent in his desire to protect Lesley from assumed mistreatment at Wellesley: "But I sha'n't refuse to be dragged into it and even to come down to Wellesley unless it is made more intelligible at once" (Fall 1917). Readers familiar with Frost's belligerent stance toward fellow artists will recognize the consistent tone of the above passage. The tone is all the more remarkable when one realizes that the cause of Frost's anger was not an academic matter but the "injustice" of Lesley's failure to make the Wellesley tennis team.

Compared to *Selected Letters* and to the Frost-Untermeyer correspondence this volume contains relatively little of Frost's ideas about poetry and writers. But the little that is available remains fascinating. Included, for example, are the poet's pronouncements on the value of Latin (Dec. 9, 1917); on how to write an essay (Feb. 17, 1919); and on prosody: "Prosody (spelled with an o) is the science of versification or meters. It is something most modern poets take pride in professing to know nothing about" (Dec. 3, 1917). Of particular interest is a long letter that amounts to a penetrating essay on the genesis of the New Poetry in which Frost urges Lesley to give full credit to Ezra Pound for shaping the movement: "But whatever you do, do Pound justice as the great original" (1934). Also included are variants of "The Aim Was Song" and "Plowmen," the beginning of an uncompleted preface to or appreciation of Hervey Allen's work which adds to the little we have of Frost's expository prose, and copies of Lesley's and Carol's poems.

But whatever the value of these statements on poetry, the volume's greatest importance surely derives from what it shows about Frost's personality. If he appears to be petty, vain, and arrogant in the other editions of the letters, he shows himself to be brave, concerned, and, above all, loving in this volume. The multiple tragedies in his family must have damaged his spirit, yet these letters suggest his strength and determination to endure. Elinor apparently believed that her husband discouraged the children from publishing poetry, and she may have been correct. But letter after letter in this edition finds Frost encouraging the children, praising a particularly good line, and in general boosting confidence. The image fostered here is that of a man with troubled, illness-prone children trying to give advice without seeming to meddle. Evidence of his tact and generosity abound. So many of the letters mention a check he has mailed: twenty-five dollars for a birthday present, one-hundred dollars a month for Carol's widow Lillian, constant financial support for Lesley's latest business venture, paying the transportation costs for the children and grandchildren to visit him. In short, the portrait of him in this volume will balance the less attractive side outlined in *Selected Letters*.

Elinor's correspondence suggests that her married life was restricted to family concerns. She is always remarking on domestic issues—sewing, moving, sending Lesley at Wellesley two dollars and the promise of a cake. The intellectual promise shown by her brilliant high school and college years seems to have been utterly negated by her obligations to the family. The letters do not show her complaining, nor do they hint that she was disappointed. Only once does she speak out: "What a curse is the obligation to write letters! I was not made with the facility about it that some people have, and I often think that trying to write a lot of letters, in addition to my other tasks, is what has brought me down so the last four or five years" (Oct. 1, 1928). Frost acknowledges Elinor's strength, for a year before her death he wrote to Lesley that she had been "too brave." And after her death, upon reading an old letter of Elinor's, he expresses surprise at the sorrow which "runs through all she wrote to you children. . . . She was not as original as I in thought but she dominated my art with the power of her character and nature. I wish I hadnt this woeful suspicion that toward the end she came to resent some thing in the life I had given her" (Mar. 1, 1939). What a long way from the comment to Untermeyer in 1917 that Elinor had never been of "any earthly use" to him.

Though *Family Letters* is an admirable volume, some minor shortcomings exist other than the absence of letters from the 1895–1914 era. A few obscurities are not cleared up by footnotes. What, for example, is the meaning of Elinor's comment to Lesley, "I know that Lillian [Carol's wife] would prefer any place to Florida, because of her fears that Carroll might break loose again over that girl, but Robert seems inclined to ignore that danger..." (Oct. 27, 1937)? What danger? Had another woman attracted Carol? The reader cannot be sure because the necessary editorial commentary is missing. More disappointingly, too few of the letters bear directly upon the family disputes and confrontations following Elinor's death in March, 1938. The Thompson biography leads us to believe that this sad time had a lasting effect upon the poet's relationships

with his surviving children, but the letters here do little to
clarify the issue. Have they been lost or omitted? The reader
cannot tell. Yet on the whole *Family Letters* is so well edited
and contains so much useful information about Frost's life that
it must be consulted if the reader hopes to have a fair assessment
of the poet's character and personality. One sentence from the
book's final letter, dated January 12, 1963, may be the place to
begin such an evaluation. With only two and a half weeks left
to live, Frost wrote to Lesley, "Life has been a long trial yet I
mean to see more of it."

Biographies

Frost has been the subject of five book-length biographies
as well as dozens of memoirs and statements of friendship published in both book and article form. This section will first
discuss the biographies and the accounts of his career as a high
school student in Lawrence, Massachusetts, and as a young
father in Derry, New Hampshire. Comment on the memoirs
and the statements of friendship will follow. Additional source
material is noted at the end of the chapter.

The problem of reliability in the early biographical publications is compounded by both Frost's tendency to mythicize
his life and the biographer's failure to substantiate facts and
anecdotes. Frost was fond of warning that his listeners could
trust him on the poetry but that they should "check up" on
him when he talked about his life. Obviously relishing the
false picture of himself as the successful poet who had to fight
extreme poverty and vindictive relatives, he often embellished
stories of his life with anecdotes which made him look better.
These false statements found their way into the earlier biographies and in turn misled the public. Frost must accept part of
the blame, of course, for some of his stories were told with such
conviction and consistency that the interviewers had no reason
not to trust him. But the initial biographers must nevertheless
assume most of the responsibility for fumbling the basic materials
of any biography, the facts. Frost's anecdotes and versions of
his life could have been checked against the facts and primary
sources to establish credibility, but such was not the case.
The result was that the myth of Robert Frost was fed by the
biographies, the very materials which could have exposed it. A
reliable account of his life was not to be had until Lawrance

Thompson published the first volume of the "official" biography in 1966.

The first full-length biography is Gorham B. Munson's *Robert Frost: A Study in Sensibility and Good Sense* (1927), published with Frost's cooperation. For an account of how Frost invited Munson to write a biography and of his subsequent annoyance at being represented as a new humanist and pure classicist, the reader may consult Lawrance Thompson, *Robert Frost: The Years of Triumph, 1915–1938* (1970, pp. 318–26). Frost was particularly irked by Munson's efforts to make him a disciple of Irving Babbitt, an argument which Munson nevertheless elaborated three years later in "Robert Frost and the Humanistic Temper" (1930).

Munson's thesis and biography are now dated, for Frost had thirty-five years yet to live when it was published. But even the treatment of Frost's life through 1927 is incomplete. The biographer all but skims over such highlights as the poet's courtship of Elinor White and his first attempts to write and publish poetry. As Munson admits, he relies heavily for details and quotations upon John Bartlett, Sidney Cox, and Elizabeth Shepley Sergeant, all of whom later wrote about Frost. He defines "good sense" as "progressive conservatism," an avoidance of "the eccentric or extravagant or fanatic" (1927, p. 20). Attributing Frost's good sense to his association with the humanistic tradition, Munson never revised his evaluation, for years later he restated it in "The Classicism of Robert Frost" (1964).

He begins with speculation about Frost's ancestors and with a discussion of genealogy which ranges all the way back to fifth-century Denmark. There is a particularly full account of the New England Frosts in the seventeenth and eighteenth centuries, including the adventures of Charles Frost, a celebrated Indian fighter in the late 1600s, who became the subject of Frost's aforementioned uncollected poem "Genealogical," first published by Professor Thompson in *Selected Letters.* But this interesting discussion of ancestors is too often marred by such superficial judgments as Munson's reason for the tragedy in Frost's poetry: "If anything planted tragedy in Robert Frost, it must have been, one surmises, the vision of his father, friend on the one hand of Buckley, the notorious blind boss of San Francisco, and on the other of Henry George, with whom for a brief time he managed a single tax newspaper" (1927, p. 26). This speculation hardly approaches the subject.

Munson's story of Frost's adult years before the trip to

England in 1912 is weakened by his ignorance of the tension in
the poet's marriage which he mistakenly describes as a "union
of singular idyllic beauty" (1927, p. 28). He does, however, correctly note the significance of the Derry years (1900–10) as an
important period in Frost's artistic career. The trouble is that
nearly all of Munson's chapter about the Derry years is in the
form of long quotations from letters and notes written by John
Bartlett and Sidney Cox. These comments make interesting reading, but Munson relies on them to the extent of avoiding the
rigors of interpretation and evaluation. Preferring to quote
Bartlett and Cox at length, he lets their statements rest unin-
vestigated and unembellished.

The primary flaw is Munson's failure to flesh out the biography. He repeatedly drops hints about an event or mentions
a series of topics which he discussed with Frost, but he ducks
his obligations as a biographer when he omits the details of these
events and topics. For example, he entices the reader with what
looks to be an especially interesting anecdote: "Frost goes on
to speak of the people he knows: of Lincoln MacVeagh and
Alfred Harcourt when they worked at Holts, of Carl Sandburg's
work and Louis Untermeyer's visits. . . . He tells of a night
spent with Paul Elmer More at Princeton. He inserts somewhere one of Padraic Colum's Irish stories" (1927, p. 81). But
this is all—Munson drops it. And we are never told *what* Frost
said about Sandburg and Untermeyer, or *why* Frost went to
Princeton, or *which* Padraic Colum story Frost told. As a result, the biography is often no more than a series of facts minus
the developed narrative passages which, if handled correctly, can
establish background to the facts and add personality to the subject.

Only in the final two chapters does Munson offer extended
evaluation of Frost's verse form and sentence sounds and of his
"classicism." Some of the ideas in these chapters were previously
worked out in his article "Robert Frost" (1925). He argues
none too convincingly that Frost is a modern representative of
the classical poet because he exhibits a balance and decorum
which have been discovered in his own experience. That is, his
"classicism" results not from adherence to a traditional canon
of literature but from devotion to his accumulation of personal
experience. Because of this classical balance, Frost does not
write exclusively from an intellectual or emotional or instinctive
center, but, instead, makes a "rude partnership" of all three.
And rather than reveal spontaneous self-expression and possibili-

ties in his art, Frost maintains his decorum by imitating nature
and by writing about probabilities (1927, p. 101). Munson's
admiration of Irving Babbitt's New Humanism weakens his
argument and distorts Frost.

In addition, these last two chapters might have been more acceptable had Munson limited his discussion to Frost. But as a
sign of his partisanship, he tries to make his case at the expense
of Ezra Pound and T. S. Eliot. This is too bad, for it has the
unpleasant side effect, intended or not, of making Frost the
sane center of modern American poetry, a kind of ballast
against the lurches of the wilder "free-versers." Rather than
rest content with the energies and rich variations of his subject, Munson gives the appearance of trying to separate the
right way to be new from the wrong. As a result, he mistakenly
places Frost on the side of the "antique" Greeks and "against"
the twentieth century. This opinion is dated—it was wrong even
in 1927.

Perhaps the most useful parts of Munson's biography for today's readers are two appendices. One quotes from a leaflet
distributed by David Nutt, Frost's first publisher, and lists
opinions about *North of Boston* from key British periodicals.
The other is a short extract of a talk on education which Frost
gave at Wesleyan University in December, 1926. On the whole,
however, this biography remains today little more than a spe-
cialty item for those interested in the early efforts of a misguided
critic to place Frost in one camp of poetry against all others.

The second biography of Robert Frost, Elizabeth Shepley
Sergeant's *Robert Frost: The Trial by Existence*, was published
thirty-three years later in 1960. Its germ is her article titled
"Robert Frost: A Good Greek out of New England" (1925),
based largely on her observations at a dinner in honor of the
poet's fiftieth birthday (really his fifty-first) on March 26, 1925,
at the Hotel Brevoort in New York. The article is useful for
its picture of Frost in his first decade of public acclaim. She disputes those who would brand his poetry as local color, and she
describes him as having a "vanishing and peripatetic look..."
and as "a good Greek disguised as a tinkering Yankee sage"
(1925, p. 144). She provides a perceptive account of his need
for isolation and for the desire to avoid such trends as Imagism
and the New Poetry. The article is full of such intelligent, telling
judgments as "the sheer clarity he gives to human lives..."
and "Frost illumines character not by comment or explanation
but through crisis" (1925, p. 146).

Her major work, however, is the full-length biography, a study which is certainly better than Munson's but not without its flaws. She confuses some of the biographical facts, and, as Lawrance Thompson points out, she inaccurately offers many of Frost's anecdotes as direct quotations even though she admits that she wrote them down from memory. For example, Miss Sergeant incorrectly calls the prologue to "La Noche Triste," Frost's high school poem about the Aztecs, a "fragment." With reference to the same poem, Professor Thompson notes that she "mistakenly represents" the meaning of Frost's comments on the battle between the Spaniards and the Aztecs (*Robert Frost: The Early Years, 1874–1915*, 1966, p. 502). Thompson also shows that Miss Sergeant wrongly points to Frost's second year in high school as the time of his first introduction to Elinor White, his future wife, when in fact they did not meet until their senior year. According to Professor Thompson, Frost caught this error in Miss Sergeant's manuscript, but was willing to let it go. She romantically, but mistakenly, tries to connect Frost's early efforts in 1890 to write poetry for the Lawrence *High School Bulletin* with his interest in Elinor. And while she correctly determines the relationship between Frost's flight to the Dismal Swamp of Virginia and North Carolina in 1894 and a rebuff by Elinor, she ruins the description with sentimental rhetoric and a misrepresentation of the season (see Thompson, 1966, pp. 504, 523): "Look at the handsome fellow, scalded by denial of worth, breaking his way through the azaleas and dogwoods of that hilly country, lashing his blazing blue eyes full of tears from the twigs and blossoms, doing minor jobs for bread, breaking his pride all the way" (1960, p. 43).

Other possible pitfalls are avoided in certain cases. When, for example, Miss Sergeant discusses Frost's association with the *Independent*, the first journal to publish his poetry, she bolsters the account by quoting complete letters. Some of the other letters she quotes add value to *The Trial by Existence* because they are not found in any of the four volumes of Frost's correspondence. A case in point is Frost's comment about the famous image in "West-Running Brook" and "The Master Speed": "My favorite theory is that we are given this light time or water for the sole purpose of standing still like a water beetle in any stream of light time or water off any shore we please" (1960, p. xxi).

Writing about the difficulty of interviewing Frost, she notes his tendency to "turn the tables" on the interviewer. He wanted to talk about his life without being pinned down, so he would often deny the truth of one of his own statements when it was read back to him. His attitude clearly complicates the process of verifying facts and anecdotes. She notes that the poet decided not to read her manuscript, though he did examine the early chapters in Parts I and II (covering the period from 1874 to 1916). Thus she admits that some of her dates may be wrong because she relied on Frost, who was often doubtful about dates. It is difficult to check the reliability of Miss Sergeant's biography even when she confesses the probability of errors because she does not include footnotes. Her book contains none of the copious notes and painstaking citations of sources which clarify and expand Professor Thompson's biography of Frost. Without these essential aids, the reader cannot determine where she got the comments by Frost's friends, either to check her sources or to read the quoted passage in its entire context.

Some of the book's better features are the first printing of "Auspex," the publication of a five-line fragment, and a short memoir of Frost by Jean Starr Untermeyer. There are also good accounts of his mother's interest in Henry George's single-tax campaign, in Edward Bellamy's *Looking Backward*, and in socialism in general, all interesting because of the contrast with Frost's own well-known conservative politics and aversion to social programs. Frost is quoted as saying, "No ... I'd hesitate to abolish poverty myself. Too much good has come of it. If it's going to be abolished, let Mrs. Roosevelt do it!" (1960, p. 21). Miss Sergeant also catches, unlike Munson, the tension between Elinor and Frost which always threatened the marriage. Although the marital problems are later completely documented by Professor Thompson, Miss Sergeant at least questions the picture of idyllic romance which was the standard description of their marriage: "A secret rivalry, which the children felt, hid beneath the situation. The farmer-teacher-poet must be primary with his wife; she must be first with the children; nor could Elinor set aside her grief" (1960, p. 74). Still, she misses, probably because Frost failed to tell her, the tragic implications of Elinor's death in 1938 and the deep-seated tensions that it revealed. In addition, there is a lively and informative account of Frost's sojourn in England and of his association with Ezra Pound, William Butler Yeats, Ford Madox Ford, Lascelles Abercrombie, Robert Bridges, and Wilfred Gibson. She takes note of, but tones down, the poet's efforts to use friends to advertise his poetry upon the return to America.

Of particular interest is her evaluation of Frost's teaching

methods, especially those used at Amherst and Michigan: his
desire to learn from students and his refusal to grade a paper for
style or to give a failing grade. She quotes him as saying, "I'm
looking for subject matter, substance in yourselves" (1960, p.
199; see the Amherst publication *Touchstone*, Feb. 1939,
for reminiscences by former students). Apparently Frost was
a natural teacher, one who could offer a variety of subjects
ranging from philosophy to pre-Shakespearian drama and English poetry from Palgrave's *Golden Treasury*. But Miss
Sergeant also documents the other side of Frost the teacher:
the late arrivals to class, the tendency to cut classes when he
could, the preference for informal sessions in his house instead of
regularly scheduled meetings. Although she reveals Frost to be
a born teacher, a man able to convince some of his students that
learning is exciting, she nevertheless points out his laziness, illustrated by his refusal to read a student's work unless it interested
him. He would say, "This is a class in seeing how long I can
keep from reading what you write." Explaining, he would tell
the students that their term grade would be determined by the
first paper they turned in, thus forcing them to accumulate
material which he never read and then make a selection near the
end of the semester. Admitting that he "escaped a lot of drudg-
ery," he claimed that he would "respond" to their work but
not correct it (1960, p. 262).

However, these strong points of *The Trial by Existence* are
once again offset by questionable documentation and shaky analysis. Part of the trouble comes from speculations like the following: "Elinor White's valedictory essay had for subject
'Conversation as a Force in Life.' Already, perhaps, she dreamed
that the very best conversation, the most elusive and least re-
cordable, was indeed to be a daily force in her own life" (1960,
pp. 24–25). Miss Sergeant refers to Frost's famous ability as a
conversationalist, but her conjecture stands alone, with no fol-
low-up information and no hint from either Frost or Elinor to
suggest how she arrived at the speculation. A similar example
occurs in her discussion of Frost's decision to enroll in Harvard
in 1897. After correctly listing the facts that Frost was at the
time a father and all but jobless, she conjectures, "Possibly his
poem 'Warning,' printed September 9, 1897, in the *Independent*
emboldened him to write Dean Briggs . . ." (1960, p. 52). In
another instance she speculates without offering evidence that
the first nine stanzas of "The Trial by Existence" might have
been inspired by Frost's memories of his father.

These and other unsupported conjectures weaken the book's reliability. In addition, the narrative line jumps around in each chapter. She describes, for example, the poet's efforts to be paid two hundred dollars for "Snow" if it appeared in Harriet Monroe's journal *Poetry*. Miss Sergeant quotes part of his letter to Miss Monroe, but she never concludes the episode, dropping it to move on to quote one of Frost's letters to Amy Lowell on an entirely different subject. At times Miss Sergeant strains for conclusions which do not evolve from the facts presented. Recalling how Frost sent "Range-Finding" to Edward Thomas who was at the British front in World War I, she notes Thomas' reply that the poem was a surprisingly good description of no-man's-land. Then she concludes, "Frost had not needed to experience war to 'see' and understand it from within" (1960, p. 189). No further comment is supplied; we are supposed to accept the conclusion as it stands. Finally, Miss Sergeant offers very little analysis of the poetry even though she quotes liberally. She often generalizes about a specific poem, but she never follows up her statement. Calling "A Soldier" one of his "absolute masterpieces of technique," she quotes the entire poem without showing why and how it rates such high praise (1960, p. 210).

In general *The Trial by Existence* is a warm and affectionate portrait of Robert Frost. The author rarely discusses the poet's ambiguities, almost as if she were unaware of them. Instead she celebrates both his life-style and his art, apparently approving of nearly everything he did and wrote. Because her admiration is so complete, her book is more an appreciation of Frost than an interpretation. The result is that she fails to catch what readers of biography like to call the "essential man."

Miss Sergeant's study is apparently a prime though unacknowledged source for Jean Gould's *Robert Frost: The Aim Was Song* (1964). The consequence is that Miss Gould repeats and paraphrases Miss Sergeant's mistakes. In addition Professor Thompson points out that Miss Gould tries to embellish Frost's anecdotes by adding her own "imaginative embroideries." He notes, for example, her false assertion, based on *The Trial by Existence*, that Frost knew Elinor during their sophomore year of high school. Miss Gould then goes on to spruce up the story by mistakenly stating that the poet and Elinor discussed Prescott's *The Conquest of Mexico* on a spring day just before Frost completed "La Noche Triste." She also tries to improve Frost's accounts of both the composition of "My Butterfly" and the trip to the Dismal Swamp. Some of Miss Gould's errors result from Frost's misrepresentation of the facts, but she could have straightened them out had she checked his story. Concerning his resignation from Dartmouth in 1892 to help his mother teach school, Professor Thompson writes that Frost often gave his recollection of this teaching experience greater importance than the facts suggest. The poet apparently claimed that he continued to teach until the end of the school year, but the facts show that he helped only though the winter term (1966, pp. 504, 515). Thus Miss Gould allows Frost to lead her astray when she accepts his version without determining its accuracy.

In general *The Aim Was Song* not only seems to be less well-informed than *The Trial by Existence*, but it also lacks Miss Sergeant's maturity. Its point of view is sympathetic, yet it fails to approach the complex qualities of the poet's character. The result is a surface appreciation, an account of the well-known facts but hardly an analysis of either the poet or his art. Calling her book a "labor of love," Miss Gould offers it as "a tribute to his courage, his indomitable will to overcome the obstacles in his path during the long struggle for recognition, and above all, to his song" (1964, p. ix). She had known Frost for nearly forty years before she wrote the biography, first meeting him in 1926 when he was Poet-in-Residence at the University of Michigan and when she was poetry editor of her Ohio high school newspaper and attending one of his sessions. Although she admits that she did not take notes during her research conversations with him in July, 1962, she nevertheless wrongly publishes many of his comments to her as if they were direct quotations. Like Miss Sergeant, she fails to supply footnotes so that it is often difficult to determine her sources. Miss Gould's inability to secure permission to publish parts of Frost's letters makes her biography considerably weaker than Miss Sergeant's because it denies her immediacy and reliability. Vivid illustration is also lost because she does not quote as liberally from the poems.

Picking up Frost's life at age seven, Miss Gould supplies only a cursory account of his parents' heritage. When she does write about the parents, she often invents feelings for them which she could not possibly know but which she uses to add flavor to her version of the San Francisco years. Recalling W. P. Frost's gambling, she writes, "If he won, he was elated; if he lost, he was grimly determined to make it up, and sometimes did. It was inevitable that he should fall into the habit of drinking, and

Belle's gentle (or vehement) remonstrances were useless; he would not change his ways" (1964, p. 15). She successfully captures the contradictory sides of Frost's nature when a child: the dreamy boy given to tales which he was not quite sure really happened, and the energetic competitor who had to prove he was not a coward. Yet she does not probe the meanings of the contradictions nor suggest their later effect on his art. Too often Miss Gould tries to improve her story with melodramatic embellishments, such as when she describes Frost facing the students in his mother's private school with "his blue eyes vague with dreams..." (1964, p. 68). Or, commenting on Frost's awareness of Elinor teaching French in another part of the schoolroom, she writes, "Rob strained to catch the music of her voice."

Miss Gould's tone is that of uncritical adoration. Like Miss Sergeant, she completely approves of the man and the poet. She glosses over the very real tensions in Frost's relationship with Elinor, and she presents an idealized version of his struggle to create, missing the apparent cost to himself and his family. She suggests that Frost would not worry if a month or two passed without a finished poem. When the tension between the thought and the mechanics of getting it down on paper became too threatening, he could "always get perspective on it by stepping out to gaze at the stars or going for a walk in a nearby wood, breathing in the fragrance of new-mown hay..." (1964, p. 79). This passage illustrates Miss Gould's idealized approach to her subject; she misses the sheer effort Frost expended to create. Following Miss Sergeant's lead, she accepts the myth that many of his poems were written in one inspired burst of creativity without changing a word. Some of her evaluations of the poems are questionable, as, for example, when she calls "New Hampshire" "great, wise, witty" and a "long, brilliant Horatian satire" (1964, p. 228). The years 1928–62 are covered in only thirty-three pages with little more than a list of the poems published in Frost's various books and a chronology of major events. Though these are the years of the deaths of his sister Jeanie, his children Marjorie and Carol, and his wife Elinor, no meaningful analysis is offered of the effect these tragedies had. While Miss Gould uses the same basic facts that Miss Sergeant draws on, she does not cover them as thoroughly or work with them as well.

Louis Mertins' *Robert Frost: Life and Talks-Walking* (1965) is the last full-scale biography of Frost to appear before the publication of Lawrance Thompson's official biography. Mertins published earlier *The Intervals of Robert Frost* (1947) in which

he provided a thirty-eight page outline of the poet's life and a
bibliographical description of his impressive collection of Frost
materials, but that book is like a dry run for the more ambitious
Life and Talks-Walking. Even the latter book is not so much a
standard biography as it is an account of Mertins' long relationship with Frost. It is valuable chiefly for its approximate reproductions of many of Frost's off-the-cuff remarks. Mertins is
primarily a collector, not a biographer, an observation which
causes Reginald L. Cook to write: "His book consists truly of
collector's items, not exacted under duress but with the amiable, if at times annoyed, compliance of the poet" (Cook,
"Robert Frost," 1969, p. 250).

The general weaknesses of *Life and Talks-Walking*, as with
other biographies examined here, result from factual errors committed when Mertins accepts Frost's version of some anecdotes
without checking for accuracy and from his tendency to mis-
lead the reader by presenting some of Frost's comments as direct
quotations when paraphrase would seem more exact. For example, Mertins reports that Frost signed the royalty contract for
A Boy's Will with Mrs. Nutt "a day or so" after leaving the
manuscript with her. But Thompson proves that while Mrs.
Nutt accepted the manuscript for publication in a letter to the
poet dated October 20, 1912, the contract was not signed until
December 16, 1912 (see Thompson, 1966, p. 585). Similarly,
Mertins claims that Frost scattered Elinor's ashes in Derry, New
Hampshire, but Professor Thompson has determined from interviews with Mrs. Lesley Frost Ballantine and Carol Frost's widow
Lillian that the ashes were kept in an urn (see Thompson, 1970,
p. 703). Thus readers of Mertins must check his account of the
facts against more reliable sources.

In his preface, Mertins explains that he first met Frost in 1932
and that for the next thirty years he kept a diary of their conversations: "The material in this book is gleaned to a great extent from our 'talks-walking' " (1965, p. viii). Frost evidently
coined the phrase "talks-walking," for according to Mertins
the poet planned at one time to use it as the name for the volume
which eventually was published as *A Further Range*.

Mertins' book has an index and photographs, but footnotes
are minimal. A further hindrance to serious readers is the lack of
dates. Except when referring to private letters, Mertins often
fails to report the specific year of an event or anecdote, so that
it is difficult to place the information in perspective.

The account of Frost's childhood gains zest from the quotation of Frost's own comments, but the zest is often at the expense of reliability. Although Mertins overgeneralizes the early years as a "nightmare" because of the uncertainty caused by a "drunken, irresponsible father," the notation that Frost thought of his father as "brave and strong and enduring" suggests a contradiction which is not resolved (1965, pp. 6, 11). Another interesting comment from Frost about his parents which Mertins offers as direct quotation, and which helps shape an intimate portrait of the poet, refers to Frost's mother: "Strict as she was, my mother was no prohibitionist, though she was always getting my father to take the pledge" (1965, p. 9). Also included are observations from Blanche Rankin Eastman, Frost's childhood nurse whom he met for a reunion when the lady was ninety-five. Mertins publishes the conversation between the poet and his old nurse, but he does not account for the direct quotation of Mrs. Eastman. The transcription of this conversation is set down as if it were a verbatim report. The question of direct quotation versus paraphrase finally detracts from the reader's interest, for one is never certain of the reliability of the quoted comments.

Though *Life and Talks-Walking* follows Frost's life chronologically, it does not repeat all of the now standard stories and facts in the manner of Miss Gould's heavy reliance on Miss Sergeant's book. While no startlingly new information is revealed, there are some different anecdotes plus Frost's comments on them which are not found in all of the earlier biographies. For example, when working for the *Lawrence Sentinel*, Frost and a group of men decided to weigh themselves. Embarrassed by his slight build, Frost slipped a lead pipe in his coat before stepping on the scales. Mertins also tries, without complete success, to construct a narrative of the poet's years on the Derry farm, interspersed with references to incidents which might have given impetus to a particular poem. This is largely unconvincing because, once again, Mertins never tells if his account of the events is strictly factual or an embellished commentary made up to provide a frame of reference for the poems which refer to farm life.

Mertins captures the contradictions in Frost's character, even though he clearly admires him and only rarely mentions the petty grudges and jealousies. He accepts Frost's side of the story when the poet braggingly related an incident from his teaching days at Pinkerton Academy. According to Frost, a history teacher commented that Frost did not stay at Harvard even long

enough to purchase a football ticket. Claiming that the insult
was premeditated and deliberate, Frost boasted how he got
revenge by denying the history teacher the position of princi-
pal of the academy and thus ruined the man's career. If this
story, given as direct quotation, is true, then Frost clearly
gloated about his "victory." This is the despicable side of Frost's
character which later comes to full light in Professor Thompson's biography, but Mertins glosses over Frost's vindictiveness
to approve of what he calls the poet's "rebuttal" (1965, pp. 98–
99).

Thus the reader must evaluate tone when using this book.
Because Mertins' tone is nearly always one of admiration, it is
difficult for him to analyze the complex relationships between
Frost's hard life, the extreme oppositions in his personality, and
the poems. When he does admit Frost's jealousy of other poets,
he implies that it is natural in artists. He quotes Frost as saying
about Edgar Lee Masters: "My verse to him is like water, as
compared with the strong drink he distills—I should say the
stagnant stuff he spigots out by the gallon" (1965, p. 146). This
is an enlightening comment on Frost, but it loses some of its
punch because Mertins does not supply an identifying date or
an analysis of what this and other similar comments suggest. Perhaps Mertins' best discussion of Frost's contradictions is the one
that recalls the poet at the Berkeley campus of the University
of California upon the presentation of Mertins' Frost collection
to the library. Picturing the poet waiting to sign the many
items, Mertins describes him as "accompanied by spleen, petu-
lance, and plain cussedness, patience and understanding, the
gamut was run" (1965, p. 364).

But despite the absence of true interpretation, the factual
errors, and the vexing problem of quotation versus paraphrase,
Life and Talks-Walking contains numerous sidelights which
make it worth reading. Many of Frost's comments about his
contemporaries, Pound, Yeats, Walter de la Mare, and Housman, are noted. Letters to Mertins from Frost's English friend
John W. Haines fill in details about Frost's 1914 stay in Dymock. There is an amusing account of Frost's meeting with
Hamlin Garland in 1932 which reveals Garland's jealousy at seeing Frost a guest of honor at Occidental College when Garland
thought of himself as the dean of American letters. There is
also a newsy, almost gossipy report, bolstered by Frost's comments and letters, of his return to California in 1947 to receive
an honorary degree from Berkeley. Many letters from the Frost-

Mertins correspondence are included and are especially valuable additions to *Life and Talks-Walking* because none of the four volumes of Frost's letters contains this correspondence. Mertins also notes the substantial changes which Frost made in some of his poems, and he publishes a complete early draft of "Nothing Gold Can Stay." Only occasionally, however, does he analyze the significance of the changes or meaningfully judge the poems. Some of his judgments are questionable, for example his insistence that in the decidedly minor one-act play, *The Cow's in the Corn*, Frost never wrote "a more artistic piece" (1965, p. 172). In short, Mertins' book, like the other early biographies, must be read cautiously. Since it is not a definitive statement about the poet's life, it should be used as a source for anecdotes and information which help to fill in the story.

There are two biographical documents invaluable for an evaluation of Frost's life before the trip to England in 1912: *Robert Frost and the Lawrence, Massachusetts, "High School Bulletin": The Beginning of a Literary Career* (Edward Connery Lathem and Lawrance Thompson, eds., 1966) and *New Hampshire's Child: The Derry Journals of Lesley Frost* (Lesley Frost, 1969). The former is required reading for those interested in the earliest examples of Frost's literary efforts. In addition to an introduction and generous notes, the book has a facsimile section reproducing each of the four issues, September through December, 1891, of the Lawrence *High School Bulletin* edited by Frost. As the editors correctly note, only rarely can the genesis of a literary career be so precisely identified. Too often, an author's initial published pieces are scattered, lost, or forgotten. Luckily, the only known complete set of the *High School Bulletin* for the years of Frost's association with it has survived. Carl Burell, Frost's high school friend, preserved his copies which are now part of the Frost collection in The Jones Library of Amherst.

The editors have reproduced the complete text of all the poems which Frost published in the *Bulletin*: "La Noche Triste" (Apr. 1890), "Song of the Wave" (May 1890), "A Dream of Julius Caesar" (May 1891), "Parting" (Dec. 1891), and "Class Hymn" (June 1892). Also reprinted is "The Traitor," which Frost published in the *Phillips Andover Mirror* (June 1892). The reproduction of these poems provides the Frost student with the earliest known illustrations of concerns which fascinated Frost the rest of his life. His continuing love of archaeological history, classical poetry, and lyric forms is foreshadowed in this verse from his teen years. Of secondary importance are most of the prose pieces he wrote for the *Bulletin*, specifically the editorials, features, and news stories. Yet his valedictory address, "A Monument to After-Thought Unveiled" (June 1892), continues to hold special interest, for in it he expresses his schoolboy interpretation of the Wordsworthian doctrine of recollection in tranquility.

Undoubtedly some readers will complain about the publication of Frost's juvenilia, citing embarrassment to the author or his family, and unnecessary exposure of his weakest work. Such is not the case, however, when the author's reputation is as firmly established as Frost's. Only periodic reevaluation of his mature work, not publication of his juvenilia, might lead to a reassessment of his current status. Messrs. Lathem and Thompson have aided Frost studies by reproducing his high school literary efforts, for they have provided an opportunity to observe a boy in the process of becoming a poet.

Of equal importance is Lesley Frost's *New Hampshire's Child: The Derry Journals of Lesley Frost* which covers the period from February 22, 1905, to August, 1909. Included are abundant photographs plus notes and index by Lawrance Thompson and Arnold Grade. Lesley Frost's introduction sets the tone of these journals covering her fifth through ninth years: "For me, life on the Derry farm was to be a long and passionate borning." In the introduction she points to the key differences between her parents. Her mother, while an agnostic, supplied a spiritual force for the family. Refusing to accept life's cruelties, she also refused to rage against them or to ask for mercy. Her father, on the other hand, was moved to self-pity, often to the extent of taking perverse pride in the assumption that God had singled him out, like Job, for special treatment, no matter how bad.

Although Frost students have long known that his children received a largely haphazard, informal education, the publication of Miss Frost's journals shows how Frost made literature a center of their early years. The list of books read aloud to the children ranges from the Bible and *Pilgrim's Progress* to all kinds of ballads and poems. Miss Frost notes that they received a "book education by night and a do-it-yourself education by day." It is easy to determine what Frost was asking the children to read by noting Lesley's references to specific poets. Admitting that poems are "very pretty sometimes," she writes that she liked "wordsworth" and "shaksperes" best, even though Lucy Gray is a "little too sad." She also approved of "Mathewarnold" because he is "loud sounding." It is interesting, too, to learn that Frost taught his young daughter to include sentence sounds in her journal notations and to create metaphor, so that as a child Lesley could write of "a swallow, like a bow that has gone off with its arrow." Some of Lesley's own early attempts to compose poems are also reproduced here. Frost apparently taught the children the difference between poetry and prose, as well as the fun of analogy and metaphor when using verse to describe something seen. Miss Frost interestingly points out in her foreword to Book IV of the journals that her father never let them know that he wrote poems.

Some of the journal notations recall specific Frost poems. Lesley's description of her father's anger at finding a hunter on his land might suggest "The Rabbit-Hunter"; and both her "Christmastime" poem for 1906 and her journal entry for December 15, 1907, might recall "Storm Fear." Today Miss Frost calls the Derry farm "a place to stand on, not only physically-in-fact but also spiritually-in-wisdom. . . ." Frost evidently felt the same way, for he often insisted that the core of his poetry came from those "free years" on the Derry farm. Captured in these childhood writings are so many of the farm experiences later immortalized in Frost's own poetry: swinging birches ("i climb," Lesley wrote, "uther threes but they dount swing as the birchis do."), applepicking, gathering flowers. The mention of these recreational activities suggests the family's isolation. Only occasionally does Lesley mention that another child came to play, or that an adult visited, or that they went to town. Her favorite places to visit were not the places familiar to most children—school, church, parties—but the alder grove or the big pasture or the brook.

The journals are valuable chiefly for their picture of these Derry years which were so important to Frost's entire family. But because Lesley's entries quite naturally contain obscure references, editorial comment is necessary. This is supplied by two sources. First, Miss Frost's general introduction and short forewords to specific sections of the journals both clarify the references and suggest the methods her father used to teach her about poetry, analogy, and spelling—subjects a more conventional parent might have considered too subtle for a child of five or six. Second, as mentioned earlier, Lawrance Thompson and Arnold Grade have supplied notes which provide historical background about Frost's relations with his family and neighbors. The notes are also designed to clarify Lesley's references to particular landmarks on the farm in order to help guide potential present-day visitors around the farm, now a state park of New Hampshire.

Among other interesting comments, the notes supply a brief history of the Derry communities and of the farm (a map of the farm is printed on the book's endpapers); an account of how "Schneider," the family dog, died; clarification of names and families mentioned in the journals; and reconstructions of some of Lesley's walks by locating the landmarks. Of particular value are some of Frost's poetic descriptions of such landmarks as the pasture, or the stream known as "Hyla Brook," or the house which became the focus of "The Black Cottage." In short, the notes and index (made for "those who like to browse") are a delight to read and an added dimension to the book. They are full, carefully researched, and meticulously detailed—characteristics which readers of Frost scholarship have come to expect when Lawrance Thompson contributes his incredible knowledge of Frost's life and times. *New Hampshire's Child* may not be necessary material for the reader interested in only Frost's poems, but it is indispensable for those who would have a picture of the whole man. If the journals are read without the notes and supporting material, the book is an endearing record of Miss Frost's girlhood. But if the journals, Miss Frost's comments, the notes, and the index are read together, the book supplies the closest thing we have to a firsthand account of Frost's crucial Derry years before he went to England.

When evaluating the biographical material on Frost, one is tempted to direct the reader to Lawrance Thompson's work as the best there is and to let it go at that: *Robert Frost: The Early Years, 1874-1915* (1966) and *Robert Frost: The Years of Triumph, 1915-1938* (1970). To begin with, Professor Thompson was Frost's "official" biographer—the poet selected him as long ago as 1939. Thompson had known Frost since his own college days at Wesleyan, and thus he had the opportunity to gather more detailed and, more importantly, accurate information than any other commentator on Frost's life. Sympathetic but not sentimental, Thompson was not afraid to challenge the public's mental picture of Frost as a beloved national hero. More than any other person, he was responsible for the destruction of Frost's public mask which the poet encouraged until he died. One need only read Thompson's authoritative discussion of the pressures Frost caused in his own family and of the resulting serious strain in his relationship with Elinor, and then compare it with the relatively rosy picture of the marriage painted by the earlier biographers to realize that only Thompson knows what he is talking about when discussing the marriage.

The work is admirably, even painstakingly documented. Volume one, for example, has seventeen photographs of Frost's parents, his children, and his life in both New England and England. The footnotes are full, judiciously placed after the text and covering 125 pages. They are as much fun to read as the biography itself and nearly as informative. Fleshing out the body of the text, the notes supply pertinent information and judgments which might have cluttered the biography for some readers but complete the tale for those who wish to be informed of all there is to know. It is in the notes that Thompson completely documents Frost's acknowledgments of his questionable treatment of Elinor and of his guilt following her death in 1938. The notes also round out such points as the marked contrast between the ideals Frost honored in his poetry and the pettiness he dramatized in his life, his careful plan to advertise his work and advance his standing in literary circles, and dozens of other equally fascinating pieces of information absolutely necessary to an understanding of Frost the man. For the general reader perhaps the most revealing discussion in the notes is Thompson's conclusive proof that Frost did not write "Stopping by Woods on a Snowy Evening" with "one stroke of the pen" as he so often claimed. Although Frost was honest enough not to "hide his traces," he nevertheless created a myth about the composition of that poem which was generally accepted as fact until Professor Thompson exposed it as false.

The index is as full as the notes, and it fulfills the expectations established by Thompson's index to *Selected Letters of Robert Frost*. It is so complete that it serves as an additional means of ordering the information along with the introduction, the central text, and the notes. As Thompson states, his index makes available some outlines and summaries not "explicitly given" in other parts of the book. Of particular interest are the forty-three topical subheads listed under "Robert Lee Frost" ranging from "Atheism" and "Fears" to "Rage," "Suicide," and "Victorian," and complete with names, dates, places, and quotations.

The introduction suggests that Thompson sees his work primarily as a demythicizing process: "Robert Frost was so fascinated by the story of his life that he never tired of retelling it. . . . whenever the bare facts troubled him, he discreetly clothed them with fictions. . . . some of his fictions amounted to mythic variations" which revealed his obsession to make the facts square with long held ideals (1966, p. xiii). Thompson tackles the delicate problem of how to use Frost's statements about his own life, and he checks Frost's versions against all of the available evidence. Knowing that documents yet to be discovered will modify certain of his conclusions, he admits that a few of the assumptions must be offered tentatively. In general this biography performs two invaluable functions: it straightens out facts confused by Frost in his myriad versions of specific incidents and accepted by other biographers taking him at his word; and it tries to set in perspective those very myths Frost manufactured about his life and about his relationships with others.

This latter function perhaps causes a small problem, for Professor Thompson's explanation of the source of Frost's mythicizing nearly amounts to a thesis directing many of his assumptions and observations. As he explains, and there is every reason to believe him, Frost came early under the spell of his mother's accounts of mythic heroes and courageous ideals. When, as a boy, he failed to measure up to those lofty standards, he became enraged, frustrated, and confused. Always a person of "excruciating sensitivities," he found that these frustrations dominated him more than they should have. Yet he could not control them. The result was that Frost continually conjured up personal myths to support ideals earlier conceived, thus injuring himself and others when he was forced to manufacture new self-deceptions to support old ones. In the introduction, Thompson cites as examples Frost's lifelong anger at both his grandfather and his wife over fictitious disloyalties and hurts which, as Thompson proves, never occurred, but which Frost expanded in his recurring mythic accounts until his belief in them finally damaged his relationships with his family. Thompson also argues convincingly that Frost often idealized certain attitudes as truths in his most personal poems, in spite of the facts which contradicted him, in an effort to "stay" the confusion he sensed in his own life. These explanations are entirely persuasive. The problem is not the validity of the argument but the way it sometimes dominates the main narrative. Established succinctly in the introduction, the argument often amounts to a thesis in the text when it is applied to numerous events in Frost's life. Even something as minor as a vomiting fit after a high school football game is described as evidence of the ordeals Frost willingly endured to fulfill his ideals of honor and glory. And, occasionally, the judgment about the tone of a particular letter—for example, that Frost showed a "note of disparagement" when commenting on Lascelles Abercrombie's review of *North of Boston*—seems forced, when compared to the letter itself, to fit the argument that Frost was jealous of his competitors (1966, p. 452).

The narrative of Frost's early years is nevertheless a model of scholarship. The first chapters offer the most detailed account to be found anywhere of Frost's parents, the influence of Swedenborg on his mother, and his life in San Francisco with an undisciplined, brilliant father and an overly devoted, moralistic mother. According to Thompson, Frost's mother unintentionally "pampered and spoiled" him with the result that the boy refused to leave her to attend public grammar schools. Even worse, hints Thompson, was the constant diet of idealistic and heroic stories she fed him—tales which, as Thompson interprets their influence, caused Frost to develop his lifelong habit of rage, self-pity, and self-defense when he found himself falling short of perfection. The biography goes so far as to suggest that Frost's fury at mistakes made when copying letters in a tablet was an outgrowth of the idealism instilled in him by his mother. Examples of the information which makes this biography so complete are the poems and stories authored by Frost's mother and discussed by Thompson in both the central text and the notes. He quotes her poem "The Artist's Motive" in its entirety, and he provides a detailed summary of her story *The Land of Crystal* to suggest the literary interests of the woman who influenced Frost for so long.

Discussing the poet's preteen years, Thompson writes of personality traits and quirks which would later become more pronounced in adulthood when they developed into deeply entrenched attitudes. For example, Frost's aversion to formal education before he reached high school foreshadows his refusal to complete his studies at Dartmouth and Harvard; or his unwillingness to keep a part-time job and his widespread reputation for shirking duties, well-documented by Thompson, look forward to his future laziness when farming or teaching school. The notes indicate that Thompson has interviewed dozens of people who knew Frost in the 1880s, as well as tracked down hundreds of leads to find the necessary authority for the story of Frost's preteen years. Just as admirably documented is the account of Frost's conversion to learning when he entered Lawrence High School.

More than any other biography or memoir, Thompson's work gives the fullest and most accurate record of Frost's complicated relationship with his high school sweetheart, and later wife, Elinor. Thompson writes in a note, "RF's known jealousy of Elinor White's capabilities is important to any biographical understanding of his complicated personality. It is apparent that this jealousy had its root in his chronic lack of self-confidence" (1966, p. 505). To begin, he corrects the popular misconception, present in both Miss Sergeant's and Miss Gould's biographies, that Frost met Elinor during his sophomore year in high school and that she very likely inspired his first serious attempts to write poetry for the Lawrence *High School Bulletin*. He proves that Frost began publishing in the *Bulletin* before knowing Elinor, whom he did not meet until his senior year. He also shows that Frost's jealousy of Elinor's talent and intellect was evident from the beginning of their relationship when he discusses the crisis caused by her decision to submit her own poems to the *Bulletin*. To ease matters she either agreed to stop writing poetry or denied that she authored those poems she submitted. In later years Frost scorned her enrollment in the "general" program, pointing out that he took the college preparatory classical course; and once he became enraged with his daughter Lesley when she jokingly told the truth that Elinor's high school average was higher than his. His fear that Elinor would find another lover seems to have reached a climax during their college years, when he dropped out of Dartmouth and then vainly pleaded with Elinor to leave Saint Lawrence. Thompson interprets their tense courtship as a classic example of Frost's passion for self-pity and easy resentment. Knowledge of the charged relationship between Frost and Elinor from high school through marriage is critical to an understanding of the ups and downs of his personality, and only *Robert Frost: The Early Years* is fully documented and reliable.

Professor Thompson also uncovers the fascinating story of Frost's trip to the Dismal Swamp in 1894 after the poet had mistakenly decided that Elinor had rejected both him and *Twilight*, the gift of his poems. Aware that earlier biographers have confused or missed details (Munson, for example, covers the journey to the swamp in one sentence), Thompson illustrates his meticulous research when he narrates what amounts to a step-by-step account of the poet's trek, explaining that Frost hoped to undergo a serious injury or even death as suitable punishment for Elinor's "harsh" treatment of him. Similar jealous behavior proved to be a pattern in his life. Frost's resentments and jealousies toward his fellow artists are well-documented, but Thompson goes beyond the standard examples to show that the same petty attitudes infected his relationships with relatives and friends who genuinely tried to help him. Two of these people were his grandfather Frost and Carl Burell, both of whom, Thompson shows, were much more generous with Frost than he was willing to admit years later. The poet's scandalous treatment of them is cited as yet another key illustration of his chronic self-doubt and inability to admit faults or to accept criticism—traits which later carried over to relationships with the artistic community.

For those interested primarily in the poems, Thompson supplies biographical information, plus dates and places of composition, for nearly every poem Frost wrote during this time, suggesting interpretations unavailable before. Thus we learn that "The Demiurge's Laugh" was written in response to Frost's queries about evolution, that "Home Burial" refers not only to the loss of Frost's first child but also to the death of Elinor's sister's child, and that many of the poems in *A Boy's Will* were composed as love poems for Elinor. Appropriately, Thompson does not deny the value of valid symbolic extension applied to those poems, but he convincingly argues the importance of the biographical and factual information he has compiled.

The volume also contains analyses of the various influences of Emerson, Thoreau, William James, and Henri Bergson, plus an especially detailed account of Frost's first months in England when he was meeting other poets and publishing *A Boy's Will*. It is an admirable biography, given added weight with the printing of some forty-odd poems which Frost either withheld from publication or never collected, including two free verse parodies of Ezra Pound and early drafts of now famous poems like "The Black Cottage."

Volume two, *Robert Frost: The Years of Triumph, 1915-1938*, won a Pulitzer Prize, and it exhibits the same scholarly care and brilliant arrangement as volume one. Besides eleven photographs, Thompson includes 190 pages of notes not only containing enough information to constitute an additional reading experience, but again placed after the central narrative and out of the way of those readers who do not wish to be bothered. The notes often carry the burden of the more analytical side of Professor Thompson's interpretation. Like the notes, the index provides an additional level of ordering for the biography, particularly the sixty-three topical subheads for the Robert Frost entries which again include names, dates, places, and pertinent quotations. In short, both notes and index do more than document the text—they round out the information by offering sidelights and anecdotes to which only a biographer of Thompson's thoroughness could have access.

In the introduction, Thompson fills in, for those who have not read volume one, the highlights of Frost's life through the sojourn in England. Calling attention to Frost's jealousies and chronic lack of confidence, he stresses, to the point of over-emphasizing, what he calls the poet's "longings for vengeance," so that even Frost's dreams of being a baseball star are said to constitute a means of retribution: "even a baseball could serve as a lethal weapon if carefully aimed at the head of an enemy batter" (1970, p. xv). Statements like this seem a little strong despite the documentation of Frost's jealousy of his fellow poets. Also stressed are Frost's deliberate efforts to cultivate influential critics and editors and to create the pose of gentle farmer-poet in order to endear himself to the public.

Robert Frost: The Years of Triumph takes up the story with Frost's return to the United States in February, 1915; his troubles with immigration officials about Edward Thomas' son who had sailed with them; and his initial introduction to the editors of *New Republic* and to a few members of the Poetry Society of America. Though Frost's subsequent efforts to flatter critics and editors are well-documented in later chapters, Thompson perhaps exaggerates when he calls these introductions Frost's "first round of campaigning," for Alfred Harcourt, head of the trade department for Frost's American publisher, all but insisted that the poet dine with the editors of *New Republic* and attend the meeting of the Poetry Society. What follows is an exciting account of Frost's subsequent entrée into the world of literary fame: publication in *Atlantic*, an invitation to be Phi Beta Kappa Poet at Tufts, reviews by recognized critics, as well as Frost's careful encouragement of reviewers and editors. Thompson pinpoints Frost's efforts with the word "manipulate" to describe how the poet used influential friends: "Oversensitive, and suffering too often under the delusion that he was being persecuted by those who might set the 'whole nation' against him, Frost needed the playful and witty support given him by many of his understanding friends, including [Louis] Untermeyer" (1970, p. 61). (Interested readers should consult Untermeyer, 1970, p. 22, for the latter's aggravated reply to the charge that Frost used him.)

Significant to this period of Frost's life is his later insistence that Elinor disapproved of his sudden public success. According to the poet, his wife would sacrifice her desires to his need to create only so long as he wrote primarily for her. Thompson points out in the notes that only Frost's side of this serious difference of opinion with Elinor is documented. More to the point may have been Elinor's conviction that Frost should give more time to writing and less time to "barding around" at various colleges. By any measure, however, volume two is especially startling because of its frankness about the poet's relationship with his wife. Thompson's narrative of Frost's campaign to gain public recognition, despite what he considered to be his wife's disapproval, and of his parallel fear of being slighted or criticized in print is so admirably documented that it should send the reader to the original reviews and articles which are mentioned.

About the same time, Thompson reports, Frost began to create the mask he mastered so well for public appearances and which the public as a whole willingly accepted, though wrongly, of course, as the real man. Those interested in the major discrepancies between the public poet and the private man will want to read this report of how Frost found his public image in the misleading descriptions of him which the first English reviewers published: that of a poor, Yankee farmer who found artistic inspiration in his farming experiences. There is also a revealing discussion, including two pages of notes, about Edward Thomas as the subject of "The Road Not Taken" and about the multiple interpretations which cropped up when reader after reader (including Thomas himself) failed to catch Frost's little joke. Considering the numerous examples of Frost's vindictiveness toward his contemporaries (see especially his double-dealing with Raymond Holden), his close friendship with Thomas is all the more meaningful as an illustration of a good relationship with a fellow artist. Equally revealing is the story of Frost's teaching ventures at Amherst and Michigan in the 1920s. Thompson shows that for all of Frost's fame as an unconventional teacher, his break with pedagogical convention was largely a matter of laziness. He avoided his teaching duties to such an extreme that his electives were often known as "gut" courses.

All of this information is significant, but perhaps the most important revelation of this volume is the story of the increasing friction between Frost and his family. Professor Thompson points out that during their stay in Franconia, New Hampshire, Elinor became highly critical of Frost's refusal to help the children with their own creative writing. Evidence is cited which suggests that he even tried to crush the poetic instinct in Carol and Lesley. In addition, husband and wife frequently quarreled about religion, for Elinor's staunch atheism challenged Frost's conservative theology and deep-seated religious beliefs. In outlining this quarrel, Thompson provides a masterful account of Frost's puritan faith which was usually hidden from the public by his little jokes and witticisms. Thompson argues that Frost's fear of death and hope of salvation were strong enough to cut through the inconsistencies created by his combination of puritanism and paganism, and that a few poems, for example, "For Once, Then, Something," were composed as answers to Elinor's taunts. Apparently embarrassed by his religious beliefs, Frost displayed skepticism in both his poems and public utterances to protect his faith from derision. (For a fascinating account of his religious beliefs, see particularly chapter 17, "Yes I Suppose I Am a Puritan.")

Professor Thompson has all the facts concerning the unbelievably numerous personal tragedies which Frost endured between 1915 and 1938. There were so many serious illnesses that the marital strains between himself and Elinor, and between daughters Irma and Lesley and their own husbands, seemed almost minor: daughter Marjorie's repeated attacks of pleurisy and tuberculosis, daughter-in-law Lillian's tuberculosis, sister Jeanie's insanity and death in 1929, not to mention his own recurring illnesses. Frost drove himself finally to these sicknesses by scheduling extensive reading tours to pay for the medical treatment of his family's chronic breakdowns. Marjorie died in 1934 following childbirth, and Elinor died in 1938 following cancer and numerous heart attacks. This part of the story is sympathetically presented to suggest probable causes for some of the poet's fears and lack of confidence. In this context, Frost's wondering if he, being an artist, should have had a family is especially poignant. Elinor's death was the greatest blow of all, and Thompson shows that his "anguish was inseparable from his guilt. . ." (1970, p. 493). The guilt resulted from the realization that since his marriage he had placed poetry instead

of family at the center of his life. Elinor had suffered during
her life with him, but she had always found a means to convey
her disapproval. Her death must have been the most serious
condemnation of all, for she never invited Frost into her
sickroom before she died. Thompson's story of these personal
tragedies is sympathetically placed in the context of Frost's
refusal to be weighed down by any death but his own, an
attitude which is not at all harsh when it is understood to be
a combination of his egotism and his faith in life after death.

When reading such impeccable scholarship, it is difficult
to point out possible flaws. But there are a few. Why is the
information that Elinor suffered a miscarriage in June, 1925,
when she was fifty-three, placed in the notes? In the central
narrative we are told that Frost misrepresented her illness as a
nervous collapse, but we have to turn to the notes to discover
the truth. One wonders if Professor Thompson felt caught
between his duties as a biographer and his obligations to the
Frost family, with the result that a compromise directed the
placement of this information in the notes. Elinor's miscarriage
at an advanced age must have contributed to the increasing
marital strain, but the reader cannot accurately determine its
effect. Thompson tells us only that the illness forced Frost
to cancel a trip to Bowdoin College. Similarly, too much of the
discussion about Frost's religion is tucked away in the notes.
Considering the importance assigned to Frost's faith, it might
have been better to have this information in the text itself.
The question for the biographer here, of course, is one of
judgment: how much supplementary information, in this case
about Frost's religion, can be included in the central narrative
without blunting the dramatic appeal of the life story? Various
readers will react to this differently, but I, for one, would
have preferred most of this information in a single discussion.
In addition, Professor Thompson states rather unconvincingly
that murder "never stayed out of Frost's consciousness too long,"
and then he goes on to list several of the poet's "enemies."
It is one thing to stress the poet's vindictiveness, but quite
another to insist that the need for revenge came close to
murder. Rather, as Thompson shows, Frost's contributions to
literary gossip and his habit of maligning his "enemies" in
letters to sympathetic correspondents served as his chief expressions of anger and rage.

One also wonders why examples of Frost's famous conversational voice are missing. When the number of talks which

Thompson had with Frost is considered, it is unfortunate that more of the poet's own descriptions and anecdotes are not included. Surely the biographer had ample opportunity to take down precise statements from the poet so that distinctions between paraphrase and direct quotation could be maintained. For some reason, however, Thompson chooses not to recreate the flavor of Frost the speaker, with the regrettable result that the poet's renowned effectiveness with informal speech is neglected. Finally, the subtitle to volume two is puzzling. How can "The Years of Triumph" be accepted literally after the reader has noted the unending series of personal tragedies which Frost suffered? Or should the subtitle be understood as having a dual thrust: an ironic comment upon the poet's life, but a literal description of these years of poetic achievement? If irony is intended, the effect seems heavy-handed, but in any case the title remains ambiguous. None of these flaws is debilitating, however. As Thompson states in the introduction to volume one, his primary goal is to "increase the general knowledge about Robert Frost, as man and as poet, so that we may improve our appreciation of his very human and yet deservedly impressive stature" (1966, p. xxiv). So much of what Thompson writes is based on evidence which he painstakingly uncovered and established that he should have good reason to believe his version of Frost's life will stand.

Memoirs

The value of the memoirs discussed here is that they preserve documented accounts of how differently Robert Frost affected a number of people who took the time to write down their impressions. They are useful supplements to the biographies because their informality encourages a more personal record of the poet. Often adulatory in tone and undiscriminating in evaluation, they nevertheless contribute to the understanding of this complex man.

Sidney Cox authored two of the better known memoirs: *Robert Frost: Original "Ordinary Man"* (1929) and *A Swinger of Birches: A Portrait of Robert Frost* (1957). Cox first met Frost when Cox was twenty-two and teaching at Plymouth (New Hampshire) High School, while Frost was employed at the nearby Plymouth Normal School. Lawrance Thompson reports that at this initial meeting Frost teased Cox to the extent

that Cox later went out of his way to avoid the poet. Frost's
attention soon flattered the young man, however, and the two
joined for tennis, walks, and long conversations about literature.
But as Professor Thompson points out, and as the letters make
clear, Frost always treated Cox ambiguously despite the fact
that their friendship lasted until Cox's death (see Thompson,
1964, pp. xvi, 313-14, 435-36). Thompson specifies 1927
as the earliest date which suggests that Cox planned to write
a biography of Frost. Elinor apparently encouraged him in 1928
when he submitted drafts of his material to her for comment.
Biographical evidence also suggests that Frost initially gave his
consent, only to withdraw it in 1928 (see Thompson, 1970,
pp. 321, 637). A few years later, in a letter dated c. April 19,
1932, Frost again tried to stop Cox: "My objection to your
larger book about me was that it came thrusting in where I did
not want you. . ." (Thompson, 1964, p. 385). Cox evidently
kept working, for Frost again protested in a letter dated
January 1, 1937, claiming that he had been ruining his correspondence with Cox "by throwing it into confusion. . ."
(Thompson, 1964, p. 435). Still this disagreement must not have
damaged their friendship too severely, for Cox served as an
honorary pallbearer at Elinor's funeral in 1938, and Frost wrote
an introduction for *A Swinger of Birches* when it was published posthumously in 1957.

Robert Frost: Original "Ordinary Man" amounts to an impression of Frost as seen by one of his most admiring friends.
This very short book has no table of contents, no index, and no
scholarly apparatus because none is needed. Cox's aim is to
create a verbal portrait of a man he obviously loves and admires. His thesis is simply stated: that it is the "ordinary" in
Frost which gives his poems "their subtle touch." By "ordinary"
he means "unspoiled manliness," acute senses, and playfulness
(1929, p. 12). Stressing what he considers to be Frost's uniqueness, Cox explains that the poet is too multifaceted to be defined.
If one calls him a Yankee, Frost can point to his California
birth. If one accuses him of being a recluse, he can quote from
the latest sports news.

This portrait is obviously idealistic. None of the jealousies,
vindictiveness, and selfish actions are mentioned. Instead Cox
pictures Frost as a man who shrugged off all obstacles in his
determination to be a poet. The reader can conclude only that
Cox considers Frost to be a perfect man. Still there are valuable
insights, offered more as springboards for further investigations

of the poetry than as conclusions to closely reasoned arguments. For example, he stresses the role of love in Frost's poems: "It is not idealized love, but experienced love. It involves difficult and never completed adjustments. And it never gets so perfect as to remove all wistfulness" (1929, p. 38). Also of interest is the discussion of Frost's religious beliefs: "God, he said, is that which a man is sure cares, and will save him, no matter how many times or how completely he has failed" (1929, p. 40). Despite these and other insights, the most prominent characteristic of this little book is Cox's worshipful attitude. Though Cox insists that Frost is an ordinary man, his portrait classifies him just this side of sainthood. The book is useful today chiefly as a means to illustrate the public pose which Frost so consciously created and which remained in vogue until Lawrance Thompson's biography all but laid it to rest.

A Swinger of Birches: A Portrait of Robert Frost is longer and more valuable because it draws on Frost's letters to Cox and on the conversations of a forty-year friendship. Frost writes in his introduction: "The author probably knew me better than he knew himself and consequently contrariwise he very likely portrayed himself in it more than me. . . . We differed more in taste perhaps than in thinking. But we stood up to each other to support each other as two playing cards may be made into a building" (1957, p. vii). Frost also gives an amusing account of their first meeting, one, he says, that Cox would have enjoyed. For according to Frost, Cox was so angered at their initial introduction that he later inquired if alcohol had prevented Frost from getting anywhere in the world.

In his preface, Cox admits that he has been trying to define his conception of Frost for almost forty years. The attitude of hero worship in the preface sets the tone for the rest of the book: "It is conditioned by the fact that all that time he has seemed to me the most lively and understanding and coherently constructive man I have known. Much of the time I have had long, hard struggles composing my conclusions with his. And I end very different from him. But, for better or for worse, I still think him the wisest man, and one of the two deepest and most honest thinkers, I know" (1957, p. xi). He also tells the reader that his book avoids biography to concentrate on ideas. Most importantly, and unlike several of the biographies, Cox distinguishes between exact quotation of Frost and paraphrase so that the book maintains reliability when Frost's own words are used.

One of the ideas Cox writes about is Frost's humor, what he

terms a "slight offishness" which will not allow Frost to be totally reverent about anything, even God. This jaunty attitude accounts for the comic tone in many of Frost's religious poems. Cox's discussion of it is especially useful when read along with Professor Thompson's chapter about Frost's religious beliefs. Another idea discussed is Frost's dislike of writing which begins with a formula (Frost points to Ibsen and Shaw) instead of with a situation and an idea which come alive in the art (Shakespeare). Also noted is Frost's disapproval of writers who strain for realistic effect in poetry when they lack the necessary experience with the character or situation they hope to express (Wilfred Gibson). Cox also documents Frost's early efforts to express, clarify, and advertise his theory of sentence sounds. As he notes, Frost did not desire to establish doctrine but to play with ideas. Since he did not want to be taken for a philosopher, he cultivated the image of himself as a prankster, a country-store sage: "He says he is entertaining some ideas, just entertaining them, not settling anything, not propounding any finalities. Give him free play, even on the highest levels" (1957, p. 19).

Frost's insistence upon fidelity to facts and reality prompts one of Cox's best discussions. Using "Birches" for illustration, he talks about Frost's need to return to earth, that is, to what he knows. He argues that reliance upon reality is the reason why Frost will not give up common sense or exchange the limitations of everyday truth for the freedoms of philosophical speculation. Frost, says Cox, would like to know the ultimate real, but he realizes it is attainable, if at all, only by a fiercely guarded relationship with particular realities like the facts of flowers, woods, or fences. As Cox shows, the poet has literally swung on birches, used a scythe, mended a wall: "He likes— and loves—the actual, and when he uses it he will not at all distort it. That is Robert Frost—for better or for worse; anything 'more' is vulgar and cheap" (1957, p. 31).

Cox admits that Frost has suffered more than his share of fear, but he emphasizes the general affirmation. Plunging to the depths and experiencing despair, the poet has always surfaced with a faith like that of the counterwave in "West-Running Brook." Cox speculates that the reason Frost refuses to give into despair, despite his acquaintance with it, is his belief that the world is generally funny. The world is seriously funny, of course, but it is funny because it *is* serious. Frost's ability to find a trace of mirth in most everything he experiences may account for the playful, often whimsical tone in many of his more serious poems which numerous critics have attacked as an indication of his failure to meet moral choices with anything except a grin and a cute wisecrack. Cox's comments on the place of humor in Frost's poetry are useful when read with an awareness that many critics disapprove of the comic touches.

Particularly interesting is the account of Frost's teaching methods, for it is full of anecdotes about Frost's classes at various schools and direct quotes from Frost on how to teach. Cox notes Frost's struggle to protect a freshman's "beliefs," his insistence that students should not be taught that education can provide "the" answer, his belief that suffering is unavoidable and that life is more of a zig-zag than a logical progression of events. According to Cox, Frost never planned a class but thought of a nucleus for the next period while walking to school. He always expressed his own judgments in class, but he refused to supply facts for memorization. He was persuasive enough to convince his students to perform *Comus, The School for Scandal,* and *The Importance of Being Earnest.* But, writes Cox, his primary goal was to give students "the freedom of their own imaginations" (1957, p. 63). Never once does Cox mention Frost's laziness as a teacher, a characteristic which other commentators have stressed. When he reports that Frost made the students throw away their composition books and then taught them to read aloud, he implies that this was a means to help the students respond to literature rather than a means for Frost to avoid written assignments which would require grading.

Finally, Cox captures the poet discussing his art—how he moves from subject matter to form, how he tries to communicate both "sight and insight," and how he wants his poetry to be understood. We get a picture of the poet speaking, musing, pondering what poetry means to him and how it can affect common experience. One of the successes of *A Swinger of Birches* is its ability to express the sense of Frost's mind at work. Cox's own colloquial style and understated approach to his subject are well suited to the man whose informality he hopes to set down on paper. The short chapters and the quick transitions from scene to scene and idea to idea make the book read easily. It is particularly good for its image of Frost just back from England, slumped in a chair, dressed in a homemade shirt, unpressed trousers, and heavy shoes, and running circles around college professors while they discussed ideas. The book's chief flaw comes from Cox's idealization of Frost. He constantly puts himself down and makes fun of his side of the discussions with Frost, almost as if he feels he must defer to the poet because of his own postgraduate education. He deprecates his own learning experience when he says that he made the mistake of going to libraries while Frost pursued truth by directly confronting life. He also glosses over Frost's now celebrated crudeness and prejudice, his inability to speak well of rivals, and his insistence on being right, when he writes that the poet was not so much crude or raw as new or original.

There is some suggestion that Frost was perfecting his pose with Cox and that Cox never saw through it. This is not necessarily a flaw in *A Swinger of Birches*, for until Professor Thompson's books the public Robert Frost was accepted by most as the real man. But while Cox's refusal to peer behind the mask may account for this portrait of Frost as a homespun intellectual complete with cows to milk and real fields to clear—certainly a valuable portrait for the Frost fan—it may also account, on the other hand, for the sense of Cox's slanted perspective which lingers after the book is read. In other words, what Cox gives us is not the man himself but *his* Robert Frost. Impressed with Frost's pose, he willingly avoids opportunities to reach the real man. For example, he writes, "When you come around to agreeing with Robert Frost he does not agree with you. I never knew that to fail" (1957, p. 43). But rather than see this attitude as one more sign of Frost's playful spirit, Cox takes it all seriously, affirming, "He is always turning tables, showing that someone had forgotten that all tables have under sides." Frost's attitude, admits Cox, illustrates his mischief, but Cox dodges commentary on the possibility that the refusal to agree is a means of having fun at his own expense. He would prefer to elevate the poet's playfulness into a consistent way of meeting the world's contraries. Thus while he correctly notes that the mischief is what saves Frost from giving into despair, he refuses to admit the element of one-upmanship in the poet's little jokes.

This extended discussion of Cox's two books is useful as an illustration of memoirs written by one who believes wholeheartedly in Frost's mask. Louis Untermeyer accepts the pose, too, but his memoirs of Frost are more balanced. His *From Another World: The Autobiography of Louis Untermeyer* (1939) is notable for its firsthand account of a gathering of Frost, Sara Teasdale, Vachel Lindsay, and Untermeyer at which Lindsay seriously proposed that at their next meeting they all bring a poem written about boxing champion John L.

Sullivan. Nothing much came of the proposal. But Frost wrote his poem and included it in a February, 1918, letter to Untermeyer. A marvelous burlesque of Lindsay's style, the poem was first published, as mentioned earlier, in Untermeyer's autobiography. Other writers have described this incident, but only Untermeyer's is a direct account. To complete the story, Untermeyer also prints Lindsay's poem in order to point out the contrast between its seriousness and Frost's playfulness.

Untermeyer's most extended discussion of Frost is the chapter entitled "The Northeast Corner." There is the standard review of well-known biographical facts, but he also includes the story of his discovery of Frost. Reading the December, 1913, issue of Harold Monro's *Poetry and Drama*, Untermeyer naturally thought that Frost, grouped as he was with Rupert Brooke, Wilfred Gibson, and Lascelles Abercrombie, belonged with the Georgian poets. But when he read "The Fear" and "A Hundred Collars" he was confused by his detection of colloquial American phrasing and idiom. The affair was soon straightened out upon Frost's return to the United States, and Untermeyer became one of Frost's most enduring and patient friends.

Frost so trusted Untermeyer that he revealed his true nature to him. As Untermeyer writes of their correspondence, "Never have letters been so personal and yet so documentary, so frankly intimate and so intense a record of the times" (1939, p. 209). He has since collected and published the letters, but *From Another World* remains a valuable complement to the correspondence. Recalling that he has known hundreds of brilliant men, Untermeyer nevertheless insists that Frost was one of only three "whose greatness rested in what they were, rather than in what they said or did" (1939, p. 210). This is a high tribute, one which sets the tone for his account of Frost: honest but uncritical of both poet and poems. His admiration causes him to gloss over difficulties in their friendship, quirks in Frost's personality, and defects in some of the poems.

One beauty of this memoir is Untermeyer's revelation of Frost's wit and the generous quotations from his funnier letters. There is a particularly amusing story of a plan proposed to Untermeyer and Frost in 1920 to abandon the United States for a Utopian community in the "purely Polynesian islands." Untermeyer cites Frost's "reply," signed "Robbered Frossed," as one of the many examples of the poet's genius for playful banter. His illustration of Frost the teaser supports his assertion that those who see him as a "grim realist" do not know him.

Although Untermeyer knew, lived with, and understood Frost's contrary complexities and the mixture of playfulness and pettiness, he chooses not to discuss them in print. Yet it is his awareness of Frost's many-sided personality which makes him doubt the success of any biography of the poet: "His life, like his poetry, is a maze of disguised simplicities and delicate double meanings" (1939, pp. 227-28). For years he was right. No biography came close to capturing the real Robert Frost until Professor Thompson began publishing the official biography in 1966.

Louis Untermeyer's other significant contribution is *Robert Frost: A Backward Look* (1964), a lecture delivered March 23, 1964, at the Library of Congress. Included is a selective bibliography of Frost materials housed in the Library of Congress with notations of manuscripts, recordings, and motion pictures. Observing that reevaluation of Frost is bound to begin now that the poet is dead, Untermeyer goes on record as affirming his belief in the ultimate high worth of Frost's achievement. Significantly, he does not blink this time at the less attractive side of Frost's personality. Aware that the publication of Frost's letters reveals the pettiness and jealousies, Untermeyer argues that the revelation should not hurt the poet's reputation. Rather it should rescue him from the danger of being "monumentally sanctified" by reminding us that he was human. Generally this memoir is a review of Frost's biography with quotes from both the poems and Frost's letters which elevate the lecture beyond a mere recitation of well-known facts. He stresses Frost's ability to keep his numerous personal griefs hidden from the public, to balance gaiety and somberness in the poems, and to reveal himself only in the letters.

A more specific memoir than Untermeyer's, and a particularly valuable record of an important incident in Frost's life, is F. D. Reeve's *Robert Frost in Russia* (1964), the story of Frost's celebrated journey to Russia in 1962. The book has eight pages of photographs but no index. Dates are loosely used so that the reader has difficulty keeping up with the time scheme of the trip. But the general story is reliable because Reeve was one of Frost's escorts. Happily the book is more than a diary of events. Reeve tries to communicate the mixture of pride, elation, and frustration which Frost felt while being toasted in a country with a culture so totally foreign to his own.

Reeve begins with some insignificant details—for example, he tells us that the State Department office in which the plans were organized had a vinyl floor and furniture of steel and plastic, but he later makes up for such irrelevancies with interesting descriptions of Russian hotels. He successfully catches Frost's wit as illustrated by his retort to Madame Dobrynin, the wife of the Soviet Ambassador to the United States, that she could not bid him "Godspeed" because Russians do not believe in God.

More important is the inspiration Frost evidently encouraged in Russian writers. According to Reeve, his greatest accomplishment "was not the political embassy he aspired to [meeting Premier Khrushchev] but the enactment of freewheeling literary activity which he, by his poetry readings and by his talk, encouraged among the Russians" (1964, p. 20). Frost discussed literature with, among others, S. M. Alyansky, Evgeny Evtushenko, Ivan Kashkin, Alexei Surkov, Alexander Tvardovsky, and Mikhail Zenkenvich (Reeve's spellings). The most memorable parts of the trip were the small dinner parties in the homes of various Soviet artists. Followers of the journey who read only the newspaper accounts were told that each day was punctuated with spectacular political comments and confrontation. The true value of Reeve's book is that it corrects this popular misconception by detailing the informal gatherings, free from observation by the press, which Frost had with these writers. A delightful description is given of the dinner with Kornei Chukovsky—like Frost, in his eighties and a recipient of an honorary doctorate from Oxford. Chukovsky donned his Oxford gown and danced "like a jester."

This book is thus a necessity for those who desire a reliable picture of the aging poet when he stepped into the international spotlight just before his death. It also clears up what many people considered to be Frost's mouthing of the conservative line regarding everything from meter and rhyme to tools and weapons when Reeve explains the difficulty the Russian writers had in catching the nuances of Frost's generalizations and the witticisms of his quips. Reeve makes his point exceedingly well, for he balances his translations of what Russian newspapermen quoted Frost as saying with accounts of what Frost really said. The more conservative papers always managed to make Frost's statements sound like a reflection of their antiliberal stance. One of the accomplishments of this little book is that it sets the record straight. As Reeve explains, the difficulties of translation often caused the wit and skepticism of the original poem to become, in Russian, moralistic platitudes on how to live and, thus, ready material for conservative Russian newspapers. Yet despite these setbacks, Frost managed to project to his audience his keen mind and stubborn independence.

Reeve also describes Frost's evening, hosted by Evtushenko, with a group of poets and intellectuals at the Cafe Aelita. He quotes in full Evtushenko's homage to Frost, "Robert Frost in the Cafe Aelita," and he notes that the poets applauded more for Frost's being there in Evtushenko's company than for understanding his poetry. The evening was a public and political gesture, and given the extreme differences in age and culture between Frost and his hosts, it could not have been otherwise. This was the summer of an apparent liberalization of the censorship of Russian writers, right before the crackdown the winter of 1962. The young artists were then confident of the significance of their work, and they recognized Frost as a sturdy representative of the independent literary tradition. But Frost let them down. As Reeve points out, Frost lacked "political elasticity." He could not respond to their needs, and he later labeled Evtushenko as the source of the trip's most disagreeable moments. According to Reeve, Frost was unable to understand how poetic spirit and political zeal could be unified as it was in these young Russians, especially Evtushenko.

Through all the poetry readings and elaborate dinners, though, Frost felt that the trip would be worthless unless he received an audience with Premier Khrushchev. Reeve says that from the beginning, even before the plans for the trip were completed, Frost expected to discuss world matters with the Russian leader. He wanted to tell Khrushchev that these two great nations should stop haggling over petty matters and get on with the business of establishing a "noble rivalry." To illustrate Frost's political naiveté, Reeve notes that the poet even hoped to persuade Khrushchev to give up East Berlin. When he finally received word that the premier would see him, Frost was extremely nervous. Reeve successfully captures the sense of what he calls Frost's commitment to a "poetic-prophetic-political role."

There is a fascinating account of their ninety-minute conversation. Frost had fallen ill with a nervous stomach, and Khrushchev, with what Reeve correctly calls "the gesture of a master," sent his personal doctor before meeting Frost. Khrushchev listened to Frost's arguments for a noble rivalry and for the establishment of political and intellectual greatness in both countries. But when the poet turned the conversation to Berlin, Khrushchev countered with the hard realities of politics, especially the threat which the Russians saw in NATO and in the growing military strength of West Germany. To Reeve's credit, he does not quote the conversation except the few lines of which he is certain. Most of his report is paraphrase, as befits a conversation in translation; yet it reads dramatically: Khrushchev's patience and political realism versus Frost's eagerness and political innocence. Reeve concludes that each man "was more affected by the other than most people suppose" (1964, p. 119). This is why the book is necessary to the Frost student— it is a firsthand account of one of Frost's greatest trips and conversations. After reading it, the controversy resulting from Frost's later interpretation of his meeting with the premier can be better set in context. It was one of the highlights of Frost's life, and it occurred just five months before he died.

A less detailed report of the Russian journey is Frederick B. Adams, Jr.'s *To Russia with Frost* (1963). At the time of the trip, Adams was Director of the Pierpont Morgan Library and an old friend of Frost's. This short book (forty-one pages) is a limited edition, expanded from a talk which Adams gave to the Club of Odd Volumes on March 20, 1963. It is a collector's item, beautifully designed, and not intended to be as full an account of the trip as Reeve's book.

Adams specifies that Reeve only hints at: that Frost was ignorant of contemporary Russian literature and that he knew too much of Tolstoy and too little of Lenin to understand either the Russian revolution or the delicate relationship between literature and the state. Adams is much more sympathetic to Yevtushenko (his spelling) than Frost is, explaining that the Russian poet's bravura was a welcome break to the "somewhat stifling" Moscow atmosphere. Both Adams and Reeve show Frost to be a grumpy traveler, easily upset by little unavoidable inconveniences to be expected when traveling abroad. Apparently he was not interested in seeing historically important sites because he believed the journey to be more than a cultural exchange. To him it was a mission of great significance for the world, since he truly hoped to discuss his plan for peace with Khrushchev. Since Adams was not present during Frost's visits to Michael Alexeiev, Anna Akhmatova, or Khrushchev, his book cannot be as informative as Reeve's.

A more general memoir than the two reports of the trip to Russia is Daniel Smythe's *Robert Frost Speaks* (1964). This book has a short index and an introduction which sets down in barest fashion the pertinent facts and dates of Frost's life. Smythe knew Frost from 1939 to 1962. Aware of the value of the poet's remarks in both letters and conversations, he learned shorthand in order to transcribe Frost's comments with reasonable accuracy. He stresses his role as a recorder, for he does not want to criticize or judge as much as he desires his book to act as a source for Frost's remarks. Despite his care, he seems to have confused direct quotation and paraphrase, and, thus, the reader cannot determine the accuracy of his recordings. It makes a difference whether Frost literally said what Smythe claims he said in various anecdotes or whether Smythe's recollections are the result of "mental notes" jotted down after the fact.

When Smythe's account of Frost's trek to the Dismal Swamp is compared to Lawrance Thompson's, for example, the problem of reliability becomes evident (see Thompson, 1966, p. 521). Frost apparently embellished his version of the trip for Smythe because Smythe reports that Frost was followed for three miles by a giant Negro who carried an axe and who might have killed him. This version is presented as a verbatim account. But, notes Thompson, some "banalities of syntax" which Frost would never use suggest that Smythe is paraphrasing from memory. The question of quotation versus paraphrase aside, however, the version of the Dismal Swamp experience which Frost told Smythe remains interesting for the melodramatic flair the poet tried to create with the introduction of the giant Negro. Professor Thompson reports that in the many variations of this experience which the poet related to him over a period of twenty-five years, the Negro man was never mentioned. Since there is no reason to doubt that Frost told Smythe about the man with the axe, we should accept the mention of the Negro as another attempt by Frost to make his life more mysterious and melodramatic than it was. First, as Thompson points out, the Negro is probably imaginary. What matters in the version told to Smythe is not the reality or unreality of the Negro man but the romantic flair which Frost tried to give the story. Second, the apparent fictitiousness of the Negro in Smythe's account points to the necessity of checking with Thompson's biography if a truly accurate report of Frost's life is desired. Frost repeatedly advised his friends to check up on him when he discussed his life, but only Professor Thompson seems to have done so consistently. This tale illustrates both the sidelights to be garnered from most of the memoirs and the need to compare these interesting variations with the official version of them in Thompson's books.

Smythe's introduction explains the book's purpose. Naming Frost "the greatest man I have ever known," he shows no inclination to judge or evaluate. He appears to be an enthusiastic supporter of Frost the man, the poet, and the myth. But evaluation is not his goal. As long as the reader is aware of both Smythe's prejudices in favor of Frost and the problem of accurate transcription, he can read *Robert Frost Speaks* with interest. Smythe's first chapter is one of the comparatively few sources for Frost's comments during the Norton lectures he gave at Harvard in March, 1936. Although Frost's contract with Harvard stipulated that he prepare the lectures for later publication, he misplaced, apparently on purpose, the typewritten transcript of the stenographic records which were taken of his lectures. Smythe does not record even one of the six lectures—far from it. But because he does describe the scene and catch a bit of what Frost said, the chapter retains interest as one of the few published recollections of that lecture series.

Frost's comments about other poets are consistently scattered throughout *Robert Frost Speaks*. As Smythe notes, Frost relished talking about his relations with or opinions about other artists. Thus Smythe's recollections of the poet's remarks about Poe, Archibald MacLeish, Sandburg, Joyce, Amy Lowell, and Pound capture some of the sparkle and opinionated barbs which distinguished Frost when he dominated conversations.

Particularly valuable are Frost's comments about some of his own poems. Often pretending that Smythe and a few others were a larger audience, Frost would give them examples of his introductory remarks to poems he would later read. About "The Pasture," for example, he mentioned how the poem expressed "the opposite of confusion. The first stanza is called 'unclouded' " (1964, p. 56). He liked to call "Dust of Snow" the "favor." He insisted that "Stopping by Woods on a Snowy Evening" was overread: "You don't go to the circus to make a lot of discussion—you go to gape. There is nothing hard in that poem, but there is a busy-mindedness that makes people want to know about a little thing like that. . . . Their teacher puts them up to it" (1964, p. 57). Even if Smythe has recorded only the sense of Frost's remarks here, as opposed to the accurate transcription his direct quotation marks suggest, he has nevertheless preserved some of the poet's opinions about his own art which any reader of Frost will find enlightening.

Frost goes on to talk about what he looks for in a poem. Claiming that he checks first to see if the rhyming flows without being artificial, he quotes quatrains by Edwin Markham, Ralph Waldo Emerson, and Walter Savage Landor to illustrate his point. In addition, he argues in favor of observation over invention in poetry, and he mentions how careful a poet must be not to use unnecessary words. These opinions, of course, are in line with his well-known disapproval of what he termed "obscure" writing. The reader interested in Frost's notions about poetry will do well to consult Smythe's record of these and other comments.

Smythe also catches some of Frost's weaknesses: his refusal to read a long book; his habit of letting friends report to him about recent books instead of reading them himself; his tendency to repeat stories to the extent that the listener wondered if he had ready-made versions of particular anecdotes. To Professor Smythe's credit, he makes no effort to chronicle all of Frost's life. He reports only those occasions when he was present with the poet, and his paraphrases of talks with one of the great conversationalists of the century are of some value. *Robert Frost Speaks* is not scholarly in the usual sense of the word. Although Smythe carefully notes dates and identifies names mentioned in the text, an informal tone happily prevails which combines nicely with the rambling informality of a conversation with Frost.

Less well acquainted with Frost than Smythe, but perhaps more perceptive in his evaluation, is C. P. Snow. His description of Frost in *Variety of Men* (1967) is a delight. In the preface Mr. Snow explains his intention as being no more than a record of personal impressions. Noting that he met all of the men he discusses except Stalin, he insists that none of them ever appeared directly in his fiction, and that only the mathematician G. H. Hardy appeared indirectly. He does admit, though, that had he known Frost when he was younger, he might have been tempted to treat the poet in a fictional manner. Finally, Mr. Snow warns that the conversations which he reports in direct quotations are more likely an accurate record of the sense of what was said than a verbatim transcription of the remarks.

First meeting the poet in England in 1957, Snow came away with the impression that Frost was "old, strong, pawky, witty," a man who "made more immediate impact on undergraduate listeners than any writer I could remember" (1967, p. 130). Like most everyone else upon first meeting Frost, Snow was immediately attracted to the poet's public persona. It was, writes Snow,

pleasant to think of this shrewd but simple artist as being above
the battle. But again, like most of Frost's acquaintances, Snow
soon discovered the gulf between public mask and private man:
"When one knew him a little better, the attractiveness remained,
but that illusion didn't: one at least realized that he was a subtle
man, with a nature difficult to reach or comprehend" (1967, p.
132). Because of this difficulty, Snow celebrates the publication
of the Frost-Untermeyer correspondence, calling it "one of the
great documents of self-revelation" (1967, p. 134). He has
learned as much or more from these letters as he did from conversations with Frost.

What follows is a short account of the usual biographical facts
but with the valuable addition of Snow's penetrating judgments
and comments. He writes eloquently about Frost's obsessive
self-doubt, the desperate need for reassurance about the ultimate
value of his poetry which led to his jealousy and envy of other
publicly recognized poets. He correctly observes that Frost believed art to be its own justification and thus warranted the sacrifice of wife and family. Lamenting the extremes of Frost's farmer persona, Snow argues that Frost would have written greater
poems had he freed himself from the pseudo-Georgian style
and had he given himself more to his periods of introspection:
"He did not trust enough in his own ultimate originality, which
was potentially as unique as Yeats's" (1967, p. 138).

Particularly perceptive are Snow's remarks concerning Frost's
long association with American universities and colleges. Commenting on the honorary degrees and financial support which the
schools gave the poet, Snow observes that these multiple honors
would have been destructive to many writers, but not to Frost.
He suggests that Frost needed neither the comfort nor the money
but relied upon the psychological support which his association
with academic life afforded. In Frost's mind, speculates Snow,
the successful affiliation with professors and students of literature
may have provided the reassurance which he constantly needed.

There are other discussions of interest: especially of Frost's
one-sided rivalry with T. S. Eliot and of the emotional memorial lecture held in Moscow after Frost's death, a ceremony at
which Snow was present. His description of it is an appropriate
climax for those who have read the accounts of Frost's trip to
Russia. Snow's chapter on Frost is far and away the best of the
shorter memoirs. Informed and exquisitely written, it is, above
all, a judicious combination of biographical facts and sane judgments. Although he does not shrink from pointing out the poet's

weaknesses, he clearly admires Frost: "With that said, I should, if I had had the luck, have chosen him for sheer company, after [G. H.] Hardy, of all the people in this book. . ." (1967, pp. 147-48).

The final memoir to be discussed is Wilbert Snow's "The Frost I Knew" (*Texas Quarterly*, 1968). Snow was a published poet and a professor of English at Wesleyan University who arranged Frost's visit to lecture at Wesleyan. He first met Frost at the celebration of the poet's so-called fiftieth birthday, March 26, 1925, and the two became good friends. Recalling that event, Snow quotes from the article he wrote for *Publisher's Weekly* to herald the celebration, "New England in the New Poetry of America," thus permitting a glimpse of his tribute to Frost the poet before he knew the man. Although he generally praised Frost in that early article, he was also gently critical of *A Boy's Will* and of "New Hampshire." Still Frost apparently liked Snow's remarks, for he made the first effort to begin the friendship.

Professor Snow's memoir is an account of how that friendship took shape, from Snow's initial efforts to entice Frost to visit Wesleyan, to commentary upon the closeness of a long friendship despite sharp debate about their political differences. This article is valuable chiefly for its recollections and paraphrases of Frost's comments about Emerson; Longfellow ("You can damn all you want to . . . Bryant, Lowell, Holmes and Whittier, but keep hands off of Longfellow,"); his experience in England; and his dismissal of Amy Lowell, Edgar Lee Masters, William Ellery Leonard, Edwin Markham, and Sandburg. Of perhaps special interest is Snow's account of Frost's ambiguous attitude toward Edwin Arlington Robinson. According to Snow, Robinson was the one contemporary for whom Frost had great respect. Yet his apparent jealousy of Robinson's prominence convinced him that they were rivals, and, thus, he could meet Robinson's generous praise of his work with only petty enmity.

Snow also recalls exchanges between Frost and Elinor about the suffering the family endured while he struggled with his unpublished poetry. These comments suggest Elinor's resentment about the sacrifice of their marriage to the demands of art. The memoir is full of little remarks by which Snow implicitly points out Frost's shortcomings: his inability to converse about poetic technique because of his need to turn a conversation into a monologue; his belief that he had "a monopoly on plain talking verse"; his inability to accept criticism even from a friend (1968,

p. 21). Yet on the whole Snow's memoir is a testimony to his admiration of Frost. He lauds Frost's genuine interest in and handling of the college boys who flocked to him. He finds a truly sensitive man when he watches Frost observe stars. And he cherishes the "sparkle and sensitivity" of Frost's personality. The article is full of direct quotations from Frost's letters, some of which are not yet collected and thus have special interest for the reader. Snow has written, in short, an informal, personable, interesting memoir from the point of view of one who knew Frost well enough and long enough to accept the strange mixture of the cantankerous, the petty, the generous, and the brilliant which made up the personality of the man whom he so fondly recalls.

The wide range of personal letters, biographical information, and memoirs discussed in this chapter indicates the complexity of Robert Frost's personality. It should now be clear that investigations of the commentary on Frost's life must be tempered with an awareness of which Frost one is reading about: the friend, the public personality, the family man, the poet, the playful prankster, the self-doubter, the egotist, the petty rival, and so on. More important, perhaps, is the necessity to avoid accepting the poet's own comments about his life as the gospel truth. For Frost enjoyed mythicizing about his life story as much as he delighted in maintaining the mask of his public personality. Readers who would know the facts must check up on him as diligently as those who write about his life. Because of the complexity of Frost's life story, perhaps the best way to approach it is to assimilate the numerous books and memoirs while using Lawrance Thompson's accurate and reliable biography as the center of information.

References

Adams, Frederick B., Jr.
  1963. *To Russia with Frost*. Boston: Club of Odd Volumes.
Anderson, Margaret Bartlett
  1963. *Robert Frost and John Bartlett: The Record of a Friendship*. New York: Holt, Rinehart and Winston.
Cook, Reginald L.
  1969. "Robert Frost" in *Sixteen Modern American Authors: A Survey of Research and Criticism*, ed. Jackson R. Bryer. Durham, N. C.: Duke Univ. Pr.

Cox, Sidney
  1929. *Robert Frost: Original "Ordinary Man."* New York: Holt.
  1957. *A Swinger of Birches: A Portrait of Robert Frost.* New York: New York Univ. Pr.
Frost, Lesley
  1969. *New Hampshire's Child: The Derry Journals of Lesley Frost.* Albany: State Univ. of New York Pr.
Gould, Jean
  1964. *Robert Frost: The Aim Was Song.* New York: Dodd.
Grade, Arnold
  1972. (editor) *Family Letters of Robert and Elinor Frost.* Albany: State Univ. of New York Pr.
Lathem, Edward Connery, and Lawrance Thompson
  1966. (editors) *Robert Frost and the Lawrence, Massachusetts, "High School Bulletin": The Beginning of a Literary Career.* New York: Grolier Club.
Lowell, Amy
  1917. *Tendencies in Modern American Poetry*, pp. 79–136. New York: Macmillan.
Mertins, Louis
  1947. *The Intervals of Robert Frost.* Berkeley: Univ. of California Pr.
  1965. *Robert Frost: Life and Talks-Walking.* Norman: Univ. of Oklahoma Pr.
Munson, Gorham B.
  1925. "Robert Frost," *Saturday Review of Literature* Mar. 28, pp. 625–26.
  1927. *Robert Frost: A Study in Sensibility and Good Sense.* New York: George H. Doran.
  1930. "Robert Frost and the Humanistic Temper," *Bookman* July, pp. 419–22.
  1964. "The Classicism of Robert Frost," *Modern Age* Summer, pp. 291–305.
Reeve, F. D.
  1964. *Robert Frost in Russia.* Boston: Atlantic–Little, Brown.
Sergeant, Elizabeth Shepley
  1925. "Robert Frost: A Good Greek Out of New England," *New Republic* Sept. 30, pp. 144–48.
  1960. *Robert Frost: The Trial by Existence.* New York: Holt, Rinehart and Winston.
Smythe, Daniel
  1964. *Robert Frost Speaks.* New York: Twayne.
Snow, C. P.
  1967. "Robert Frost" in *Variety of Men.* London: Macmillan, pp. 130–50.
Snow, Wilbert
  1968. "The Frost I Knew," *Texas Quarterly* Autumn, pp. 9–48.

Thompson, Lawrance
1964. (editor) *Selected Letters of Robert Frost.* New York: Holt, Rinehart and Winston.
1966. *Robert Frost: The Early Years, 1874–1915.* New York: Holt, Rinehart and Winston.
1970. *Robert Frost: The Years of Triumph, 1915–1938.* New York: Holt, Rinehart and Winston.
Untermeyer, Louis
1939. *From Another World: The Autobiography of Louis Untermeyer.* New York: Harcourt.
1963. (editor) *The Letters of Robert Frost to Louis Untermeyer.* New York: Holt, Rinehart and Winston.
1964. *Robert Frost: A Backward Look.* Washington: Library of Congress.
1970. "Book Forum, Letters from Readers," *Saturday Review* Sept. 5, p. 22.

Selected Additional Readings

Adams, J. Donald
1959. "Speaking of Books," *New York Times Book Review.* Apr. 12, p. 2.
Baker, Carlos
1957. "Frost on the Pumpkin," *Georgia Review* Summer, pp. 117–31.
Bartlett, Donald
1946. "A Friend's View of Robert Frost," *New Hampshire Troubadour* Nov., pp. 22–25.
1966. "Two Recollections of Frost," *Southern Review* Oct., pp. 842–46.
Beach, Joseph Warren
1954. "Robert Frost," *Yale Review* Winter, pp. 204–17.
Bennett, Paul A.
1966. "Robert Frost: Best Printed U. S. Author and His Printer, Spiral Press," *Publisher's Weekly* Mar. 2, pp. 82–86.
Clark, Sylvia
1946. "Robert Frost: The Derry Years," *New Hampshire Troubadour* Nov., pp. 13–16.
Cook, Reginald L.
1947. "Poet in the Mountains," *Western Review* Spring, pp. 175–81.
1949. "Frost Country," *Vermont Life* Summer, pp. 15–17.
Cox, James M.
1963. "Stamp of a Heroic Life," *Saturday Review* Oct. 5, pp. 43–44.

Cox, Sidney H.
1946. "Robert Frost at Plymouth," *New Hampshire Trouba-dour* Nov., pp. 18–22.
Dendinger, Lloyd N.
1969. "Robert Frost: The Popular and the Central Poetic Images," *American Quarterly* Winter, pp. 792–804.
Eberhart, Richard
1966. "Robert Frost: His Personality," *Southern Review* Oct., pp. 762–88.
Fairlie, Henry
1973. "Camelot Revisited," *Harper's* Jan., especially pp. 72–74.
Farjeon, Eleanor
1954. "Edward Thomas and Robert Frost," *London Magazine* May, pp. 50–61.
Fisher, Dorothy Canfield
1926. "Vermont" in *Bookman* Dec.; reprinted in *Recognition of Robert Frost*, ed. Richard Thornton, pp. 103–7. New York: Holt, 1937.
Fitz Gerald, Gregory, and Paul Ferguson.
1972. "The Frost Tradition: A Conversation with William Meredith," *Southwest Review* Spring, pp. 108–16.
Flint, F. Cudworth
1966. "A Few Touches of Frost," *Southern Review* Oct., pp. 830–38.
Francis, Robert, et al.
1963. "On Robert Frost," *Massachusetts Review* Winter, pp. 237–49.
Grade, Arnold E.
1968. "A Chronicle of Robert Frost's Early Reading, 1874–1899," *Bulletin of the New York Public Library* Nov., pp. 611–28.
Haines, John W.
1935. "England" in *Gloucester Journal* Feb. 2; reprinted in *Recognition of Robert Frost*, ed. Richard Thornton, pp. 89–97. New York: Holt, 1937.
Holmes, John
1936. "Harvard: Robert Frost and the Charles Eliot Norton Lectures on Poetry," *Boston Transcript* Mar. 21; reprinted in *Recognition of Robert Frost*, ed. Richard Thornton, pp. 114–19. New York: Holt, 1937.
Howarth, Herbert
1966. "Frost in a Period Setting," *Southern Review* Oct., pp. 789–99.
Joyce, Hewette E.
1966. "A Few Personal Memories of Robert Frost," *Southern Review* Oct., pp. 847–49.
Kahn, Roger
1963. "Robert Frost: A Reminiscence," *Nation* Feb. 9, pp. 121–22.

Kennedy, John Fitzgerald
1964. "Poetry and Power," *Atlantic Monthly* Feb., pp. 53–54.
Kenny, A.
1963. "Robert Frost: RIP," *National Review* Feb. 12, p. 100.
Laing, Dilys
1966. "Interview with a Poet," *Southern Review* Oct., pp. 850–54.
Lathem, Edward Connery
1963. *Robert Frost: His American Send-Off.* Lunenburg, Vt.: Stinehour Pr.
Lathem, Edward Connery, and Lawrance Thompson
1963. (editors) *Robert Frost: Farm-Poultryman.* Hanover, N.H.: Dartmouth Publications.
MacLeish, Archibald
1964. "The Gift Outright," *Atlantic Monthly* Feb., pp. 50–52.
Meixner, John A.
1966. "Frost Four Years After," *Southern Review* Oct., pp. 862–77.
Moore, Virginia
1931. "Robert Frost of New Hampshire," *Yale Review* May, pp. 627–29.
Morse, Stearns
1973. "Lament for a Maker: Reminiscences of Robert Frost," *Southern Review* Winter, pp. 53–68.
Newdick, Robert
1936. "Robert Frost and the American College," *Journal of Higher Education* May, pp. 237–43.
1936. "Robert Frost as Teacher of Literature and Composition," *English Journal* Oct., pp. 632-37.
1937. "Robert Frost and the Dramatic," *New England Quarterly* June, pp. 262–69.
1939. "Robert Frost Looks at War," *South Atlantic Quarterly* Jan., pp. 52–59.
1940. "Robert Frost and the Classics," *Classical Journal* Apr., pp. 403–16.
Poole, Ernest
1946. "When Frost Was Here," *New Hampshire Troubadour* Nov., pp. 10–13.
Robson, W. W.
1966. "The Achievement of Robert Frost," *Southern Review* Oct., pp. 735–61.
Rosenthal, M. L.
1959. "The Robert Frost Controversey," *Nation* June 20, pp. 559–61.
Sampley, Arthur M.
1971. "The Myth and the Quest: The Stature of Robert Frost," *South Atlantic Quarterly* Summer, pp. 287–98.

Samuel, Rinna
   1961. "Robert Frost in Israel," *New York Times Book Review*
   Apr. 23, pp. 42–43.
Stanlis, Peter
   1973. *Robert Frost: The Individual and Society*. Rockford, Ill.:
   Rockford College Pr.
Stewart, Bernice
   1922. "Michigan" in *Detroit Free Press* June 25; reprinted in
   Recognition of Robert Frost, ed. Richard Thornton, pp. 108–11.
   New York: Holt, 1937.
Thomas, Helen
   1956. *As It Was* and *World Without End*. 2 v. in 1. London:
   Faber and Faber.
Thompson, Lawrance
   1967. *Robert Frost*. Minneapolis: Univ. of Minnesota Pr.
Trilling, Lionel
   1959. "A Speech on Robert Frost: A Cultural Episode," *Partisan
   Review* Summer, pp. 445–52.
Untermeyer, Louis
   1946. (editor) *The Pocket Book of Robert Frost's Poems*. New
   York: Washington Square Pr.
Van Dore, Wade
   1970. "Native to the Grain," *Yankee* Aug., pp. 172–75.
   1972. "Robert Frost: A Memoir and a Remonstrance," *Journal
   of Modern Literature* Nov., pp. 554–60.
Van Doren, Mark
   1936. "The Permanence of Robert Frost," *American Scholar*
   Spring, pp. 190–98; reprinted in *Recognition of Robert Frost*,
   ed. Richard Thornton, pp. 3–13. New York: Holt, 1937.
Whicher, George F.
   1937. "Amherst College" in *Amherst Record* July 14; reprinted
   in *Recognition of Robert Frost*, ed. Richard Thornton, pp. 98–
   102. New York: Holt, 1937.
   1943. "Out for Stars: A Meditation on Robert Frost," *Atlantic
   Monthly* May, pp. 64–67.
Yevish, Irving A.
   1968. "Robert Frost: Campus Rebel," *Texas Quarterly* Autumn,
   pp. 49–55.

CHAPTER 2

The Early Criticism of
Robert Frost

The material generally considered to constitute the early Frost criticism covers a little more than a decade, from 1913 to 1925. During this period, Frost published four volumes of poetry—*A Boy's Will* (1913), *North of Boston* (1914), *Mountain Interval* (1916), and *New Hampshire* (1923)—not a prolific production, perhaps, but enough to secure his fame. Most of the early Frost criticism is made up of reviews of these four books. Since this was also the time of an extraordinary ferment in British and American poetry, many of the longer commentaries discussed in this chapter focus on Frost as a leader in what was then called the New Poetry or the "modern poetic renaissance." When read together, the reviews of individual volumes and the longer, more general essays complement each other in such a way as to document the foundations of Frost's first decade of public recognition.

In a manner which seems incredible today, these first evaluations sparked active controversy in literary circles. First of all there was the matter of Frost's publication in England. Because both *A Boy's Will* and *North of Boston* were initially published in London, Frost found himself in the middle of the traditional argument about British recognition of neglected American authors. Generally the British reviewers hailed his achievement, particularly *North of Boston*. When he returned to the United States, he became the subject of a multi-edged dispute. Some critics used Frost to comment upon the sorry state of American publishing, lamenting that native artists of exceptional merit had to find publication in a foreign country because American publishers and editors were blind and deaf to the newer movements in poetry. Other commentators disagreed. Attacking Frost for his so-called British-made reputation, these critics used the poet's work as a transition to a more general argument that the American public should not patronize an American artist just because the English think well of him.

These two points of view generated a second controversy about the ability of American editors and publishers to recognize and support native talent. Critic after critic came to Frost's support, but they mixed praise of his poetry with disgust at the overall atmosphere facing American artists in 1913. Because Frost had waited so long for recognition, he genuinely feared that these attacks, many of them acid-edged, would turn American editors against him just when he was beginning to publish regularly. Additional arguments developed over his sense of humor and his use of New England themes. Frost claimed publicly that he did not bother with commentaries on his work, but like most authors he was affected privately by criticism.

This chapter will take into account his more pertinent comments about the early criticism. The only collection of these materials, *Recognition of Robert Frost*, edited by Richard Thornton (1937), will be discussed first. Although published in 1937 and actually beyond the scope of this chapter, *Recognition of Robert Frost* nevertheless remains the only volume in which the reader can find a sampling of the first British, American, and continental evaluations. Following commentary upon this book will be discussions of first the British and then the American essays on Frost which were published between 1913 and 1925.

Recognition of Robert Frost was printed by Frost's publisher in honor of the twenty-fifth anniversary of the publication of *A Boy's Will*. Because the editor's goal is to present a composite picture of Frost the man and to offer an introduction to his poetry and philosophy, a good many biographical sketches have been included. These pieces are aimed at students. Unfortunately Thornton has shortened some of the articles, apparently believing that the collection would be better with more essays than with complete ones. There are nine pages of photographs and a selected chronology of Frost, but no index.

Thornton has grouped the articles according to subject and theme so that the reader can turn to the selections he needs after glancing at the table of contents. Mark Van Doren's well-known essay "The Permanence of Robert Frost" introduces the volume. The groupings which follow Van Doren's article have such general titles as "Early Recognition," "Tribute in Verse," "Home Places," "Bibliographical," "Portraits," "The Idea," "Continental Recognition," and "Four Prefaces to a Book." Aware of the problem facing those who want to investigate the important early criticism of Frost—often scattered in obscure reviews and foreign periodicals—Thornton has included some of the notices more difficult to find. The "Tribute in Verse" section reprints poems by Wilfred Gibson and Edward Thomas, while "Home Places" includes articles about Frost's years in New Hampshire, England, and Michigan, and at Amherst College and Harvard.

Especially important in this latter section are the two notices of Frost's Norton Lectures at Harvard in 1936 and the essay by John W. Haines. First, the accounts of the Norton Lectures are significant because very few reports of those talks were preserved. Although his contract with Harvard called for the eventual publication of his lectures, Frost misplaced, apparently on purpose, the stenographic records of his remarks. Knowing that he made a stronger impact on the audience when he spoke informally, and mixing his rambling comments with sayings from the poems, Frost refused to write down a lecture. He also knew that a stenographic record of his remarks would be an injustice to his platform performances at Harvard because the secretary would capture only the words while missing the nuances, tones, and gestures. The point is, obviously, that the poet frowned on publication of his lectures. Thus, when the records of these lectures were "misplaced," Frost students lost an opportunity to investigate one of his most important series of talks. *Recognition of Robert Frost* reprints an anonymous editorial from the *Harvard Alumni Bulletin* (Mar. 20, 1936) which celebrates the overflowing audiences that turned out to hear an American poet (as opposed to the usually more popular European artists), and a more specific article by John Holmes, first published in the *Boston Transcript* (Mar. 21, 1936), which lists the titles for the six lectures and paraphrases some of Frost's remarks. The article by John W. Haines, first published in the *Gloucester Journal* (Feb. 2, 1935), is rewarding for its recollection of Frost during his stay in the Dymock section of England. The essay is important not for its revelation of facts but for its firsthand account of Frost's period in England written by a friend who joined the poet for many walks and discussions.

The most important essay in Thornton's "Bibliographical" section is Frederic Melcher's "Robert Frost and His Books," which originally appeared in the *Colophon* (part II, May 1930). Though from today's perspective the article is dated, it remains nevertheless an informative record of the publishing history of Frost's books and poems through *West-Running Brook*. The "Portraits" section includes, among others, Elizabeth Shepley

Sergeant's well-known essay "Robert Frost: A Good Greek Out of New England" (originally published in *New Republic*, Sept. 30, 1925, and discussed in chapter 1 of this book) and Sidney Cox's review of *Mountain Interval* (first appearing in *New Republic*, Aug. 25, 1917). Cox praises Frost's "sincerity," his skill at capturing tones of speech, and his ability to set down what he sees, never pretending to "see what isn't there. . . ." Eighteen articles are grouped in "The Idea" section, most of them concerned with general analyses of Frost's idiom, subject matter, and style. Among the most important notices represented are those by Louis Untermeyer, G. R. Elliott, Percy H. Boynton, and James Southall Wilson. None of the essays in this section can be called "scholarly" evaluations of the poet's achievement, but all are significant for the serious Frost student because they illustrate the foundations upon which later, more incisive comment is based.

The "Continental Recognition" section contains translations of three articles written by French and German critics. Of particular interest is Albert Feuillerat's essay (first published in *Revue des deux mondes*, Sept. 1, 1923) which stresses, understandably, the "Americanness" of Frost's poetry: "No mistake could be made about this: Frost's work could have been written only by an American" (Thornton, 1937, p. 269). Though Feuillerat argues that Frost's poetry has a "limited horizon," he praises the poet's skill at communicating the essence of a particular people and the infinity of small, exact details.

Just as interesting as the essays by the continental critics are the prefaces grouped under "Four Prefaces to a Book." Written by W. H. Auden, C. Day Lewis, Paul Engle, and Edwin Muir, these articles make up the preface to the 1936 English edition of *Selected Poems of Robert Frost*. Auden writes of Frost as "almost the only representative" today of nature poetry, stressing the poet's stoical attitude which frees him to describe what he sees without comment. C. Day Lewis similarly praises Frost's "peculiar intimacy with nature" which prevents him from being "openly didactic." Commenting on his own experience in America, Paul Engle lauds Frost's skill at describing what he knows so that the reader can feel and see it. And Edwin Muir analyzes "The Ax-Helve" to illustrate Frost's poetic method.

All of these groupings of essays and commentary have their value, but perhaps the most significant section for today's reader is "Early Recognition." It begins with an 1894 letter from Maurice Thompson to William Hayes Ward, editor of the *Independent*, in which Thompson praises "My Butterfly," Frost's first

published poem, while advising Frost to abandon poetry because of the inevitable discouragement he would face. Readers
can find this letter in Lawrance Thompson's edition of *Selected
Letters of Robert Frost* (1964), but more difficult to track
down are the first reviews of *A Boy's Will* and *North of Boston*.
Thornton has collected a few of these early comments so that
the reader can determine the specific qualities of Frost's poetry
which attracted influential critics and encouraged them to advertise his work. The anonymous review, for example, first published in the *Academy* (Sept. 20, 1913), praises Frost's simple,
lucid, and yet experimental lines: "One feels that this man has
seen and *felt:* seen with a revelation, a creative vision; felt personally and intensely; and he simply writes down, without confusion or affection, the results thereof" (Thornton, 1937, pp.
19–20). Lawrance Thompson reports that Frost "relished" this
particular review (see *Robert Frost: The Early Years, 1874–
1915*, 1966, p. 426). More important are the reviews by Englishmen Lascelles Abercrombie, Edward Thomas, and Edward
Garnett, and by Americans William Dean Howells, Amy Lowell, and Ezra Pound, each of which will be discussed later in
this chapter.

The value of *Recognition of Robert Frost* is not simply that
it gathers together some fifty or so comments and essays which
highlight Frost criticism through 1936. The collection, of
course, does ease the task of those who want a sampling of this
early commentary. But of perhaps greater importance is the
editor's care in tracking down and publishing essays which
might otherwise remain unavailable to most general readers and
to many libraries. Amy Lowell's notice in *New Republic* and
William Dean Howells' comment in *Harper's* are easy enough
to find, but the little magazines like *Poetry*, which published
Ezra Pound's key reviews of Frost, and the commentaries from
English and continental writers are not so readily available.
Aware of this problem, Thornton has happily gathered the
best known as well as some of the best of the more obscure
articles in order to provide a representative collection of early
Frost criticism.

The English Criticism

Although Frost received encouragement from English poets
and publication by an English firm, the first notices of *A Boy's*

Will in English journals were disappointing. The anonymous "Notices of New Books" in the *Athenaeum* (Apr. 5, 1913), for example, contained only two sentences. Noting that Frost intended the poems to depict a progression of the boy's outlook upon life, the reviewer concludes that Frost does not succeed: "The author is only half successful in this, possibly because many of his verses do not rise above the ordinary, though here and there a happy line or phrase lingers gratefully in the memory" (1913, p. 379). The anonymous commentator in the *Times Literary Supplement* (Apr. 10, 1913) was a little more favorable, but once again the notice was only two sentences, far too small to attract attention. Praising the "agreeable individuality" of the poems, the reviewer notes that some lines make the reader "stop and think." Yet he concludes that a few thoughts are so feebly expressed as to render obscure an otherwise striking poem, like "The Trial by Existence."

Brief as they are, these were two of the most important notices of *A Boy's Will* for several months. Frost's understandable disappointment is reflected in a letter which Elinor wrote to Margaret Bartlett: "Rob has been altogether discouraged at times, but I suppose we ought to be satisfied for the present to get the book published and a little notice taken of it. Yeats has said to a friend [Ezra Pound], who repeated the remark to Robert, that it is the best poetry written in America for a long time. If only he would say so publicly, but he won't, he is too taken up with his own greatness" (*Selected Letters of Robert Frost*, c July 3, 1913).

Norman Douglas' review gave more positive encouragement. Revised for his book *Experiments* (1925), this short piece was originally published in slightly different form in *The English Review* (June 1913). Echoing the standard European opinion of the time that nowhere is more "derivative nonsense printed under the name of poetry" than in America, Douglas gives credit to Frost for breaking with the standard drivel. He especially likes the "wild, racy flavour" of the poems in *A Boy's Will* because they suggest a response to nature which shows that Frost is a true lyric poet. Although this notice is short and general, Frost was proud of it. He wrote to John Bartlett that he valued it "chiefly for its source" because the editor himself (Douglas) wrote it for the influential journal *The English Review* (*Selected Letters of Robert Frost*, c June 16, 1913).

Like the anonymous review in the *Academy* mentioned in the above discussion of *Recognition of Robert Frost*, F. S. Flint's

comments in *Poetry and Drama* (June 1913) supplied the praise
Frost needed. Though Flint finds lapses of diction in some of
the poems, he believes that their "intrinsic merits" are great. The
book's charm, writes Flint, derives from its simplicity which allows Frost to create the complete expression of one mood or
emotion in each poem. In Flint's opinion the most general characteristic of the poems is "direct observation of the object and
immediate correlation with the emotion. . . ." Frost needed a
notice like this one. It goes beyond superficial remarks about
the book's arrangement to comment with understanding on the
kind of poetry Frost was trying to write. Still there was one
sentence which worried him. Noting that Frost had found his
first publisher in England, Flint implicitly criticizes American
editors for forcing one of their own poets into "a constant
struggle against circumambient stupidity for the right of expression." Ezra Pound had already leveled this charge in his
review of *A Boy's Will,* and Frost began to worry about alienat-
ing the editors and publishers he would need upon his return
to America. Consequently, in a letter to John Bartlett, whom he
was trying, as mentioned earlier, to persuade to advertise *A
Boy's Will* in the United States and Canada, Frost included
copies of the most favorable reviews with the stipulation that
Bartlett omit the "slams" at American editors (*Selected Letters
of Robert Frost,* Aug. 6, 1913).

Succeeding reviews of Frost's poetry were more and more
favorable, perhaps because many of them were written by his
closest English friends. Louis Mertins writes that Frost admitted
as much when he commented that his poet friends in England
made his books a success. According to Mertins, Frost claimed
that these poets thought of him as a "lost puppy straying far
from friends and relations," and that they gave *A Boy's Will*
greater praise than it deserved (see Louis Mertins, *Robert Frost:
Life and Talks-Walking,* 1965, p. 109). Although his second
book, *North of Boston,* was generally received with acclaim
and enthusiasm, the anonymous reviewer for the *Times Literary
Supplement* (May 28, 1914) began where he left off a year
earlier in his remarks about *A Boy's Will.* Now giving Frost
five sentences where earlier he had assigned him only two, the
reviewer again has it both ways. He either guardedly praises
North of Boston or gently criticizes it, depending on the reader's point of view. Again commenting on the "agreeable and
naive individuality" of the poems, he decides that the "unpreten-
tious" aim of the book is to present unembellished pictures of

ordinary human life which have little significance. "Sometimes certainly the episode narrated is so unimportant that it seems to have no significance at all and to arouse no interest" (1914, p. 263). He is willing to admit, however, that in "The Death of the Hired Man" emotion is "very subtly conveyed." Considering the immediate fame which the speech rhythms and blank verse of *North of Boston* earned, it is surprising that this commentator limits his observation to only a mention of Frost's "natural speech." The revolutionary verse form seems to have escaped him.

More perceptive than the *Times* reviewer, and highly qualified to determine and discuss what is new in the poetry he reviews, Lascelles Abercrombie comments in the *Nation* (London, June 13, 1914) on Frost's poetic spirit which is so "shy and elusive" that an analytical reader must wonder if the notional existence for Frost's poetic impulse can be separated from "expressive substance." He compliments Frost on his method which frequently accomplishes something remarkable and which invites the reader to participate in the poetic experience. This is a shrewd comment, for it refers to the reader's need to sense the "sentence sounds" before the poem can be fully appreciated. The effect of the poems, writes Abercrombie, is not long lasting, but it is memorable: "It burns out, as a rule, rather quickly; but while it is burning, substance and fire are completely at one, and at the end we are not left with embers, but with the sense of a swift and memorable experience" (1914, p. 423).

Abercrombie also observes that while Frost is an American, he stands against the tradition of American poetry because he is capable of writing about common life in his own country. Noting that Frost's pictures of New England life are not greatly different from farm life in England itself, Abercrombie nevertheless pinpoints the key difference. Rural life, as Frost portrays it, is hardier, lonelier, more "reflective and philosophical" than in England. Yet unlike many American reviewers of *North of Boston*, Abercrombie correctly sees that a "queer, dry, yet cordial, humor" is present along with the loneliness and tragedy.

The most valuable discussion in Abercrombie's review is his analysis of the technical achievement in Frost's second book. He remarks on the proximity of the blank verse to good prose, and he suggests that the similes and metaphors are scarcely more elaborate than good conversation. Yet Frost's metaphors and analogies are usually striking because of the "concrete familiarity of the experiences they employ." More importantly, writes

Abercrombie, his verse is new and vigorous because of the *way* he uses simple language and concrete images. What follows is the first and still one of the best incisive comments on Frost's blank verse. As Abercrombie explains, those who look for the kind of metrical modulation usually found in poetry will be disappointed, for the rhythms are not intended for aesthetic decoration. Instead Frost introduces a novel use of meter which "can only be designed to reproduce in verse form the actual shape of the sound of whole sentences." Though the difficulties of indicating accent by verse movement occasionally cause monotony, the usual result, insists Abercrombie, is "decidedly exciting." He correctly points out that while Frost's intention is not new, such total reliance upon it as the primary element of technique is indeed rewarding. He then compares Frost's poetry to that of Theocritus, an original observation in 1914 which has been accepted as standard today: "Poetry, in this book, seems determined, once more, just is it was in Alexandria, to invigorate itself by utilizing the traits and necessities of common life, the habits of common speech, the minds and hearts of common folk" (1914, p. 424). Abercrombie's discussions of Frost's verse form, of the use of sentence sounds, and of the closeness to classical Greek bucolic poems were especially perceptive. Later, more elaborate analyses could expand upon his comments but not discredit them, for his essay laid some of the groundwork for future Frost studies.

Ford Madox Hueffer's essay in the *Outlook* (June 27, 1914) is not as penetrating as Abercrombie's, but it represents another boost to Frost's early work by an important critic. In the first half of his review, Hueffer mentions neither Frost nor his poetry, directing his remarks to a partly serious but largely tongue in cheek put down of America in general and of Pennsylvania farming in particular. Nothing that really matters, writes Hueffer, occurs there in the realm of art, ideas, politics, or law. As for the farming, it is primarily a matter of chasing the sheep out of the corn field before retiring to eat watermelon, only then to shoo them out of the waterhole before returning to the watermelon. But New England farmers are different—the unfertile land and the harsh climate make them suffer. Hueffer describes them as provincial, old-fashioned, and often a little mad.

Turning to *North of Boston*, Hueffer says that the volume is valuable as a book of travel because of "the revelatory light that it casts upon the nature of this queer population. . . ." He also uses the word "queer" to describe the verse form: "But

Mr. Frost's verse is so queer, so harsh, so unmusical, that the most prosaic of readers need not on that account be frightened away" (1914, p. 880). To anyone who has read Abercrombie's informed and intelligent comments, it is clear from Hueffer's witty review that he does not understand Frost's achievement nearly as well. He brims with enthusiasm, ranking Frost higher than Whitman, but his appreciation seems mixed with bewilderment. Quoting the first seven lines of "Mending Wall," he insists that they can hardly be called blank verse. He describes the line "Where they have left not one stone on stone" a "truly bewildering achievement." Although he never suggests that Frost write free verse, Hueffer wonders why he does not. But in the long run he does not care how Frost gets his effects as long as he continues to create them: "He may use rhymed Alexandrines for all I care."

This enthusiastic review gave Frost needed support in an influential journal. Yet unaware of Frost's experiments with sentence sounds and of his efforts to break with the "te tum" effect of conventional blank verse, Hueffer can only admit that he is baffled by what he so obviously likes. Considering the newness of *North of Boston* in 1914, his bewilderment is perhaps understandable. Neglected for decades, Frost was in no position to hold out for understanding appreciations of his innovations with technique—enthusiastic reviews like Hueffer's were enough. Apparently brushing aside the suggestion about free verse, the kind of comment which would later anger him, Frost wrote to John Cournos: "I have just read Hueffer's article and I like every word of it. What more could anyone ask for a while" (*Selected Letters of Robert Frost*, July 8, 1914).

One of the most influential reviews of *North of Boston* was Wilfred Wilson Gibson's "Simplicity and Sophistication" (*Bookman*, July 1914). Focusing upon the so-called simplicity of Frost's verse which nearly every reviewer comments on, Gibson insists that this celebrated simplicity contains sophistication of a high order. He praises the "quiet and unsensational" qualities of *North of Boston*, calling it the most "challenging" book of verse to have been published for some time, and he distinguishes between the sophistication of the connoisseur and the sophistication of the artist. The former collects poetical phrases and then betrays his comparative artlessness by the use of artifice, but the latter's art is revealed by the avoidance of poetical tricks. The challenge of Frost's work, writes Gibson, "lies in its starkness, in its nakedness of all poetical fripperies" (1914, p.

183). Still Gibson expresses one reservation. While appreciating the deliberate art which conceals sophistication in its apparent simplicity, he wonders if Frost has not discarded too much in his determination to strip his verse of poetic frills. He particularly misses the "exhilaration of an impelling and controlling rhythm." Because this complaint remains underdeveloped and buried in the end of the review, it would seem that Gibson includes it only to protect his remarks from the appearance of unqualified praise. His admiration for Frost's achievement is evident throughout, and his comments are intelligent and perceptive.

A little more than a month following its first review of *North of Boston*, the *Times Literary Supplement* published a second (July 2, 1914). Using the theme which Wilfred Gibson develops in more detail, the anonymous reviewer lauds the "naked simplicity" of the poems while simultaneously reiterating that the verse form is often monotonous. A more serious charge is leveled when the writer accuses Frost of vagueness and obscurity in "The Fear" and "A Hundred Collars." He evidently wishes the ambiguity of the two poems to be cleared up even though most readers would agree that too much clarity would ruin the tension of "The Fear." But the significance of this second *Times* review is not the restatement of supposed flaws but the declaration of approval. Perhaps the *Times* reviewer has rethought his earlier opinions under pressure from the enthusiastic statements by influential commentators like Abercrombie, Hueffer, and Gibson, or perhaps the *Times* has a new reviewer. Whatever the reason for the change of heart, this column now praises Frost with a statement which has become well known in Frost circles: "Poetry burns up out of it—as when a faint wind breathes upon smouldering embers" (1914, p. 316). None of these remarks is developed in depth, but with his appreciation of the humor in "The Code" and of the last lines of "The Wood-Pile," this reviewer calls attention to deserving poems other than the consistently praised "The Death of the Hired Man" and "Home Burial."

The notice in the *English Review* (Aug. 1914) by Frost's close friend Edward Thomas is significant because it initiates a different area of discussion. With his usual perception, Thomas goes right to the heart of the newness of *North of Boston*. He notes Frost's skill in writing poetry without the trappings of poetic diction, and he urges the reader to appreciate the combination of the lyric and dramatic modes. More importantly,

Thomas is one of the first to point out the differences between
Frost's poems of rural life and Wordsworth's. Suggesting that
North of Boston marks more than the beginning of a new experiment, he argues that Frost knows the life he writes about
better than Wordsworth. The result is that Frost sympathizes
where Wordsworth contemplates. The plain language and the
intense simplicity often fool the reader into thinking he is reading prose, and only at the end of the best poems like "Home
Burial" and "The Wood-Pile" does the reader realize that the
poems are "masterpieces of deep and mysterious tenderness"
(1914, p. 143). For today's student of Frost, this review can
serve as a starting point for a discussion of Frost and Wordsworth. The article became well known in America, and parts
of it were often quoted to illustrate the English support of Frost.

Just as influential in the growing critical acclaim for Frost
was Harold Monro's review in *Poetry and Drama* (Sept. 1914).
It is short, not because he finds nothing to say about *North of
Boston*, but because the initial shock of World War I has stag-
gered him. As he reads the new books of poetry, Monro is intrigued by the signs that they were all written before the war.
Suggesting that it would be an injustice to the authors to discuss their books before the public is ready to think about poetry
as well as war, Monro limits his comments on Frost to a few incisive sentences. He finds the blank verse "remarkable." Unlike
the reviewer for the *Times Literary Supplement*, he detects no
trace of monotony in the rhythms and word choice. Monro is
perceptive enough to see that the irregularity of Frost's verse is
caused by the subordination of regular rhythm to the demands
of emotional value and colloquial speech. These comments were
another boon to Frost, for they were written for a prestigious
journal by an acknowledged leader of the new literature. Interestingly, Abercrombie, Hueffer, and Monro all focus on Frost's
unusual verse rhythm, unlike many of the later American reviewers who stress what they call Frost's grimness.

By 1915 Frost had returned to America, and some British
notices like Edward Garnett's in the *Atlantic Monthly* (Aug.
1915) began to comment upon Frost's achievement thus far instead of reviewing his individual books. Written by a prominent
English critic for a widely read American periodical, Garnett's
article is the earliest significant essay, as opposed to review, to
appear on Frost. He begins by asking the same question other
commentators had raised and of which Frost seemed leery: why
was *North of Boston* issued by an English instead of an Ameri-

can publisher? Although he does not press his disapproval of American editors in the manner of F. S. Flint, his implicit criticism is clear enough. The problem of American poets going to England to find publication may seem minor today, but it was a touchy point of debate from 1905 to 1915. In those years most American editors and publishing houses expressed their disapproval of anything new in poetry by refusing to publish it. Given the ferment then growing in the arts, resentment by American artists and puzzlement by their British counterparts were indeed understandable. Thus a note of irony, which Frost did not miss, can be seen in the fact that Garnett's essay was published in the *Atlantic*, for that journal was one of the prestigious magazines which had previously rejected Frost's work, only to accept him when he made it big.

Garnett goes on to remark that the true question is not the place of Frost's publication or the influence detected in his work, but whether or not the author is a "fresh creative force, an original voice in literature." He decides that Frost's newness is authentic, not only original in tone and vision but also confident in image and insight. The opening lines of "Mending Wall" are worthy of Wordsworth, while the whole of "The Death of the Hired Man" breaks new ground. Admitting that some diehards used to poetry of romantic fancy and lyrical tone will question whether a poem that looks and sounds like "Hired Man" can be genuine poetry, Garnett quotes from Goethe to the effect that what counts is not the artist's definition of poetry but his closeness to a true natural vision of life. No subject is unpoetical, writes Garnett of "A Hundred Collars." If the life the poet perceives is prosaic, the triumph is all the greater for his ability to seize and represent the enduring human truths of its familiarity. Important also is Garnett's remark about Frost's humor. Like most of the British critics, he praises the "ironical appreciation of grave issues," whereas so many American commentators miss the use of humor to stress the sadness.

This is not to say that Garnett underplays the tragedy. He devotes a good deal of his discussion to "Home Burial," of which he says "that for tragic poignancy this piece stands by itself in American poetry" (1915, p. 218). He is also perceptive enough to note that the book's triumph is due in large measure to Frost's brilliant handling of blank verse. Knowing that some purists will complain about the variations in the pentameter rhythm, Garnett argues that a great poet is not judged by his adherence to a metronome but by his comprehension of when to give and take a beat. And while he names Frost one of the few new original poets among hordes of literary poets, poetical poets, and drawing-room poets, he is not afraid to criticize the excessive figurative language of "The Self-Seeker" or the long-windedness of "The Generations of Men."

The appearance of this essay was a tremendous breakthrough for Frost, for it marked his acceptance by the more conservative but powerful American journals. "Birches," "The Road Not Taken," and "The Sound of Trees" are published following the article. Frost, of course, was ecstatic about the essay, and he realized its importance. But he was characteristically worried by Garnett's criticism of both American editors for ignoring him and American readers for their inability to accept anything new in poetry. Still Frost privately agreed with Garnett. Writing to thank the Englishman, he betrayed his impatience with the American reading public by admitting that his first draft of the letter "ran off into the unpatriotic . . . it has been a long fight with editors, my rage has gathered considerable headway and it's hard to leave off believing the worst of them" (*Selected Letters of Robert Frost*, June 12, 1915). Frost was also well aware of the publicity created by Garnett's essay, for he comments on the good effect the article will have.

Of all of Frost's contemporaries, Edgar Lee Masters was most often compared to him during the first decade of his acclaim. Padraic Colum's review of *Mountain Interval* in the *New Republic* (Dec. 23, 1916) is not a comprehensive study of the two poets' work, but it discusses Frost's book in such a way as to shed light on the comparison. Repeating the commonplace assertion that both write about American local life, Colum argues that to "go from 'The Spoon River Anthology' to 'North of Boston' is to go from the court-house into the fields" (1916, p. 219). This difference exists because, unlike Masters, Frost is not interested in satire or social judgment. If Masters had written "A Servant to Servants," he would have left a judgment to be inscribed on the pathetic woman's tombstone. But not Frost. His interest lies in the current of life which still moves: "And as that life expresses itself we feel only sympathy with a soul that does not judge and which is beyond our judgments" (1916, p. 219). The same holds true for "The Self-Seeker." Masters would have seen the opportunity for irony in the insurance company's compensation, but Frost depicts the "reserves of a soul."

These are shrewd comments, worthy of elaboration in a comprehensive essay. Colum is particularly good when he notes that while both poets create a sense of community, Frost excels in giving life to the inanimate things around him. Rather than catalogue these things, he reveals their spiritual history. Unlived-in black cottages, walls, woodpiles, a solitary mountain, apples—all of these things mean more after reading Frost's poems. He finds the same genius in *Mountain Interval*, and he is especially impressed with "The Hill Wife." This article retains its value because Colum's comparison of Frost and Masters and his analysis of Frost's poetry go beyond the usual remarks to suggest new areas for consideration.

Frost's return to America and his subsequent publication by an American firm all but halted the steady output of British commentary. He was not ignored in England—far from it; but he was now written about as an established leader of the new poetry instead of as the newly discovered author of original verse. John Freeman's essay in the *London Mercury* (Dec. 1925) illustrates this changed point of view. He begins with the questionable statement that Frost seems to have a firmer grasp on English tradition than any other contemporary American poet. This is a curious opinion, for Freeman was writing in 1925 after four of Frost's books had been published and after dozens of critics had praised his close ties with American tradition. Of the four volumes, Freeman agrees with those who name *North of Boston* the best. He detects a weakness of form in *A Boy's Will* primarily because of the "common lyrical measures of English verse. . ." (1925, p. 177). Nevertheless he praises the vision and tone of the first book because its affirmation thankfully contrasts with what he calls the despair and negation of modern poetry.

Like most commentators following the publication of Edward Thomas' review, Freeman points to the echo of Wordsworth in Frost's poems. But he also offers the novel, though unsupported opinion that British poet Coventry Patmore is another strong influence. He does not pursue the suggestion because of his more pressing interest in showing how Frost's genius is distinct from that of other poets. Following Garnett, whose essay he mentions, Freeman singles out "Home Burial" and "A Hundred Collars" for special praise, and he picks up Garnett's term *"genre* poetry" to describe the uniqueness of *North of Boston*. The most valuable part of this essay, however, is the discussion of Frost's ethical concerns. Freeman argues that Frost's puritan moralism often amounts to an "ethical stigmatism" which spots his lens and confuses his impressions (1925, p. 184). Yet this moralism can just as easily strengthen the poetry. The problem is that Freeman never specifies the poems in which he detects the negative or positive effects of Frost's ethical concerns, and the result is an intriguing suggestion left unconvincing by its vagueness. A summation of Frost's theory of sentence sounds and of its application to blank verse concludes this generally laudatory essay. Freeman quotes Frost's definition of the function of a "good sentence," and he paraphrases some of the poet's remarks on the importance of catching tones instead of inventing them. His most perceptive observation is the comment that Frost's theory must have been deduced from the poems, for such fine poetry could not have been founded upon theory. Elaboration of this suggestion would have made the essay truly significant.

The American Criticism

The earliest known remarks about Frost's poetry occur indirectly in the short series of letters dated from April, 1894, to December, 1896, which the poet wrote to Susan Hayes Ward, sister of the editor of the *Independent* which first published one of his poems. Especially interesting is his response to her apparent attempt to introduce him to Sidney Lanier's poetry and theory of verse (*Selected Letters of Robert Frost*, June 10, 1894).

The first significant American notices of Frost's poetry, and still among the most famous, are the two reviews which Ezra Pound wrote for Harriet Monroe's periodical *Poetry: A Magazine of Verse*. With characteristic gusto, Pound opens his review of *A Boy's Will* (May 1913) with a scornful comment about the "great American editors" who neglected Frost for so long that he had to find a publisher in England. Noting that the book is "a little raw," he nevertheless praises its sincerity, observation, and lack of sham. Pound then catches Frost in an embarrassing moment, for he publishes a false impression which Frost had given him about his relatives. Quoting "In Neglect," he writes, "It is to his wife, written when his grandfather and his uncle had disinherited him of a comfortable fortune and left him in poverty because he was a useless poet instead of a money-getter" (1913, p. 74). Frost, of course, was elated that the eminent Pound would write about him in a leading periodical of the new poetry, but his opinion of the review was finally mixed. Although he would later regret the slam at American editors

which was to become a kind of rallying cry for those who supported the newer poets, he was immediately upset by the inaccurate details about his relatives. Frost often misrepresented them
in order to make himself look better, but he did not want to see
the false impression in print. He felt that the article was too personal, and he claimed that Elinor cried when she read it.

In the second article on Frost, this one a review of *North of
Boston* (Dec. 1914), Pound once again begins with an attack on
the unimaginative American editors: "There was once an American editor who would even print me, so I showed him Frost's
'Death of the Hired Man.' He wouldn't have it; he had printed
a weak pseudo-Masefieldian poem about a hired man two months
before, one written in a stilted pseudo-literary language, with all
sorts of floridities and worn-out ornaments" (1914, p. 127). Pound
then celebrates Frost's honesty for writing about what he knows
instead of "cribbing" themes from Ovid. He praises Frost's success with natural speech rhythms and his refusal to make fun of
the people he writes about. Most important, in light of the many
comments on Frost's tragic vision which would soon follow,
Pound notes Frost's humor. He particularly likes the comedy
of "The Code," which he describes as "the humor of things as
they are, not that of an author trying to be funny. . ." (1914,
p. 130). With typical Pound phrasing, he concludes his remarks by noting that Frost's "stuff sticks in your head."

The subsequent falling out of Pound and Frost over clashes
between both personalities and theories of poetry is now literary
history. What is not well known is Pound's disgruntlement when
American editors began advertising the false view that Frost
made it on his own in England. He published his protest in a
letter (Aug. 1915) to the *Boston Evening Transcript*. Noting
that he was more destitute than Frost upon arrival in London, he
continues, "I reviewed that book in two places and drew it [to]
other reviewers' attention by personal letters. I hammered his
stuff into *Poetry*, where I have recently reviewed his second
book, with perhaps a discretion that will do him more good than
pretending that he is greater than Whitman." He rejoices that
Frost has "caught on," but he resents the neglect of his own efforts to help Frost as well as the misrepresentation that Frost
made it on his own (D. D. Paige, ed., *The Letters of Ezra Pound:
1907–1941*, New York: Harcourt, 1950, pp. 62–63).

The second review of *A Boy's Will* to appear in an important
American journal was written by William Morton Payne. Short
and perhaps negligible, it was significant to Frost because of its

publication in the *Dial* (Sept. 16, 1913). Payne is entirely appreciative of the lyrics, especially of the quiet passion expressed
in the poet-figure's passive acceptance of the world. Rather than
gay sunlight, Payne finds the "more gracious charm" of twilight.
Like most of today's readers, he is particularly impressed by
"Flower-Gathering" and "Reluctance." He concludes by declaring that if these poems suggest melancholy, "there is at least
nothing morbid about it" (1913, p. 212).

A less favorable notice appeared in the *Dial* a year later with
Alice C. Henderson's review of *North of Boston* (Oct. 1,
1914). She approves of Frost's "sympathetic, kindly, but keenly
humorous vision," and she likes his unromantic, more primitive
sense of the earth. This latter observation is seminal. In showing
that Frost is interested in the natural object as it is instead of as
a symbolic shape or as a means to a romantic, mystical experience, Miss Henderson publishes one of the first analyses of the
difference between Frost's nature poetry and that of the nineteenth century. And yet she seems uninformed about his experiments with voice tones and blank verse, for *North of Boston*
reminds her more of a new novel than of a book of poems. She
concludes that his rhythms are monotonous, but purposely so
because of the type of life he portrays: "Doubtless there will
be many readers who will find Mr. Frost dull, and who will object to his verse structure. There is no denying that his insistent
monosyllabic monotony is irritating, but it may be questioned
whether any less drab monotory of rhythm would have been so
successful in conveying the particular aspect of life presented"
(1914, p. 254).

Miss Henderson's misguided comment illustrates the confusion which Frost's revolutionary blank verse caused among many
serious readers. But this review in the *Dial* and the two in *Poetry*
remained the most important American notices of Frost's work
until his return from England in 1915. Sylvester Baxter publicized Frost's return in his column for the *Boston Herald* (Mar.
9, 1915). Written like a gossip column, this article is a newsy
account of Frost's all but triumphant sweep through Boston
literary circles. Hailed as another Masefield and as the originator
of a new note in poetry, Frost is described as one of "the most
loveable men in the world." Baxter reports that the poet dined
with such luminaries as Alice Brown, Ellery Sedgewick, Professor Hocking of Harvard, and Amy Lowell. This kind of
treatment was strange to Frost, but needless to say he recognized
the opportunity to further his reputation. As editor of the

Atlantic Monthly, Sedgewick soon published three of Frost's poems, and Baxter and Miss Lowell helped Frost's cause by writing widely circulated articles.

Baxter's essay was published in *American Review of Reviews* (Apr. 1915). Though he is not as pungent as Ezra Pound, he retells the false story that Frost was cut off from bright material prospects when his relatives branded him a ne'er-do-well. His article is more an account of Frost's life through the English visit than a review of the poems or an analysis of technique. Describing Frost as if he were the archetypal artist who struggled against the odds and made it, Baxter all but idealizes the poet. His article is especially interesting in the light of Lawrance Thompson's biography, for it sets down the mythic overtones which Thompson was to expose fifty years later. If Baxter is to be believed, Frost was a misunderstood rebel, an inspiring teacher, a loving family man, a brilliant poet, and a deserving recipient of international acclaim. Writing of Frost's reception in London, he comments: "Perhaps if Walt Whitman himself had chosen England for his advent and there dawned unheralded upon the world the effect would hardly have been more electrical" (1915b, p. 433). This was hardly the case, but both the remark and the entire article illustrate the false pose which Frost encouraged and which the public believed until Thompson exposed it.

Baxter's essay is typical of the way Frost used willing columnists to promote an idealized picture of himself. Many more examples can be found in the invaluable collection of interviews edited by Edward Connery Lathem, *Interviews with Robert Frost* (1966). Mr. Lathem has gathered together the most important interviews of Frost's career, from his return to America in 1915 to just before his death in 1963. Two of the most significant of these early interviews, one of which is republished by Lathem, are those conducted by William Stanley Braithwaite for the *Boston Evening Transcript*. The first appeared April 28, 1915, under the title "A Poet of New England: Robert Frost, A New Exponent of Life." Apparently ignoring the possible reaction which some critics would soon initiate against the stinging attacks on American publishers and editors made on his behalf, Frost used the first Braithwaite interview to solidify his reputation as a poet who had to leave the United States to make his own way. Braithwaite evidently did not know about Pound's support, for he wrote, "He has accomplished what no other American poet of this generation has accomplished, and that is,

unheralded, unintroduced, untrumpeted, he has won the acceptance of an English publisher on his own terms, and the unqualified approbation of a voluntary English criticism" (1915a, p.
4). This is the article which prompted Pound's aforementioned
angry letter to the *Transcript*, for Pound knew well the false-
hoods in such a story.

The second Braithwaite interview, which is included in *Interviews with Robert Frost* (Lathem, 1966, pp. 3–8), was published in the *Transcript* May 8, 1915. In this article, Frost supplies Braithwaite with comprehensive discussions of his theory
of sentence sounds. The interviewer cooperates by quoting long
passages from these definitions. Today's readers will find this
interview significant, not only for its illustration of the way
Frost advertised his work, but also for the explanation of Frost's
theory of poetic sound which is largely in his own words.

The reaction against the continuous praise of Frost for first
succeeding in England found expression in more conservative
sources than Pound's angry letter to the *Boston Evening Transcript*. For example, the January, 1915, issue of the *Bulletin of
the Poetry Society of America* mentions that two selections
from *North of Boston* were read at the previous meeting. The
anonymous reporter then continues with evident sarcasm: "Mr.
Frost has been greatly acclaimed by prophets of new poetic
cults in England, but his work could hardly be said to have
found sympathizers in the Poetry Society." This statement may
reflect the society's traditional disapproval of innovative poetry,
but it also suggests the disgust with which some commentators
were reacting to the incessant celebration of Frost's English success. Jessie B. Rittenhouse, the secretary of the Poetry Society,
soon after reviewed *North of Boston* for the *New York Times
Book Review* (May 16, 1915). Trying to mute her anger, she
begins by noting that Frost has fortunately lived down the "fulsome and ill-considered praise" which followed his success in
England. But she soon reveals that the English reputation antag-
onizes her, complaining, "Just why a made-in-England reputation is so coveted by the poets of this country is difficult to
fathom, particularly as English poets look so anxiously to America for acceptance of their own work" (1915, p. 189). In her
opinion, Frost is not nearly as important as Whitman, no matter
what the English say, and she wonders if the short story would
not be a more appropriate form for the poet's material. What
praise Miss Rittenhouse expresses is directed toward the poet's
command of psychology, particularly in "The Death of the

Hired Man" and "Home Burial." Perhaps her most valuable comment is that Frost's truest studies are of women, as illustrated by his success in capturing the combination of grimness and tenderness in these isolated New England farm wives.

Frost's reaction to Miss Rittenhouse's censure was swift. On the same day that her article appeared, he wrote to Sidney Cox, explaining that perhaps she was right insofar as intemperate praise was hurting his reputation. Accordingly, he asks Cox not to let his admiration run away with him. But true to his inability to accept criticism in any form or from anybody, he lashes out at Miss Rittenhouse's "nastiness" for calling the English reviews "fulsome." "There she speaks dishonestly out of complete ig-norance—out of some sort of malice or envy. . . . She has no right to imply of course that I desired or sought a British-made repu-tation" (*Selected Letters of Robert Frost*, May 16, 1915). Frost tells the truth up to a point. He did not sail to England with the idea of making a reputation with British critics, but once the opportunity presented itself, he cultivated it at every turn.

Alfred Harcourt's editorial in the *New York Times Book Review* (Aug. 8, 1915) resulted from Frost's aggravation at Miss Rittenhouse's review. The poet was primarily upset not so much by her comments about the favorable English reviews as by the implications that he had sailed to England to escape the stupidi-ties of American editors. He was worried that the continued sniping at American publishers would ruin his chances with those like Ellery Sedgewick who were just beginning to support him. Thus he appealed for aid from Alfred Harcourt, his editor at Holt, who used his influence to publish a denial in the *New York Times*. Because Harcourt accepted Frost's version, the editorial was partly untruthful: "Writing to his present Ameri-can publishers he tells them that he happened to be in England when the idea came to him of collecting his poetry manuscripts into a volume. . . . He declares, moreover, that he 'never offered a book to an American publisher, and didn't cross the water seek-ing a British publisher.' The thing 'just happened.' And, so, there is not 'another case of American inappreciation' to record" (1915, p. 284). It is true that Frost never offered a book to an American publisher, but it is wrong to suggest that he did not plan to find a British publisher once he arrived in London. Frost was using Harcourt to smooth over an unpleasant row.

This argument was soon overshadowed by another, originating in the first lengthy essay on Frost written by an American, Amy Lowell's portrait in *Tendencies in Modern American Poetry*

(1917). The discussion there is an expansion of her review of *North of Boston* which had appeared in the *New Republic* (Feb. 20, 1915). This is the review which Frost first noticed on the newsstand upon his return from England. Echoing the cry of the day, Miss Lowell wonders about the perspicacity of American publishers, and she welcomes the American edition of *North of Boston*. She calls it the "most American volume of poetry which has appeared for some time," but she, like Alice Henderson, finds it remarkable that Frost should have chosen to tell his stories in verse. Setting up the point of view which she later develops in *Tendencies*, Miss Lowell mistakenly remarks upon Frost's lack of humor and upon the way *North of Boston* details the disease and degeneration of rural New England. Her point, wrong to begin with, loses its punch because of the over-emphasis: "For Mr. Frost's is not the kindly New England of Whittier, nor the humorous and sensible one of Lowell; it is a latter-day New England, where a civilization is decaying to give place to another and very different one" (1915, p. 81). She concludes with enthusiastic praise of his observation, simplicity of phrase, and metrical rhythms. If much of Miss Lowell's article is on the wrong track, it at least testifies to her understanding of what Frost was trying to do by taking such unaccustomed liberties with the rigors of blank verse. But Frost was disturbed by her denial of his humor, and in a letter to Edward Thomas he comments, "Amy Lowell says I have no sense of humor, but sometimes I manage to be funny without that gift of the few" (*Selected Letters of Robert Frost*, Apr. 17, 1915).

In its day, and indeed for some years after its publication, Miss Lowell's essay in *Tendencies* was considered to be one of the two or three best evaluations of the poet. In *Some Contemporary Americans: The Personal Equation in Literature* (1924) for example, Percy Boynton lists it along with articles by G. R. Elliott, Edward Garnett, and Louis Untermeyer as the best essays on Frost's work. Today's readers no longer share this opinion. The articles by Elliott, Garnett, and Untermeyer continue to be appreciated, but Miss Lowell's essay is now thought of as a kind of wrongheaded curiosity. Especially erroneous are her arguments that Frost writes poetry limited to New England themes, that his poems are always tragic, and that he cannot understand how to create speech tones in poetry because he fails to use dialect. These observations will be more fully commented on in the next chapter which discusses Frost's negative critics; the other points in her long essay will be mentioned here.

She begins with a comparison of Frost and Edwin Arlington
Robinson, suggesting that where Robinson is intellectual and of
an older New England, Frost is intuitive and of the present.
She also declares, without amplification, that Frost is the only
contemporary writer of true bucolic poetry. So far, so good;
but she ruins her generalizations when she writes that Frost is
"plastic and passive" about the world, permitting the world "to
make upon him what imprint it will" (1917, p. 80). None of
these comments is developed, for Miss Lowell then turns to an
account of Frost's biography. Like all the critics of the day, she
mistakenly lists 1875 instead of 1874 as the year of his birth.
Her replay of biographical facts takes up approximately one-
half of the essay, and it outlines the chronology of his life which
was not generally known in 1917. It is interesting to note, however, that while she discusses his early life in San Francisco and
his years in England, she insists that these two parts of the world
have had no effect upon his work: "He, who has proved himself
extraordinarily receptive to environment, seems to possess that
receptivity only in regard to one environment" (1917, p. 83).
The result of these statements is her unintentional limitation of
the poems to a superior brand of local color. *North of Boston*
is thus judged a "very sad book," one which reveals the disease
and death of New England. Reading this, one wonders if Miss
Lowell closed her eyes to the humor of "A Hundred Collars"
(which she calls "dull") or to the rough joke in "The Code."

Still, Miss Lowell's enthusiasm for the poems dominates the
essay. She likes what she has read of Frost, and she is open with
her praise. She especially approves of Frost's accurate observation, of the "perfect simplicity of phrase," and of the words
which are "simple, straightforward, direct, manly." These observations were astute in 1917, but less perceptive is her statement that Frost's blank verse is "halting and maimed like the
life it portrays, unyielding in substance, and broken in effect"
(1917, p. 128). Miss Lowell correctly points out, however, that
the blank verse of *North of Boston* was revolutionary enough
to shock what she calls the "elder taste." Today's readers often
underestimate the surprise which greeted the iambic pentameter
of a poem like "The Death of the Hired Man." She does Frost
a service by showing how his verse rhythms work. So great is
her pleasure with *North of Boston* that she believes *Mountain
Interval*, Frost's latest work before *Tendencies* appeared, will
add nothing to the poet's achievement. This point of view,
which in my opinion seems wrong, became standard years later

when many critics argued that Frost's poetry following *North of Boston* was anticlimatic. Thus Miss Lowell can conclude her essay with the questionable suggestion that his art, while surely brilliant, is painted on a canvas so "exceedingly small" that he can never equal the achievement of a man with a wider vision. She has, unfortunately, let her opinion that Frost writes about only New England shape her observations about his themes, his blank verse, and his vision.

Although it is obvious that Miss Lowell intended her portrait of Frost to be balanced and yet full of praise, the poet was privately infuriated. In a 1917 letter to Louis Untermeyer, he points out the numerous errors in her biographical account of his first forty years (Louis Untermeyer, *The Letters of Robert Frost to Louis Untermeyer*, 1963, pp. 61–63). More to the point is his resentment of her portrayal of him as a disillusioned recluse who writes only tragic poems about decaying New England. And he again voices his anger at her insistence that he lacked a sense of humor. But what he really disapproves of is the "mistake" about Elinor. Miss Lowell accepts the standard but incorrect opinion about Frost's marriage—that it was an idyllic union given solid support by the silent, understanding wife. Reading this, Frost explodes to Untermeyer: "That's an unpardonable attempt to do her as the conventional helpmeet of genius." Although Frost unburdened himself to Untermeyer, he covered his anger with a thin veil of praise when he wrote to Miss Lowell. Thanking her for her generosity, he devotes the rest of the letter to a list of corrections which she could make in the second edition. He takes her up on everything from biographical data to the spelling of Elinor's name to her charges about his lack of humor and dialect: "He says he doesn't put dialect into the mouths of his people because not one of them, not one, spoke dialect" (*Selected Letters of Robert Frost*, Oct. 22, 1917). Some of his anger is justified, for Miss Lowell's opinions are often dead wrong. But the fact remains that her essay was more than full of praise; it was influential enough to direct judgments about Frost in both critical and general audiences. Frost's inability to accept criticism in any form resulted more from a lack of confidence than from specific points in her remarks.

Also critical of Frost's poetry is O. W. Firkins, whose review of the American edition of *A Boy's Will* in the *Nation* (Aug. 19, 1915) is not as laudatory as the British notices two years earlier. This may be because *A Boy's Will*, which does not measure up to the rest of his volumes, was published in the United States after *North of Boston*. It was bound to be a disappointment to those American critics who read *North of Boston* first. Firkins notices three distinct elements in *A Boy's Will:* vigorously sketched landscapes, trenchant feeling, and "superadded interpretations." The third element is the most important. Somewhat sharply, he criticizes Frost for trying to force meanings into his lyrics which the lines will not bear: "Mr. Frost is a poet by endowment; he is a symbolist only by trade. The meaning he personally attaches to landscape seems quite unrelated to the meaning by which he hopes to enlist the sympathies of his readers. His philosophy, in a word, is propitiatory; it is Mr. Frost's apologetic bow to a supposedly intellectual public, and I am uncourtly enough to wish that the obeisance had been withheld" (1915, p. 228). This is a pointed enough remark to bother most poets and readers of poetry, and it may well be true. But Firkins hurts his own case by refusing to specify titles or to analyze particular lines. The result is that the reader never knows which poems, lines, and symbols are examples of what Firkins considers a propitiatory philosophy. In the remainder of the review, Firkins attempts to soften the blow. Unlike most commentators, he approves of the prose glosses to the poems, and he praises the emotions which Frost conveys. His final evaluation, however, is negative. Although he thinks that Frost, whom he mistakenly calls a young writer, has a future in poetry, he regrets the poet's choice of a "crabbed syntax" and a "jolting meter." The devices may be intentional, writes Firkins, but he is not consoled. He hopes, therefore, that Frost will learn his lesson by climbing the slopes of Parnassus in a "wagon without springs."

One of the most important of Frost's early notices was written by William Dean Howells for *Harper's* (Sept. 1915). Writing with the confidence of an established and venerated critic, Howells begins his remarks about some of the newer poets with a few ironic barbs. He notes that nearly every publishing house which has a poet or two under contract feels obligated to announce the publication of each new volume of poetry with a statement about the current poetic renaissance. If the publishers are to be believed, writes Howells, who has no wish to dispute them, then the present "poetic sunburst" is a phenomenon not seen within "something like a geological period." Such high praise is unfortunate for a critic like himself because he is "at a loss what to say of poets and poetry already so sung, so sound-

ed, so, as it were, dinned into us" (1915, p. 634). He wonders
if the poets need his comments, so used are they to being assured of their worth.

Putting aside his irony, Howells promises his readers that most
of the current poetry is neither new nor good. He believes that
the best of the newer poetry is found in that which uses traditional forms, and he reminds the reader that Walt Whitman
was writing rhythmical free verse sixty years before Amy Lowell and Edgar Lee Masters found fame with shredded prose:
"Freak for freak, we prefer compressed verse to shredded prose"
(1915, p. 635). For this reason he singles out *A Boy's Will* and
North of Boston for special praise because Frost's poems deserve the acclaim they have been accorded. He acknowledges
the breaks in traditional rhythms, but unlike Firkins he approves. Particularly affected by the expressions of New England life, Howells believes that Frost has extended the bounds
of sympathy and knowledge. He discounts the book jacket
blurbs about the new poetry in order to celebrate Frost's as
"the old poetry as young as ever . . . ." For all of Howells'
insight, however, it is interesting that he fails to mention what
makes Frost's poems, especially *North of Boston*, so refreshing. Nothing is said about the metaphors, the sentence sounds,
or the blank verse. One finally wonders if Howells singles out
Frost for praise *because* the poet uses traditional verse forms.
Frost, nevertheless, was what he called "overwhelmed" with
Howells' interest. In a letter to Edward Garnett, he thanks
the British critic for calling his work to Howells' attention
(*Selected Letters of Robert Frost*, June 12, 1915).

Although George H. Browne's essay in the *Independent*
(May 22, 1916) does not enjoy the prestige of Howells' article, it is significant for two reasons: it is published in the journal which first printed a Frost poem in 1894, and it makes use
of direct quotations from Frost to explain and illustrate sentence sounds. Browne believes, probably correctly, that readers
enjoy Frost's poetry because it is written in language they themselves speak. He goes on to explain how Frost's sentences do
double duty when they convey the necessary information as
well as the tones and inflections which supply imaginative and
emotional vitality. His most significant comment is that verse
like Frost's succeeds because "in form as well as in substance
it is true to life" (1916, p. 283). Although he does not develop
the idea, his attention to the form of Frost's poetry is something which was needed among the squabbles about old and new

poetry and about the English reputation. Browne urges the
reader to read aloud and to listen as well as watch how the poetic form takes shape. By today's standards the brief account
of Frost's life is idealistic, but the several direct quotations from
Frost about his technique make the essay informative, especially
this definition of sentences: "living expressions flying around."

Harriet Monroe, editor of *Poetry: A Magazine of Verse*,
published two articles on Frost which are more important for
their place of publication than for their content. The appearance of Frost's *Mountain Interval* and of Edgar Lee Masters'
The Great Valley prompts Miss Monroe to contrast the two
poets in the first review (Jan. 1917). She finds them both
"telling the tale of the tribe," Frost better than any past New
Englander and Masters better than Middle Western writers.
But she hardly goes beyond this superficial observation. Pointing out the verisimilitude of Frost's granite-souled characters
and the integral role of nature, she gets down to the business
of analysis only when she writes about "Snow," awarded a
prize by her journal. With just a few comments, she shows that
conversation, not statement or description, is at the heart of
Frost's account of a winter tempest. She is not as laudatory
about Masters because of his "spirit of careless abundance" which
denies him Frost's selectivity. Never once in this article does
Miss Monroe exhibit the perception of Padraic Colum when
writing about the same two poets.

Her second essay (Dec. 1924) begins with a little more insight. Indirectly challenging those like Amy Lowell who would
limit Frost to a poet of New England, she argues that however
"loyally local," he transcends his environment to seize the
essential things in life itself. She drops this potentially fruitful
subject, however, in favor of a brief account of biographical
facts. Writing of the trip to England, she inadvertently reopens
the English publisher controversy when she attacks the publisher in his own country who had "refused him a hearing." A
kind of general introduction to Frost's work follows, valuable
to those who are taking up the poet seriously for the first time.
Perhaps the more rewarding part of her essay is the division
of his poetry into four general categories: the rural background
("Birches" and "The Wood-Pile"), farm life ("Mowing" and
"Mending Wall"), dialogues of human character ("The Code"
and "Snow"), and the more personal poems ("Storm Fear" and
"Flower-Gathering"). Since Miss Monroe never develops any
of her good ideas, the article remains on the level of a surface
appreciation.

A far more incisive and even famous article is G. R. Elliott's "The Neighborliness of Robert Frost" in the *Nation* (Dec. 6, 1919). Investigating in depth what Harriet Monroe mentions only briefly, Elliott takes on those critics who persist in calling Frost a regional poet. He sees the wider significance of Frost's art in its spirit of neighborliness. Yet anyone who has read Frost carefully knows that he was skeptical of human brotherhood. As mentioned earlier, Louis Untermeyer has reported that Frost could not say "brotherhood" without sneering. But Elliott does not mean "brotherhood" when he writes of neighborliness. Insisting that Frost's realism saves him from notions of brotherhood which limit more idealistic poets, he defines neighborliness as "the spirit which enables people to live together more or less fruitfully in a small community, and which, with all its meannesses, comprises the basal conditions of the wider human brotherhood" (1917, p. 713). Frost is conscious of this wider ideal, but he always writes about it in local terms. In this way he can be "faithfully local" and still be "more deeply represen tative" than other poets who hope to express the spirit of the age.

Elliott finds a perfect illustration in *A Boy's Will*. When Frost details the poet-figure's growth from isolation to acceptance of the world, he portrays a change from the poetry of romantic longing to the poetry of neighborliness. The youthful figure, says Elliott, learns to embrace not human brotherhood in general but the lessons to be experienced from everyday relations with both people and nature. "Mowing" and "A Tuft of Flowers" illustrate the volume's true "social standpoint." Elliott could have added "The Vantage Point" and "Reluctance," but his point is made. He finds the same theme more brilliantly developed in *North of Boston*. In this book Frost expresses the spirit of labor and the spirit of sympathy: "The diverse modes of the poet's art are harmonized in his persistent spirit of patient, laborious neighborliness" (1919, p. 714).

His definition of neighborliness complete, Elliott takes to task those critics who misinterpret the implications of this spirit of neighborliness. In particular he singles out Amy Lowell for exaggerating Frost's grimness and Louis Untermeyer for stressing his gladness. Frost is in between these extremes, writes Elliott. The "burdens of the neighborhood" prohibit happiness, but faith in the neighborly spirit prevents sadness. Unlike Edgar Lee Masters, Frost does not resort to cynicism when writing about human limitations. And unlike Wilfred Gibson, he avoids mysticism when concerned with fellow laborers. "He is more dispassionate and more veracious than his fellow-craftsmen when contemplating the limitations of common life" (1919, p. 714). The rest of the essay is devoted to illustration of the argument with, understandably, "Mending Wall" serving as the key example. This essay is one of the few early pieces of Frost criticism to retain significance. The date of its publication, 1919, is important, for it points to the fact that the article was written years before Frost turned more and more to social and political subjects. Without the lesser "editorials" and purely political poems like "Build Soil" to guide him, Elliott succeeds in discussing with clarity and good sense a theme which was to become obvious in Frost's later books. Frost liked the article, describing it to William Stanley Braithwaite as "one of the most understanding things ever written about me" (Lawrance Thompson, *Robert Frost: The Years of Triumph, 1915–1938*, pp. 153, 569). He also praised it in a letter to Elliott himself: "I had begun to be afraid certain things that had been said about me in the first place (and in praise, mind you) by people who had hardly taken the trouble to read me would have to go on being said forever. You broke the spell" (*Selected Letters of Robert Frost*, Mar. 20, 1920). Today's readers who are interested in either Frost's conservatism or his more socially oriented poetry will do well to consult Elliott's perceptive essay.

Elliott's other important article, published in the *Virginia Quarterly Review* (July 1925), extends his discussion of Frost's neighborliness, for it begins with both an epigraph from "Mending Wall" and the statement that Frost "moves in neighborly fashion among modernistic thinkers and poetic extremists, and writes passages that they love" (1925, p. 205). Elliott continues to be upset by the sympathetic but erroneous criticism which, reading Frost superficially, stresses his drab realism, New England idioms, and "earthy tang." Too often, insists Elliott, his humor is overlooked. The problem may be that Frost's humor is not characteristically American. Elliott suggests that it is "quite un-American in its slowness to 'register,' in its very quiet and gradual way of 'intriguing' the reader" (1925, p. 206). Unlike the smart satire and obvious jokings which all readers immediately recognize, Frost's humor is subdued enough to encourage soundless laughter once the reader has read with care. Frost remains "the good neighbor," kindly and withdrawing, humorously taking note of the values in everyday life. By overlooking this quiet humor, readers have misinterpreted the peculiar quality of his solitariness of mood. Rather than the brooding loneliness which some critics read into his poems, Frost creates the kind of loneliness which is neighborly—that is, the kind which stands off a bit from life in order to observe it with amusement. This ambiguous humor, neither intimate nor aloof, is nicely illustrated in "The Census-Taker." Loneliness and realism may be particularly evident in some of the poems in *North of Boston*, but in the two latest volumes, *Mountain Interval* and *New Hampshire*, the mingling of "genial and shivering" humor dominates, especially in "Paul's Wife," "The Witch of Coös," and "Snow." Humorously wary of fixed approaches to life, Frost refuses to commit himself: "He glances into the philosophic and romantic avenues of the Soul, and turns away. He reapproaches his neighbors with a deepened sense of his and their elusiveness . . . and a more pungent humor for meeting them while there is still 'a time to talk' " (1925, p. 212). Elliott's cogent remarks are particularly useful when read in the context of the early Frost criticism which stresses his grimness and tragedy. The failure to perceive Frost's humor is bothersome; Elliott's article remains vital to those interested in pursuing this neglected phase of Frost's achievement.

Written by one of Frost's most faithful supporters among critics, Louis Untermeyer's *The New Era in American Poetry* (1919) celebrates the poetic renaissance which saw the publication of so much truly fine American poetry. In his introduction Untermeyer laments the sorry standards used to evaluate and popularize American poets as late as 1900. Singling out Edmund Clarence Stedman's *An American Anthology* (Greenwood, 1901), Untermeyer correctly describes that nine-hundred-page book as a "gargantuan collection of mediocrity and moralizing." He points out that of the nine hundred pages, no more than ten pages of genuine American poetry are included because writers like Whittier are given twice as much space as true poets like Whitman. Untermeyer attempts to remedy that situation by writing analyses of poets who were contemporary in the 1910–20 period. Although he discusses writers like John Hall Wheelock and Charles Erskine Scott Wood who are forgotten today, he also assigns complete chapters to such giants as Ezra Pound, Edwin Arlington Robinson, and Frost.

The chapter on Frost begins the study. Noting that a poetic feeling for the ordinary things in life is the bond that unites most of the poets he discusses, Untermeyer writes that "in none is it expressed so simply and yet so richly is in the work of Robert Frost" (1919, p. 16). He uses "Mowing," particularly the now famous line, "The fact is the sweetest dream that labor knows," to illustrate the difference between Frost's use of common events and that of the average writer who begins honestly but ends on the edge of banality. The average writer, argues Untermeyer, betrays his "ordinary" material with poeticisms and clichés, while Frost succeeds because he never tries to "amplify" the fact. Because Frost's "casual quality" confuses many of his critics into stammering such pompous phrases as "whether or not this is poetry, it is still good," Untermeyer devotes much of his chapter to an explanation of how Frost's apparently simple verse breaks new ground. His argument may seem commonplace today, but its value will be quickly noted once we remember that at the time Untermeyer was writing, Frost had been back in the United States only four years. Poems like "The Death of the Hired Man" were then refreshingly new, so much so that they were often mistaken for free verse. Untermeyer hopes to straighten out the confusion, explaining that in Frost's poems after *A Boy's Will* there is a "total absence of fine feathers and fustian, of red lights and rhetoric, of all the skillful literary mechanics that we have been used to" (1919, p. 22). No one except Synge, writes Untermeyer, has so successfully captured in dramatic poetry what he calls the "sharp tang of life." Frost has so potently created the illusion of reality that the standard elements of poetry seem to be missing. This quality enables Frost to capitalize on what Untermeyer calls the "great gift of concentration," the ability to set a stage and to begin a dramatic incident within the space of a few lines, as in the beginning of "The Fear."

Concerning "The Fear," Untermeyer makes some shrewd comments. He points to the apparent ease with which Frost communicates the woman's very real fear and to the successful build-up of dramatic tension. More importantly, he criticizes those who would insist on making a "bloody melodrama" out of the poem. Calling attention to the consciously created anticlimax, he argues correctly that the power of "The Fear" comes not from physical violence, though that has been expected, but from the reader's realization at the end of the poem that nothing can be as fearful as the woman's "mental uncertainty and the fact that nothing happens." Not all of Untermeyer's judgments are as judicious as this one. He suggests, for example, that "Mending Wall" documents the struggle between "a pagan irresponsibility and a strict accountability" (1919, p. 25). Yet, for the most part his readings of the poems clarify ambiguities as well as counter wrongheaded criticism.

Similarly, Untermeyer's insistence that Frost is not a "grim realist" helps to offset one of the consistent charges brought against his poetry in the 1910s. He shows that Frost can be grim, matter-of-fact, or fanciful, depending upon the mood he hopes to invoke. The grimness of "The Fear" is balanced by the humor of "The Mountain." Untermeyer also challenges another questionable opinion, current at the time, that Frost's speech tones are unsuccessful because he does not use dialect. Quoting primarily from Frost's letters, he defines the theory of sentence sounds to show how Frost has reproduced human tones, as opposed to a specific dialect, and how the "very kind and color" of the words help the reader determine the tone Frost desires. From today's perspective, it is plain that Untermeyer draws on much of the material, the colorful comments, and the succinct definitions of poetry which Frost fed him in letters and conversations. Reprinted here, for example, is the now famous proverb that poetry "begins as a lump in the throat"—a definition which comes from a Frost letter to Untermeyer (see *The Letters of Robert Frost to Louis Untermeyer*, Jan. 1, 1916). But at the time Untermeyer published *The New Era in American Poetry*, Frost's letters had not been printed, and the controversies over his verse form, grimness, and speech tones had not been resolved. By using the poet's own definitions and explanations of what he was trying to accomplish, Untermeyer clarifies much of the confusion surrounding Frost's poetry in 1919. His chapter on Frost is more than a defense of the poet written by an unfailing friend: it is the clear, balanced, and informed analysis which was needed at the time.

Waldo Frank is one of those commentators whom Untermeyer and G. R. Elliott might criticize for overemphasizing Frost's dark side. In his foreword to the American edition of *Our America* (1919), Frank explains that this book came about as the result of World War I. During the war, France sent artists to the United States to make their country known to Americans. In an effort to clarify something about America for Frenchmen, Frank was asked to write a book about America and its artists. His comments on Frost are included in a chapter entitled "The Puritan Says 'Yea' " in which he analyzes the ambivalence of the Puritan world which pits the denial of life in "tearing down" against the affirmation of "building up." He argues that this ambivalence speaks today most "clearly in the art of Robert Frost."

Frank obviously likes Frost's poetry, but he finds in it an excellence "hard to catalogue." Calling it lyrical, dramatic, and philosophic, he wonders why artists the high caliber of Frost (in addition to Whitman, Dreiser, Masters, and Anderson) first have to find support in England before America will acknowledge them as serious writers. Echoing an old charge, he feels that the answer lies in America's deafness to new voices. America is too full of "repressive and pervasive academics" to recognize groundbreaking art like Frost's. "When the unregenerate American utterance is heard, this potent group resists it as a sure attack upon the dominion of the Puritan and Colonial point of view" (1919, p. 159). Although Frank may have been generally correct in 1919, his biting comment illustrates the kind of opinion Frost feared when it was published for all to read. Agreeing that his verse deserved a more favorable treatment from journals and editors before the English pointed out its value, but afraid of the charge that he fled to England in order to find a publisher, Frost continued to shudder at the possibility of retribution from American editors who might take offense at strongly worded attacks like Frank's.

Frank then stresses the grimness in Frost's poetry. In a marvelously written catalogue of the kind of people Frost writes about in *North of Boston* and *Mountain Interval*, he argues that the poet's admirers are usually unaware of the sterility, the sullenness, and the silence which define the characters in Frost's longer poems. He correctly notes that Frost neither distorts nor moralizes about them. And yet, writes Frank—and here Untermeyer would agree—Frost somehow manages in the process to make "their sullen silence sing." The poems may depict a "starved, sick world," but they show that New England is not dead since Frost is so much alive: "One comes to feel that after the long repose of bitterness and failure, lying upon New England, a new Beauty is being born" (1919, p. 161). This opinion, of course, recalls Amy Lowell's.

As a final estimate, however, Frank decides that the repressiveness of New England diminishes the vitality of Frost's verse and thus accounts for the ambivalence: "His poems are fiercely vital, but like New England their vitality is repressed: it has not burst into dynamic life" (1919, p. 161). As a result, Frost's poems lack aspiration and faith. He is a true artist, but his art must be incomplete because it is a "direct intuitive reaction" to the sterile life about him. Although Frank's estimation is concisely put and closely argued, it suffers from the false assumption that the poet and his home region are in perfect accord. Frank would not use the phrase, but his comments make Frost little more than a local colorist who writes strictly about New England. Nothing is said about the universality of the poet's themes or about the humor which, as Untermeyer points out, balances the grimness. One can conclude only that Frank has allowed his specific judgment of the poet to be swayed by his more general estimation of New England which he hopes to communicate to the French.

Also concerned with Frost's Puritanism, but less controversial than Frank, is Carl Van Doren's "The Soil of the Puritans, Robert Frost: Quintessence and Subsoil," published in the *Century Magazine* (Feb. 1923). Van Doren distinguishes between two kinds of poetry in Puritan New England: that of the gentry (Holmes, Longfellow, Lowell) and that of the subsoil (Thoreau and Frost). The problem has been that from Thoreau's death to Frost's appearance, a span of fifty years, the Yankee farmer and the small New England communities which make up the "subsoil" have been treated in verse as if they were "mere museums of singular customs and idioms. . ." (1923, p. 630). Inarticulate themselves, these people invited obscurity and misinterpretation. Frost's poems, however, have given this segment of the population a voice.

Turning to a comparison of Frost and Robert Burns, two poets who expressed the life-styles of their own rural communities, Van Doren points to a key difference. Burns grew up among traditional ballads and peasant songs and thus could include lyric rhythms in his poetry. But other than "Yankee Doodle," songs have not flourished in the small townships of New England. Unlike Burns, then, Frost turns to accepted habits of speech as the basis for his poetry. Using understatement and casual syntax, he rescues an entire people from obscurity by capturing their folk-speech. The point, writes Van Doren, is that in his most characteristic poems Frost talks instead of sings. Just as important is the fact that he not only talks like a Yankee poet but also thinks like one. This is especially evident in his close attention to the objects of his rural world. When he writes of mowing, he does so not as one who has seen the work done but as a mower who has swung the scythe himself. Like G. R. Elliott, Van Doren suggests that it is this rapport with his subject matter which allows Frost to be a good neighbor. Experiences from daily Yankee affairs have taught him as much about life as about poetry: "He is neighbor, in a Yankee fashion, both to the things he sees and to the beings he sees into" (1923, p. 635). The difference between Elliott and Van Doren is that the latter points out the absence of "general humanitarianism" in Frost. He does not criticize the poet for this lack, but he does insist that while Frost's neighborliness permits him to accept the friendship of those he encounters in the business of daily affairs, it prevents him from making wider acquaintances or from cultivating broader sympathies.

Finally, Van Doren suggests that for all the drabness and loneliness in Frost's poetry, it is also full of quiet fun. The poet may write about the Puritan tradition, but he avoids those strict codes of judgment. The result is a canon which includes humorous poems about sin and witchcraft and other departures from Puritan codes of life. Most of all, Frost dodges the old Yankee curse of preaching. Van Doren notes that New England literature traditionally comments instead of creates. Frost, however, refuses to moralize. He writes about people who "would rather talk than sing, but who would also rather work than talk" (1923, p. 636). This shrewd comment is indicative of the essay, one of the best general evaluations of Frost's work before 1925.

It should now be clear that by the 1920s more and more critics were challenging Amy Lowell's assertion that Frost wrote about only New England. His volume *New Hampshire* (1923) gave support to these countercharges. In an essay review of *New Hampshire* written for *Poetry* (Mar. 1924), Dorothy Dudley points out that the title poem shows Frost playing with themes more common to life in general. The "obtuse" have persisted in limiting him to a poet of New England, but this book should settle the issue. For in the title poem, he leaves "his own counties" to touch on "the enormous fevers of the day—business, communism, sex—or rather, the frantic admission of it to the American program" (1924, p. 331). Miss Dudley finds the shorter narratives and lyrics more "intimate," capable of holding within them tears, smiles, and mysteries. Refusing to psychoanalyze New England, Frost remains the poet of "voices, postures, appearances." The "crucial" facts of life lurk in his poems so that, reading them, we are taken along the road of the familiar to the edge of the unknown.

A broader estimation which places Frost in the literary atmosphere of the times is found in Percy H. Boynton's *Some Contemporary Americans: The Personal Equation in Literature* (1924). Boynton begins his study by observing and lamenting the ignorance about their own literature which most Americans shared in the 1920s. The reasons are the timid self-consciousness of American culture and an outmoded university system which neglects its native literature. The situation was so serious at the time Boynton was writing that he could say without fear of contradiction, "Not one eminent university man in this country today has devoted his whole career to studying or teaching the literary history of America" (1924, p. 5). Because Americans expect condescension from foreigners when American literature is mentioned, they all but encourage it. The result is that they apologize for Whitman while fearing that they are like Tom Sawyer. This problem of the neglect of American literature is similar to the one Untermeyer speaks of in *New Era in American Poetry* when he deplores the sheer ignorance in otherwise educated Americans about their own literature. Like Untermeyer's book, Boynton's study is aimed at countering the ignorance. Each of the chapters in *Some Contemporary Americans* was first published in article form; by bringing them together Boynton offers a comprehensive study of modern American literature from Edwin Arlington Robinson through 1920.

He begins his chapter on Frost with an idealized description of the poet's so-called casual approach to publishing. If we listen to Boynton, then Frost was never "impatient for a hearing" nor "inclined toward putting his own hopes or fears or special convictions into print" (1924, p. 35). Today's serious student of Frost now knows that Boynton's statement is wrong. But the significance of this idealized description is not its error but its contribution to the myth of Robert Frost. For comments like Boynton's were just the sort of thing Frost encouraged—he liked the image of himself as a gentle farmer-poet above the pettiness of bigtime literary circles. This mask, which the public believed, has now been exposed, but it was unchallenged in the 1920s when Boynton was writing.

More to the point are Boynton's remarks about the general state of versification in modern poetry and about Frost's in particular. With amused irony he notes the efforts of certain critics to prove that every line of poetry must literally conform to a certain measure—that all iambic pentameter lines must have five stresses and ten syllables. The result is that poetry has been forced into a straitjacket of "Te tum, te tum, te tum, te tum, te tum." In this context, Boynton supplies an informed analysis of Frost's ideas about rhythm, complete with paraphrases of the poet's statements and examples from "The Runaway." He shows how Frost merges the freedom of conversational tones with the regularity of poetic rhythm. Though brief, his remarks on Frost's prosody are so clear and to the point that they can still be used as a reliable introduction to an investigation of the poet's irregular iambic pentameter line. When Boynton turns to the poems, he stresses the characteristic which Louis Untermeyer claims is over-emphasized: the sadness of Frost's people. "They live in a country which has come to old age on arid tradition. They are unacquainted with mirth or song or play" (1924, p. 44). This charge is similar to the one Waldo Frank makes in *Our America*, but Untermeyer is correct when he argues that such a view of Frost's poems is too narrow. When poems like "A Hundred Collars," "The Generations of Men," "A Cow in Apple Time," and "Brown's Descent"—all published before Boynton wrote his chapter—are considered, Frost's playfulness and amused point of view are in full view to balance the grimness which so many of the early critics emphasized. Boynton's essay, then, offers a good brief analysis of Frost's rhythms, but it goes astray when it considers Frost's public persona and the general tone of his poems.

Even more off the mark is Gorham B. Munson's essay "Robert Frost" in *Saturday Review of Literature* (Mar. 28, 1925). This essay is Munson's original article on Frost which led to *Robert Frost: A Study in Sensibility and Good Sense*, his 1927 biography of the poet discussed in chapter 1. Acknowledging the validity of earlier critical remarks which praise Frost for his economy, simplicity, perception of landscape, and insight into people, Munson insists that these qualities are secondary. He proposes to push to the heart of Frost's work, and in so doing he expresses his thesis—Frost as a classicist—which was to determine the direction of his work on the poet for the next forty years. The flaws in Munson's remarks have been explored in depth in the previous chapter on the biographical materials. But it should be remarked here that by slighting T. S. Eliot and Ezra Pound, he overemphasizes his argument that Frost is "the purest classical poet of America." In Munson's words, Eliot is full of "sentimental melancholy," wistfulness, and obfuscation, while Pound expresses only "the irritations and discomforts of a sensitive being" (1925, p. 626). The remainder of the essay is a fleshing out of the argument, highly influenced by his acceptance of Irving Babbitt's New Humanism. Munson republishes the essay almost verbatim in his biography, and he makes the same error there as here: trapped by his thesis and overemphasizing his point, he mistakenly places Frost on the side of the ancient classical writers and against both contemporary poets and the modern world.

Clement Wood returns to an old point of dissension in *Poets of America* (1925). Calling his chapter on Frost "The Twilight of New England," he joins Amy Lowell in picturing Frost as the poet of "one moribund phase" of New England: "It is of

this dimming of the old noon that Robert Frost is the laureate" (1925, p. 143). Also like Miss Lowell, he mistakenly
limits the poet's accomplishments to New England themes and
settings. Although noting Frost's San Francisco birth, his father's interest in the Old South, his mother's Scotch tales, the
experiences at Dartmouth and Harvard, and the sojourn in England, Wood incredibly states that because Frost does not write
about these experiences his poetry reflects only "the dodder-
ing senility and decadence of the land that fathered eleven
generations of Frosts" (1925, p. 146). He calls attention to "Into
My Own" and "The Sound of Trees," and he decides that these
two poems illustrate Frost's choice to flee the city and "lose himself in a world of trees. . . ."

If we believe Wood, then the poems are sad because the poet
is: the "saddest things" in Frost's work are "doubly sad for the
sad-eyed man who tells them" (1925, p. 150). With all of this
emphasis on tragedy, senility, and sadness, it is surprising that
Wood finds most of the poems beautiful. He says that every
word in "Mending Wall" is "precious." He finds instances of
Frost's "finest beauty of phrase" in "The Death of the Hired
Man." He calls "The Mountain" "a leisurely gem." And though
he seems to have been influenced by Miss Lowell's evaluation as
expressed in *Tendencies in Modern American Poetry*, he nevertheless perceives the humor of "A Hundred Collars" and "The
Code." He also disagrees with Miss Lowell when he suggests
that Frost's art is "lifted further" in *Mountain Interval*.

Turning to the sound and speech rhythms, Wood specifically
alludes to Amy Lowell, mentioning "one critic" who has pointed out the lack of dialect. But he goes even further, saying that
the limitation is more than the absence of authentic dialect: Frost
misses "the general contraction and elision that accompanies the
usual spoken word" (1925, pp. 159–60). According to Wood,
the speech rhythms in Frost's poetry are less a transcription of
conversation than a reproduction of the poet's own speech habits. The result is precise voice tones but not the "tang and
twist of the undiluted Yankee tongue" (1925, p. 160). Today's
readers find hard to understand this persistent outcry that Frost
failed when he avoided Yankee dialect, but they need only realize that it stems from the more fundamental error of limiting
Frost's themes and visions to a New England milieu. Those, like
Amy Lowell and Clement Wood, who restrict him to a poet
of New England are almost forced by the narrowness of their
judgment to require dialect from him. Wood, nevertheless,
names Frost one of the "great masters" when it comes to writ-

ing iambic pentameter because the poet is not afraid to let the speech rhythms violate the rigidity of a standard iambic line. His chapter is not nearly as knowledgeable as Untermeyer's about Frost's theory of poetry, nor as informative as Miss Lowell's. Though he places Frost's poetry with that of the first rank, he joins the sizable list of early Frost critics who restrict him to a poet of limited vision writing about only a dying New England.

More to the point is Llewellyn Jones' discussion of Frost in *First Impressions: Essays on Poetry, Criticism, and Prosody* (1925). Jones believes Frost's art to be great because it does not depend upon "something big"—the sensational or the spectacular. Coming close to the little events of daily life, Frost brushes aside artificialities to show reality in its "original movement." Jones is particularly pleased with Frost's union of free speech rhythms with the demands of metrical beats. Explaining a point which still needed to be clarified in 1925, Jones shows how the subordination of metrical patterns to speech cadences fooled many readers into placing Frost within the free verse movement. He illustrates how Frost's lines scan, and he instructs misguided readers to scan them not as Latin or Greek but as English verse. His point is well taken, for today, as well as in 1925, readers with a preconceived notion of scansion have difficulty with Frost's dramatic dialogues.

The analysis of some of the poems in *A Boy's Will* is especially good. Jones warns against a literal reading of "The Trial by Existence," insisting that these poems should not be read as autobiography or as material for psychoanalysis. Particularly interesting for later readers is his discussion of "In Equal Sacrifice," a poem on the theme of Douglas carrying the heart of Robert Bruce to the Holy Land. Although originally published in *A Boy's Will*, "In Equal Sacrifice" is not included in subsequent editions of Frost's collected works. Thus Jones' comments about it are valuable for those who want to investigate Frost's lesser known poems. Like most of the earlier commentators, Jones believes *North of Boston* to be Frost's best, though, unlike Amy Lowell and others, he detects a "widening of subject and of interest" in *Mountain Interval* and *New Hampshire*. Considering the popular opinion of the day that Frost's subject and vision are limited because he depicts only New England, Jones' comment is as refreshing as it is correct. Again like many of his fellow critics, he alludes to Miss Lowell—"a New England poetess"—when he disputes those who would deny the humor of Frost's poetry. Jones points out that Frost has always shown humor, sometimes explicitly and sometimes with "just a faint shade." Writing in 1925, he can choose "New Hampshire" to illustrate the humor, a poem unavailable to Miss Lowell, who published her essay in 1917. But Jones is correct when he writes that Frost's lighter side has been evident since *A Boy's Will*. He makes no attempt to analyze the poems in technical terms or to discuss Frost's theory of poetry. More an appreciation than an argument, his essay is a sane balance to the mistaken assumptions of some of his fellow commentators.

This analysis of the Frost criticism published during the first decade or so of his recognition shows that his poetry initially enjoyed near unanimous acclaim. Following the very first doubtful remarks in British journals about *A Boy's Will*, most English and American critics praised Frost's poetry with such vigor that he returned to the United States an acknowledged leader of the new literature. There were, of course, certain areas of dispute, particularly about such matters as the British-made reputation, the presence or lack of humor, the New England themes, and the absence of dialect. Yet even those critics who pointed out what they considered to be flaws in his poetry nevertheless celebrated his overall achievement. The result was a period in which both critical and popular readers agreed about the high quality of his art. In later years Frost's eminence would be challenged, and a relatively small but articulate strain of negative criticism developed which continued through the appearance of *In the Clearing*, his last book.

References

Abercrombie, Lascelles
   1914. "A New Voice: *North of Boston*," *Nation* (London) June 13, pp. 423–24.
Anonymous
   1915. *Bulletin of the Poetry Society of America* Jan.
Anonymous
   1913. *Times Literary Supplement* (London) Apr. 10; reprinted in *Recognition of Robert Frost*, ed. Richard Thornton, p. 54. New York: Holt, 1937.
Anonymous
   1914. "*North of Boston*," *Times Literary Supplement* (London) May 28, p. 263.
Anonymous
   1913. "Notices of New Books," *Athenaeum* Apr. 5, p. 379.

Anonymous
   1914. "Some Recent Verse," *Times Literary Supplement* (London) July 2, p. 316.
Baxter, Sylvester
   1915a. "Talk of the Town," *Boston Herald* Mar. 9, p. 97.
   1915b. "New England's New Poet," *American Review of Reviews* Apr., pp. 432–34.
Boynton, Percy H.
   1924. *Some Contemporary Americans: The Personal Equation in Literature.* Chicago: Univ. of Chicago Pr., pp. 33–49.
Braithwaite, William Stanley
   1915a. "A Poet of New England: Robert Frost, A New Exponent of Life," *Boston Evening Transcript* Apr. 28, pt. 3, p. 4.
   1915b. "Robert Frost, New American Poet," *Boston Evening Transcript* May 8; reprinted in *Interviews with Robert Frost,* ed. Edward Lathem, pp. 3–8. New York: Holt, Rinehart and Winston, 1966.
Browne, George H.
   1916. "Robert Frost, A Poet of Speech," *Independent* May 22, pp. 283–84.
Colum, Padraic
   1916. "The Poetry of Robert Frost," *New Republic* Dec. 23, pp. 219–22.
Douglas, Norman
   1925. *Experiments.* New York: McBride, pp. 161–62.
Dudley, Dorothy
   1924. "The Acid Test," *Poetry: A Magazine of Verse* Mar., pp. 328–35.
Elliott, G. R.
   1919. "The Neighborliness of Robert Frost," *Nation* Dec. 6, pp. 713–15.
   1925. "An Undiscovered America in Frost's Poetry," *Virginia Quarterly Review* July, pp. 205–15.
Firkins, O. W.
   1915. "Poets of the Day," *Nation* Aug. 19, pp. 228–29.
Flint, F. S.
   1913. Review of *A Boy's Will, Poetry and Drama* June, p. 250.
Frank, Waldo
   1919. *Our America.* New York: Boni and Liveright, pp. 158–62.
Freeman, John
   1925. "Contemporary American Authors: Robert Frost," *London Mercury* Dec., pp. 176–87.
Garnett, Edward
   1915. "A New American Poet," *Atlantic Monthly* Aug., pp. 214–21.
Gibson, Wilfred Wilson
   1914. "Simplicity and Sophistication," *Bookman* (London) July, p. 183.

Harcourt, Alfred
  1915. Untitled editorial on Robert Frost, *New York Times Book Review* Aug. 8, p. 284.
Henderson, Alice C.
  1914. "Recent Poetry," *Dial* Oct. 1, p. 254.
Howells, William Dean
  1915. "Editor's Easy Chair," *Harper's* Sept., pp. 634–37.
Hueffer, Ford Madox
  1914. "Mr. Robert Frost and 'North of Boston,'" *Outlook* June 27, pp. 879–80.
Jones, Llewellyn
  1925. *First Impressions: Essays on Poetry, Criticism, and Prosody*, pp. 37–52. Reprinted 1968, Freeport, N.Y.: Books for Libraries Pr.
Lathem, Edward Connery
  1966. (editor) *Interviews with Robert Frost.* New York: Holt, Rinehart and Winston.
Lowell, Amy
  1915. "*North of Boston,*" *New Republic* Feb. 20, pp. 81–82.
  1917. *Tendencies in Modern American Poetry*, pp. 79–136. New York: Macmillan.
Mertins, Louis
  1965. *Robert Frost: Life and Talks-Walking.* Norman: Univ. of Oklahoma Pr.
Monro, Harold
  1914. "New Books," *Poetry and Drama* Sept., pp. 296–97.
Monroe, Harriet
  1917. "Frost and Masters," *Poetry: A Magazine of Verse* Jan., pp. 202–7.
  1924. "Comment: Robert Frost," *Poetry: A Magazine of Verse* Dec., pp. 146–51.
Munson, Gorham B.
  1925. "Robert Frost," *Saturday Review of Literature* Mar. 28, pp. 625–26.
  1927. *Robert Frost: A Study in Sensibility and Good Sense.* New York: George H. Doran.
Payne, William Morton
  1913. Review of *A Boy's Will, Dial* Sept. 16, pp. 211–12.
Pound, Ezra
  1913. "*A Boy's Will,*" *Poetry: A Magazine of Verse* May, pp. 72–74.
  1914. "Modern Georgics," *Poetry: A Magazine of Verse* Dec., pp. 127–30.
Rittenhouse, Jessie B.
  1915. "*North of Boston:* Robert Frost's Poems of New England Farm Life," *New York Times Book Review* May 16, p. 189.

Thomas, Edward
1914. Review of *North of Boston, English Review* Aug., pp.
142–43.
Thompson, Lawrance
1964. (editor) *Selected Letters of Robert Frost.* New York:
Holt, Rinehart and Winston.
1966. *Robert Frost: The Early Years, 1874–1915.* New York:
Holt, Rinehart and Winston.
1970. *Robert Frost: The Years of Triumph, 1915-1938.* New
York: Holt, Rinehart and Winston.
Thornton, Richard
1937. (editor) *Recognition of Robert Frost.* New York: Holt.
Untermeyer, Louis
1919. "Robert Frost" in *The New Era in American Poetry.*
pp. 15–40. New York: Holt.
1963. (editor) *The Letters of Robert Frost to Louis Untermeyer.* New York: Holt, Rinehart and Winston.
Van Doren, Carl
1923. "The Soil of the Puritans, Robert Frost: Quintessence
and Subsoil," *Century Magazine* Feb., pp. 629–36.
Wood, Clement
1925. "The Twilight of New England" in *Poets of America,*
pp. 142–62. New York: Dutton.

Selected Additional Readings

Anonymous
1923. "The Literary Spotlight: Robert Frost," *Bookman* (London) May, pp. 304–8.
Anonymous
1915. "Short Stories in Verse," *New York Evening Post* June
11, p. 14.
Benjamin, Paul L.
1920. "Robert Frost—Poet of Neighborliness," *Survey* Nov. 27,
pp. 318–19.
Bradley, William Aspenwall
1915. "The New Freedom—In Verse," *Bookman* (London)
Apr., pp. 184–95.
Jones, Llewellyn
1915. "Robert Frost," *Chicago Evening Post* Apr. 23, p. 11.
Lowell, Amy
1922. *A Critical Fable,* New York: Houghton Mifflin, pp. 21–25.
Untermeyer, Louis
1915. "*North of Boston,*" *Chicago Evening Post* Apr. 23, p. 11.
Van Doren, Mark
1923. "Robert Frost," *Nation* Dec. 19, pp. 715–16.

CHAPTER 3

Frost and His Negative Critics

". . . no poet has had even the range of his work more
unforgiveably underestimated by influential critics of
our time. . . ."

RANDALL JARRELL
"To the Laodiceans"

The above passage, taken from the best "appreciation" of
Frost ever published, is not meant to disparage the opinions
of those critics whose work will be mentioned in this chapter.
Many of these critics justly celebrate various parts of Frost's
achievement, but they all feel that his poetry shows serious
weaknesses in execution or philosophy which prevent him from
attaining true greatness. Jarrell's statement is meant, rather, to
call attention to the substantial body of negative criticism which
cropped up almost as soon as Frost returned from England in
1915, and has continued to appear after his death. It is true that
some "influential" readers have underestimated Frost and have
dismissed him as a holdover from the nineteenth century, a poet
unworthy to be called "modern" in the same breath that names
Eliot or Stevens. Our business is not with those opinions. Yet
to gain a balanced awareness of Frost's art and of his value as a
modern poet, it is necessary to face the negative criticism.

What makes Frost a particularly controversial subject is the
enormous number of honors heaped on him during his lifetime.
No American author in recent decades has been accorded such
a sustained reception by both serious and casual readers, and the
word "sustained" is the point. Unlike other writers who enjoyed critical and popular success in their lifetime—say Fitzgerald or Faulkner—Frost never had a period of low reputation. It
seems inevitable that such a reaction must set in, now that he is
dead, before we can begin the tentative steps toward an objective evaluation, but this process has not yet begun. He remains
one of the three or four most respected American poets of the
century, and his work continues to challenge intelligent readers
to better and more incisive interpretations. The case for or
against Frost is far from over.

A writer's final worth cannot be judged by the honors he

receives—certainly many great authors fail to win a single award. However, with Frost the honors are so numerous that they do indicate a measure of his success. A common way to honor a writer is to give him an honorary degree, but Frost was awarded forty-four (see Lawrance Thompson, *Selected Letters of Robert Frost*, pp. 623–24, for a list of his honors). He is the only poet to win four Pulitzer Prizes. He was honored with numerous distinguished medals for achievement in the arts, including those from Congress, the American Academy of Arts and Sciences, the National Institute of Arts and Letters, the Poetry Society of America, the Signet Society of Harvard, and New York University. He was given several highly coveted cash awards, including the Huntington Hartford Foundation Award, the Bollingen Prize, and the Russell Loines Poetry Prize. He was Phi Beta Kappa poet once at Columbia and William and Mary and twice at Harvard and Tufts. He was visiting professor or writer-in-residence at various schools, among them Amherst, Michigan, and Harvard. He was saluted by the U. S. Senate on the occasion of his seventy-fifth (in reality his seventy-sixth) birthday, and he said "The Gift Outright" at the inauguration of President Kennedy. The one important award that eluded Frost was the Nobel Prize. Most critics agree that these honors, plus all those not mentioned, are deserved for at least two reasons. First, Frost wrote consistently superior poetry. Second, his poetry challenged and appealed to all kinds of readers in a country whose general public ignores its artists.

Given this wide-ranging, long-lasting acceptance, it is significant that a substantial number of good critics dissent. This chapter looks at these dissenting opinions in an attempt to sort out the various criticisms so that the main negative arguments can be known. Some of the "answers" to these essays will also be discussed. But it is not the purpose of this chapter to defend Frost against each specific charge, for such a defense would require an essay of approximately equal length for each of the articles mentioned. The intent, rather, is presentation. The following survey of criticism should make the serious Frost student aware of the body of negative commentary about one of the most celebrated poets of our day. By reacting to these opinions, the reader may be better able to determine Frost's strengths and weaknesses and the poems in which they are illustrated.

The earliest critics who pointed out what they thought to be faults in Frost's art did so primarily in reviews rather than in full-fledged essays. Thus, most of them are concerned with specific books of poems, not with his theory or philosophy or his poetry as a whole. Amy Lowell, for example, was one of the early reviewers of *North of Boston*, and she later expanded her remarks to essay length in *Tendencies in Modern American Poetry* (1917). (See chapter 2 for a fuller account of her comments.) Although she generally approves of the poetry, she commits what has to be one of the classic examples of misreading in American criticism. Recognizing Frost's realistic depiction of manners and scene, she mistakenly assumes that his poetry is a kind of glorified local color. She sees Frost's characters as isolated old farmers, morbid, and giving way to insanity, and she wonders why the farmers of other countries live isolated lives without going insane. Miss Lowell's mistake is her tendency to limit the range of Frost's poems, and as an error it is relatively minor. But the conclusions she draws from it are devastating to her criticism. She fails to understand that while Frost uses a New England setting, his themes in *North of Boston* are universal: love, fear, death, communication.

She makes a more serious error when she comments that although Yankee characters and locale impress Frost, the speech does not. Misunderstanding the experiments with sentence sounds, she wishes that he would concentrate on genuine dialect poetry similar to that of James Russell Lowell, and she even suggests that Frost ignores this Yankee dialect because he lacks an ear for the peculiarities of speech. Miss Lowell concludes that while Frost's work is finished, these faults limit his scope and thus prevent him from writing poetry of the first rank. Reading criticism such as this, we wonder if she truly read the poems. Her misunderstanding of Frost's principle of sound is especially curious because of the pains he took to advertise and explain it at every opportunity. Miss Lowell's review is so wrongheaded that it has gained a kind of notoriety. It is by far the least valuable criticism to be examined in this chapter, but it is outlined here to illustrate the small body of very early Frost criticism which expresses some negative evaluations.

More serious attacks were levied by Granville Hicks and Frederic I. Carpenter in their reviews of Frost's 1930 edition of *Collected Poems*. In "The World of Robert Frost," written for the *New Republic* (Dec. 3, 1930), Hicks wonders why Frost violates the generally accepted literary principle which holds that great literature is created only when the artist and his moment in time reflect each other. Hicks admits that Frost has written poetry as fine as that of any contemporary American, and he praises the poet for not slipping into silence or mediocrity after early success. But the fact remains that despite Frost's intense and sustained power he exercises his creative faculties independent of circumstance. Hicks suggests that this is because Frost occupies himself with a limited experience instead of "yielding himself to the casual inspirations of unrelated phenomena" (1930, p. 77). Many poets have their own private world, but Frost's is different because it is not an intellectual abstraction. His is so closely related to the real world that his characters take on three-dimensional qualities and his figures of speech are always concrete.

Examining the collected poems in the light of Frost's private world, Hicks finds an absence of such powerful modern forces as industrialism, scientific hypotheses, and Freudianism. On the other hand, Frost can write about comic conflicts, dramatic tensions close to tragedy, and objects of natural beauty. Hicks is not so much attacking Frost as probing for reasons why he is not a better poet: "he cannot contribute directly to the unification, in imaginative terms, of our culture" (1930, p. 78). Frost's limited private world has the advantage of furnishing him with subjects and images less complicated than the major events, ideas, and forces of modern times. We would be, writes Hicks, considerably poorer if he had not created poetry based on rural New England. But Frost can never be grouped with the great poets of the ages because he fails to write about the world in which most people of the twentieth century find themselves.

Frederic I. Carpenter is much more pointed in his negative evaluation of Frost's *Collected Poems*. Attempting to make his review in *New England Quarterly* (January 1932) sound like praise, Carpenter welcomes the collection of Frost in a single volume. As the first of Frost's collected editions, this book offered the critics of the day an opportunity to examine his poetry as a body rather than as separate publications. Carpenter takes the first tentative steps toward a broader judgment than that offered by reviews of the single books when he notes that *Collected Poems* challenges the critic to reevaluate Frost's reputation. The trouble is that he begins by criticizing Frost for not being prolific. He complains that Frost's complete poems occupy only 350 pages, much of it in the form of narrative poems and none of it printed very closely. From this observation, Carpenter decides that Frost lacks "fertility"—implying that a better poet would have written more. Claims such as this get the review off on a bad foot, so that when he steps back a little in the next paragraph to say that quality, not quantity, is

important, we tend to question where his emphasis really is. His
call for judgment based on quality is undercut by the weight
of his previous comments.

Carpenter then celebrates what he considers to be the high
points of Frost's quality: its perfect modulation, its range of
feeling, its use of various rhythms, its perfect technique, and its
"exquisite" feeling for the right word. From such high praise
he concludes that Frost is a "poet's poet," but that this is not
enough. To praise Frost's accomplishment in such terms, he
argues, is to consider him only as a poet, and it is here that Carpenter spells out his main criticism: that Frost looks at life from
only a poetic viewpoint. He suffers by comparison with the
"cosmic imagination" of Whitman, the "tragic imagination"
of Jeffers, the "epic imagination" of Stephen Vincent Benét,
and the "dramatic imagination" of Robinson. Carpenter implies that Frost achieves limited perfection because he does not
write like these poets, and that by writing in his own style he
cuts himself off from the possibility of "absolute greatness."
From this criticism, never really developed, he concludes that
Frost has denied the "American way" by choosing quiet perfection and happiness over the possibility of what he calls "tur-
bulent greatness." Frost, thus, lacks the power to be the great
American poet.

The problem remains, however, of determining which criter-
ion Carpenter uses to evaluate a poet—quantity or quality. His
appreciation of Frost's strong points suggests that he believes
many of the poems to be perfect. But the nagging suspicion remains that he would give Frost a higher mark had the poet used
his perfect technique to write more poems, especially the kind
of long, book-length poems that Robinson, Jeffers, and Benét
have published. At any rate, Carpenter's short review opens the
door to what has become a standard criticism of Frost—that he
does not write like his contemporaries.

Robert Hillyer and Stewart Mitchell (*New England Quarterly*, April, 1932) jump on Carpenter's review to refute his
argument and to defend Frost. Hillyer's main quarrel with Carpenter is over the definition of "power." Examining the comparisons Carpenter makes with Whitman, Jeffers, Benét, and
Robinson, Hillyer defines what these poets mean to him and then
agrees that Frost does indeed write differently. He concedes
that Frost does not create the self-indulgent private world of a
Whitman or display the "disordered power of a wrenched
mind" of a Jeffers, and he is thankful that Frost lacks those lev-

els of power. Hillyer dismisses outright Carpenter's complaint that Frost lacks the epic imagination of Benét and the dramatic imagination of Robinson. Noting that Frost has no intention of creating an epic, he remarks that Frost cannot be faulted for "tasks he has not undertaken." And Hillyer insists that neither Robinson nor Frost can be called dramatic poets. Seizing the fault by which Carpenter leaves himself open to attack, Hillyer criticizes him for unconsciously equating power with bulk or quantity: Frost is not equal to the other four because his list of titles is not long and his poems are generally shorter. Hillyer celebrates Frost's restraint as a kind of power as equally valid as the definition Carpenter supplies. Mitchell's reply to Carpenter follows a similar line. He suggests that a literary critic's first duty is to recognize a poet at first sight and then "act accordingly," but Carpenter fails the test.

The tone of these early negative comments is generally mild. It is almost as if Frost's detractors were afraid to lash out too strongly at a poet who was already approaching the status of a national institution. Such was not the case, however, when Frost published *A Further Range* in 1936. Appearing in the middle of the depression, with World War II on the horizon, fascism rampant in Europe, and the Russian revolution a failure in the minds of many intellectuals, *A Further Range* infuriated a number of influential critics who believed that Frost's conservatism and playful approach to serious problems of worldwide scope were an insult. The comments by Newton Arvin, Horace Gregory, Rolfe Humphries, and R. P. Blackmur about this particular book form the core of the first true attack on Frost's art. Frost would never again enjoy the near unanimous approval of literary critics.

In his review of *A Further Range* written for *Partisan Review* (June 1936), Newton Arvin disputes those who claim that Frost is the spokesman for New England. He does not deny that Frost's poems represent an authentic expression of that region, but he distinguishes between the major and minor strains of Yankee life and culture. According to Arvin, Frost is the laureate of "nasalized negations, monosyllabic uncertainties, and noncommittal rejoinders"—the spokesman for the New England of unpainted farmhouses and "arid" sitting rooms (1936, p. 27). Militancy, positiveness, conviction, and struggle are qualities which have long been characteristic of New England, but Frost has never succeeded in expressing them. Arvin is clearly disappointed with Frost's subject matter in general, even though he is fair enough to admit that his remarks only qualify, but do not minimize, what he calls the poet's "admirable achievement." But his disappointment with *A Further Range* in particular is another matter. Suggesting that in this volume, more than in the previous books, Frost pays the price for cultivating a "fruitless and rather complacent skepticism," Arvin finds the warmth and freshness of the earlier books degenerating into dryness, emptiness, and "caprice." He grants that a dozen of the poems are so good that no other poet could have written them. But while criticizing Frost for writing from extreme bias, Arvin reveals his own personal point of view when he fails to name some of those dozen poems which merit his approval. Rather than credit Frost for the best work in *A Further Range* or discuss the poems which catch his fancy, he singles out the weaker ones for comment. Most readers would agree that "Build Soil" and "Two Tramps in Mud Time" are among Frost's lesser achievements; but, hopefully, most reviewers would not dwell on them to the exclusion of the better poems. Yet this is what Arvin does. The result is an article which reveals Arvin's own bias for a poetry of social commentary and which weakens his serious charge that Frost is out of touch with the times.

Writing for the *New Republic* (June 24, 1936), Horace Gregory strikes out as strongly at Frost's supporters as at the poet himself. He argues that Frost's critics have done him a major disservice when they assure the public that Frost is the current inheritor of the New England tradition of Emerson and Whittier, and he points out that Frost would be embarrassed if he pretended to such eminence. For if he were to walk the paths of Emerson and Whittier, he would have to shoulder the load of social responsibility—a burden he prefers to avoid. Frost should not be seen as a New England writer but as the last survivor of the English Georgian movement. In advancing this original thesis, Gregory makes the even more startling point that *A Boy's Will* is "easily the best" of the poet's earlier books. He notes that the poet has never lost his ear for common speech and his skill in using it, traits which are still very much present in *A Further Range*, and he laments that rather than extend the "Georgian" beginnings of *A Boy's Will*, Frost unfortunately has listened to those who place him in the socially active New England tradition. Gregory finds the socially oriented poems of this volume "self-defensive and ill informed," particularly "Build Soil," "To a Thinker," and "A Lone Striker." His judgment of these poems seems correct. But more importantly, Gregory catches Frost in a contradiction: if the poet truly wants to remain noncommittal about the pressing issues of the day, why does he "trouble his head about further ranges into politics, where his wisdom may be compared to that of Calvin Coolidge?" (1936, p. 214). Gregory believes that Frost has allowed his supporters to convince him that he merits the inheritance of the New England tradition when in fact he does not. Unlike Arvin, however, Gregory illustrates a fuller awareness of *A Further Range* as a whole when he names "The Master Speed" and "Provide, Provide" as "memorable examples" of Frost's better abilities.

A much sharper commentary on *A Further Range* is Rolfe Humphries' "A Further Shrinking" published in *New Masses* (Aug. 11, 1936). Humphries really lets Frost have it. Writing for *New Masses*, he might be expected to criticize Frost for his reactionary politics, but this does not seem to be the point. "Sedentary," "obdurate," and "homey" to the point of affectation are the characteristics which Humphries applies to the Frost of the earlier books. Yet he accepts them as part of the man who offers shrewd observations and a measure of real life in his poems. But when Frost turns to politics, as he does in *A Further Range*, Humphries finds that his latent penchant for didacticism surfaces, causing his manner to become unbearable. The result is that Frost falls short as a poet because his quarrel with others is too strong: "the new didacticism lacks authentic organic originality; it seems applied to the verse instead of pervading it. . ." (1936, p. 41). Humphries goes so far to insist that *A Further Range* catches Frost in the act of being what he constantly boasts not to be—"fuddled, garrulous, deaf, and ordinary."

The problem is that Humphries makes the mistake of not analyzing specific poems to illustrate his censure—he does not even name titles. His generalities are so strongly worded that they amount to a kind of shrill outcry. When he writes about the "tendency to prolong argument after the demands of art are satisfied," the inability to reject bad material, and the homilies which "sound like Guest," the reader needs to know which poems and lines these strictures refer to. Some of the poems are as bad as he suggests, but surely the entire volume is not a uniform disaster—not even Arvin or Gregory goes that far. But Humphries remains content with generalities, some of which, like the accusation of didacticism, would have carried greater weight had he included some analysis. Rather than pin the blame on Frost's critics, as Gregory does, Humphries points to the poet's university audience as a prime cause for the weakness of

A Further Range. He believes that Frost has been corrupted by "an admiring yokelry," and that Frost now substitutes reputation for art.

In the final negative review of *A Further Range* to be considered, R. P. Blackmur (*Nation,* June 24, 1936) criticizes Frost for some of the qualities which Frederic I. Carpenter praised four years earlier: technique and craft. Arguing that the political and social subjects of *A Further Range* result in poetic failures, Blackmur suggests that the weaknesses in this particular book reflect shortcomings which mar most of Frost's work. He feels that the flaws stem from one source: Frost's inability to assume the correct attitude toward his art. More a bard than a poet, Frost cannot transform his instincts into true poetry. Blackmur defines a bard as an "easy-going versifier of all that comes to hand," a man who never masters his casually selected subjects. A poet, on the other hand, is defined as a maker of images, a man who can express the reality of experience and who can distinguish between true subjects and "the false host of pseudo-subjects." Blackmur illustrates his point by suggesting that Swinburne is a bard who is also a poet while Yeats is a real poet. Frost fails to measure up to either because he writes with only a bard's discipline.

His main criticism is that Frost relies on instinct to carry him through the creative act rather than on the entire range of the rational imagination. Frost does not push himself to see the actuality of experience, and thus he cannot express it in his poems. Blackmur suggests that poetic craft is not limited to meter, rhyme, or matters of phrasing—but must also include "the relish and hysteria of words" which help reveal experience. Frost has a good line here and there, but they only call attention to the bad. Blackmur illustrates by referring to two poems, "Build Soil" and "Desert Places." He calls the argument in the former indifferent, and he dismisses the poem as dull verse. This evaluation of "Build Soil" may be justified; it is far from being one of Frost's better poems. But his choice of "Desert Places" as an example of Frost's lack of craft is fuzzy because he never makes clear his objections to the poem. All we can be sure of is that he does not think the final two stanzas measure up to the first two due to a failure to use the experience described in the first pair of stanzas.

One of Blackmur's problems is that he opens up charges which the limited scope of his review cannot handle. He lacks the room to develop and support his negative criticisms not only of the book he is reviewing but also of Frost's work as a whole. Many readers would agree that parts of *A Further Range* are weak. But while Blackmur says that Frost fails in his handling of these new subjects in such a way as to reveal faults in the earlier poems, he never substantiates the point. He simply lacks the space to do so in a short review. An even greater problem with his remarks is that he ignores most of the lyrics of *A Further Range*. Not all of them are first rate, naturally, but some are among the best of American poetry: "Neither Out Far Nor In Deep," "Design," or "Provide, Provide." Blackmur's chief contribution to the negative criticism of Frost is his insistence that Frost writes by the dictates of his instinct.

Writing a year and a half later, Bernard De Voto answers Blackmur's charges with what has to be one of the most stinging replies in American criticism to another critic (*Saturday Review of Literature*, Jan. 1, 1938). The occasion of De Voto's response is a review of Richard Thornton's *Recognition of Robert Frost* (1937), but he expands the review into a major essay that lashes out at those modern critics who judge Frost—and other poets—by preconceived theories of what poetry ought to be. Rather than objectively examine Frost's work, De Voto argues, these critics compare him to those poets who fit their definition of poetry, and thus they naturally find him lacking. De Voto is particularly miffed at Blackmur and other reviewers of *A Further Range*, and he pulls no punches when referring to Blackmur. Exclaiming "Oh, the hell with scholarly reservations," he calls Blackmur's review "the most idiotic of our time. It is one of the most idiotic reviews since the invention of movable type." He grants that Blackmur and the other negative reviewers (especially Newton Arvin and Horace Gregory) read *A Further Range*, but he criticizes them for reading any writer with a preconceived theory of poetry placed between them and the printed page. Such methods, writes De Voto, force literary criticism into the realm of mathematical processes because they depend on logic rather than on instinct and experience with literature for their judgments.

As he reviews the various essays in Thornton's collection, De Voto discusses some of the so-called right ways to create poetry which have blossomed and withered in twentieth-century criticism. For example, Frost was first given critical approval because it was thought that he joined the Imagists in revolt "against something." But when Pound threw over Imagism, the theorists decided that poetry had to mirror the techniques of Pound and especially of Eliot. De Voto sarcastically comments that this kind of poetry required prose explanations, "about a hundred pages of theory to one page of text." Frost was, of course, held at a distance by these new critics because his poems neither looked nor sounded like Eliot's. But the theorists were not alone in their disdain of Frost. A rival group which insisted that poetry be concerned with social problems held up Auden, Spender, and Day Lewis as the correct models for all poets to follow. Since Frost failed to fit the mold, he was damned again.

The remainder of De Voto's essay evaluates Frost's poetry in such a way as to illustrate how poetry can be seriously read free from the confining burdens of specific literary theories. He is surely correct when he argues that the clear surface of a poem does not mean that surface is all there is to it. But not every superior poem has to find its roots in *The Golden Bough*. Particularly impressed by Frost's lyrics, De Voto suggests that the negative critics could find surprising rewards if they would bring to these shorter poems the same energy and reverence with which they approach "The Hollow Men." In many ways this angry article is a transitional piece in the development of the negative criticisms of Frost because it defends Frost from some of the early charges as well as foresees many of the opinions that the negative critics after 1938 would hold. His point is that Frost's reputation should depend upon an intelligent reading of the poetry and not on the ways his work either adheres to or diverges from particular critical theories of how poetry should be written, nor on the way his art differs from that of other successful moderns, especially Eliot.

This later criticism, beginning roughly in 1944 with an article by Malcolm Cowley, takes two general points of view in its negative reading of Frost. The first is a development of the tendencies De Voto notices. Comparing Frost to the poets who are usually accepted without question as modern—Eliot, Yeats, Pound, and Stevens—these critics argue that Frost's art is not equal to theirs because he does not approach contemporary themes the way they do. This point of view usually involves a preconceived opinion as to what themes twentieth-century poetry should be concerned with and how they should be articulated in poetry. The second general point of view refers specifically to the kind of poetry Frost writes. Noting the stone walls, birch trees, and brooks, these readers criticize his handling of social problems or the problems of modern urban society as opposed to those of the rural world. It all boils down to what they consider to be fallacies in Frost's "social philosophy." Although they disagree about the value of his man-nature poems, they all feel that Frost represents a skeptical view of collective human effort because he advocates to a fault individual responsibility. They argue that Frost is cut off from enduring human values because the rural world of his poems oversimplifies human experience. Thus, his poetry degenerates to a poetry of evasion, incapable of exploring fundamental modern issues since Frost himself refuses to meet them.

Malcolm Cowley's "The Case Against Mr. Frost" (*New Republic*, Sept. 11, 18, 1944) is the earliest of these articles. Beginning with a list of Frost's honors, Cowley admits that the awards are deserved and that most of his poems are a pleasure to read. Still, he believes there is room for a "dissenting opinion." The first half of his essay is a well-deserved attack directed against the overzealous admirers of Frost who do not really like his poetry, but who use Frost's art as a banner behind which they dismiss the more obviously modern poets as dangerous, degenerate, and disciples of foreign influences. Cowley argues that such narrowly conservative readers point to Frost as 100 percent American, a poet worthy of the pure American tradition passed down by Emerson and Hawthorne. Cowley would not rank Frost as high as these nineteenth-century giants, but comparisons of this sort are not his concern in the essay's first half.

In the second half, however, he shifts his sights from readers of Frost to take direct aim on Frost's poetry. Admitting the achievement with narrative and lyric poems, Cowley criticizes what he calls the "social philosopher in verse." There can be little doubt that the long poems like "New Hampshire" and "Build Soil," his satiric "editorials," and his poems on various political subjects are his worst, but Cowley nevertheless uses them to construct a case against Frost's political and social conservatism in an attempt to prove that Frost is a poor representative of the liberal New England tradition. He insists that Frost is opposed to innovation in art, science, and politics, that he dismisses Freud, and that he objects to inventions and improvements which bring change. The problem, as Cowley sees it, is that Frost is too caught up in the past and that he will do nothing positive to relieve social problems, preferring to leave things pretty much as they are. He suggests that Frost's brand of self-reliance is misconstrued if labeled Emersonian because Emerson wanted to reform the individual in order to reform society.

But it is not just Frost's handling of social questions that dis-

turbs Cowley. He also believes that Frost dodges all opportunities to explore the self by building barriers between himself and
the infinite. Strictly interpreting the woods of Frost's poems as
"the uncharted country within ourselves," Cowley argues that
when a narrator in one of the poems refuses to enter the trees, he
metaphorically rejects the chance for inner exploration. Thus,
Frost cannot examine with meaningful depth either the inward
experience of the individual or the outward experience of society. Cowley clearly believes that a poet has a duty to recommend social action—since Frost does not do so, he cannot be a
major poet. In addition to using many of Frost's worst poems for
illustration, Cowley tends to wrench lines out of context to make
his point. He selects, for example, these lines from "A Considerable Speck" to show that Frost denies "Christian charity" and
the idea of a "universal brotherhood under God:"

> I have none of the tenderer-than-thou
> Collectivistic regimenting love
> With which the modern world is being swept.

To do so, however, is to ignore the playful context. The poem
has nothing to do with human relations but with the narrator's
reaction to a microscopic speck which crawls across a sheet
of paper. The narrator leaves it alone because he is glad to
recognize "Mind when I meet it in any guise." Yet Cowley
uses this poem, plus others such as "Two Tramps in Mud Time,"
to suggest that Frost is not a poet of the great New England
spirit, but one who celebrates the "New England of the tourist
home and the antique shop in the abandoned gristmill." Cowley's liberalism clashes with Frost conservatism with the result
that Frost is named a weak poet.

George F. Whicher takes issue with Cowley's conclusions by
arguing that Frost has survived so well because he refuses to
acknowledge allegiance to any particular age (*American
Scholar*, Aug. 1945). He suggests that Eliot likewise rejects
the liberal tradition when Eliot embraces three citadels of conservatism: the Anglican church, royalist politics, and classicism
in literature. Whicher examines Cowley's article point by point
in order to counter each of the charges. He is not too concerned
with the complaints that Frost is a conservative nationalist and
that Frost's skepticism of foreign influences in art prevents him
from belonging to the great New England tradition. Claiming
that Frost is no more than a well-wisher of the United States,
Whicher argues that while Emerson, Thoreau, and other nine-

teenth-century New Englanders read every bit of foreign literature they could find, especially Oriental literature, they were
more concerned with supporting and rounding out their own
ideas than with learning the fundamentals of Oriental mysticism.
Thus, Frost's skepticism of Freud and his tendency to poke fun
at Darwin cannot be made to illustrate his divergence from the
liberal opinions of his Yankee forerunners.

Whicher devotes the greatest part of his essay to a refutation
of Cowley's charge that Frost lacks human charity and concern
for his fellow man. Calling attention to Frost's celebrated "neighborliness," he points to the obvious reason for Cowley's dislike of Frost—Frost is a poet while Cowley is more of a social
scientist. Frost's refusal to support the New Deal and later social
programs has been misconstrued to mark him a disbeliever in
brotherhood. What most disturbs Whicher is Cowley's method
of illustration. It is clear that the lines from "A Considerable
Speck" are read out of context, but an even greater fault is the
misreading of "Two Tramps in Mud Time." Giving his interpretation of the poem, Whicher goes on to compare it to
Wordsworth's "Resolution and Independence," suggesting that
if Frost is insensitive to human needs in his poem, then Wordsworth is too for not "rushing home to write a plea for old-age
pensions." In other words Cowley's response as a social scientist
is one point of view, but it is out of place when applied to the
reading of a poem. No major poet can be totally concerned
with the specific social problems of a particular era. To do so is
to limit his scope. He must be committed to examinations of experience in such a way as to comment on universal problems and
values. Finally, Whicher dismisses Cowley's objection that Frost
is not interested in exploration of the inner self, suggesting that
while Frost is not part of the American Gothic tradition, such
poems as "Desert Places," "Acquainted with the Night," and
"An Old Man's Winter Night" say enough about inner problems
to exonerate him from the charge of being only a gentle nature poet.

Despite Whicher's objections to Cowley's criticism, the complaint that Frost is out of touch with tragic human problems
gained supporters. Louise Bogan raises the issue again in *Achievement in American Poetry: 1900–1950* (1951). Although her
book is a literary history of modern American poetry, her remarks on Frost are very brief, covering only five pages, and generally negative. Like nearly every critic, she approves of the
approximation of speech tones in *North of Boston,* but she be-

lieves that Frost possesses "humane realism and insight" in only
that one book. She seems to place the blame on Frost's avoidance of the problems brought on by industrialization. According to Miss Bogan, he leaves the potential tragedy of New England "dangling and incomplete" when he skirts the issues raised
by the mills and the immigrant population. She may be correct
when she writes that Frost dodges certain important contemporary issues, but her insistence that this is the cause for a diminishing tragic vision remains questionable. The problem is that
Miss Bogan wants Frost to write a series of *North of Bostons*,
for she states that Frost's later work never "realized the tragic
power that *North of Boston* promised" (1951, p. 49). Skipping
Mountain Interval and *New Hampshire*, she names *West-Running Brook* as the beginning of his role as country philosopher.
We do not learn whether she thinks the two intervening volumes to be beneath comment or outside the scope of her thesis.
Whatever the case, she roundly attacks all of his work since
North of Boston for what she calls his "unthinking timidity."
If we believe Miss Bogan, then Frost has held so tightly to his
"views that they at last have very nearly wiped out his vision"
(1951, p. 51). Like R. P. Blackmur before her, she grants him
no more than the role of bard. Such a sweeping denunciation of
all of Frost's work since *North of Boston* is eccentric enough to
be treated gingerly. Her criticism is so broad as to arouse the
suspicion that she just does not care for Frost. Worse, Miss Bogan's remarks remain only generalizations, for she never analyzes
poems or lines to show how she arrives at such questionable conclusions.

   Harold H. Watts is a more articulate commentator on Malcolm
Cowley's suggestion that Frost has a faulty social philosophy. In "Robert Frost and the Interrupted Dialogue" (*American Literature*, Mar. 1955), Watts argues that Frost does establish a successful relationship with nature, and that he tries to do
so with society, only to fail because he too often resorts to
whimsical conversation which confronts serious issues with cute
wisecracks. Using "West-Running Brook" as the focal poem in
his essay, Watts suggests that this poem shows man and nature
as part of a common creation, both coming from the same un-
named source. If this interpretation is valid, then Frost misrep-
resents man's place in his world when he dismisses the man-society dialogue as unequal in value to the man-nature dialogue.
Watts believes that Frost sets up a kind of either-or situation
which is a false dilemma—man must have a fixed negative re-

sponse to social dialogue or he cannot hope for a meaningful dialogue with nature. Frost, then, evades the man-society relationship. He gains valuable insights from his investigations of nature, but he denies the same sympathetic attention to human processes. Thus, he refuses to follow up what his perceptions of the common origin of man and nature tell him in "West-Running Brook." He cannot completely ignore the man-society dialogue because humanity keeps breaking in ("The Egg and the Machine"), but he will not grant that man's efforts in society are as instructive as his examinations of nature.

Instead, Watts argues, Frost begins a new dialogue which is especially evident in his late books, *A Witness Tree, Steeple Bush,* and the *Masques.* In this second dialogue, Frost is "a less apt and flexible observer" because he will not use the insights gained from his original dialogues with natural processes to reckon with the enormous problems which society also poses for man. Toward all philosophical systems and social reforms, Frost displays two attitudes—skepticism for man's efforts and a tentative "as-if acceptance." Watts' major contention is that the dialogue with society is forced on all men by the urgencies of the times, but that Frost refuses to learn from it. He chooses the weakest poems for illustration, but his argument is that these poems are inferior because Frost's view of society is faulty. "The Bear" suggests Frost's skepticism of philosophical systems, while "A Lone Striker" reveals his attitude toward social organization. These poems, and the others like them, are witty, but for Watts they are also slight, trivial editorials. Frost shows concern for the universal themes of birth, death, isolation, and the need to take a stance in the face of natural processes, but he will not use his skills to picture man maintaining the same stance against social dilemmas. The final part of Watts' essay is a quarrel with Frost's politics and with his skepticism toward religion and science. He concludes that the poet puts his talents "only obliquely in the service of mankind" because Frost will not grant that social process is as valuable as natural process.

Watts joins Cowley in his belief that to be of major stature a poet must recommend social action. A similar criticism forms one of the main lines of attack in what is probably the most famous of the negative evaluations of Frost: Yvor Winters' "Robert Frost: Or, the Spiritual Drifter as Poet" (*The Function of Criticism: Problems and Exercises,* 1957). Winters echoes Cowley on at least two minor counts: he admits that Frost is a talented poet (though overestimated), and he insists that

Americans like Frost because his rural subjects give them a nostalgic feeling for the past. His major concern is also similar to Cowley's because he attacks Frost for what he believes to be a poor social philosophy. The key difference is that Winters bases his criticism on a disavowal of Frost's claims to an Emersonian discipleship. According to Winters, Frost is a spiritual drifter because he assumes discipleship without Emerson's religious convictions. Thus he drifts, taking the easy way out whenever he faces what should be formative decisions.

Winters implies that Frost's themes are minor because they deal with stone walls rather than with contemplation of death and eternity. His poems are good, but they do not go far enough. His whimsical decisions, his failures to develop serious moral choices in the poems, cut him off from a sensitive understanding of human experience. Selecting "The Road Not Taken," "The Sound of Trees," "The Hill Wife," and "The Bearer of Evil Tidings" for illustration, Winters insists that Frost uses "devious evasions" to convince himself that he is wise when in reality he confuses whimsical impulse for moral choice. In the bulk of his essay, Winters follows the negative critics before him when he selects the didactic, satirical poems to support his thesis. Citing such poems as "The Bear" and "To a Thinker," he argues that Frost dismisses reason in favor of instinct, and that he advocates both a retreat from cooperative action and a casual approach to what, in Winters' mind, should be formative decisions. Winters also uses "Build Soil," a poem first read in 1932 before the New Deal, to show that Frost advises "against any kind of political activity in a time of national collapse." Calling this attitude political drifting and a retreat to passivity, Winters stretches his reading of "Build Soil" to insist that Frost favors national development only if things are allowed to fall where they may. Frost's regard for nature is as sentimental as his dislike of the machine, and both attitudes reflect his objection to social cooperation.

Summing up his discussion of the satirical poems, Winters decides that Frost is at odds with normal human experience for the following reasons: he elevates impulse over reason; he brings a casual approach to important decisions; he encourages retreat from cooperative action; he advocates self-reliance to an extreme; and he denies the seriousness of good and evil. These are serious charges, and if they were all true, it is doubtful that Frost would have had any reception at all from intelligent critics. Winters follows this summation with an admission that Frost has a "genuine gift for writing" which shows up best in his later work. In poems like "On Going Unnoticed," he believes that Frost reveals increasing melancholy at mutability and at man's smallness, and he cites "The Most of It" as a significant unsentimental view of nature. But these poems fail to salvage Frost for Winters. In his final paragraphs, he admits that in some respects his remarks have been unfair because the didactic poems are Frost's worst, but he rationalizes his approach by arguing that these longer poems offer the best clues to Frost's thought. He appreciates many of the descriptive lyrics, but even here he feels that Frost shows a "sentimental obscurantism" which leads away from a meaningful investigation of human experience. Winters concludes that Frost is a good poet but a dangerous influence because he openly supports the principles which have hampered his development and which could cause the deterioration of the United States: "the principles of Emersonian and Thoreauistic Romanticism. . . ."

The extremes of Winters' attack are caused for the most part by his notion of what poetry ought to be. He is more interested in establishing and defining his belief that poetry must have a definite social function, a deliberate concern for specific contemporary issues, than in examining Frost's good poems for strengths and weaknesses. Winters and Cowley are almost angry in their evaluations. One begrudgingly admits Frost's talent while the other even says that the honors are deserved, but both seem to resent the general and critical receptions given a writer who does not conform to their definitions of what a twentieth-century poet ought to be.

Roy Harvey Pearce also feels that Frost has serious limitations, but he does not base his criticism on the weaker poems or on Frost's social philosophy (*Kenyon Review,* Spring 1961). Rather, he discusses what it means to "accept" Frost's art in an age of modern criticism. Observing that Frost knows himself and the world of his poetry perfectly, Pearce feels that this knowledge may be the reason why Frost is able to perfect his work in a way none of his contemporaries has been able to match. But for Pearce perfection is not necessarily good because it tempts him to speak of Frost as a "minor poet." The point is, he argues, that Frost's work is perfect because its world view and range are severely limited. Frost's world is so rural that it cannot be readily meaningful to his readers. Rather than write about the urban, industrialized, overpopulated world that engulfs twentieth-century man, Frost chooses to portray a pastoral community in which individuals resist the changes they would have to experience if they were to live in the urban society and still retain their individuality. It is not that Frost necessarily celebrates rural life—he often writes about the great cost to those who isolate themselves by refusing to meet the modern world. But for Pearce this is not enough. He feels that readers are forced to deny Frost's world not because Frost cannot speak their language but because modern readers cannot speak his. This is because Frost renounces the complications of twentieth-century life to find a wholeness and a measure of perfection in simplified surroundings.

Acknowledging Frost's debt to Emerson, Pearce nevertheless argues that Frost uses Emerson's doctrine of freedom in his own individual way. Emerson broke with the past to look forward, while Frost does so only to examine the present, to stabilize a point and then withdraw for consolidation of his strength. This is a kind of freedom, but only a freedom to define the self rather than one to move ahead. Frost is sure of himself because he rarely ventures into unknown regions. The beautiful clarity of his poems—difficult enough to achieve—is gained at the expense of ignoring some of the conditions of modern life. Using "The Most of It" for illustration, Pearce writes that the very detail which makes his poems effective also makes readers aware of the gulf between the two worlds. Frost's world is so individual that contemporary society does not exist as "an immediately conditioning factor" in his poems, a remark which recalls Granville Hicks' article. By way of final comment, Pearce sees as Frost's chief weakness his unwillingness to chance unknown thoughts. But this limitation is also a kind of strength, for it allows Frost full possession of the small world beyond which he refuses to go.

Irving Howe also questions Frost's status as a modern poet. In his well-written, closely argued essay (*New Republic*, Mar. 23, 1963), he tries hard not to let his liberal political bias interfere with his evaluation of Frost's art. His main interest is determining the extent of Frost's modernity, and he decides that the poet belongs in the company of modern poets "almost against his will." Although he criticizes Frost for lacking the technique and temperament of the moderns, he finds that Frost shares their "vision of disturbance." What follows is an expression of Howe's qualified approval of Frost. Completely at odds with a critic like Louise Bogan, he points to a dozen or so lyrics as the height of Frost's achievement, poems more original and distinguished than the best of the dramatic dialogues in *North of Boston*. He admits that his judgment may seem outrageous, but he wants it to be taken as praise.

In the first half of the essay, Howe lists and illustrates the weaknesses he finds in Frost's poetry. Like most readers, he believes Frost to be at his worst in poems like "New Hampshire," the longer poems which unite sarcasm and didacticism. He dislikes the public pose of the poet found in the *Masques* and in most of *Steeple Bush*. Most of all, he denounces the garrulousness, the conservative decline into "smallness of mind," and the "vanity" of pronouncement he finds in so much of Frost's work. Commenting on parts of *A Masque of Reason*, Howe writes: "Frost permits himself such mindless flippancies because he knows that by now his audience has been trained to admire his faults at the very point where they become magnified by cleverness" (1963, p. 23). When he turns to the lyrics, Howe challenges standard critical opinion by naming "Mending Wall," "Birches," and "The Death of the Hired Man" as second-rate. These poems rely too much upon what he calls "stock sentiments" and the "mode of false pastoral." In these poems, Frost panders to our nostalgia for the idyllic rural setting and to our false belief that wisdom is to be found in tight-lipped farmers and village eccentrics.

But, says Howe, if this were the extent of Frost's achievement, then we would have no choice but to accept Yvor Winters' broadside attack. Primarily because of lyrics like "Acquainted with the Night," "After Apple-Picking," "Stopping by Woods on a Snowy Evening," "The Most of It," and several others, Howe has no intention of agreeing with Winters. He notes that Frost requires complicated critical evaluation because so many of his best poems are also his most popular. It is in these lyrics that Frost confronts basic human troubles without offering false security or solace: "They focus upon a moment of intense realization, a lighting-up of hope and a dimming-down to wisdom" (1963, p. 26) At his best, Frost reveals the kind of wisdom which refuses to settle into the "comforts" of an intellectual system. And by sharing in the loss of firm assumptions, writes Howe, Frost joins other modern poets who seek some tentative basis, some "momentary stay," for life itself. Howe concludes by quoting "The Most of It," which he correctly names "one of the greatest poems ever written by an American." This essay remains one of the best of those which are direct and precise in their negative evaluations of Frost's achievement. Howe does not like the bulk of Frost's canon, and he is quick to say so. But because he supports his argument with analysis, and because he willingly praises those poems which do appeal to him, his article reflects the thoughts of a reader who hopes to express his own complicated response to the poetry instead of publishing a hatchet job.

An equally fine essay is Isadore Traschen's "Robert Frost: Some Divisions in a Whole Man" (_Yale Review_, Oct. 1965). Traschen essentially agrees with part of Roy Harvey Pearce's thesis when he writes that Frost neither "risks" his life nor faces the "deepest" experiences. But unlike Pearce, he believes that despite Frost's reputation for being a whole man who is able to integrate life, his poetry reveals damaging divisions. In the case of the nature poems, for example, Traschen senses a division between the "man who is involved" and the one who observes the action. While Frost can render nature faithfully, he often fails to unify his "idea of it with his feeling." The scenes described are too often followed by abstract comment. Traschen admits that this fault is absent in the dramatic narratives where the action is better sustained and in a few superior lyrics like "The Silken Tent" and "The Most of It," but he insists that these poems are exceptions.

Second, Frost's rhythms and subjects show division. Refusing to vary the intensity of his rhythm with his subject, Frost uses the same rhythm in poems as different as "Mending Wall" and "An Old Man's Winter Night." From this Traschen concludes that Frost's tone is too level, producing the effect of understatement which tricks the reader into thinking he has listened to wisdom. Such level tones prevent Frost from expressing what Traschen calls "the tragic Howl" of great poets who "risked everything." And this lack marks a further division, the "separation of fact and feeling" which is part of his sentimentality as expressed in a poem like "The Road Not Taken."

The fourth division is between Frost and nature. Traschen argues that Frost holds back, that he refuses to lose himself in nature in order to grow from the experience as D. H. Lawrence and Dylan Thomas do. He remains outside, unchanged, always the observer who looks at the terror and offers solutions. Calling this kind of art "a poetry of isolationism," Traschen goes on to say that Frost avoids real modern crises because of his role as observer: "Uninvolved, Frost paralyzes us with merely passive or stunned responses to modern terror, as in 'Design,' 'Bereft,' or 'Once by the Pacific'. . . ." (1965, p. 66). As is usual with most of the negative criticism of Frost, Traschen's com-

plaint really focuses on the question of whether or not Frost
avoids the social entanglements and the intellectual issues of
contemporary times. He criticizes Frost for not approaching
modern dilemmas the way Yeats would have, or Eliot, Lawrence, Thomas, Kafka, and Camus. When Frost does meet modern issues, Traschen suggests, he is "inadequate" because he
manages only commonplace remarks. Traschen reaches the questionable conclusion that Frost writes in a "historical vacuum,"
saying little about modern alienation and fragmentation.

This article touches on what seem to be the two main points
in the negative criticisms: Frost's relationship to modern social
problems and his way of handling modern intellectual themes
as compared to the methods other contemporary poets use. A
sane, low-key evaluation, Traschen's essay contrasts with the
more biting attacks by Cowley and Winters. While Cowley
and Winters often seem angry with the way Frost writes and
with the attitudes he assumes, Watts, Pearce, and Traschen lament that he fails to do better. These three critics believe that
had Frost committed himself to the social and intellectual crises
of his day he might have been capable of the development which
characterizes Yeats and Eliot.

W. W. Robson agrees. Published in an issue of the *Southern
Review* (Oct. 1966) devoted entirely to Frost studies, his "The
Achievement of Robert Frost" is a long, intelligent evaluation of
a body of poetry which he finds lacking. This is not to say that
the British critic disapproves of Frost's art, but only to remark
that he does not think Frost worthy of the highest rank. According to Robson, Frost is no longer widely read in England:
"My own impression, for what it is worth, is that if Frost is
mentioned at all, it is as a worthy but dull poet of about the
rank of Masefield" (1966, p. 735). If he is correct, then Frost
has suffered a spectacular loss of favor since the days of his first
publication in London and of the near unanimous support of influential British critics, all of which culminated in his receipt of
honorary degrees from Oxford and Cambridge in June, 1957.

Robson recalls some of the flavor of Frost's early fame in
British literary circles when he quotes from Edward Thomas'
review of *North of Boston*. Drawing on Thomas' remarks about
Frost's technical innovation, he summarizes how Frost cut across
the grain of the *verse libre* movement with the union of meter
and speech cadences. This summary is useful to those who are
not acquainted with the history and practice of Frost's sentence
sounds. Robson correctly argues that speech tones are not the

whole of Frost's innovation. The colloquialism may be famous, but close reading reveals how much of the traditional literary language Frost retains. No one can read "The Silken Tent," for example, and call it colloquial. The point is that Frost does not necessarily associate speech tones with informal diction or syntax.

Following an analysis of Frost's relationship with the Georgian poets, Robson gets to the heart of his essay. He wonders, once he grants the value of Frost's technical innovation, if the poet achieved anything more than a "quiet and sensible" style—did Frost ever write a "really considerable poem?" Like so many of Frost's negative critics, Robson believes that the poet's supporters have done him a disservice by institutionalizing him as a national hero and, therefore, as a poet whose total achievement is not open to rigorous judgment. Refusing to honor the critical "protection" of Frost, Robson compares him to Wordsworth and finds him wanting. He detects a "certain thinness" in Frost's poetry, a lack of "poetic intensity." "The Death of the Hired Man" falls short of the tragic destiny found in Wordsworth's "Resolution and Independence" or "Michael." Robson's analysis is worthy of consideration, but his argument is weakened when he suggests that the famous moonlight passage in "Hired Man" is "curiously extraneous." Disappointingly, he falls back on the old charge that Frost's art is "more akin to that of the short story writer than the poet." He finds the significant difference between Wordsworth and Frost in the pastoral quality which the two poets evoke. Without elaborating his point, he writes that Wordsworth achieves universality by using pastoral with complete seriousness, while Frost uses pastoral for irony.

This potentially fruitful distinction fails to be completely convincing for want of fuller analysis. It does lead, however, to Robson's negative evaluation of Frost's characters. The problem, he feels, is that they "are not related to anything greater than themselves" (1966, p. 753). Frost communicates sympathy and understanding for them, but these qualities are not enough for a great poet. There must also be the suggestion of a larger perspective, of "the wider and finer mind," but Frost is content to detail the particulars of the scene. Reading this, one wonders if Robson has carefully read "A Servant to Servants" or "Home Burial." He decides that this absence of a larger perspective results in a lack of technical and personal development. Frost may have the advantage of continuity, but he simultaneously suffers from the inability to distinguish between manner and mannerism. And it is Frost's playful manner which most irritates Robson. Referring to the poet's least satisfactory work, poems like "Build Soil," he asks why we should take the ideas seriously if the poet apparently does not. This observation is reminiscent of Cowley's and Winters' censures, and one which needs more complete investigation.

Robson concludes his essay with a short analysis of the poems he does like. Suggesting, with justification, that Frost's best poems are those in which the poetic persona is not strongly felt, he names "Gathering Leaves," "Dust of Snow," and "Neither Out Far Nor In Deep" as examples of Frost's true achievement. The poet's strength lies in these "short poems [of] human transcience," for he possesses a deep sense of life's brief span. These poems are good because Frost avoids wistfulness. Eschewing nostalgia, he forces us to realize that each generation must discover its own relationship with the universe. Robson argues that these poems are marginal in Frost's work and that they suffer when compared to the more ambitious efforts of other poets. Yet they are highly distinctive and worthy of our attention. This essay clearly shows that Robson celebrates many of Frost's poems. Instead of developing a sweeping denunciation of the poet, he seems more interested in trying to decide why Frost fails to equal the standard of the very greatest art. His suggestions about Frost's use of pastoral and about the disturbing effect of the poet's persona are significant, but to be convincing they need elaboration. Perhaps he means for his article to be a kind of starting point for a reassessment of Frost's canon—if so, he has succeeded. For his calm tone and knowledge of Frost's general development invite the reader to pursue his conclusions even if he disagrees with them.

The criticisms thus far discussed are in review or essay form, but by far the most developed of the negative criticisms is George W. Nitchie's book *Human Values in the Poetry of Robert Frost: A Study of a Poet's Convictions* (1960). Like Traschen's essay, Nitchie's study focuses on both of the major theses put forth by many of these critics: Frost's avoidance of crucial social themes and his approach to modern intellectual questions. Nitchie's book is so patiently documented, so carefully worked out, that all readers of Frost, whether those who admire or those who disapprove, must confront it if they hope to get a full picture of how Frost's poetry has been accepted.

A good statement of Nitchie's point of view can be found in his concluding chapter. Admitting that Frost is a first-rate poet, a writer whose work is both good and important, Nitchie says that the question is not one of being first- or second-rate, but rather one of why such a significant poet should "take refuge in the arch, the cute, the complacent, the trivial, gradually abandoning areas of proven strength. . . ." And for Nitchie, Frost's strength lies in the dramatic narratives of the earlier books and in such poems from the later collections as "The Subverted Flower" and "Directive." He agrees with most of the negative critics that Frost oversimplifies human experience and values by writing about man in a simplified setting. Man's situation in the poem is thus an individual concern, solitary and basically antisocial, one which permits him to avoid the pressing problems of the times. The milieu of the poems, writes Nitchie, is essentially Edenic, and the freedom man has in it is only a questionable freedom from the pressures of social life. Given this Edenic setting, the freedom Frost celebrates is more a freedom from restrictions than a freedom to create. Nature is the bedrock of the Edenic myth, but as significant as it is in Frost's poetry, the concept of nature is too limited. Rather than an object of philosophical theorizing, nature is used for an evasion of fundamental problems, a "place" which simplifies crises. Nitchie's point is not that nature suggests ready-made answers, but that it offers a world in which situations involving difficult choices are stripped of their complexities and seen in black and white. Free of complicating factors, human values are based on choices of only what road to take or whether or not to join the sound of the trees. Thus, argues Nitchie, there is a fundamental evasion in Frost's poetry because human dilemmas, other than those in isolated instances, are avoided. As a result the poems rely on the cute wisecrack or on the arch attitude rather than on the unity that metaphor affords.

Although Nitchie seems to be echoing Winters, he does have a different argument. Winters believes that Frost reduces human values to the point at which choices can be made on impulse, and that Frost confuses these whimsical decisions with moral choices. Nitchie agrees, but he hesitates to use Winters' criticism as an overall approach to the poems. Instead he suggests that Winters overlooks a basic contradictory theme, that of an impulse to drift whimsically with life joined with an urge to find commitment and unity. The problem, as Nitchie sees it, is that while either position is clear within the individual poems, the reader never knows where Frost stands generally. Frost cannot decide between the two, and Nitchie insists that the failure to choose is a philosophical indecision on Frost's part. He is either

unwilling to make or incapable of making the choice. He lacks
the coherent myth that structures the work of Yeats, Eliot, and
Stevens. Nitchie readily admits that this failure does not keep
Frost from writing good poems. But he also maintains that while
many of Frost's characters heroically reveal their integrity in
their ability to face reality, they never know what reality is because Frost does not know. The poems show only isolated men
facing problems in a world they never try to understand.

In the final chapter Nitchie summarizes his argument. He finds
that Frost's stature diminishes when compared with Yeats, Eliot,
Auden, and Stevens primarily because he lacks a myth which
would enable him to make significant, coherent propositions
about man and his reality with enough consistency to prove that
he is seriously concerned with the fundamental issues of the human condition. Nitchie admits that examination of the problem
of unsatisfactory art is speculative, but he believes that the problem must be tackled. The trouble is that in comparing Frost's
art with that of other modern giants on similar subjects, Nitchie
often puts Frost's worst up against their best. It makes no difference to him that Yeats' myth of reality is absurd—Frost still fails
to commit himself to a myth. The reader does not have to accept the particulars of Yeats' myth to see that they enable him
to write about man in a larger, richer context than Frost does.
The same goes for the other modern poets mentioned. Nitchie
does not blame Frost for not having a coherent value system,
but he believes that if Frost had developed one he could have
offered "an embodied vision of man." Frost, then, has real importance, but only the "aptness" for consistently great poetry.

Unlike most of the critics discussed, Denis Donoghue is more
concerned with Frost's style and with the ways his writing differs from that of other poets. Donoghue simply does not like
Frost, or at least his essay gives that impression despite his statement that to call Frost a master of the "middle style" is both to
praise him and to point out limitations. So concerned is he with
constructing his case against Frost that he has published at least
three variations of his essay. The first agrees with Pearce and
Traschen that Frost does not speculate enough, and that he
shows an "intellectual slackness which often takes the camou-
flage of disengagement" (*Twentieth Century*, July-Aug. 1959).
But what Donoghue is really interested in is Frost's style which
he terms "middle" as opposed to "high" and "low." This style
appeals to the ideal Frost reader who, says Donoghue, is as uncommitted as the poet is. A poem like "Fire and Ice" gets across

to its reader, but while the communication is rich, it is also lim-
pid. His middle style prevents him from using the "Art of Ele-
vation" which allows major poets to "move into charged meditation." When Frost tries to elevate his style, suggests Donoghue,
he falls into the rhetoric of a poem like "The Gift Outright"
which Donoghue incredibly dismisses as a slogan. He also criticizes Frost for writing about only what he knows so that the
modern theme of isolation, for example, degenerates into self-
pity in poems like "Acquainted with the Night." He complains
that Frost is a lesser poet because he does not handle subjects
the way Yeats and Eliot do. Writing about the common ground
he knows exists between himself and his readers, Frost relies on
a middle style based on no more than a "shared sense of humane
fact."

The second version of this essay is still concerned with Frost's
middle style and with why he does not write like Yeats, Eliot,
and Stevens (*Yale Review*, Winter 1963). Donoghue also repeats his opinion that Frost evades problems by writing about
subjects too familiar to him and his ideal reader. Admitting that
he likes "A Servant to Servants," "The Fear," and " Out, Out
— ", Donoghue nevertheless feels that Frost lacks the full range
of poetic resources. The negative readings of Frost articulated
in the two essays are essentially the same except for a paragraph
added to the second version. With it Donoghue tries to soften
his attack by excusing Frost for not being God. Instead he
charges him with the lesser offense of "conniving" with the habit in man to set up "a closed circuit" which links some key
points of experience at the expense of others.

The third version of the essay is in his book *Connoisseurs of
Chaos: Ideas of Order in Modern American Poetry* (Donoghue,
1965). Even more than the articles, this variation shows more
interest in comparisons among poets than in examinations of
Frost's poetry. Noting that Eliot's poetry has some disagreeable
qualities, for example his dislike of ordinary people, Donoghue
excuses Eliot's weaknesses because he believes that Eliot spent
his life "trying to get things straight" while all Frost did was
create a pose. He would rather speculate on the way Eliot might
have written "Provide, Provide" than evaluate the poem in detail. But this time Donoghue specifically names "The Most of
It," "An Old Man's Winter Night," and "After Apple-Picking"
as poems worthy of the three named in the earlier versions. He
drops "limpidly" from his description of how "Fire and Ice"
communicates. And he admits that "Acquainted with the Night"

is impressive while continuing to identify the speaker with Frost
and remarking that the poem's conclusion reveals self-pity. The
last eight pages are an addition to the first two versions of the
essay, and they are obviously tacked on. Discussing the relationship between Frost and the ideas of Social Darwinism, Donoghue
decides that Frost is complacent about such problems as war and
waste because he is one of the strong who has survived in a "survival of the fittest" doctrine. This point of view causes Donoghue to miss the emphasis of "Pertinax" and the irony of "Our
Hold on the Planet" and "Bravado."

These, then, are some of the crucial points in the major negative readings of Frost's accomplishment. This is not the place
to develop a coherent defense against the wide range of charges
levied against him, but the survey presented here should suggest
the extent of the published criticism which questions the ultimate value of a much honored poet. While such studies must
be reckoned with if a balanced awareness of Frost's achievement is to be had, they cannot be entirely dismissed by his admirers nor wholly embraced by his detractors. Each essay
should be read in its entirety and evaluated on both the merits
of its thesis and the interpretations offered of the particular
poems. Yet some general observations can be made.

Traschen begins his essay by naming the admirable qualities
of Frost's poetry and by asking a key question. Noting that
Frost is such a fine poet, he wonders why "he needs to be de-
fended so often." Traschen then mentions Randall Jarrell's article "To the Laodiceans" (*Poetry and the Age*, 1953) as an
example of an appreciative essay which begins by acknowledging Frost's limitations. True, Jarrell admits Frost's weaknesses,
but he also says that they are no more damaging than those of
the contemporary poets who are held up as models for Frost to
follow. Jarrell complains of those critics who say that Frost is
no more than a bard when compared to a true modern poet like
Eliot, or Stevens, or any of Frost's contemporaries one cares to
substitute. Frost's poetry deserves to be read and evaluated on
its own merits, free from the critic's preconceived theories
about what modern poetry ought to be. The same goes for his
handling of contemporary themes and issues. It seems absurd to
dismiss the terror of "Design" and "An Old Man's Winter
Night," or the alienation of "The Hill Wife" and "The Most
of It" simply because Eliot would have approached the subjects
differently. We can treasure Eliot and Stevens and still grant
Frost the admiration he deserves.

This is not to gloss over Frost's shortcomings. His didactic poems are weak and his short "editorials" are even worse. These are the poems which Winters describes as the lesser part of Frost's achievement, yet he still uses them to build his famous attack on Frost's so-called social philosophy. But to take the satirical poems so seriously as to see them as a perfect mirror of Frost's thought is to miss the humorous tone which most of them have. It seems poor reading to stress those qualities of a poem which fit a thesis at the expense of those which might alter the critic's point of view. Frost's tendencies to play sage, to preach, to indulge in Yankee cuteness, in short to act the public pose so many readers think of when they remember him, are his greatest faults. But for the most part these liabilities are limited to his obviously weaker poems.

A poet of Frost's accomplishment deserves to be judged on his best work, those poems which need no defense and which by themselves repudiate the weaker poems. How can we read *A Witness Tree* and *Steeple Bush* as signs of Frost's diminishing powers when these collections include "The Silken Tent," "Come In," "The Most of It," "The Subverted Flower," "The Gift Outright," "November," "The Rabbit-Hunter," "Directive," and "Take Something Like a Star"? To list good poems, however, is not to make a definitive statement. Any selection suggested here has to be partially subjective, and I certainly do not expect anyone to adopt it without question. A calm hold on our critical faculties should allow us to challenge many of the opinions outlined in this chapter. Pearce's essay, for example, is worthy of serious contemplation, but it could be argued that rather than a minor accomplishment, Frost's is of the first rank. To know one's inner self in the fragmented twentieth century, even at the cost of retreating a little, must surely be one of the major crises of our time. We could also differ with Pearce's evaluation of poems like "The Most of It." This poem's details may be drawn from a simplified rural world, but the problems they depict refer just as much to the contemporary issues which so many of these critics, including Pearce, feel that Frost avoids. The concluding words of "The Most of It" ("and that was all") can be read not as a sign of satisfaction but as an expression of the poet's despair at the protagonist's failure to interpret correctly his relationship with nature.

Similar questions of interpretation can be raised about Traschen's essay. Of "The Onset" Traschen writes that while the poem is finely wrought, it is ultimately unsatisfactory because Frost fails to see that death is organic to life. Yet the celebration

of spring's return in "The Onset" may be read as ironic because of the snake and the white-color imagery which unifies
the two stanzas. Such matters of interpretation are highly significant because they illustrate and support the critic's thesis.
Traschen says that Frost has reminded us of many stable things
such as birch trees and oven birds, and he is grateful for the reminder. But, he insists, trees and birds are not enough because
these objects are common to any age and are thus not the particulars of our own. If Frost's poems were limited in this sense
as, say, Kilmer's "Trees" is, then we would have to agree. But
it seems to me that Frost uses these common objects to make a
point about our time. The literal level is followed by deeper
levels of meaning so that the rural settings and descriptions
function as a vantage point from which Frost can make significant comments about the issues of the day.

One could also argue that while many of the dramatic narratives are excellent, Frost's lyrics reflect his best effort. Thus one
would not agree with those critics who feel that he never realized the tragic potential of *North of Boston* and, to a certain
extent, of *Mountain Interval*. Once Frost developed his dramatic narratives to such a high standard, he turned more to the
lyric and to the satirical poem. Regarding the dramatic narratives, how could he do better than "The Death of the Hired
Man," "Home Burial," "A Servant to Servants," "The Fear,"
"The Mountain," and "Snow"? Frost's superior lyrics are so
varied in subject, technique, and detail that he avoids the definite myth or system to which many readers wish he had fastened
himself. He shares with his contemporaries so many of the concerns which dominate art in this century: loss of stable values,
fear of alienation, inability to communicate, distrust of traditional religious doctrine, and the fear that man may count for
nothing when measured against the universe. His lyrics which
reflect these themes are often as ironic and ambiguous as the best
work of the century's other major poets. What finally counts
is the value of the poems themselves and not just their relationship with the specific problems of 1913–62. The particulars of
that era will pass from memory to be replaced by new crises,
but the poetry will remain if it has intrinsic value. That Frost
has written numerous poems destined to survive as poetry of
the first rank is so obvious that it seems ludicrous to call attention to them once again. Since he has lodged more than a few
poems where they "will be hard to get rid of," we should be
more than grateful.

References

Arvin, Newton
1936. "A Minor Strain," *Partisan Review* June, pp. 27–28.
Blackmur, R. P.
1936. "The Instincts of a Bard," *Nation* June 24, pp. 817–19.
Bogan, Louise
1951. *Achievement in American Poetry: 1900–1950*, pp. 47-51. Chicago: Regnery.
Carpenter, Frederic I.
1932. Review of *Collected Poems, New England Quarterly* Jan., pp. 159–60.
Cowley, Malcolm
1944. "The Case Against Mr. Frost," *New Republic* Sept. 11, 18, pp. 312–13, 345–47.
De Voto, Bernard
1938. "The Critics and Robert Frost," *Saturday Review of Literature* Jan. 1, pp. 3–4, 14–15.
Donoghue, Denis
1959. "The Limitations of Robert Frost," *Twentieth Century* July-Aug., pp. 13–22.
1963. "A Mode of Communication: Frost and the 'Middle Style,'" *Yale Review* Winter, pp. 205–19.
1965. *Connoisseurs of Chaos: Ideas of Order in Modern American Poetry*, pp. 160–89. New York: Macmillan.
Gregory, Horace
1936. "Robert Frost: New Poems," *New Republic* June 24, p. 214.
Hicks, Granville
1930. "The World of Robert Frost," *New Republic* Dec. 3, pp. 77–78.
Hillyer, Robert
1932. "Robert Frost 'Lacks Power,'" *New England Quarterly* Apr., pp. 402–4.
Howe, Irving
1963. "Robert Frost: A Momentary Stay," *New Republic* Mar. 23, pp. 3–28; reprinted in *A World More Attractive: A View of Modern Literature in Politics*. New York: Horizon Pr., 1963.
Humphries, Rolfe
1936. "A Further Shrinking," *New Masses* Aug. 11, pp. 41–42.
Jarrell, Randall
1953. "To the Laodiceans" in *Poetry and the Age*. New York: Knopf.
Lowell, Amy
1917. *Tendencies in Modern American Poetry*. New York: Macmillan, pp. 79–136.

Mitchell, Stewart
1932. "Notes on Nightingales," *New England Quarterly* Apr., pp. 404–7.
Nitchie, George W.
1960. *Human Values in the Poetry of Robert Frost: A Study of a Poet's Convictions.* Durham: Duke Univ. Pr.
Pearce, Roy Harvey
1961. "Frost's Momentary Stay," *Kenyon Review* Spring, pp. 258–73.
Robson, W. W.
1966. "The Achievement of Robert Frost," *Southern Review,* n.s., Oct., pp. 735–61.
Thompson, Lawrance
1964. (editor) *Selected Letters of Robert Frost.* New York: Holt, Rinehart and Winston.
Thornton, Richard
1937. (editor) *Recognition of Robert Frost.* New York: Holt.
Traschen, Isadore
1965. "Robert Frost: Some Divisions in a Whole Man," *Yale Review* Oct., pp. 57–70.
Watts, Harold H.
1955. "Robert Frost and the Interrupted Dialogue," *American Literature* Mar., pp. 69–87.
Whicher, George F.
1945. "Frost at Seventy," *American Scholar* Aug., pp. 405–14.
Winters, Yvor
1957. "Robert Frost: Or, the Spiritual Drifter as Poet" in *The Function of Criticism: Problems and Exercises.* Denver: Alan Swallow; also published in *Sewanee Review,* Aug. 1948, pp. 564–96.

CHAPTER 4

The Literary Heritage of Robert Frost

The English language authors with whom Robert Frost is most often compared are William Wordsworth, Ralph Waldo Emerson, and Henry David Thoreau. Frost is on record as having carefully read all three, and he gave public talks celebrating their art. Yet the question is not so much one of direct influence between these Romantic authors and Frost as it is one of literary heritage. Frost does not write "like" Wordsworth, nor is he a Transcendentalist as were Emerson and Thoreau. But there is an intellectual kinship among these artists based on the ways they write about common men and nature, and on their uses of language.

Accordingly, this chapter will have four divisions: Frost and Wordsworth, Frost and Emerson, Frost and Thoreau, and Frost and New England in general. The first of these has received the least scholarly attention. Although many critics have remarked upon the affinity between Frost and Wordsworth, only a few significant studies have as yet been published. These plus Frost's public lecture on Wordsworth are all that is available despite the numerous promising shorter comments on the resemblance which began to appear in the early reviews of *A Boy's Will*. A happier situation exists with the Frost-Emerson-Thoreau relationship, for enough critical studies have been published to suggest the question's scope. Yet significant analyses of Frost and Emerson did not appear until about 1940, while the Frost-Thoreau kinship was generally underdeveloped until the centennial of *Walden* in 1954. Critical debate on these subjects is far from over, a fact which prompted Lawrance Thompson to remark in 1966, "Much has been written on the kinship between RF and Thoreau and Emerson; but not enough. The task which remains is to separate likenesses and differences" (*Robert Frost: The Early Years, 1874–1915*, p. 550). No one has yet arrived

at a definitive statement, although most of the better articles clear
the way for further analysis. As a result, the drama of disagreement and reply, the give and take associated with the negative
criticism or the early criticism is absent, because thus far there
are fewer areas for serious critical dissent. Except for several
disagreements with the essays of Malcolm Cowley and Yvor
Winters, critics have not taken to sniping at each other over
opinions about how Frost adapted his literary heritage. The
most serious area of contention focuses on Frost's place in the
New England tradition, specifically upon the question of
whether or not he is a worthy successor to the past, great spokesmen of Yankee thought: Emerson, Thoreau, and Hawthorne.

Frost and Wordsworth

Any study of Frost's relationship with William Wordsworth
should begin with Frost's "A Tribute to Wordsworth" (*Cornell
Library Journal*, Spring 1970). This publication is the transcription of a talk which Frost gave at Cornell University on April
20, 1950, as part of the university's exercises commemorating
the centenary of Wordsworth's death. Since Frost's remarks
are in the form of an informal talk, they do not follow the lucid,
orderly progression of ideas which we expect when reading
literary criticism. They have, instead, a lucidity of another kind
—Frost's rambling but penetrating observations about both specific lines of poetry and Wordsworth's general achievement. He
begins, for example, like the poet he is and unlike a literary
critic when he distinguishes between meditation and contemplation. Leaving meditation to those who would analyze poetry, he
urges his listeners to contemplate glory.

Turning to Wordsworth, Frost reminds the audience that the
English poet never attempted the "very rhetorical." He describes Wordsworth's verse as "simple simony"—by which he
means a clarity and tone approximating the innocence of childhood. To make his point, he quotes from Robert Southey and
Wordsworth, for he believes that both poets "got up a theory"
from Wordsworth's spirit. Frost is especially impressed with
the tune and "naive" accent of Wordsworth's lyrics. He uses
words like "insipidity" and "paternal severity" to describe why
the lyrics are lovely in a "strange, banal way." The Wordsworth
he cares for—what he calls the essential Wordsworth—has a level
of banality which penetrates "right down into the soul of man,

and always, always there'll be one line in it that's just as penetrating as anything anybody ever wrote" (1970, p. 86). The
poetic tone may be sweet and insipid, but Frost does not use
"insipid" in a pejorative sense. He apparently senses an affinity
between his own poetry and Wordsworth's lyrics.

The "other" Wordsworth he calls "intellectual." Frost believes that the English poet turned to intellectual poetry as the
result of worrying about both the lukewarm reception given his
simpler lyrics and the state of the British nation. Although he
says that he would prefer to read "Michael," a poem he very
much admires, he continues to remark upon the poems Wordsworth wrote when he was "bothered by his own time." One
poem which Frost admits influenced him is "Ode to Duty" because it discusses the two kinds of will: inspiration and discipline. His comments about this poem suggest that he uses it as an
excuse for his own change from youthful rebel to adult conservative, a change which he sees in Wordsworth. This recorded
lecture is far from a definitive statement of Frost's relationship
with Wordsworth's poetry. But it is indispensable for those interested in investigating the particular poems and tones in
Wordsworth which Frost finds significant. Although conclusions
about influence cannot be reached from a reading of these remarks, the article should be the starting point for any analysis
of Wordsworth's effect on Frost.

John Lynen's approach in *The Pastoral Art of Robert Frost*
(1960), is, naturally, much more analytical. To use Frost's
terms, Lynen meditates about the question while Frost contemplates. This excellent book, which will be discussed more fully
in a later chapter, is concerned with how Frost has assimilated
the ancient pastoral tradition to the demands made upon him as a
modern poet. In pursuing this question, Lynen does not focus
upon Wordsworth's influence, but he does say enough about the
problem to make his remarks useful. To begin, Lynen adds Frost
to a short list of writers—Burns, Wordsworth, Hardy, and Faulkner—who succeed in employing local materials for pastoral purposes. Both regionalism and pastoral are concerned with the
contrast between the rural world and the complex urban society,
but regional art becomes pastoral only when the contrast is
"properly exploited." This is an important distinction, and Lynen carefully elaborates to make his point. He argues that most
regional writing is second-rate at best because the authors do not
take the contrast seriously. Instead of projecting themselves
into the scene and looking with the rural point of view, writers

like James Russell Lowell maintain too great a distance. As a result, regionalism is not exploited for pastoral purposes, a higher art, for it never gets beyond charming, peculiar, sentimental local color. Both Frost and Wordsworth dodge this flaw because they use regional traits in such a way as to make them universal. The materials which seem unique to a particular locale become, in the hands of masters like Frost and Wordsworth, suggestions of realities present in all experience.

Lynen correctly points out that one of the key lessons Frost learned from Wordsworth was the connection between the mind and the land. This unity is a general trait of Romantic poetry, but Wordsworth is Frost's particular model for how characteristics of landscape and individual psychological qualities can be associated. For example, Michael's dignity is related to the glory of the Lake Country mountains, just as the clear gaze of Frost's Yankee persona is related to the crisp air of New England. There remains, however, a significant difference between the two poets. As Lynen notes, Wordsworth's relation to the specific locality is always individual. His concern with revealing the basic processes of the mind is usually expressed through "a minute examination of his own experience" (1960, p. 61). For this reason, his best character is himself—when he tries for more complex characterization, he fails. Frost's regionalism, on the other hand, is "thoroughly social." It is more concerned with the rural experience and with the sense of values which the local society shares than with scenery or the intuitions of the poet's mind. The speaking voice in a Frost poem normally depends upon membership in the community for its identity. Lynen concludes that this difference explains the reason why Frost, unlike Wordsworth, can sparkle in both lyric and dramatic poems. Frost can express the communication between characters who share a regional ethic, as well as reveal personal emotion. As Frost's particular adaptation of the pastoral mode fosters his dramatic talent, it also encourages his impulse to philosophize. But, as Lynen shows, Frost the philosopher is quite different from other poets like Wordsworth who "deal in general ideas." In Wordsworth, for example, the speaker is often solitary, wrapped in his own thought, and, thus, meditative or rhapsodic. But in Frost's philosophical poems the speaker is usually conversational. He may be exchanging opinions or speaking alone, but his ideas are always directed toward others—what Lynen calls "speech rather than unspoken thought translated into words" (1960, p. 130).

Lynen's most extended discussion of the two poets is in his

chapter "Nature and Pastoralism." Arguing that Frost's view of nature is unique, he admits that many modern readers may not accept the uniqueness because their attitudes toward nature poetry have been determined by the English Lake Poets. The problem, then, is that today's readers often approach Frost's nature poetry as if it were Wordsworth's—that is, they believe the same concept of nature shapes Frost's poems as well as Wordsworth's. Yet, as Lynen suggests, these readers have mistakenly overlooked Frost's bleak landscapes and sharply outlined imagery which mere differences between localities cannot explain. In addition, Frost's nature poems do not "evoke the same variety of emotional response." Frost manages to write about nature "without exploiting the emotional effects which, however fine they are in Wordsworth and the other Romantics, seem rather shopworn in more recent poets" (1960, pp. 141–42). Lynen willingly admits that no contemporary poet can break completely with the Romantics' treatment of nature. But Frost's freedom or lack of freedom from it is not the point. More important is the way he has adapted tradition to the demands of his own vision.

The key difference between Frost's approach to nature and Wordsworth's is that Wordsworth stresses the union of mind and external reality by suggesting the merger of thought and the natural scene, and by calling attention to the affinity between that scene and moral values. For this reason his descriptions of natural objects, such as streams, trees, and birds, are purposely vague. Lynen suggests that this imprecision is intended because it is the "medium in which thought and object merge." Using Frost's "The Wood-Pile" to illustrate similarities, he agrees that its approach to nature recalls Wordsworth's in "Resolution and Independence." Frost's manner may be anecdotal, while Wordsworth's is didactic, but their attitudes are nevertheless similar: the poet wanders through the landscape as a means to the "mysterious instruction of the soul." Both poems suggest a high seriousness or an ethical purpose, and both hint that a revelation from nature will come to the poet-figure. Yet for all of these key similarities, the differences are more telling. Frost's figure finds not "an image of the spirit immanent in man and nature" as Wordsworth's does, but rather a symbol of the human spirit's ability to rise above the physical landscape. Unlike "Resolution and Independence," the meaning of "The Wood-Pile" is found in the difference between man and nature. The cedar swamp has no meaning or design except that which can be imposed on it by man. Nowhere do we discover Wordsworth's faith in the kinship between man and nature, but we do find everywhere in Frost's poetry the gulf separating the two. Frost's true subject is always humanity. Lynen concludes that those who persist in thinking Frost a "sketcher of pleasant landscapes" should contemplate poems like "The Most of It." Reading these useful arguments, one wishes that Lynen could have further pursued the matter of Frost and Wordsworth. His primary topic, Frost's pastoral art, prevents a more extensive comparison of the two poets, yet his remarks remain among the best analyses in print. Indeed, though the matter itself has been generally ignored, Lynen's discussion is good enough to encourage more detailed critical investigations.

In *The Poetry of Robert Frost: Constellations of Intention* (1963), Reuben Brower takes steps to expand our awareness of Frost's relationship with Wordsworth. He begins by expressing the widely held opinion that Wordsworth and Emerson, especially Wordsworth, were for Frost's contemporaries the poets who most shaped concepts of nature poetry. When Frost was a young beginner in the 1890s and 1900s, Wordsworth's poetic voice was persuasive, just as the vision it asserted was convincing. Neither Wordsworth nor Emerson liked to admit doubt when expressing their moments of vision. As a result, the standard reading of their poetry in the late nineteenth century emphasized assurance, optimism, and beneficence. As Brower notes, today's readers are too influenced by what he terms the "age of ambiguity" to accept those assurances without pointing simultaneously to evidences of doubt in the poems, but in Frost's youth expressions of doubt were foreign to readings of Wordsworth. The English poet's definition of nature was so pervasive that it dominated matters of both form and vision. Frost's problem, then, was not to find "concepts" of nature but to discover a form and role which could express his own experience. Readily granting that Frost "triumphantly" found his form, Brower explains that the point of his analysis is to determine how Frost's own "poetic revelation relies on and diverges from the poetic revelations of Wordsworth and Emerson" (1963, p. 42). His discussion of this question remains the best general commentary on Frost, Wordsworth, and Emerson published as of this writing.

To find some answers to his broader question, Brower raises several significant subordinate queries which shape his chapter: what roles do the two nineteenth-century poets create for themselves when in the presence of a natural fact; what tones and rhythms, images and metaphors do they use; what attitudes toward nature do they express? Having already mentioned that

Frost lacks the assured tone usually associated with Wordsworth, Brower begins with a crucial distinction: that Wordsworth is more "seer than naturalist." The English poet has little desire to detail the exact location of the natural scene. More interested in the "marvelous transformation" which takes place when he casts his eye on nature, Wordsworth combines the role of the lone visionary with that of a man who has an intimate, easy relationship with natural processes. Nature often acts as a catalyst for the later recreation of joy through recollection of the mystical experience. Brower's point is that while Wordsworth celebrates the imagination's power, the poet longs for a state in which he would not need it. In a succinct summation, Brower writes: "Even when Wordsworth's nature lyrics start from a specific human situation, there is a subtle imprecision—managed with great tact—that allows him to move into the declarations of faith we all remember and yet find so hard to assign to particular poems" (1963, p. 45). The poet may use ballad rhythms and colloquial phrases, but he easily jumps from "expostulation to expressions of belief, from the English spring to Universal Spring."

This is a significant comment for readers interested in Frost's relationship with nineteenth-century poetry, and one which Brower uses to good effect. For in his following chapter he emphasizes as a key difference between the two writers the fact that Wordsworth begins with a natural object and uses it for a mystical experience, while Frost focuses on the human observer. "To a Butterfly," the Lucy poems, "Tintern Abbey," and "The Prelude" are briefly analyzed for illustration. "Tintern Abbey," for example, is described as a "brief rehearsal" for the main concerns of "The Prelude," which are defined as how nature encourages the mind to grow from coarse pleasure to joy, and how "love of nature leads to love of man." As Brower notes, there may be an acknowledgment of doubt and a "Johnsonian realism," but "the effect of facing the alternatives is hardly that of twentieth-century 'double vision' . . . [and] scarcely ironic in intention or effect" (1963, pp. 53–54). Wordsworth's tranquility often seems inextricable from the coldness, but his faith is usually based on "ennobling experience." The poet, finally, is interested not so much in the natural fact as in the vision, often mystical, to be gained—the physical fact is secondary in both Wordsworth and Emerson because the inner vision finally changes the butterfly or tree or brook.

Brower suggests that Emerson goes even further. When considering Frost's attraction to Emerson, his success in finding his

own form and vision seems all the more remarkable. Emerson's
tendency to subordinate the specific natural object to the generic whole causes him to doubt the primacy of the real world
even more than Wordsworth—a situation, writes Brower, which
often makes poetry and even expression impossible: the best
poem is silence. Two of Emerson's better poems "Uriel" and
"Brahma," deny ordinary concepts of nature and morality, and,
significantly, both poems meant a good deal to Frost. But as
Brower correctly notes, Frost turned to these poems not when
he was thinking of nature but when he was "speculating on evil
and good, on 'the nature of things' in the large Lucretian sense"
(1963, p. 57). Emerson wrote a few poems in which he begins
with the reality of a rural locale, but more often than not he is
interested in the generic characteristics. This is why his nature
scenes are rarely as memorable as Frost's—they seem to be included in the poem only to accompany the "truths." The individual poems have many good lines, but the descriptions of
nature are usually weaker than the eye-catching lines, an observation which explains why the truths can be detached so easily
from the poem. Brower illustrates by showing how "The Rhodora" has not quite "earned" the final line ("The self-same Power that brought me there brought you"). The poem is reminiscent of Wordsworth's "The Daffodils," but its vision is less
mysterious, just as its unity of vision and description is less convincing. Brower concludes with the standard remark that only
in the essays and journals could Emerson consistently balance
his awareness of the observed fact with his evaluation of feeling. He then moves on to a short but useful discussion of Frost
and Thoreau which is centered on two generally accepted conclusions: that Frost learned about the expression of "commerce
with things" from Thoreau's prose; and that Thoreau saw and
admitted darkness as one example of nature's inexhaustible variety.

All this might seem of marginal interest to the Frost student
were it not for the following chapter. Brower's remarks about
Wordsworth and Emerson provide the context needed to examine Frost's nature poetry in the light of what went before it.
Taken together these two chapters form an extensive evaluation
of how Frost adapted the style and vision of nineteenth-century nature poetry to the demands of his own art. Brower begins by calling attention to Frost's voice, that "odd blend of
speech and song," as the feature which most clearly reveals the
poet's attitude toward nature. Most readers of Frost realize that
he comes closest to Romantic reverence in the lyrics of *A Boy's*

Will. Brower points to "Rose Pogonias" as an example of an early lyric which has a tonal kinship with "To a Cuckoo" and "The Rhodora." Yet even in this poem Frost shows signs of developing his own style and vision, for unlike Wordsworth and Emerson, he does not lose himself in lonely contemplation of the natural scene. Unlike Wordsworth who, says Brower, "blurs" the difference between the social and visionary voices, Frost sees in this difference the potential for a dramatic clash, and he later exploits it in his better poems. This is a significant remark, for Brower calls attention to the importance of the voice Frost uses to express a concept of nature which obviously differs from that of his predecessors. The "I" of Frost's poems may ring of Wordsworth's visionary, but it has a "distinctive and bleak note of isolation." Wordsworth suggests that his speaker's isolation is pleasant, a means of separating himself from society in order to pursue deeper values. But Frost's lone speaker is more severely alone because his natural scene does not act as an agent for mystical, beneficent visions. The call to lament in "Come In" is rejected, and the mysterious pull toward the dark trees in "Stopping by Woods on a Snowy Evening" is ignored. Brower is surely correct when he argues that while Frost might appreciate Thoreau's remark that "Silence is the universal refuge," he could hardly accept it "in transcendental calm": "His integrity is not that of the visionary, but of the ironist," a role he was beginning to form as early as "Pan with Us" (1963, p. 77).

There are other reasons why Frost's view of rural life should not be confused with that of Wordsworth or Emerson. "The Need of Being Versed in Country Things" is perhaps too clearly defined, but it illustrates Brower's opinion that Frost celebrates not rustic, humble people but country sophistication. Frost's rejection of the "urban sophistication of pastoral" allows him to dismiss the pathetic fallacy. The point is that his rural intelligence comes from a country world entirely different from Wordsworth's or Emerson's. Frost rarely identifies with his farm characters, and, unlike Emerson especially, he realizes that country people use their idiom to "compress meaning and over-meaning." The Romantic belief in the divinity of rustics, idiots, and children is foreign to Frost's art. Frequently, the higher value is pragmatic, the action in the moment itself, as expressed in "Mowing." Emersonian transcendence or Wordsworthian vision is not needed to affirm the value.

This refusal to accept the mystical power of nature permits Frost to question the beneficence of natural processes in a manner which would startle his predecessors' faith. Like them, he glimpses nature's eternal cycles, but he does not find evidence of lasting benevolence in the cyclical order. In many of Frost's poems, terror rather than faith rests at the center of the cycle, for he realizes that nature's cyclical movement guarantees perpetual loss. Perhaps Brower's most important comment here is his remark that Frost "maintains no simple attitude, even of ironic disillusionment, toward the possible malevolence of the natural world"(1963, p. 89). This is because his most "deeply felt" relationships are dramatic. His observations in the presence of nature belong to the moment, free of visionary commitment. The uncertainty of vision, the lack of that surety expected in Wordsworth and Emerson, is nicely expressed in "The Mountain," for in that poem Frost approaches the observed fact not as a poet but as a farmer. Refusing to discover "reality," he sees only what is there. The doubt which Wordsworth admits and yet finds disturbing is finally celebrated by Frost. In "A Boundless Moment," for example, the positive act associated with the vision is not the development of the illusion but the realization that it is false.

Paraphrase is always an injustice to a carefully worked out argument, but it is perhaps an even greater sin when applied to Professor Brower's book. His long discussion of Frost's relationship with Wordsworth and Emerson is so clearly written and so patiently documented that the remarks made here barely indicate its value. He writes in the preface that he reread both nineteenth-century poets while working on the book. His willingness to do so has freshened his evaluation of Wordsworth and Emerson with the result that he is better able to discuss the influential nature poetry out of which Frost fashioned his own. Because this readiness to analyze the context of Frost's nature poetry is joined to consistently superior readings of the individual poems, Brower's discussion of how Frost differs from Wordsworth and Emerson remains one of the most useful sources currently available to the Frost student. Other critical essays go deeper into more specific areas of investigation, but Professor Brower's is the best available for commentary on the question's general scope.

Frost and Emerson

Those who want to pursue Frost's relationship with Emerson have, happily, the same advantage as those who plan to study the poet and Wordsworth, for Frost also gave a talk on Emerson which has been preserved: "On Emerson" (*Daedalus*, Fall 1959). The occasion (Oct. 8, 1959) was the presentation, by the American Academy of Arts and Letters, of the Emerson-Thoreau medal to Robert Frost. His acceptance speech was not the standard declaration of thanks, but rather an expression of his ideas about Emerson. Although his remarks were revised for publication in *Daedalus*, the reader must nevertheless remember that, like the reproduction of his speech on Wordsworth, this article is not intended as a formal essay.

With typical verbal facility, Frost begins by admitting that he is glad for the admiration of himself even though he is "here" because of admiration for Emerson and Thoreau. He calls attention to the first edition of Emerson's poems which he has in his pocket, and he declares his intention to be, on this occasion at least, "as much of an Emersonian as I can." This remark alone shows Frost's own awareness of his crucial differences from Emerson's ideas and art. He expresses his appreciation of Emerson at the outset when he includes him with Washington, Jefferson, and Lincoln as the four greatest Americans, and he describes Emerson with what is now a well-known phrase: "a poetic philosopher or as a philosophical poet, my favorite kind of both" (1959, p. 713).

A summation of Emerson's importance to Frost's mother follows, leading to the poet's remarks about Emerson's first direct influence upon himself. Protesting that he has never been submissive enough to be a follower, he nevertheless admits that Emerson caught him with the line, "cut these sentences and they bleed." Frost explains that he "never got over that" because the line helped to shape some of his own thinking about language. Of special significance to him is the passage from "Monadnock" beginning, "Yet wouldst thou learn our ancient speech," for with it Emerson came "pretty near" to making him an "anti-vocabularian" (1959, p. 713). Frost then turns to a discussion of Emerson's "Brahma," using his comments as a means to express indirectly his disapproval of ambiguous poems which need notes. (Once again he alludes to his famous dislike of T. S. Eliot's work.) "Brahma" proved to be extremely difficult, but he says that he returned to it again and again, "without help from dictionary or encyclopedia," until he could read all but a line or two. The significant distinction made is between his dislike of "obscurity and obfuscation" and his approval of "dark sayings I must leave the clearing of to time."

In the second half of the talk, Frost moves from Emerson's

poetry to his ideas. He explains that he owes more to Emerson than anyone else "for troubled thoughts about freedom." Approving particularly of Emerson's disavowal of converts and followers, Frost defines his own notion of freedom as shaped by Emerson: "nothing but departure—setting forth—leaving things behind, brave origination of the courage to be new" (1959, p. 715). Emerson taught him the need to exchange attachments for attractions. These remarks are certainly interesting, but Frost does not develop them. Rather, he uses them as the lead to the best-known part of the talk—his observation that "probably Emerson was too Platonic about evil" (1959, p. 717). Reemphasizing his opinion that Emerson's "Uriel" is the best Western poem, Frost quotes the line, "Unit and universe are round." Then he demurs, arguing that another poem could be made from that line to show that only ideally is this circle round. In reality the circle is an oval with two centers, Good and Evil: "Thence Monism versus Dualism." With this opinion he clarifies a remark made five pages earlier, when he said that it bothers his friends to think of him as an Emersonian, "that is, a cheerful Monist." Frost was not a cheerful Monist, and his remarks on Emerson testify to his careful reading of a writer who held a lifelong fascination for him. His own belief in the reality of evil, which he admits here, pinpoints the difference between himself and the man he so admired, and it is for this reason that post-1959 investigations of Frost and Emerson should begin with this talk.

Lawrance Thompson's most extensive treatment of the two writers is the little-known limited edition *Emerson and Frost: Critics of Their Times* (250 copies originally published in 1940; reprinted in 1969). His general argument is that these two poets cannot be relegated to the dusty shelves of romance as well-meaning idealists too far removed from the realities of everyday affairs, because they took the trouble to be "plain-spoken in their criticism of the American scene. . . ." He believes that Frost and Emerson illustrate the abstract quality known as the "American spirit," and he describes them with a puzzling and undefined phrase: "the most permanent poets" which American democracy has produced. Answering the inevitable protest that the poets no longer speak to our age, Thompson suggests that we should listen to them because they have proved themselves adept at the processes of rigorous thought.

Like all great thinkers, Frost and Emerson are able to solve complex problems by perceiving a common denominator among the various parts. In each case the common denominator is metaphor. The correspondence between the ways each poet relies on metaphor has been noted again and again, but Thompson provides a new slant when he suggests that an understanding of their uses of metaphor is the key to an appreciation of how the two poets can be critics of their times. Accordingly, he quotes from Emerson's well-known "Nature" and from Frost's lesser-known "Education by Poetry" to outline their primary opinions of metaphor. Each author clarifies fundamentals by using metaphorical reasoning. Although the matter is generally known today, Thompson was one of the first to call attention to the echoes of Emerson's "Nature" in Frost's "Education by Poetry." Both suggest the necessity of cultivating man's inner harmonies before considering political or economic remedies for the ills of the day. But the most important point in the first part of this book is Thompson's observation that the two artists arrive at this conclusion by opposite means. Both insist on the primacy of metaphor and on the supremacy of the individual, but Emerson reaches these conclusions from "a philosophic idealism which is essentially Platonic," whereas Frost rejects Platonism to rely on a "skeptical realism" (1940, p. 12). This distinction may seem obvious today, but in 1940, when Thompson was writing, it was a stimulating opinion. Thompson was the first critic to insist upon significant differences between the two which nevertheless did not deny the similarities recognized by earlier readers.

Thompson explains the primary reason for this difference between Platonic idealism and skeptical realism: the times which nurtured the two writers. Emerson's "picnic-land of opportunity for the individual" had become the land of labor problems, urban crises, and wars during Frost's best years. It was "inevitable" that the America which fostered Emerson produced an optimist, just as it was "almost inevitable" that the America of several decades later produced a skeptic. Nevertheless, both men agreed with the fundamental that "the hope for the individual and the nation in any time was 'men thinking' " (1940, p. 13). Thompson describes Emerson's idealistic statements as "pretty" ideas and as opinions which were more likely to apply to Emerson's time than to ours. This is not to say, writes Thompson, that Emerson ignored the daily realities which challenged his ideals as he grew older, for he did attack both President Andrew Jackson's administration and "shallow Americanism." But he also continued to insist upon idealism, and he recognized possibilities for the common man in Jacksonian democracy. To illustrate Emerson's criticism of the times, Thompson quotes long passages from the journals and essays in which Emerson outlines his opinions concerning the right relationship between the informed individual and his government. For those familiar with Frost's disapproval of the New Deal, it is obvious that Thompson is preparing for a discussion of the poet's well-known social conservatism when he discusses how Emerson's idealism was founded on a clear-eyed appraisal of the day. He insists that Emerson was "far too shrewd to let mercy grow into sentimentality" (1940, p. 18). Unwilling to supply necessities to the stupid and lazy, Emerson declared in "Self-Reliance" his opposition to a humanitarianism which, in Thompson's words, "went about its task in tears." The government was at fault for failing to regulate the balance between supply and human needs, but the individual deserved blame for looking to government to solve his problems. Thompson supplies long passages from the essay "The Young American" to illustrate Emerson's position.

Turning to Frost, Professor Thompson points out that although the poet joins Emerson in championing the "sacredness of the inner man," he nevertheless lacks Emerson's "evangelical passion" (1940, p. 23). Thompson quotes from Frost's "Introduction" to Edwin Arlington Robinson's *King Jasper* to illustrate the poet's witty criticism of Platonism. Perhaps his most perceptive comment about Frost's skepticism is his observation that the skepticism balances the poet's mutual inclinations toward the extremes of both faith and agnosticism. This middle course is less a result of Stoicism than an outgrowth of a "genuinely mystical New England Puritanism," a heritage which Thompson describes as a direct link between Emerson's day and Frost's. Like his predecessor, Frost distrusts all methods of reform except that of encouraging the individual to take advantage of his own potential for greatness. True progress comes primarily from the ideas of a few developed individuals. Thompson's evaluation of Frost's individualism is surely correct, but when reading this discussion it is nevertheless easy to understand the grounds on which Malcolm Cowley would later attack Frost's conservative social ideas, and why Yvor Winters would brand Frost a "spiritual drifter" for lacking Emerson's intense religious convictions. The more important difference between the two poets, of course, is that Frost lived in a time when "the odds were stacked high against the individual." Thus, his faith in individual potential was bound to be colored by his skepticism about the possibility for meaningful personal development. In Thompson's words, "His objective is to make the best of hardship even though the results may require a grim acceptance of gains that are little more than failures" (1940, p. 26). Because his times are worse than Emerson's he knows that he must create from the struggle a defense, a "momentary stay," against the daily confusions.

In the remainder of this little book, Thompson elaborates his ideas about Frost's definition of the self's relationship with society and about the easy transformation of idealism to skepticism. He quotes from "Build Soil" to illustrate the poet's distaste for brotherhood, and he correctly notes that neighborliness, not brotherhood, is the "keynote of Frost's social outlook." Thompson does not mention G. R. Elliott's essays on Frost's neighborliness, but he seems to have Elliott's definition in mind (see chapter 2 for a discussion of Elliott's articles). Poems like "The Exposed Nest" and "Love and a Question" are quoted to show Frost's inability to answer the thorny question of how far the self should involve itself in the sufferings of others.

Aside from the questionable technique of including too many long quotations from Emerson and Frost, many of which are not identified, the chief flaw in this short book may be Professor Thompson's point of view. He so obviously sides with Emerson's and, especially, Frost's social and political conservatism that the reader feels thankful for Cowley's disapproval of Frost's "Emersonianism" published a few years later. Reading again Frost's use of the Bible to prove that the poor are always with us, one wonders why Thompson does not point out the poet's blindness to the need for some government aid. Instead he quotes from "A Roadside Stand," one of Frost's weaker poems, and he glosses over the poet's easy acceptance of poverty to comment on his outspoken criticism of "those government programs which encourage professional poverty on the one hand and professional 'greedy good-doers' on the other hand" (1940, p. 39). These are Thompson's words, not Frost's, and one is thus prepared for the book's conclusion in which Thompson places both Frost and Emerson on the side of the "Old Guard" Republicans against the New Deal Democrats as the lesser of two evils. Still, one cannot quarrel with the impressive knowledge of both authors which Thompson exhibits. It cannot be said that this book sets the stage for the future studies of Frost and Emerson because its limited edition prevented wide circulation in 1940. But from today's perspective, it is clear that Thompson's evaluation of the two authors' relationships with their times is penetrating and correct.

Thompson's discussion of Frost and Emerson in *Fire and Ice: The Art and Thought of Robert Frost* (1942) is less developed. Though published more than thirty years ago, this book remains one of the best general analyses of Frost's art. Readers approaching Frost seriously for the first time would do well to consult it, for Thompson's commentary on the various subjects necessary to an understanding of Frost form the foundation for later, more elaborate investigations. Such is the case with his chapter titled "The Sound of Sense," for it is here that Thompson offers a concise summation of nineteenth-century attitudes toward poetic diction which Frost found so distasteful. For our purposes, his discussion of the reasons why Frost turned to Wordsworth and Emerson is particularly relevant.

Reacting against the "sonorous artificialities" of Tennyson and Longfellow, Frost looked to the art of Wordsworth and Emerson for an example of the poetic use of speech rhythms. But as Thompson points out, there is a difference between Wordsworth's "plainer and more emphatic language" and Frost's sentence sounds. Wordsworth tried to reflect in poetry the emotions present in common speech. Frost, however, hoped to convey the gradations of meaning through sound. Aware that the spoken word has two levels of meaning, the denotative and the connotative, he uses the word "sense" to suggest the connotations communicated by tones of voice. Frost argues that every meaning has its own sound-posture. He points to Emerson's "Monadnock" as an earlier statement of what he later termed the sound of sense. In the lines beginning "Now in sordid weeds they sleep," Emerson writes about the highly communicative tones of meaning which "rude poets of the tavern hearth" could utter. Thompson should also have pointed out that Emerson did not write poetry which used sentence sounds. It was, rather, Emerson's statement in "Monadnock" about the possibilities of voice tones which attracted Frost. Finally, as Thompson notes, Frost follows Wordsworth and Emerson in his consideration of common speech for two other reasons: the proverbial turns of phrase and the natural cadence which folk speech illustrates. In this short discussion, Thompson clearly does not try to write a definitive study of the relationship between Frost's poetic sound and that of Wordsworth and Emerson. His remarks do, however, outline the points needed to be known by those who plan a more thorough investigation of how Frost developed his concept of sentence sounds.

Hyatt Howe Waggoner's seminal essay "The Humanistic Idealism of Robert Frost" (*American Literature*, Nov. 1941) is the first penetrating analysis in article form of Frost and Emerson. Waggoner lists the few critics who, by 1941, had recognized the intellectual affinity between the two writers, but he correctly notes that not one of them had investigated the implications of the relationship. (Thus one sees how important Thompson's *Emerson and Frost: Critics of Their Times* would have been with a wider circulation.) He plans to clarify the issue by examining the philosophy in Frost's poetry in light of both the tradition which the poet carries on and the current trends which he opposes. Waggoner's advantage over other commentators is that he took the trouble to consult Frost himself. The paraphrases and quotations of Frost's comments add immeasurably to the value of this essay.

Waggoner begins with Frost's entrance to Harvard in 1897 and with his skepticism toward the two sets of ideas which then dominated Harvard's intellectual life: the pessimism of naturalism and the supreme importance of science. According to Waggoner, Frost quickly turned to Emerson's poetry and to William James as "an antidote for the poison of scientism and disillusion." Because Frost has never grown away from their ideas, his poetry "cannot be completely understood except against this background of the tradition of pragmatic idealism" (1941, p. 210). Waggoner may be overstating his case, for insistence on the importance of pragmatic idealism in the poet's philosophy contradicts Thompson's belief in Frost's skepticism, as well as apparently ignores other influences as various as Vergil, Wordsworth, and the English Georgians. But once this overemphasis is understood, Waggoner's remarks are indeed helpful, even when he expresses questionable opinions, such as his statement that the Emerson of "Self-Reliance" and "The Poet" remained "Frost's master." He suggests that Frost was particularly struck by Emerson's emphasis upon the importance of the individual, the necessity of self-reliance, the relation of experience and scholarship, and the reality of spiritual and moral values. If we accept his interpretation of Frost's life, then we are forced to believe that the poet left Harvard because Emerson and James convinced him to spurn the then current intellectual disputes and return to New Hampshire to write poetry based on human experience. Frost's decision to leave school is thus seen as the act of a self-reliant individual following the advice of "his beloved Emerson."

The desertion from Harvard did not mean, as Waggoner correctly notes, that the poet embraced a cheerful optimism to combat pessimistic naturalism, or that he ignored the "thought-currents" of his day. Waggoner refers to Frost's increasing tendency, from the publication of *New Hampshire* (1923) on, to use science as a specific subject. Revealing his own skepticism toward scientific discoveries, he argues that Frost does not dismiss science as much as deny its supremacy over humanism. Frost's poems expose his doubts about the validity of all scientific knowledge, his fears of the scientist's power, and his refusal to believe that anything new has been discovered. Waggoner challenges the opinions expressed by many of the negative critics, whose articles are examined in the previous chapter, when he writes that Frost is not so much out of touch with the times as he is skeptical about "current tendencies and interpretations." Poems like "The Star-Splitter," "At Woodward's Gardens," and "The White-Tailed Hornet" are cited for illustration.

Frost's antidote for the overemphasis on science is an Emersonian idealism, and his definition of man's relationship with nature is "essentially" that of Emerson's in "Fate." Waggoner quickly points out that Frost never finds nature "wholly benevolent and purposeful," but he also insists on Frost's belief in the ability of mind "partially to control and utilize nature" (1941, p. 217). The latter observation is certainly crucial to a reading of Frost, and Waggoner's comparison of "Fate" and "Sand Dunes" to show how each writer celebrates the power of mind to grapple with the impersonal universe is worth reading. Frost never conceals the terror encouraged by suspicion of an alien universe, but more often than not he dismisses the problem humorously, as not worth worrying about when the importance of day-to-day crises is considered. Unlike Yvor Winters, then, Waggoner detects none of the whimsey and cuteness which Winters accuses Frost of using to dodge serious issues. Rather, Waggoner believes that while both Frost and Emerson can accept life's limitations without hatred or despair, only Frost willingly expresses his awareness of the limitations. The essay concludes with a short explanation of his opinion that words like "democratic," "humanistic," and "mystical" best describe Frost.

The article's chief problem derives not so much from what is said as from tone. First, Waggoner is so confident that Frost's philosophy is correct that he seems guilty of the sin, later exposed by Malcolm Cowley, of using Frost as a kind of banner to celebrate the conservative element in modern American poetry. He divides the reactions to science's influence into two roads: the one which takes as "its starting point" the method of the implications of science and which is traveled by Mark Twain, Edwin Arlington Robinson, and William Vaughn Moody; the other which keeps close to human experience and which is traveled, if Waggoner is to be believed, only by Robert Frost. This kind of exaggerated praise hurts his argument. Second, Waggoner refuses to admit that Frost's poems about science are decidedly weaker than the better lyrics and dramatic dialogues. He writes as if all of Frost's poems are of high value. When a poem like "At Woodward's Gardens" is cited as an example of a telling retort to science's claims, one wonders about the critic's standards of judgment. Waggoner's remarks may seem commonplace to today's readers who have already investigated the relationship of the two writers, but even with these two weaknesses they remain enlightening to those who need a beginning.

Not everyone has accepted Frost's relationship with Emerson as affirmatively as the critics thus far discussed. Although most argue for a positive connection between the two writers, a few demur. Those who disagree with the generally held opinion that Frost successfully adapts Emerson's writings to his own needs usually express negative views about Frost's overall achievement—to them the Emerson issue is just one more example of Frost's unsuccessful art. The preceding chapter deals more fully with these negative critics, but two of them, Malcolm Cowley ("The Case against Mr. Frost," *New Republic*, Sept. 11, 18, 1944) and Yvor Winters ("Robert Frost: Or, the Spiritual Drifter as Poet," in *The Function of Criticism: Problems and Exercises*, 1957) should also be mentioned here.

Cowley argues that Frost has no business in the company of the great writers of the New England tradition: Emerson, Hawthorne, and Thoreau. When Frost is measured beside these giants, his stature is noticeably diminished: "it is almost as if a tough little Morgan horse, the best of its breed, had been judged by the standards that apply to Clydesdales and Percherons." But even if Frost could stand shoulder to shoulder with these writers, he still fails to express the New England spirit. Cowley believes that Frost's aversion to modern ideas and foreign influences causes him to fall prey to the New England flaw which

Emerson, Hawthorne, and Thoreau avoided: a "narrow and
arithmetical" spirit. The problem, as Cowley sees it, is that Frost
makes the mistake of accepting the older customs of New
Hampshire as immutable laws. This constricted point of view
diminishes the possibility for superior poetry. Too walled in
by the past, he expresses outrage when anyone proposes to
change or to improve the quality of New England life. He
preaches only half of Emerson's doctrine of self-reliance, refusing to accept Emerson's inclusion of the community along with
the individual. Thus, where Emerson develops the concept of
self-reliance to help society, Frost dismisses its application to social improvement. His inability to distinguish between separate-
ness and self-centeredness disqualifies him from the position of
the twentieth-century inheritor of the New England tradition.

Yvor Winters agrees. Noting Frost's claims to an Emersonian
discipleship (Winters seems unaware of Frost's disavowal of being a follower of anyone), he argues that the claim cannot be
honored because Frost lacks Emerson's religious convictions.
For this reason the poet's celebration of personal impulse lacks
direction and meaning. Unlike Emerson, Frost does not acknowledge God as the source which gives authority to Emerson's
definition of impulse. And since his relativism does not derive
from religious convictions, it results "mainly in ill-natured eccentricity and in increasing melancholy." Winters rarely refers
to Emerson again in the remainder of this famous essay, for he
concentrates his remarks on developing the argument that Frost
is a "spiritual drifter." Taken together, however, Cowley and
Winters make a formidable combination to combat the suggestion that Frost belongs in the Emersonian tradition. The one
compares Frost's ideas about social action to Emerson's and finds
him lacking, while the other notes the absence in Frost's poetry
of Emerson's intensely felt religious beliefs. Curiously, neither
discusses the two writers' ideas about nature or their definitions
of the nature poet—the two most fruitful topics when comparing Frost and Emerson. That Frost's conservatism blinded him
to the need for meaningful social action can hardly be denied.
Similarly, his public skepticism about religion protected his rather traditional personal beliefs so that he never openly echoed
Emerson's faith. But while these two matters suggest his differences from Emerson, enough similarities remain to warrant comparisons of the two, even if the results conclude that Frost radically changed rather than mirrored Emerson's ideas.

In "Emerson and Frost: A Parallel of Seers" (*New England
Quarterly*, June 1958), Reginald L. Cook begins with a dis-

missal of Winters' remarks, insisting that Winters does not successfully distinguish between the two writers. Quoting liberally from his private talks with Frost as well as from the poet's public statements, Professor Cook discusses the meaningful differences between the two writers in order to show how the authors parallel each other. His analysis of the physical and temperamental differences is less important than his comments about the ideological differences. He correctly points out that their pictures of reality differ in source and expression. Frost's comes directly from experience, whereas Emerson's is a priori. This is to be expected, for Frost relies on rational insight for moral inspiration, while Emerson looks to suprarational insight. For this reason, writes Cook, Emerson's tendency to make thoughts symbols of things is reversed in Frost, who typically uses "objective realities" as symbols of thought. From these significant observations, Professor Cook expresses the standard conclusion that Emerson's attitude toward experience is more consistently optimistic. Despite Emerson's acknowledgment of "the odious facts," his optimism is to be expected, for it grows naturally from his faith in suprarational insights. Frost, on the other hand, is more of a relativist, a poet who believes time and place to be key variables when determining the meaning of experience. Emerson and Frost may share a quality of wit, but, as Cook points out, Frost's expressions of "the comedy of man" are much more robust because he laughs at the man who hopes to make the universe adjust to him.

Still there are significant similarities between the two men. Cook names their belief in individualism, their refusal to structure a formal pattern of ideas, their use of a supple intellect to connect remote ideas and to express them in proverbial statements, and their ability to renew tradition rather than repudiate the past. Realizing the danger of assigning too much influence from one poet to another, he terms Frost "an emancipated traditionalist," an artist who, like Emerson, hopes to show the vitality in what the past has to offer rather than look back to it. Frost may be less of a rebel than his predecessor, but both "reflect a forward thrust." Readers of Frost criticism will recognize how Cook's belief in Frost's forward thrust clashes with the opinions of most of the negative critics who argue that Frost is complacent about the present and uninterested in the future. Yet Professor Cook neither challenges these negative opinions nor clarifies his suggestion.

Instead he turns to a discussion of Emerson and Frost as analogists. Referring primarily to "Nature" and to "Education by

Poetry," Cook analyzes how Emerson uses relationships to express the final unity, and how Frost, on the other hand, uses analogy to look at old things in new ways in the hope of pointing out a fresh insight. He quotes Frost's comment that the poet wants to surprise the reader "by trying to show a connection of two things in the universe" which the reader has not suspected (1958, p. 210). It follows that Frost's and Emerson's primary similarity as analogists can be found in what Cook calls "their common addiction to metaphor." Cook quotes Frost to illustrate the poet's distrust of "mystification" in metaphor, and he shows how Frost's delight in a functional metaphor, as in "The Silken Tent," differentiates him from Emerson's love of the cryptic and the oracular. The essay concludes with the opinion that Frost is just as interested in the social and political movements of his day as was Emerson. This may be so, but Cook does not point out that Frost's pronouncements upon contemporary issues are decidedly less helpful, less positive, and, in some cases, surely less intelligent than Emerson's. He is most certainly correct, however, when he says that Frost respects Emerson's intellectual freedom above all else: "What I think has impressed him most is the sense of rangy freedom of mind—the independence and bold play at 'the dangerous edge of things'— the stimulation for example that comes from an unsystematized attitude" (1958, p. 216). This valuable comment suggests perhaps the correct approach to a study of Frost's influences: that is, analysis of how he assimilates Emerson's ideas instead of arguments about how he echoes this point precisely or warps that idea wrongly. This article does not analyze Emerson's influence upon Frost's thinking about the art of poetry, but it nicely discusses the similarities and differences between their basic principles, opinions, and idioms.

In "Frost and Emerson: Voice and Vision" (*Massachusetts Review*, Oct. 1959), Alvan S. Ryan investigates the relationship between Frost's and Emerson's art. Writing in 1959, he has, of course, the advantage of a foundation already set by the earlier, more tentative speculations about Frost's possible debt, and he mentions some of the previously published opinions to illustrate the critical controversy. For some reason, however, he believes most of the parallels between the two writers which other critics have pointed out to be no more than "superficial similarities." Such things as their agreement on the importance of metaphor, their keen sense of correspondence, their interest in rural subjects, and their experiments with meter are dismissed in one paragraph as surface considerations. This comment, in my opinion, shows better than anything how far Frost-Emerson criticism has come since the first serious considerations of the question appeared in the early 1940s. The basic point, Ryan suggests, concerns their poetic theories and practices of poetry. One may quarrel with Ryan's refusal to treat areas other critics have correctly noted as important to a study of Frost and Emerson, but after reading this essay, one cannot help but appreciate his analysis of voice and vision in the two writers. Quite simply, Ryan's essay is one of the best on the subject.

To begin, he distinguishes between Emerson the bard, prophet, and seer, and Frost the maker of poems. Those readers familiar with R. P. Blackmur's negative evaluation of Frost, discussed in the previous chapter, as a poet with no more than the instincts of a bard, will appreciate the thrust of Ryan's statement. He outlines the traditional role of the poet in the nineteenth century, and he finds Emerson fitting it as a poet who both apprehends the inner reality of things and announces his discovery to man. As he correctly notes, there is nothing of this in Frost because Frost is more interested in the sheer challenge of making poems. Like Reginald Cook before him, Ryan believes that the two writers meet primarily in their emphasis on "emblem, symbol, and analogy," and he points to what every serious reader of Frost knows: that Frost believes metaphor will finally break down.

More important than these similarities, writes Ryan, are the differences. Their theories may suggest resemblances, but their poems are substantially different. Accordingly, he examines the structure, the use of image and symbol, and the matter of meter and rhyme in their poetry. His first significant observation is that Emerson's poems fail to achieve immediacy because of their "panoramic" quality. "Vague" and "general" are words to be applied to "The Rhodora," but not to the typical Frost poem. For unlike Emerson, Frost permits his characters to "see and to move through the medium of literal action—action which more often than not turns finally into symbolic representation or significant generalization" (1959, p. 10). This comment should be extremely useful for further studies of the relationship. The argument is convincing because Ryan contrasts poems like "Woodnotes" and "The Oven Bird" to show how Emerson prefers to be suggestive, whereas Frost usually develops the poem around a single sharply sketched event: "Emerson's unifying principle is ideational, Frost's metaphorical." Although Ryan does not mention F. O. Matthiessen's famous reading of "Days" (see Matthiessen, *American Renaissance*, Oxford, 1941, 1968), he follows Matthiessen's lead when he suggests that only in a few poems like "Days" does Emerson approach the tightly organized poem typical of Frost.

Ryan then turns to the vision of "interpretation of experience" which he finds in the work of each writer. Aware that this issue has spawned sharp critical debate in recent years, he points to the problem of reconciling the early Emerson of "Nature" with the later one of "Experience" as an example of the difficulty facing those who would write about an artist's vision. Specifically, he discusses Newton Arvin's "The House of Pain: Emerson and the Tragic Sense" (*Hudson Review*, Spring 1959) and Lionel Trilling's "A Speech on Robert Frost: A Cultural Episode" (*Partisan Review*, Summer 1959) to illustrate important recent essays which have muddied the waters by challenging the common view that both Emerson and Frost are "amiable, inspiriting, optimistic writers, who prefer to look on the pleasanter aspects of life" (1959, p. 15). Ryan argues that a balance needs to be maintained among the opinions which praise them for their optimism, denigrate them for the same reason, and stress their confrontation with evil. Thus, the final third of his essay is concerned with the two writers' views of nature, of man's relation to society, and of evil and suffering. He points out, for example, that with the essay "Experience" Emerson indicates a clear shift between his early intuitive contemplation of nature and the later more rational response. No such shift is discernible in Frost because he has always kept up the dialogue between feeling and thought. Unlike Emerson and the English Romantic poets, Frost does not "invest so heavily" in nature when he concerns himself with the correspondence between man and nature. This, of course, is a crucial distinction, one accepted as a general truth today. But in 1959, when Ryan was examining the question, the issue was still debatable. He shows how Frost defines a "human attitude" when faced with nature's mutability, and how Frost's speakers are usually moved by the opposing urges to identify with nature and yet to draw back toward a "properly human self-definition." The point is that in Frost's nature poems the emphasis is almost always upon the human figure instead of upon the natural scene.

These different approaches can be seen in the style and technique of the two writers. Emerson works in sermons and monologues, whereas Frost characteristically chooses dialogue. Emerson is often oracular, exhorting the reader to virtue, able to arrive at conclusions. But Frost sacrifices conclusions and resolutions in favor of drama, immediacy, and realism. In Ryan's words, he is "more tentative but also more objective" (1959, p. 21). And it is in the dramatic narratives that Frost is least Emersonian, for the frustration, failure, and pathos so characteristic of these poems are absent from Emerson's work. Ryan even defines the dialogue poems as closer to those of the Metaphysicals than the Romantics, but, unfortunately, he does not elaborate. He concludes that Frost may resemble Emerson in some ways, but not at all the Emerson most readers have in mind when comparisons are made. This important article may not be definitive— as Ryan himself notes, many of the points he mentions invite fuller development in other essays. Yet from today's advantage, his study can be seen as pivotal in the continuing analysis of Frost's relationship with Emerson, for Ryan takes advantage of the then new arguments by Arvin and Trilling, and the fact that the two authors reveal a greater feeling for the tragic than has been generally accepted. This is not to say that no one before 1959 had pointed out the darker side of Emerson's and Frost's visions. But Ryan is correct when he writes that general evaluations of these writers have too often stressed their supposed optimism and sunny good cheer.

Radcliffe Squires also denies Frost's so-called genial world view. In *The Major Themes of Robert Frost* (1963), especially in the chapter "Grounds: Back and Fore," Squires notes that while Frost seems different from most modern poets, he fits the general pattern of the New Englander. This region is bound to affect its artists because there is a "greater continuity, a braver changelessness" about New England than about any other part of the country. People there seem to be frugal and spare because New England demands much from them while supplying little; yet they are usually proud in their poverty. Their general certainty of what is right accounts for what Squires calls the "weird optimism" which characterizes so many New Englanders. Emerson, of course, is the prime example from the past, and Squires finds "something of Emerson's optimism" in Frost's poetry.

It is not that Emerson's poetry influences Frost, but that the poetry of both turns from the "tight-lipped and tight-fisted" people of New England to investigate nature: "Nature, as a matter of fact, often takes up the rôle deserted by human beings in the poetry of Frost and Emerson" (1963, p. 9). This is a debatable statement when applied to Frost, for only a very few of his poems fail to focus on the human participant. Human beings do not "desert" their role in most of his poems. There is, of course, a significant difference, one which rises primarily from Emerson's belief that the moral world and nature are united. Emerson's faith in this unity prevents him from including the specific details of nature. As Squires observes, he does not have to bother with details because the moral statements in his poems serve the same purpose. Similarly, because moral law and nature are merged, Emerson does not go to nature to learn. Believing that he is a part of the natural world, he is instructed by the very fact of his unity with nature. For this reason, writes Squires, Emerson feels no need to conclude a poem—the conclusion is implied in the parts. Frost, however, is not primarily a philosopher or an optimist. Specific detail constitutes a major part of his poetry, and he works hard to arrive at recognizable conclusions. Thus, for all of the obvious relationships between Emerson and Frost, the kinship makes better sense if two other New England poets, Emily Dickinson and Edwin Arlington Robinson, are also considered.

Squires believes that Dickinson's "grand" isolation in New England caused her to express herself not only through nature but also to it. Living in an atmosphere which encouraged inner vision while discouraging outer expression, Dickinson turned to nature as the object of her need for communication. The difference between her and Emerson is that Dickinson identifies natural occurrences with a mood or desire, whereas Emerson identifies nature with an abstract idea. Robinson is somewhat different. Where Emerson and Dickinson turn to nature because communication with humans is unlikely, Robinson focuses on the incommunication itself. He is rarely concerned with nature except as setting. Squires' point is that too many readers mistakenly believe the difficulty of communication to be a particularly modern theme, when in fact it has been implicit in New England literature for a century. As part of this heritage, Frost partakes of and modifies all of these attitudes. Squires argues that his work is greater than that of the other three because of its versatility: "At its best it has all of these things together." So superbly does Frost fit the idea of the New England poet that Squires is not tempted to pin the label on him.

Philip L. Gerber's comments are much less challenging than Squires' or Ryan's or Brower's. Like most of the books in the Twayne series, Gerber's *Robert Frost* (1966) is written for those who need a general introduction to a specific author. Although Professor Gerber's book seems a better example of a Twayne study, it nevertheless follows the standard outline for that series. A chapter on the highlights of the poet's biography is followed by chapters on Frost's career, craft, theories, and themes. Gerber also includes a general chronology composed chiefly of publication dates, notice of awards, and various appointments, and a selected annotated bibliography. Unfortunately, the book was published before Lawrance Thompson began releasing the official biography, and, as a result, Gerber must rely on less reliable work by Elizabeth Shepley Sergeant, for example, for a good deal of factual information.

Professor Gerber's discussion of Frost and Emerson covers two short subdivisions of the second chapter which are titled "Emerson and Thoreau" and "Heritage from the Nineteenth Century." Nothing of much value, however, is said of the relationship. Gerber tells us that Thoreau's subjects are often Frost's, and that Frost is "less the scientist and more the conscious artist." He paraphrases some of the key ideas in Emerson's concept of nature, and he suggests that "Departmental" is a versification of Emerson's prose description of ants. But nothing is analyzed or probed, and we are left with a superficial overview. Even the intriguing suggestion that Frost has more affinity with Walt Whitman "than appears on the surface" remains undeveloped. Although the reader aware of the relationship between Frost and Emerson will learn nothing here, the uninitiated or beginner could profit from the argument that Frost inherited at least "four vital attributes" from the nineteenth century: the need for a personally experienced perception of the universe, reliance upon intuition, a sense of his national identity in literature, and expression of self-reliant individualism. The trouble is that Gerber does not explain how Frost adapts these attitudes or why these "vital attributes" belong especially to the nineteenth century. He seems content with saying that Frost is a traditionalist because of his reluctance to innovate. This is a curious opinion when we remember the poet's insistence that tradition must be renewed, not copied, and when we recall the puzzled response to his experiments with blank verse and sentence sounds. This book is useful in the later chapters in which Professor Gerber discusses Frost's craftsmanship, theories, and themes, but the reader should turn elsewhere for an analysis of Frost and Emerson.

But perhaps one should not turn to William Chamberlain's

"The Emersonianism of Robert Frost" (*Emerson Society Quarterly*, Oct.-Dec. 1969). Although the title suggests an especially useful evaluation of the question, the final effect of the article is disappointing. This is so, not because the essay is wrongheaded, but because it does not take advantage of the better material on Frost and Emerson already published. Ryan's and Brower's discussions, for example, are so full of insights that they invite further investigations. Their articles open critical doors, as it were, and point to the complexity of the problem, as well as offer useful conclusions. Chamberlain suggests interesting readings of "West-Running Brook" and "Directive," but a fuller analysis might have supplied the authority his article lacks. His thesis is that Emersonianism is the key to Frost's concept of a momentary stay against confusion, which he terms the "core of Frost's philosophy of poetry." For those who need the reminder, Chamberlain quotes the famous definition of the "momentary stay against confusion" from "The Figure a Poem Makes." From this he concludes that both Frost's and Emerson's theories of creation can be classified as Romantic. The two authors resemble each other because they believe in the passive, intuitive reception of inspiration and because they subscribe to the notion of organic development. Chamberlain is certainly correct, as far as he goes, but one wishes for a more detailed analysis. Nothing is mentioned, for example, of revision and of the way it would affect the ideal of organic creation, though as Lawrance Thompson has shown, many of Frost's revisions have survived. Nor is anything said about the apparent discrepancy between the intuitive reception of inspiration and Frost's short editorials, poems which are direct responses to specific social issues. The most interesting point which Chamberlain makes about the momentary stay refers to his identification of it with Frost's strategic retreat. He defines the stay as "a reorientation of the mind by which new departures are made possible" (1969, p. 62).

Like Hyatt H. Waggoner before him, Chamberlain then briefly discusses how Frost modifies Emerson's teachings with the help of William James' pragmatism. The intriguing suggestion that Emerson's own skepticism can be traced through James to Frost is offered but never developed. Instead Chamberlain turns to an interesting discussion of the ladder image in Frost which he sees as a metaphor for the "future-creating essence of his 'stays' . . ." (1969, p. 63). Although the ladder suggests aspiration, its rungs are the limitations which help man to define his possibilities. The form which self-definition encourages acts to resist the chaos—in other words, Frost sees limitations as a means to create order. Good enough, but Chamberlain never explains why or how this idea is necessarily Emersonian. He seems content with pointing out that Frost's use of form and chaos reflects Emerson's "idea of 'a stupendous antagonism.' " His argument that the poem itself is a stay against confusion is then applied to a reading of "Directive." If the reader understands that "stay" does not mean stasis but rather regrouping for future movement, then, says Chamberlain, he can see how wrong those writers are who insist that Frost prefers to stabilize experience. Though interesting, the reading of "Directive" leaves questions unanswered. Concerning Frost's line that we should "pull in" a ladder road if we are now lost enough to find ourselves, Chamberlain interprets it to mean that one must "become passive to a mode of perception other than one is accustomed to. This state can be defined as the Jamesian-Emersonian reorientation of the mind mentioned in the preceding discussion" (1969, p. 64). Fine, but what about the obvious reference in that line to Christ's dictum of gaining one's life by losing it? The problem is that Chamberlain's readings of the poems, while often stimulating by themselves, are compared to short passages from Emerson and James to illustrate the authors' affinity, but no real analysis is offered. Thus, the conclusions seem to misrepresent the complexity of the question.

Frost and Thoreau

Along with Wordsworth and Emerson, Henry David Thoreau is one of the most frequently mentioned authors when Frost's relationship with the nineteenth-century literary tradition is discussed. Once again the Frost student is lucky. For as he did with his comments on Wordsworth and Emerson, Frost permitted some of his remarks on Thoreau to be recorded and published. The occasion of "Thoreau's 'Walden': A Discussion between Robert Frost and Reginald Cook" (*Listener*, Aug. 26, 1954) was the one-hundredth anniversary of the publication of *Walden*. Although J. Isaacs mentions in his introduction some of the more obvious parallels between the two writers, such as rugged independence, spokesmen for New England, communion with nature, and rebellion against authority, the heart of the article is the conversation between Frost and his friend Reginald Cook.

Frost's comments on Thoreau are a delight to read. Grouping *Walden* with *Robinson Crusoe* and *The Voyage of the Beagle,* he explains that these three tales of adventure have a "special shelf in my heart." He especially approves of the way they combine a declaration of independence with a "gospel of wisdom." He admits that Thoreau's immortality may depend on this one book, but he does not mind because all of Thoreau's greatness is in *Walden*: "Nothing he ever said but sounds like a quotation from it. Think of the success of a man's pulling himself together all under one one-word title. Enviable!" (1954, p. 319). Branding himself a "Thorosian," Frost says he would refuse an offer to spend a year at Walden Pond because to leave his own place in Vermont would be to violate the spirit of Thoreau's lesson. Thoreau believed in finding the world in his own backyard, and thus, says Frost, he "saved himself a journey to the Arctic to see red snow by waiting at home till red snow fell in Concord" (1954, p. 320). Perhaps the most useful parts of the discussion are Frost's comments about freedom. Defining Thoreau's general theme as freedom, he explains that Thoreau desired an independence that "seems to stop short somewhere of Liberty with a capital 'L' " (1954, p. 320). In Frost's words, it is a "one-man revolution." Here Frost pinpoints a significant parallel between his ideas and Thoreau's, for he argues that Thoreau was more concerned for daily liberties than with the "liberty brightest in dungeons and on the scaffold. . . ." Both artists value most of all the kind of freedom called personal independence. Frost distinguishes between the civilization of nineteenth-century Concord, a village which tolerated eccentrics, and utopian schemes which crowd everyone together. And he is convinced that Thoreau would join him in celebrating the separation of the parts instead of the connection: "But in Thoreau's declaration of independence from the modern pace is where I find most justification for my own propensities" (1954, p. 320). This article is especially helpful to those who are interested in the ideas of Frost and Thoreau rather than in an analysis of their writings.

Ten years after this discussion, Professor Cook published a critical evaluation of the two authors. In the opening paragraph of "A Parallel of Parablists: Thoreau and Frost" (in *The Thoreau Centennial,* ed. Walter Harding, 1964), Cook summarizes the highlights of Frost's comments on *Walden* in order to set up the foundation for his argument that the two writers are "complementary parablists." The emphasis falls on "complementary," for as Cook shows, Frost does not mirror Thoreau's art.

Thoreau's parable is "aspiratory," whereas Frost's is speculative. Cook defines his terms when he explains that Thoreau's parables (of Kouroo or of the lost bay horse, for example) are introspective and idealistic, and that Frost's are "commonly an imaginative means of objectifying *felt* experience" in a more realistic era (1964, p. 66). The following two sections of the essay are built around examples and analyses of first Thoreau's and then Frost's parables.

The key to Thoreau's parables, writes Cook, is his affinity with Transcendentalism. Because his world is emblematic, he usually begins his parable with a correspondence between "the data of sense and spirit." Thus, he can easily find clues to what he calls the "laws of ethics" in daily natural phenomena, enabling him to turn the insights gained from a close observation of nature into parables. Cook recalls Thoreau's insistence that he hoed beans not because he believed in the economy of beans but "for the sake of tropes and expression, to serve a parable-maker one day." The remainder of this section on Thoreau amounts to a catalogue of his parables, especially those found in the *Journals*. Cook's emphasis seems to be on citing examples instead of directing analysis. Accordingly, he calls attention to Thoreau's well-known counsel to Harrison Blake and to his description in *A Week* of how a town is "planted." The entirety of *Walden* is designated as Thoreau's "classic" parable of self-realization. Cook is surely correct when he notes that Thoreau's concern for being instructive negates the need for a gloss. There is no dialectic of the kind found in Frost, for the moral implications clarify the heart of his writings. Turning to Frost, Cook points to "The Demiurge's Laugh," "The Tuft of Flowers," "Range-Finding," "Birches," "The Wood-Pile," and others as examples of Frost the parablist. Whether lyric or narrative, serious or humorous, writes Cook, the key to Frost's "parable-like poems" is their way of releasing an idea through an action from common experience. As an example, he describes "The Demiurge's Laugh," rightly refusing to pin a specific meaning on the poem's "untrue god." Suggesting that Frost's parables often hint, leaving the reader to supply meaning, he writes of "The Demiurge's Laugh": "This particular parable does not aim to contrast ignorance and enlightenment" (1964, p. 74).

Professor Cook is also interested in distinguishing the differences within this parallel of parablists. Once again, he stresses Thoreau's penchant for "aspirative perfectionism"; "His dominant mode is the evocative excursus of the lyric statement in an expository passage" (1964, p. 75). This is a shrewd comment, for it suggests the undercurrent of nostalgia often present in Thoreau's better work. Frost, however, is more speculative than evocative, more interested in "a play of mind," more dramatic than nostalgic. These differences, of course, result from different temperaments and techniques. Although the point needs amplification to be entirely convincing, Cook seems correct when he suggests that Frost's relaxed approach to experience differs radically from Thoreau's more systematic exploration. If the reader accepts this point, then he will have no trouble agreeing with Cook that Thoreau's parables reflect "an intimate, passional intensity" in his attempt to clarify the correspondence between himself and nature, whereas Frost's parables illustrate the "continuous dialectical act of intelligence." In poems like "Birches" and "Directive," typical of Frost's parables, there is always the alternative of withdrawal and return. Perhaps Cook's most useful comment is his suggestion that the "idea comes to a crisis *in* the parable and not in a statement about the crisis. Natural insight suffices. . ." (1964, p. 76).

The most fundamental difference between these two "parablists" is in their vision of reality. Although Cook does not say so, most readers would probably comment that this difference is also the most obvious. Frost simply is not a Transcendentalist, and thus he does not subscribe to Thoreau's faith in a beneficent universe guided by divine sanctions. Any close reader of Frost knows that the poet is skeptical about ultimate answers. Though Cook may overemphasize his contention that Frost avoids "mystique" in his vision of reality, he is generally correct when he writes that Frost contemplates nature with "becoming detachment." This difference alone, of course, would account for the varied examples of the parable in Thoreau's and Frost's art. The reader of this essay soon wonders if the title is misleading, for the differences are more important than the parallels. Cook does not say that Frost's idea of nature is as benign as Thoreau's, but he nevertheless underestimates the role of possible universal evil in Frost's poems when he writes that the evil in "A Servant to Servants," "The Housekeeper," and others is man-made. This may be so, but what about poems like "Lodged," "Bereft," "Once by the Pacific," and "Desert Places" —surely the alienation and fear as expressed in these poems are not man-made. To say, as Cook does, that the alienation "only serves to intensify the capacity of human endurance" is to acknowledge Frost's qualified optimism, but it is also to underplay the very real fear expressed in so many of Frost's "nature" poems. Still, this article is one of the key essays in the continuing study of Frost and Thoreau. It is valuable because it illustrates how their parables should constitute another area for analysis. And while Cook does not answer all of the questions, he offers enough intriguing suggestions to stimulate further reading.

Nevertheless, Frost's remarks about Thoreau remain curiously ignored. Indeed, the entire relationship between the two writers —ideas, art, approaches to nature, and life-style—continues to be an unexplored area of criticism. As S. P. C. Duvall wrote in 1960, the probability that Thoreau's work was a genuine inspiration to Frost has been "so far only glancingly noted." Critical articles about the relationship have been published, of course, but most readers continue to rate Emerson as a more primary influence. Two of the better, more specific studies are Duvall's "Robert Frost's 'Directive' out of *Walden*" (*American Literature*, Jan. 1960) and James P. Dougherty's "Robert Frost's 'Directive' to the Wilderness" (*American Quarterly*, Summer 1966). Though both obviously use "Directive" as a focal point, the approaches differ. Duvall's article is a close reading of Frost's poem in the light of *Walden*, whereas Dougherty is concerned with placing "Directive" in the context of a familiar theme in American literature, the retreat to the wilderness.

Professor Duvall begins his excellent article with the complaint that those who emphasize "idea and aphorism" when evaluating Frost's literary antecedents often lead the reader away from the poetry. In a footnote he specifies Reginald Cook's essay on Emerson and Frost, but he does not elaborate. Instead, he suggests that we should concentrate on the art itself, and he points to "Directive" as a poem which "bears the unmistakable imprint" of *Walden*. What follows is Duvall's reading of "Directive" with particular emphasis on the poem's detail, imagery, and meaning, and their parallels in *Walden*. A line by line paraphrase of Duvall's reading is not appropriate here, but some of the more general points should be noted. The ghosts in "Directive," for example, which serve as reminders of those who previously walked down the road, are reminiscent of two chapters in *Walden*: "Former Inhabitants" and "Winter Visitors," which emphasize Thoreau's "former occupants." Similarly, such details as the broken drinking bowl, the cellar dents, and the children's flowers are significant in both poem and book. As Duvall notes of *Walden*, "such an extravagant excursion is ad-

venture near the height of poetry," calling to mind Frost's
phrase in "Directive," "the height of adventure" (1960, p. 484).
His point is that both works suggest the need to withdraw from
confusion in order to refresh one's self at the spirit's "watering
places." Surely he is correct to insist upon the close connection
between *Walden* and "Directive" when he calls attention to
the fact that both artists direct us, if we are to be wise men, to
dig our cellars close to water; or when he points out the way
both urge us to simplify and to search for lost cultures.

More important is Duvall's suggestion that the two writers
consider metaphor, "the cross of matter and spirit," to be the
true height of adventure. Inevitable obscurities result in artistic
creation because art represents adventure into the imagination.
Thus, as Thoreau rejects in his concluding chapter the demand
that artists speak so that all can understand, so Frost writes of
putting a spell on the broken drinking goblet so that the wrong
ones can't find it. Duvall's interpretation of the goblet as a metaphor for poetry, or even as a metaphor for metaphor, is supported by his quotation of Frost's own reading of the reference
to St. Mark: "It seems that people weren't meant to be saved
if they didn't understand figures of speech" (1960, p. 487).
Only after Duvall has examined the parallels in Frost's and
Thoreau's art does he turn to a short outline of similarities in
their ideas. Self-withdrawal, insistence on independence, pur-
suit of the present moment—all are themes both share. He concludes by stating flatly that Frost should be aligned with Thoreau instead of with Emerson. When Frost directs us back to our
sources, he also invites us to return to *Walden*—one of the "great
watering places of American literature."

James P. Dougherty's equally fine article begins with a con-
trasting evaluation of "Directive's" opening line. Whereas Duvall describes the line as "a near perfect line poetically," Dougherty refers to its "constricted words and stumbling cadence."
Yet he is not concerned with matters of vocabulary and meter.
Rather, he is interested in showing how Frost's poem illustrates
a familiar theme in American literature: "the retreat out of
some complexity into the simplicity of a lonely encounter with
wilderness" (1966, p. 208). Dougherty believes that Frost departs
from his usual stance in this poem, and that the poem "returns
through the categories of New World experience to rejoin the
traditions of world literature, rather than appealing directly to
the Old World as Eliot does in *The Waste Land*. . . ."

This essay is admirably documented and argued. Seizing the

poem's first line with its emphasis on "going back," he calls attention to studies of this theme in American literature by R. W. B. Lewis and Henry Nash Smith. In doing so, he places "Directive" in the context of earlier American writing which generally expresses a myth of the wilderness—that is, the idea that the Golden Age exists, that retreating in time can be gained by moving back in space. Dougherty correctly shows that this theme has been standard in our literature from Franklin, Jefferson, and Thoreau to Frost, Hemingway, and Salinger. Unlike Duvall, however, he points to a crucial difference between Frost and Thoreau. Calling attention to the normal reading of Transcendentalism with its emphasis on a "benevolent nature-spirit" and on a "mood of cosmic optimism," he insists that in "Directive" Frost's view is closer to Melville than Thoreau. From the "ominous" simile of the crumbling graveyard stones established in the opening lines, Frost describes a landscape in which nature has been too much for man. Dougherty's point is well taken, and it seems doubtful that many contemporary readers would confuse Frost's view of nature with that of Thoreau and other Transcendentalists. Yet he quickly points out that Frost's scene in "Directive" is not "an arid desert" like that in *The Waste Land* but rather "a wilderness in the American sense, fertile land resisting cultivation" (1966, p. 211). The poem's nature imagery suggests neither the harmony of Thoreau nor the malevolence of Melville. Instead, Frost sets up nature as an adversary which has both the advantage of strength and the assurance of certain triumph. In "Directive," then, Frost runs counter to the American literary tradition of returning to a beneficent, spirit-healing forest. Dougherty's reading has merit, though one wonders if he does not overemphasize when he includes remarks like "the figure of man is crushingly secondary to the wilderness."

Perhaps his most significant point is that the poem's climatic moment is as much a part of world literature as American literature. That is, the poem employs a progression of tensions which is generally American (Dougherty names past and present, innocence and experience, space and time, etc.), but the poem's conclusion that self-knowledge is gained by a "paring away of relationships" to achieve "at last a clear self-definition" is kin to universal literature. There is nothing particularly American about Frost's expression of the "balked rage to which such tensions goad" the man who would cut free from encumbering attachments. The remainder of the essay is not specifically concerned with Frost and Thoreau or Transcendentalism. Dougherty shifts instead to a close analysis of "Directive" as a poem in which Frost turns from his usual poetic stance of showing man rejecting the pull of the dark woods. Because Frost, in effect, enters the woods in "Directive," he achieves a deeper level than most literary works employing "the frontier image." In short, he shows man rejoining nature instead of "opposing himself to it." His poet-figure finally recalls Thoreau or Ishmael, for all three return from nature to share their discoveries with those who can understand. There is not an article in my opinion which better places one of Frost's most important poems in the context of a primary tradition in American literature—the theme of retreat to nature.

Another article which traces Frost's use of a particular image also found in Thoreau is Daniel G. Hoffman's "Thoreau's 'Old Settler' and Frost's Paul Bunyan" (*Journal of American Folklore*, July-Sept. 1960). Hoffman's note is of much narrower scope than either Duvall's or Dougherty's essay, and, consequently, it is not as useful to the general reader. But its interesting and convincing evidence warrants attention from those concerned with the full range of the Frost-Thoreau relationship. A specialist in folklore, Hoffman focuses on a possible primary source for Frost's poem "Paul's Wife." As he notes, his first suggestion, made in 1952 in *Paul Bunyan, Last of the Frontier Demigods*, held that Frost found the story of Bunyan's wife in Ida Virginia Turney's *Paul Bunyan Comes West* (1916). In this article, however, Hoffman discusses a probable source "closer in spirit" to Frost's idealization of the Bunyan materials which he "indubitably" found in Turney's book. He quotes the well-known passage near the end of the chapter "Solitude" in *Walden* in which Thoreau describes the occasional visits he had from "an old settler and original proprietor." Citing the parallels between Thoreau's old settler, reported to have dug Walden Pond, and the folklore of Paul Bunyan creating the "geographical features of the landscape, particularly its lakes and waterways," Hoffman points to a key distinction between Frost's lumberman and the giant of American folktales: in "Paul's Wife," Bunyan is not the outgoing hero of the tales but, like Thoreau's mysterious settler, secretive and shy.

There is an analogue in "Solitude" even for Paul's wife. Hoffman quotes the passage which describes Thoreau's second visitor, the elderly dame. Admitting that Thoreau's dame does not physically resemble Frost's vision of Paul's wife, he nevertheless speculates that Thoreau's description of the dame's youth could have shaped Frost's image of the lumberman's wife. If so, the point is that Frost humanizes the materials rather than mythologizes them. Hoffman insists that the humanization results in a contradiction, for Frost leaves us with an unresolved contrast between the "moody lyricism of [Bunyan's] marriage to the wood-sprite and the jovial exuberance" of the logging feats (1960, p. 237). The article concludes with a short discussion of Thoreau's use of folk materials and with a reemphasis on Frost's decision to reduce the scale of the mythic characteristics in his poem. Though not an important article, the evidence cited is solid enough to be of interest.

An entirely different approach to the Frost-Thoreau relationship is Thornton H. Parsons' "Thoreau, Frost, and the American Humanist Tradition" (*Emerson Society Quarterly*, Oct.-Dec. 1963). Because Parsons' primary emphasis is on Irving Babbitt's New Humanism, the article is not completely relevant to those interested only in Frost's art. Yet it is valuable for readers familiar with Gorham Munson's earlier efforts, discussed in chapter 1, to make the poet a disciple of Babbitt. Unfortunately, Parsons fails to mention Munson's work and thus deprives the reader of the opportunity to know what he thinks of Munson's oft-challenged thesis. Parsons' essay seems much the fairer, for he does not force Frost's ideas or art into the Babbitt mold. Rather, he first outlines Babbitt's humanistic position and then specifies how Thoreau and Frost adapt it. The article's key weakness for the Frost student is its long exposition of Babbitt's humanism. Though Parsons hopes to account for this emphasis when he explains that Irving Babbitt is so largely forgotten as to necessitate a restatement of his position, the continued paraphrases of New Humanist thought do not seem to me justified.

The article's first half does little more than summarize Babbitt's ideas. It is true that most of today's readers need this refresher information, but Parsons carries it to such lengths that Thoreau and Frost seem ignored until the reader wades through the discussions of Babbitt's work. Parsons is unquestionably well-acquainted with New Humanism ideas, and he clearly defines Babbitt's affirmation of "old-fashioned" virtues like will, control, responsibility, and individuality. According to Parsons, Babbitt set himself the goal of "shoring up the defenses of Western Civilization against the naturalistic and nihilistic dogmas of the modern world" (1963, p. 34). He hoped to establish "poise" between the extremes of pseudo-classicism and Romanticism. Parsons describes Babbitt as a man who sought "mediation between the phenomenal and the noumenal." This is not the place to paraphrase Parsons' restatements of Babbitt's theories. Suffice it to say that he willingly admits Babbitt's flaws, especially in the humanist's thoughts about nature. As a humanist, Babbitt should have "asserted the legitimacy" of a love of nature which encourages a heightened consciousness, but he "felt so intensely the moral shallowness of the time that he erred on the side of strictness of conscience" (1963, p. 35). The result, of course, is that his work ignores Thoreau.

Parsons outlines the affinity between Babbitt's and Thoreau's ideas about nature, democracy, and reform, and he correctly insists that Babbitt made a mistake when he dismissed Thoreau's writing as an example of "Romantic egocentricity." What follows is a longish restatement of Thoreau's ideas in which Parsons praises the writer for both his willingness to accept nature's wildness and his refusal to apply human standards to nature. This idea leads to a discussion of Frost's poems in which the implication seems to be that Babbitt could also have accepted Frost as a New Humanist if he had not misunderstood the artistic uses of nature. The connection of Frost and the New Humanist tradition is, however, less successful than that of Thoreau and Babbitt's thesis. Parsons' reading of "The Road Not Taken," for example, mistakenly emphasizes the "celebration of the self-reliance that enabled Frost to resist the temptations of conventional life and to become a poet" (1963, p. 39). Most readers know now that Frost intended "The Road Not Taken" to be an ironic comment on Edward Thomas' reluctance to accept a decision once it was made. Similarly, Parsons' suggestion that the last stanza of "Two Tramps in Mud Time" echoes a passage from Thoreau's "Life without Principle" is interesting, but his description of Frost's poem as an "eloquent and dramatic" tribute to spontaneous consciousness seems questionable. And although he correctly names wildness as one of Frost's major themes, he overemphasizes the "tonic of wildness" in "A Lone Striker." One of Frost's decidedly weaker lyrics, "The Brook in the City," is praised as "a poem that powerfully implies what may happen when the fact of wildness in us is ignored" (1963, p. 41).

Indeed, the rest of the essay is essentially a discussion of how Frost and Thoreau handle wildness. Parsons concludes that American humanism, particularly as expressed in this century, has been mistakenly viewed as a polemical struggle. Insisting that Frost's general position resembles Babbitt's, he nevertheless points to the key differentiating factor: Frost is the true exemplar of the American humanist tradition because he, unlike Babbitt, keeps his "poise." To be persuasive, Irving Babbitt needs the corrective of the poet's lyrical humanism.

George Monteiro's "Redemption Through Nature: A Recurring Theme in Thoreau, Frost and Richard Wilbur" (*American Quarterly*, Winter 1968) illustrates the impact of Reginald Cook's seminal work on Frost and Thoreau, for Monteiro cites it in his opening paragraphs. But his approach to the problem is unusual, to say the least. Establishing the relationship between Emerson's "Nature," Thoreau's *Walden*, and Frost's "The Ax-Helve," he plans to show how these related works illuminate the poems of Richard Wilbur. He begins by quoting a passage from one of Frost's letters (July 15, 1915), known to all Frost students, in which the poet praises "the beautiful passage about the French-Canadian woodchopper" in *Walden*. Also quoted is part of Frost's interview, published in the *Public Ledger* (Philadelphia, Apr. 4, 1916), in which he compliments Canadian woodchoppers for whittling their own ax handles by following the curve of the grain. With this evidence for support, Monteiro can confidently understate the resemblance between parts of *Walden* and "The Ax-Helve" as "persuasive." He willingly admits that parallels such as the way both Thoreau's and Frost's Canadian woodchoppers love to take time with their work, or the manner in which both have trouble with English, are elementary. A deeper affinity can be found in the way both authors use the carefully made helve as a metaphor for the way a man should grow.

Equally significant is the fact that both "The Ax-Helve" and *Walden* question the Romantic notion that these natural men of the woods are embodiments of virtue. Monteiro writes, "That Frost's Baptiste and Thoreau's woodchopper are themselves unaware of the implications of the serpent in Eden . . . reaffirms the idea that men of undeveloped spirit endanger human culture and the fostering of its values" (1968, pp. 799-800). He continues by pointing out that Thoreau's basic complaint about "economy" in society reappears in Frost's poem. The machine-made ax-helve may be economical, but it is also artificially crooked. Baptiste prefers the true product which "grows crooked." Monteiro's suggestion challenges the more standard readings of these two passages, but it is never clarified. After raising the issue of how Frost and Thoreau confront the Romantic notion of natural man, he drops it, leaving the reader wishing for further analysis and additional illustration. Instead, he turns to a discussion of the ways both *Walden* and "The Ax-Helve" criticize the machine. Thoreau's dismissal in "Housewarming" of the small cooking stove and his praise of the open fireplace are evaluated as illustrations of his argument in "Economy" against all forms of overuse. Thoreau, as always, pleas for a return to the more natural, more "economic" life-style necessary for spiritual renewal. Similarly, Frost's poet-figure in "The Ax-Helve" is uncomfortable in Baptiste's overwarm kitchen. Monteiro then interprets the rocking of Baptiste's wife beside the hot stove as a metaphor for the erratic movement of the earth, in danger of destruction caused by rocking too close to the sun. Both the earth and Baptiste's wife right themselves in time and thus avoid "overwarmth."

The key to all this, as Monteiro notes, is the definition of education which Thoreau and Frost illustrate. Just as the machine makes overheated stoves or brittle ax-helves, so false education ignores the natural growth of a man by attempting to impose form from without. Emerson shares this idea—we all remember his commitment to nature and his warning to avoid the library and the scholar's lamp. But, as Monteiro writes in perhaps his most useful observation, Frost's poem "seems to say that Baptiste's art is also knowledge, but knowledge that, significantly, is in itself evil *and* good" (1968, p. 802). The resemblance here between Frost's Baptiste and Thoreau's artist of Kouroo is obvious. Quoting from "Higher Laws," Monteiro recalls Thoreau's dual emphasis upon spiritual instincts and savage qualities which corresponds to Frost's "perception of the 'Edenic' moment, the poet's encounter with the great 'Adversary' in the midst of 'natural' wisdom and 'good' organic form" (1968, p. 803). Monteiro goes on to suggest that the snake-like shape of the ax-helve is good because the snake can represent human consciousness and thus the possibility of spiritual development. Baptiste, of course, remains unaware of these weighty matters, but Frost invites the reader to pursue them. The remainder of this essay completes Monteiro's progression of Thoreau, Frost, and Wilbur, and thus is outside the concerns of this chapter. Suffice it to say that the critic believes "The Ax-Helve" to have an immediate relationship to Wilbur's "Junk," just as *Walden* "fostered" Frost's poem. A similar line of development is convincingly suggested for Thoreau's plumbing the depths of Walden Pond, Frost's "For Once, Then, Something," and Wilbur's "Digging for China."

At first glance this article might appear to be just one more study of two or three writers which points out similarities in order to imply influence. But such is not the case because Monteiro takes pains to differentiate between superficial and fundamental resemblances. His attention to surface affiliations acts as a springboard to more significant discussions of how Thoreau and Frost write about education, knowledge, and good versus evil. As with all current studies of Thoreau and Frost, this essay encourages further speculation and analysis. This is because the entire matter of Frost's relationship with Thoreau was generally ignored until roughly 1960. The studies of the question published thus far must necessarily first call attention to various resemblances and correspondences between the two artists, for only when the foundations are laid can more definitive investigations be completed. Perhaps Monteiro could have made his remarks a little clearer, but his essay remains a good one on a subject Frost students have only begun to examine.

Frost and New England

The final section of this chapter focuses on Frost's relationship with other New England authors and with the New England heritage in general. His association with New England was more than a matter of just living there. He seemed to bring the New England spirit to life and to export its qualities all over the world when he traveled. To many readers, Frost *was* New England, the Northeast Corner made flesh. Such was not the case, of course. But it is interesting to note the various evaluations and descriptions of Frost as New Englander which contribute more than their share to the shaping of the myth of Robert Frost. Writing in 1926, Charles Cestre ("Amy Lowell, Robert Frost, and Edwin Arlington Robinson," *Johns Hopkins Alumni Magazine*, Mar. 1926) is understandably interested in the revitalization of American poetry which was so noticeable in the 1920s. Like most students of American literature, he points to Walt Whitman as the prime factor in the move to free American poetry from the imitation of English literature. Yet he does not believe that the writers of the New Poetry in the 1920s are followers of Whitman. Many are distinctly American, as is Whitman, but in Cestre's words, their work is more "delicate," more "refined." Although his essay examines three of these newer original poets, Amy Lowell, Edwin Arlington Robinson, and Frost, our business is only with his remarks about Frost as a New England writer.

At first glance it seems as if Cestre ignores Frost's relationship with Wordsworth, Emerson, and Thoreau, for he argues that Frost "takes his cue from the great realistic movement that has swept the domain of fiction, in the last seventy years, all over the world" (1926, p. 369). This curious opinion is understandable when we recall that Frost's ties with Wordsworth, Emerson, and Thoreau were not generally accepted until years later. Cestre's remark seems directed more toward an illustration of Frost's break with the "poetic" diction and rhythm of a Tennyson or a Swinburne than toward a denial of relationships with these past giants of Romanticism. When he turns to a discussion of New England and Frost, he echoes the opinion of many critics of the day—that Frost is "the poet of the New England country and of nothing else." Little wonder, then, that he uses phrases like "rather narrow boundaries" or "the limitations of genre-painting." Cestre nevertheless likes Frost, and he believes that the poet has achieved a "notable" success within his limited scope. Echoing Amy Lowell's essays on Frost (see chapters 2 and 3), he suggests that Frost is the poet of a diminishing New England. If Cestre is to be believed, then the best of the New England population emigrated West, leaving Frost with narrow minds, rude manners, and obstinate wills as a basis for poetry. Cestre's analysis here is so wrongheaded that he finds himself distinguishing sensitivity to beauty according to sex: the New England man is "dull to the beauty of his fells, ponds, heaths, or mountain intervals," whereas the women may notice "natural loveliness" (1926, p. 370). He correctly states that the poet is more interested in the human drama than in the natural landscape, but his descriptions of New England suggest ignorance about both the region and Frost's poetry. When Cestre discusses the way Frost sets up the details in a poem, he seems more convincing. But he always returns to his true subject— Frost as a New England author.

Never once is Cestre critical of Frost's subject matter or of what he considers to be the poet's limited scope. Unlike Amy Lowell, he recognizes the fact that while the poet's subject and locale are of New England, his concerns are the universally human: "The circumstances of moral or religious life and the local coloring is [sic] primarily New England and broadly American; the emotional complications reverberate in the hearts of all readers, whatever their national manners, prejudices, or associations" (1926, p. 372). But, Cestre continues, because Frost is tied to the ethical and historical circumstances of New England, he must necessarily emphasize the unattractive traits previously mentioned. With a thesis as questionable as this one, it is not surprising that Cestre misreads when he finally gets to the poems. Of "The Death of the Hired Man," he writes that Warren "feels no sympathy for a wastrel who works only on the sting of hunger. . . ." He brands the husband in "Home Burial" with "hard-grained feelinglessness" and the wife with an undefendable flight. And the woman in "A Servant to Servants" is said to lack stamina. The interpretations are either oversimplifications or dead wrong, but they result more from Cestre's misjudgment of Frost's New England ties than from an inability to read poetry.

Closer to the mark is Sidney Hayes Cox's "New England and Robert Frost" (*New Mexico Quarterly*, May 1934). It takes him only one paragraph to challenge Cestre's contention that New England men are "dull" to natural beauty, for Cox begins his short essay by elaborating his claim that "all New England loveliness is peculiarly a triumph." Similarly, his description of New England natives differs entirely from Cestre's. Instead of pointing to obstinate wills and narrow minds, Cox finds New Englanders to be "tough, sinewy, difficult, exacting, full of sap." If they seem slow to act, writes Cox, it is because they prepare decisions "with exceptional commitment and awareness of the fatal finality of deeds" (1934, p. 91). Comparing Cox's remarks with Cestre's, we wonder if a single description of New England is possible. Yet the point here is not the validity of their statements about New England but the ways these statements affect their readings of Frost's poems. In this sense, Cox is more reliable than Cestre.

Pointing out that Frost knows both the man and the earth, Cox explains how the poet uses his New England material. He avoids the debate about Frost's supposed narrow boundaries, and he concentrates on how the poet tells a story instead of generalizing. According to Cox, Frost "has both the Yankee tendency to turn things over in his mind and see if he can't extract some hint for later exigencies and the Yankee inclination not to say much but wait until he sees" (1934, p. 92). This is why, says Cox, Frost's statements in the poems often sound tentative and casual. Instead of spelling out meanings, the poet tries to "in-

veigle" us to take a deeper look. Some readers may suppose that
Frost has committed himself to slight significance when he
stresses his own ties to the New England setting, but those kinds
of readers are in touch with only the poem's surface. Cox challenges those who argue that Frost escapes modern predicaments
by retreating to the Yankee region. As he says, it would be
truer to show how the poet demonstrates the significance of
looking for possibilities within the limiting conditions symbolized by the New England life-style. The frustrating conflicts
which often illustrate life in New England should be read as
analogies with the general difficulties of living anywhere: "And
is not New England just a good synecdoche for earth?"

This article typifies Cox's work on Frost because it tends
toward idealization. Yet while it underplays the harshness, tragedy, and sterility present in so many of Frost's "New England
poems," it is a more reliable analysis than Cestre's. The essay's
primary weakness is the absence of references to the poems. It
is obviously not the kind of article which develops incisive analyses of specific poems, but one misses, nevertheless, the designa-
tion of a title or two for illustration and support.

An entirely different kind of article is Gladys Hasty Carroll's "New England Sees It Through" (*Saturday Review of
Literature*, Nov. 9, 1935). A New England author herself, she
writes of the status of New England letters in the 1930s from
the point of view of one who is concerned with the varying
value of the region's literature. The article is both informative
and entertaining, and it focuses more on New England writing
in general than on Robert Frost in particular. Yet it has value for
the Frost student because it tries to pinpoint what Frost (as well
as other writers) means to the Yankee spirit. If the article has a
specific point of reference, it is Sarah Orne Jewett. Miss Carroll is very likely correct when she writes that many felt the
loss of New England's strength when Miss Jewett died in 1909.
But Miss Carroll is less interested in Miss Jewett's art than in
showing how her death marked just one more turning point in
a long series of ups and downs for New England vitality. As she
remarks, "It is a curious thing how often this Northeast Corner
has been declared dead." Such changes as from wooden ships to
steel, from whale oil to kerosene, from carriages to trolley cars
were all pronounced as symbols of New England's demise. But
Miss Carroll refuses to accept the predictions. She correctly notes
that the "temper of a race" can be reflected in the "works of the
poets and novelists who are *in* and *of* the race itself, living in the

usual houses, sharing at least some of the current opinions, laboring under many of the popular delusions, setting down what they see and hear and feel, what they themselves are (1935, p. 4). Thus, she calls on New Englanders to turn from Whittier, Longfellow, Lowell, and Holmes, whom she designates polite but not great writers, and to accept the new spirit of literary vitality first illustrated in American letters by Whitman and Twain. These two authors may not have been invited to tea in Boston's social circles, but "America was tired of tea; it wanted meat."

Miss Carroll pulls no punches—she probably angers some of her New England devotees when, dismissing the "polite" poets, she writes, "We were closer to literary oblivion than we knew, here in New England, around the middle of the nineteenth century" (1935, p. 4). She sees Sarah Orne Jewett's association with *Atlantic Monthly* as the first step toward revitalization. But she also believes that this rebirth of New England letters was slowed by the substitute of passion and heat for control and form in the novels of Dreiser, Anderson, and Lewis. Though not New England authors, these writers dominated the literary scene of the day: "There was no place for New England in such an America as this." Miss Carroll overestimates the "silence" of potential New England writers when faced with Dreiser or Lewis, but she is on sure ground when she points to the counterbalance provided by the "new" poetry of Frost and Robinson. Although she does not directly state it, her point seems to be that New England's desire for form and control found new expression in Frost's poems. He captures the New England scene and its speech, yet he maintains traditional rhythms and verse forms. Most of all he expresses Yankee vitality.

Writing in 1935, Miss Carroll distinguishes between Frost's early and late work. By "early" she probably means only *A Boy's Will*, for she claims that its "still peace and patience" should be laid away like a keepsake. Since it is difficult to see how these words could be applied to *North of Boston*, we are probably safe in assuming that the vitality she detects in Frost's "later" work occurs in all of his books except the first. She does not analyze Frost's poems to show how the control is used or in which lines the sense of life is expressed, but close reading of specific poems is not her concern. Her primary interest remains the general status of New England letters in 1935, and her informal approach to this question is entertaining.

One finishes Miss Carroll's essay with a feeling for the bright future of New England life and letters. She carefully refrains from making predictions, but her optimistic appraisal of the renewed vitality of Yankee living and of the faith in the then current New England writing suggests her hope. Not so with Merrill Moore. Although his short review of *A Further Range*, "Poetic Agrarianism: Old Style" (*Sewanee Review*, Oct.-Dec. 1937) is not intended to be a general evaluation of New England literature, it is nevertheless interesting to note his disagreements with Miss Carroll's assessment. Writing only two years after the publication of her essay, Moore says nothing about rebirth and revitalization. Instead he detects a calmness in *A Further Range* which he attributes to Frost's affinity with the soil. And rather than interpret Frost's poems as illustrative of New England's new found strength, he writes that in "Build Soil" Frost "clings to the older faith." The reason for this difference of opinion, of course, is the book of poems being reviewed, for Miss Carroll published her essay before *A Further Range* appeared. Yet it is interesting to note how two commentators, both sympathetic to Frost, can express such varied evaluations of Frost's relationship with New England. Miss Carroll praises Frost's expression of New England's current life-style, while Moore insists that there is a "faint, almost pathetic, tinge to his lines suggestive of an old order of life which is passing away" (1937, p. 508). To Moore, "A Lone Striker" suggests complacency more than vitality. Frost is so much a New Englander that he remains unruffled by national problems. Moore's review is otherwise insignificant, and he seems unaware of the furor, discussed in chapter 3, which *A Further Range* caused. But his remarks might interest some Frost students because of their variations on the continuing discussion of Frost's relationship with New England.

A full treatment of the subject is Robert P. Tristram Coffin's *New Poetry of New England: Frost and Robinson* (1938) which was originally a series of lectures given at the Johns Hopkins University. In the first chapter, "The World That Is Gone," Coffin defines American poetry of the nineteenth century in order to set up a frame of reference for his remarks about Frost and Robinson. Casting his eye back over Bryant, Longfellow, Emerson, Lowell, Holmes, and Whittier, he finds unity in their tendency toward oration. All of them felt the need to preach the serious message of truth: "To be a poet was to be on a rostrum, head and shoulders above life" (1938, p. 5). The poet might touch upon common life, but when he did so the village blacksmith assumed the eloquence of the man in the pulpit. In addition, says Coffin, American poetry of the past century expressed romantic adventure in a decorative style now known as "poetic." But behind the exotic subjects and the artificial style lay the "rather outmoded doctrine of the improvement of life." Coffin attributes this doctrine of steady improvement to the Puritan heritage which all of the poets had to deal with, whether or not they accepted its teachings. He suggests that this Puritan tradition was significant not so much for its support of taboos but for its lessons about the inevitable enlargement of man. Not only did the faith in progress result in the religious aura of past American poetry, it also encouraged men to believe in unlimited opportunity. Thus, the poetry of that day generally expressed hope, a faith in the future which remained unshakable until after the Civil War.

Coffin summarizes his ideas with one phrase when he names nineteenth-century American poetry the "poetry of confidence" (1938, p. 14). Unaware of the psychology of the unconscious, and unwilling to accept scientific theories which denied the beneficence of the universe, these poets devoted themselves to principles which never called for reexamination. The characters in their poems may have led isolated lives, but this isolation did not cause the kind of spirit-numbing loneliness which Frost would later detail. Life in a virgin wilderness is not as lonely as that in a place which has been deserted by its inhabitants. If Coffin is correct, then Frost's "The Census-Taker" could never have been written by a nineteenth-century American poet. This is not to say that Coffin sees the current poets of New England as prophets of the hopeless. But he does suggest in his opening chapter that Robinson and Frost particularly are not mere holdovers from a past poetic tradition. Their perspectives, styles, and tones are radically different from that of their precursors.

Turning to the two writers themselves, Coffin argues that Frost is the "happier" poet. His distinction may be legitimate, for he correctly observes that Robinson has found "more of his eloquence in men's failures." Yet use of the term "happy" to distinguish the poets is a disservice to both Frost and the reader. The term may call needed attention to Frost's comic poems, but by using it Coffin both overlooks the numerous poems of doubt and fear and neglects Frost's tone of what can only be called qualified affirmation. Frost may celebrate more sureties than Robinson, more "things in life to feel well about," but a greater measure of confidence does not make him the "happier" poet. The key chapter on Frost, as opposed to those which com-

pare Robinson and Frost, is titled "The Poet in a New World."
Coffin's portrait of the poet typifies the idealistic view of Frost
which literary criticism perpetuated prior to the publication of
Lawrance Thompson's biography. Misrepresenting the poet as
an active farmer, Coffin describes him doing small but necessary
jobs around the farm while picking up poems everywhere. The
seasons, frost, and rain are described as the poet's "friends," and
the daily chores are defined as "rituals of lovely and loyal living"
which make a man feel good enough to forget sorrow and death
(1938, p. 53). Reading this peaches and cream version of Frost,
we can perhaps understand why Coffin calls him the happier poet.

Coffin is better informed when he discusses the fresh images
and tones Frost brings to the standard New England subjects.
He calls attention to Whittier's "Snow-Bound" and to Frost's
"Snow" to illustrate the superiority of the latter's knowledge of
New England winters. The point is that Frost knows the particulars—he can put "the real country into words." He communicates the difficulties of New England farming in such a way as
to comment upon general trials by existence. Because he knows
both the correct names of things (for example, stone-boats, and
fox-grapes) and the way natural processes act against a wall or
within a brook, his poetry, more than that of his New England
predecessors, is "exact and expert." Coffin correctly insists that
Frost's fidelity to life's particulars does not mean that his poems
are realistic photographs of New England life. The objects
which Frost details always mean more than they seem. Yet Coffin
fails to expand his observation into a true analysis of the poems.
Rather than show how Frost moves beyond the realistic use of
common details, and what he thus accomplishes, Coffin generalizes about Frost's accurate way of seeing. It is not that Coffin is
wrong—indeed, his comments are usually rich enough to prod
the reader to pick up the poems. But instead of providing a full
discussion of what he means by a "new kind of symbolism" in
Frost's poetry, he suggests only that a poem like "Stopping by
Woods on a Snowy Evening" can bear the weight of multiple
readings. This weakness holds true for his otherwise valuable
discussion of Frost's "people." His generalities seem correct:
"Frost's people are no better than they should be. Some are
worse"; or "But unlike Robinson's people, they almost never
brood or shut themselves away from life" (1938, p. 66). But this
is all we get—promising general comments without analysis of
the poetry. Surely Coffin is correct when he writes that Whittier and Longfellow missed the poetic possibilities in the people

around them because they never took the time to discover them properly. Yet the specific discussion which this statement calls for is not forthcoming.

Coffin's admiration unfortunately leads him to hold up Frost as a model for other writers. He suggests, for example, that Frost is a "first-rate proletarian poet" because he puts real people into books. Although the term "proletarian" when applied to Frost surely cannot mean the same thing when it is used to describe Steinbeck, or Dos Passos, or other writers of the 1930s, Coffin fails to specify the difference. Equally questionable is the assertion that Frost, not Cummings, Eliot, or Joyce, is "the real radical among modern poets." Disapproving of the experimental writers' subject matter, which he calls "the novelty of grafting healthy tissue on the dead," he dismisses them as pseudo-radicals. The same approach holds when Coffin compares Frost to past poets. Beside Frost's description of nature, for example, Spenser's is "concocted" and Shakespeare's is "a game of carving hearts on trees." Wordsworth's people are "too whole and too picturesque," and Keats' country loveliness is too "theatrically unusual." Claims such as these are the reason why some later critics argue that Frost's supporters perform a disservice when they use him as a rallying point against different kinds of poetry. It is as if Coffin believes Frost's way to be right—the achievement of other poets is lesser because they do not write the way Frost does.

This attitude carries over into Coffin's discussion of Frost's language and pattern of poetry. Thus, he claims that Frost is a better user of words than most modern poets because he is not obscure. Coffin correctly notes Frost's belief that poetry is a "renewal of words," but he seems to define the phrase to mean only the new simplicity of wording which his poetry illustrates. Once this objection is noted, however, the reader can investigate with profit Coffin's analysis of why Frost uses simple words and phrasing. As he points out, Frost is not just reacting against the florid style of the late nineteenth century. Formulating his doctrine of sentence sounds, the poet finds that he relies upon simpler words and more colloquial phrasing in the attempt to catch speaking tones. Coffin writes, "Oral prose idiom is full of poetry" (1938, p. 79). He offers the interesting theory that Frost fears words. As a New Englander who believes in the virtues of understatement and of concealing emotions, Frost relies on a simple vocabulary because he does not want words to betray him into saying more than he should. Unfortunately this fruitful suggestion is not supported by analysis of the way words work in specific poems. "Neither Out Far Nor In Deep" is quoted, but with only the comment that the words are so exact and "hard" that they can "hardly be called poetical."

The remainder of the book is a discussion of such varied topics as the universality of Frost's poetry, Frost's humor, and the general state of contemporary New England poets. Coffin's advantage is that he himself is a New England poet. When he discusses Frost, Robinson, and the literary history of that region, he can rely on broad knowledge nourished by familiarity. Though he is a college teacher, his approach in *New Poetry of New England* is that of a poet appreciating the art of fellow writers. Perhaps this is why these lectures do not have the kind of literary analysis we expect when reading criticism.

Although not as wide-ranging as Coffin's collection of lectures, Charles Howell Foster's "Robert Frost and the New England Tradition" (in *Elizabethan Studies and Other Essays*, Oct. 1945) is the most comprehensive single essay on the subject to be published by 1945. Well aware of the growing body of Frost criticism with a negative slant, Foster wryly notes how negative critics like Malcolm Cowley rarely attack Frost's poetry. Unable to criticize Frost the poet, they challenge Frost the New Englander. Claiming that Frost refuses to participate in the critical issues of the age, these critics dismiss all claims that the poet is a worthy expresser of the great New England spirit. Foster, however, tackles Cowley and the others head on, insisting that such opinions reveal a failure to "examine the great New Englanders and Frost with care." To begin, Foster argues that Cowley (see chapter 3) overestimates Hawthorne's status as a reformer. He willingly grants Cowley's opinion that Hawthorne campaigned against brutality on American ships and that the novelist was dissatisfied with the lot of the poor, but he nevertheless insists—with lovely sarcasm—that Hawthorne was "rather far from the spirit of *The New Republic* . . ." (1945, p. 371). Rather than reform society, writes Foster, Hawthorne hoped to develop the individual soul. He argues convincingly that Hawthorne would have greeted with sympathy Frost's cry for a "one-man revolution." And as for Cowley's objection that Frost prudishly drapes his love affairs, or that he treats adultery only when it is very old or wrapped in brown paper, Foster reminds us that the adultery in *The Scarlet Letter* is two hundred years old. He admits that Frost does not seek "paradoxical depths" in the manner of Hawthorne, but he correctly points out that the two New England writers are very much alike in their preference for "psychological ramifications" rather than naturalistic shocks. Frost's poetry is closer than Cowley thinks to the Hawthorne of the *American Notebooks*, "Snowflakes," and "The Old Apple Dealer."

This convincing argument against the pervasive claim that Frost's dislike of social reform disqualifies him from the New England tradition does not mean that Foster finds strong echoes of Hawthorne in Frost. He quickly points out, for example, that Frost does not participate in Hawthorne's tragic vision. Read superficially, "The Witch of Coös" might seem to belong in the Hawthorne tradition, but its effect is finally comic. Frost does not care to endow it with the "intense seriousness" reminiscent of Hawthorne because "the problem of sin does not touch off his imagination" (1945, p. 374). This observation does not mean that Foster, like most readers in 1945, underplays Frost's tragic poems. On the contrary, he points to "Out, Out—" and to "Desert Places" as prime examples of Frost's tragic mood. But he believes Frost to be "too much in the tradition of Emerson and Thoreau for the tragic note to be major" (1945, p. 374).

Foster is surely correct when he notes that the Yankee tone of voice and the Yankee character are often humorous. Frost's skill in communicating this tone and character keeps him from expressing a universal tragic note. Like the great nineteenth-century New England writers, Frost is nevertheless interested in universalities. Poems like "Birches" and "West-Running Brook" "approximate those passages in Thoreau's *Journals* where meditation on some natural event or fact is lifted into speculation and observation on life" (1945, p. 375). Like Thoreau, Frost urges man to turn inward if he would cultivate his intellectual life. And like most New England writers, Frost celebrates the common man. He shares with Thoreau especially the intense interest in man working, in quirks of speech, in illustrations of eccentricity, and originality. But, as Foster notes, there is less analysis and criticism in Frost than in Thoreau and Emerson. Frost's Baptiste ("The Ax-Helve") may recall Thoreau's woodchopper, but Frost does not measure his character intellectually or spiritually. And the greatest difference of all between Frost and Thoreau is that Frost is not a Transcendentalist.

Frost's refusal to embrace the radical politics of Thoreau does not mean that he is as conservative as his critics claim. He may be a political conservative, but he, like Emerson, knows that one

cannot duck behind walls and avoid change. Once again, Foster
suggests that the question of liberal or conservative politics has
very little to do with evaluations of Frost's place in the New
England tradition. More significant is the absence of "intellectual complication" in Frost. As Foster shows, Emerson embraced
all ideas, past and present. From Oriental thought, Plato, and
Plotinus, to Shakespeare and Swedenborg, Emerson sampled the
world's great ideas. Frost may be a follower of Emerson, but he
lacks his predecessor's interest in the chief intellectual forces
which have shaped the world. And yet, if Frost lacks Hawthorne's tragic vision, Thoreau's "mystic awareness," and Emerson's intellectual interests, he is nevertheless a contemporary example of the New England tradition because these qualities are
"less a matter of tradition than of special endowment." In matters of independence, originality, metaphorical thinking, delight
in the common man, and faith in the beauty of art, Frost remains very much a part of the heritage from which Cowley and
others would disqualify him: "Not only has he translated into
poetic drama attitudes and habits of thought one finds in the
prose of Emerson, Thoreau, and Hawthorne, but he has shaped
the Yankee talk of Lowell and Whittier to a poetic style unmis-
takably his own, and achieved an art of great subtlety and perfect modulation" (1945, p. 380). Frost does not echo the New
England tradition—he extends it. Foster's essay is entirely convincing. His arguments are well illustrated and calmly stated,
and he clearly has a thorough knowledge of American literature.
The Frost student who wonders about the contrast between
Frost's conservative politics and the more socially active ideas
of the classic New England writers must consult this essay. More
importantly, Foster shows the problem to be only one consideration in a host of others which should be examined when Frost's
relationship with New England is discussed.

   Foster's analysis of the New England intellectual and artistic
tradition is one way to approach the question of Frost and his
home region. Another is W. G. O'Donnell's, who, in "Robert
Frost and New England: A Revaluation" (*Yale Review*, Summer 1948), concentrates on Frost's poetry. The two approaches
complement each other to provide a rather full investigation.
O'Donnell wants to reevaluate Frost for several reasons. First,
the poet's fame is unusual. Next, the attacks on Frost for what
negative critics consider a homespun philosophy need to be countered. Finally, enough of Frost's work has been published to
warrant a reappraisal. These are certainly legitimate reasons, but

it is interesting that in the course of the reappraisal O'Donnell falls for Frost's public pose. Listing Frost's "gifts" other than the poetry, O'Donnell exposes his ignorance of Frost the man when he assigns to him a personality of "extraordinary charm and integrity." The Frost whom O'Donnell praises is that of the public entertainer, the man on the platform who gives the impression of wisdom and horse sense while breaking up those in the front row with his little asides. And yet O'Donnell is aware of what this pose has meant to Frost's public, for he realizes that the poet's performance contributes more to his reputation than to an understanding of the poetry. Add to this observation the fact that most readers know Frost primarily from anthology pieces, and the problem arises of a well-known poet whose full artistic range remains unappreciated. One of the problems, writes O'Donnell, is that unlike Yeats or Eliot, Frost has declined to furnish signposts to his own development. Because he has refused to supply notes or extended essays directly analyzing his own poetry, he has inadvertently fostered the false opinion that he has not developed at all. In O'Donnell's words, the "clarity of his verse has obscured the complexities of his development." Too many serious readers who ought to know better continue to think of the poet as one who remains smugly sure of all he thought was true. O'Donnell plans to remedy the situation by discussing Frost's books in the order of their publication.

Immediately branding *A Boy's Will* a "failure as a collection," he complains that it lacks unity of tone. This is a curious charge, for, as most students of Frost know, the poet was highly conscious of the overall tone and organization of his books. *A Boy's Will* in particular was arranged to communicate the drama of a youth finding his way (see Donald T. Haynes, "The Narrative Unity of *A Boy's Will,*" *PMLA*, May 1972). Closer to the mark is O'Donnell's criticism of the book's poetic diction. Nearly every contemporary reader will flinch when he reads, for example, of the youth "fain to list." Yet *A Boy's Will* established Frost's ties with New England: "Not since Thoreau had anyone responded so sensitively to the particularities of a rural landscape" (1948, p. 701). According to O'Donnell, the problem with Frost's use of the New England scene in the first volume is that the poet makes the special value of the native detail an end in itself. Frost has "not yet developed his later ability to make the local truth in nature an integral part of the over-all purpose of a poem" (1948, p. 702). This is a shrewd comment, one which seems valid when the use of New England details in

North of Boston is compared with that in *A Boy's Will*. For in
his second book, Frost selects his New England scene to reflect
the decline of Yankee prosperity. His characters know more
of paying off a mortgage or of holding a rock-infested farm
together than of mid-nineteenth-century Concord.

O'Donnell includes several paragraphs of statistics to support
his argument for a declining New England, and he insists, correctly in my opinion, that *North of Boston* should be read
against the background of what he terms this "social and economic disturbance." Those who think of Frost as an affirmative
voice have not read "Home Burial" or "A Servant to Servants."
And yet it is obvious that Frost loves the Yankee region. One
of O'Donnell's best comments is that the heart of the experience
in *North of Boston* can be found in "this complicated double
movement of rejection and acceptance" (1948, p. 704). In other
words, the second Frost book shows both a rebellion against a
rigid way of life and a mature adjustment. The double movement saves his later affirmation from the sentimentality and nostalgia found in Masters' *Spoon River Anthology*. O'Donnell's
discussion of *North of Boston* continues for several pages, and
it remains one of the best shorter analyses ever published. He
challenges those who believe that Frost should protest more
against the harsh Yankee farm life when he writes that Frost is
not a pamphleteer but a poet. He dismisses the argument which
holds that Frost admires the alienation interpreted so vividly
in his poems. And he shows how the obviously youthful accents
of *A Boy's Will* give way to the mature vision of *North of
Boston*.

By the publication of *A Witness Tree* (1942), Frost's sev-
enth volume, the poet's voice has developed to become that of
a "man who has lived many years beyond the tragic discovery
and is now looking back upon life. He did not go bounding
through existence from one happiness to another" (1948, p.
707). "Happiness Makes Up in Height for What It Lacks in
Length" illustrates, by contrast with "Going for Water" from
A Boy's Will, the change. Recalling T. S. Eliot's return to
New England in 1932, and Henry James' in 1904, O'Donnell
shows how these two great artists failed to penetrate the surface of Frost's Northeast Corner. Eliot found nothing but failure and defeat, a scene "more desperate than the desert," whereas James discovered primarily the beauty of the wealthy summer folk, a scene out of touch with the realities of the local
inhabitants. Frost sees the same failure and defects which so

discouraged James and Eliot. But unlike them, he realizes that while much of the older New England has been lost forever, something of value has endured—a vitality, a sense of life strong enough to meet the challenge of the conditions. The author of "Home Burial" and of "A Servant to Servants" is the same man who writes some of our loveliest lyrics, and both types of poems grow from his Yankee background.

O'Donnell is a good enough critic to go beyond the debate over Frost's status as a New England writer. As he notes, Frost remains a minor figure if he is defined as a voice of New England. But to the extent that "he makes his New England universal in meaning and implication, he is a significant writer" (1948, p. 710). Frost's ability to portray local truths must be allied with an ability to speak in terms of experiences "that are valid for those who know New England only as a small territorial division on the map of the United States." And it is here that O'Donnell feels the poet falls short. Other than in *North of Boston* and in a few later poems, Frost, according to O'Donnell fails to achieve a significant universality. In the weaker poems like "A Roadside Stand" and "Build Soil," he establishes an unpleasant dichotomy between city and country. But in "Birches," "Spring Pools," "Stopping by Woods on a Snowy Evening," "Directive," and about three dozen more, he curbs his declamatory voice and reaches the heights of true poetry. This nicely written essay retains its value today primarily because O'Donnell has no ax to grind. He is fully aware of Frost's shortcomings, and he willingly admits them. Happily, however, he believes that an artist has the right to be judged on his best work, and thus he evaluates the poet's relationship with New England in the light of what he considers to be Frost's most successful book, *North of Boston*. Readers of this article may not agree with O'Donnell's emphatic praise of the second volume, and they may regret his easy acceptance of Frost's public pose, but they will certainly realize the value of his remarks. His essay is as pleasurable to read as it is informative.

Equally impressive is James M. Cox's "Robert Frost and the Edge of the Clearing" (*Virginia Quarterly Review*, Winter 1959). His article is primarily concerned with the relationship between Frost the poet and Frost the public figure. Professor Cox suggests that the key character in many of Frost's poems is the same figure who dominates the stage when giving a lecture: "For Frost's primal subject is always poetry and the poet— *his* poetry and himself the poet" (1959, p. 87). In this way Frost has cultivated the position of literary man as public entertainer, a role last successfully played by Mark Twain. Cox's conclusion, intriguing yet debatable, is that Frost the public figure is a natural extension of the poetic career, rather than a calculated addition to it. While developing these ideas, Cox adds to the critical appraisal of Frost as New Englander.

To begin, Cox believes, unlike O'Donnell, that Frost has successfully endowed his provincial center with universal significance. Like William Faulkner, the poet has created a myth about his home region. The myth's hero is the New England farmer who wears the "anti-mask of the traditional poet." Cox's first important point for our purposes is his suggestion that Frost's ability literally to be a farmer-poet distinguishes him from Wordsworth: "Wordsworth played the part of the Poet concerned with common man, but Frost has persistently cast himself in the rôle of the common man concerned with poetry" (1959, p. 75). This stance may cut him off from the philosophical poetry which Wordsworth developed, but it nevertheless permits him to excel in matters of irony, wit, comedy, and dramatic narrative. This is a significant observation, one which should invite more study of Frost's relationship with British and American Romantic poets.

Professor Cox points out what so many readers continue to miss—that despite Frost's fame for depicting his region realistically, he has never been a "mere reflector" of the New England scene. Rather he has "managed to create the illusion of making the world he describes, and in his hands the region north of Boston becomes a self-sustaining yet surprisingly inclusive microcosm with the character of Frost himself at its center" (1959, p. 77). In other words, Frost reshapes the New England region as an extension of himself. Even his celebrated skill in reproducing Yankee speech mannerisms is seen as a means by which the central character, Frost, stamps his signature upon the created locale.

Cox's argument was new in 1959, and it offers an exciting counterpoint to the other articles thus far discussed in this chapter. He illustrates by paralleling Frost to Emerson and Thoreau, who also cast their shadows "upon the landscape" they surveyed. As Cox shows, Frost avoids Emerson's and Thoreau's delight in abstract thinking while assimilating many of their methods and attitudes. Like them, he is determined to know his world. But, significantly, unlike them, he does not begin with the assurance that definite assumptions exist: "His work has been no experiment to test himself, but the venture of a lifetime" (1959, p. 78).

Similarly, Frost advances far beyond another New England poet, Longfellow. Both are able to write about past experiences, but Longfellow unfortunately retreats "back into nostalgia." Cox picks up one of Frost's key images—the woods—to explain that the poet forces a clearing in the woods "which Longfellow declined to enter." Interpreting the clearing as the world between the wild and the tame, Cox uses "The Last Mowing" to show how Frost points out beauty in this meeting place of order and chaos. The woods are always moving to reclaim the clearing, forcing the poet to match his strength against the "alien entanglements" which they represent. This drama recalls Emerson's lesson of self-reliance. The difference, of course, is that while Frost may accept "the antagonists of the Emersonian drama," he nevertheless lacks Emerson's religious serenity. Thus, he writes of a more fearful chaos, showing how the "drama of existence" becomes man's ability to place himself in the clearing and confront the dark woods. Unlike Emerson, Frost "knows that the material of the unwrought poem inheres in that wilderness" (1959, p. 80). Cox argues that the literal facts of Frost's New England are important, not for themselves but for the way they supply the poet with the materials needed to create a "scenic analogy against which the Frost character performs his act. . . ." In the remainder of the essay, beyond the concerns of this chapter, Cox analyzes some of Frost's "woods" poems and those like "A Servant to Servants" and "An Old Man's Winter Night" which illustrate how hard it is to hold the clearing once it is won. He supplies especially interesting readings of "Stopping by Woods on a Snowy Evening" and "Directive." This impressive article remains valuable to both the general reader and the scholar, for it offers a persuasive interpretation while remaining free of the burdening rhetoric of many critical essays.

J. Albert Robbins' "America and the Poet: Whitman, Hart Crane, and Frost" (*American Poetry*, 1965) is not nearly as informative about Frost as Cox's or O'Donnell's articles, but it offers another point of view on the question of Frost and New England. The title is misleading, for it suggests an analysis of the three poets. Instead, Robbins focuses upon Whitman, using Crane and Frost as examples of more contemporary poets in the Whitman tradition. His remarks about Frost are fascinating, if only because they insist upon a connection between Frost and Whitman which most readers deny. Frost himself is on record as describing Whitman's style as "bumptious" (*Selected Letters of Robert Frost*, Mar. 10, 1924). Robbins is, of course, correct when he writes that to accept Frost as an "updated Longfellow" is to misread him. His primary point regarding Frost is that the poet both belongs to and is independent of the tradition of Emerson and Whitman. This observation would not be worth noticing were it not for the inclusion of Whitman.

Robbins writes that Frost resembles "Whitman in his sense of brotherhood and his faith in American character and purpose" (1965, p. 61). The problem is that Robbins fails to define "brotherhood." This is not quibbling, for many readers of Frost recall Louis Untermeyer's statement that Frost could not say "brotherhood" without sneering. Perhaps Robbins means "neighborliness," a quality in Frost first celebrated by G. R. Elliott (see chapter 2), but we are never certain. Surely, one could argue that the Frost of, say, *A Further Range* seems very far indeed from Whitman's famous expressions of brotherhood. Similarly, one wonders what Robbins means by "faith in American character and purpose," for in so many of the later poems, particularly those in *A Further Range* and *Steeple Bush*, Frost seems highly critical of the America he sees about him. Consequently, one can only question Robbins' statement that if Frost in any way combines the qualities of both Emerson and Whitman, "it is in merging Emerson's intellectuality and tight poetic form with Whitman's insistent love for men and his poetry of feeling" (1965, p. 61). A few of the critics discussed thus far might challenge the suggestion that Frost illustrates Emerson's intellectuality, but nearly all would find debatable the implication that Frost reflects Whitman's brotherly love.

Robbins seems more convincing when he shows how the land means as much to Frost as it does to Whitman. Woods and stars for Frost, roads and seashores for Whitman—in either case the imagery is used to communicate a deeply felt response to the physical demands of the land itself. Yet, as Robbins points out, there is a crucial difference in tone: "The often tense insistence of Emerson and Whitman is gone, and with Frost we are persuaded by calm insights—all illumined with a humour that flickers at the rim of sobriety" (1965, p. 63). Robbins' discussion of Whitman and his disciple Hart Crane is finally more persuasive than the remarks about Frost. For all of his insights concerning what Whitman has meant to American poetry, he never really clarifies why he includes Frost in this essay.

Although Barton L. St. Armand's "The Power of Sympathy

in the Poetry of Robinson and Frost: The 'Inside' vs. the 'Outside' Narrative" (*American Quarterly*, Fall 1967) is more a comparison of two Yankee poets than a discussion of Frost's relationship to New England, it says enough about Frost's handling of New England characters to warrant comment here. In this convincing and nicely written essay, St. Armand begins with the common subject matter of Robinson and Frost—a decaying New England locale and its wracked people—and goes on to show the differences between the ways the two poets communicate sympathy. As he points out, both poets roam the same countryside, but their psychic journeys remain "miles apart." The poetry of defeat which we recognize in Robinson becomes the poetry of survival in Frost. St. Armand's most significant conclusion is that Robinson gets "inside" his New England characters, whereas Frost prefers to stay "outside." These different points of view naturally affect the measure of sympathy generally communicated in the poems. Selecting "Captain Craig" to illustrate Robinson's handling of a New England personality, St. Armand argues that the difference between Craig and the hardened dilettantes who adopt him results from Craig's Emersonian optimism. He quotes from Emerson's "The Poet" to show the parallels between Craig's philosophy of life and Emerson's beliefs. More important is St. Armand's analysis of Robinson's technique, for he denies that "Captain Craig" is a character sketch. It is, rather, a "poetic psychograph," an "inside" narrative. The poem supports this definition because it explores Craig's mind and that of his disciples. And because Robinson succeeds in establishing an interaction between these different states of mind, he is able to develop both an intellectual and an emotional dialectic. Attitudes change in the poem, especially as the narrator becomes responsive to what St. Armand calls Craig's "Existential-Emersonian commitment." Thus, sympathy is the poem's "key notion," communicated by the narrator's growing compassion which matches his new understanding of Craig's philosophy.

Frost's poems exhibit the same high level of craftsmanship as Robinson's, but they develop from a radically different point of view. Whereas Robinson's narrative poems usually express the inside of his characters' minds, Frost's narratives reflect the outside. This is an interesting interpretation, later made convincing by St. Armand's development of it. For he points out that Frost, being more of a "terse" New Englander, will not let the reader into the minds of his Yankee characters. This is not to say that we fail to know his people. We learn a great deal

about them, but that knowledge usually comes from watching
the results of their action rather than from observing the work-
ings of their minds. Unlike many of the characters in Robinson's narratives, Frost's often hold themselves in, refusing to
communicate, and finally inflicting "pain and misery on their
own souls and the souls of others" (1967, p. 570). St. Armand
uses "Home Burial" and "The Hill Wife" for illustration, certainly good choices to point out the problem of communication
in Frost's poetry. Discussing the final barrier which will always
separate Amy and her husband ("Home Burial"), he argues that
we can only guess at its cause. Similarly, we do not experience
the wife's loneliness in "The Hill Wife" but rather the "chilling
finality of the results of that loneliness." Thus, concludes St.
Armand, we cannot feel compassion for Frost's characters, the
way we do for Robinson's, because Frost will not let us. No
value judgment is implied—two New England poets handle the
same material differently. The tension in Frost's narratives results from "a concrete external conflict of the self with something outside the self, which in turn results from some internal
conflict within the self which is rarely, if ever, glimpsed" (1967,
p. 572). The result is that our sympathies are less with Amy or
the hill wife than against the undefined "thing" which hurts
them so. As far as it goes, this analysis is persuasive. But discussion of only one poem from Robinson's canon and two from
Frost's shows that the study is limited.

Perhaps it is fitting that the last article to be discussed in this
chapter is also one of the most comprehensive. In "The New
England Tradition" (*American Libraries*, July-Aug. and Oct.
1971), Hayden Carruth is concerned with what it means to be
a New Englander and with how that particular tradition affects
Yankee artists and thinkers. Clearly his scope goes beyond a
special interest in Robert Frost, yet readers of Frost will find
useful the way he places the poet in the New England tradition. He admits immediately that this heritage cannot be defined:
"No, the New England tradition is not in what I say about it,
but in my poems, and then in all the poems and other imaginative works of all the other and greater artists who have inhabited
this region from the beginning, in their concretely articulated
feelings, and finally in the works of the greatest artist of us all,
the common New England mind that has generated, and continues to generate, our language and our lore" (1971, p. 692).

In the first part of this long essay, Carruth analyzes the effect
of Puritanism upon the New England mind. Challenging the

popular misconception of the Puritans as shallow, hypocritical, and negative, he concludes that the Puritans were "actually as good a company as any nation could hope to have for its progenitors" (1971, p. 697). He concedes that their opposition to the arts militated against the fledgling country's creativity, but he nevertheless believes that their virtues continue to help shape the mainstream of American development. For better or for worse, Puritanism was the base of New England culture. For this reason Carruth "wipes out" the whole New England eighteenth century with one stroke, for he does not believe that the people of that era contributed anything "genuinely formative" to the New England heritage. Similarly, he "jettisons" the nineteenth-century Yankee intellectuals associated with Boston and Cambridge. Brownson, Longfellow, Lowell, Holmes, Howells, and Henry James are all dismissed. He bases this surprising exclusion of them from the New England tradition not on aesthetic considerations but on his conviction that their development, though rooted in Puritanism, "was away from New England and toward nationalism and internationalism, i.e. toward cosmopolitan high culture" (1971, p. 697). Reading this, one can only wonder if Carruth exhibits the same narrowness of mind with which popular history brands the Puritans. How can one write about the New England tradition and exclude nineteenth-century Boston and Cambridge? Yet Carruth defends his position well. He admits that Boston-Cambridge has always been the capital of New England, but he insists that beginning in the last century it "lost touch with its own constituents." Developing his unusual point of view, he argues that the true vitality of New England has originated not in metropolitan drawing rooms but in the rural landscape. The key date may be 1835, for that was the year that Emerson turned his back on Boston-Cambridge and established himself in Concord. What follows is a lengthy discussion of Emerson's intellectual positions, most of which is outside the concern of this chapter. Perhaps Carruth's most important conclusion about Emerson is that the Concord sage was repairing Puritanism by restoring "vitality of faith" to New England. Emerson may have been rhapsodic where the Puritans were rational, but, says Carruth, his "spiritualized morality, his awareness of the spiritual unity of meaning and being, and his view of the natural world as the mask of spiritual reality, were close, at least functionally," to Puritan beliefs (1971, p. 698).

After a short commentary on Thoreau, Robinson, and Charles Ives, Carruth turns to Frost. Most of the essay's second part is devoted to Frost, for, as Carruth notes, "in his poetry every element of the tradition is combined, there to be given the thrust of his sometimes hot and sometimes vacantly, terrifyingly cold personality" (1971, p. 944). Happily, Carruth decides that he need add nothing to the "reams" already published about Frost's closeness to nature or about his New England "cultural relevance." Instead he begins his discussion of Frost with an analysis of a generally ignored poem, one which Carruth considers among Frost's best, "The Vanishing Red." He comments upon the end-stopped lines and upon the successful blend of speech patterns and metrical rhythms. But his most significant observation concerns the Miller's laugh, which he correctly points to as the heart of the poem. In what must be one of the best short analyses of "The Vanishing Red" yet published, Carruth offers the unusual reading that the laugh reflects the center of Frost's poetic temperament: "the blackest, bitterest despair in three hundred years of New England tradition." Insisting that there is nothing to match this laugh in Hawthorne, James, and Robinson, he argues that one must go back to Wigglesworth's *Day of Doom* (1662) to find an acceptable parallel of a man destroying himself. Carruth names "The Hill Wife," "Neither Out Far Nor In Deep," "Acquainted with the Night," and others as additional examples of Frost's vision of mankind doomed. Yet the poet's greatness comes from his refusal to shriek—"the vision is so quietly reported that the horror almost skips past us, and that itself adds to the horror" (1971, p. 945). Carruth overemphasizes the place of doom in Frost's poetry, but his discussion of the way the poet handles horror and fear is sound. Like so many commentators in the past two decades, he points particularly to those poems which challenge the false myth of Frost as a gentle nature poet.

Frost also illustrates what Carruth calls New England's "persistent trace of Emersonian spiritual aspiration," except that in Frost's poetry it is more a stand against despair than a temptation to hope. Noting that many of the poems allude to this trace, Carruth nevertheless believes that the poems which do are "demonstrably" weaker than those which report horror. As examples he names "For Once, Then, Something" and "The Strong Are Saying Nothing." His comment about the latter is correct— that the poem is too explicit, too lacking in Yankee understatement to rank with Frost's best. But his criticism of the former— that the final lines need a "solider tone"—remains unclear. Still, his primary interest is not in the poems themselves but in the way the better ones illustrate Frost's mastery of the Yankee penchant for understatement. Carruth believes that Frost is at his best when the poet describes the ultimate failure, "the failure of love. The earth is rich, the flowers will bloom, men and women will love one another—and it changes nothing" (1971, p. 947). At its bleakest, Frost's despair is finally colder than that of any other major poet. With this comment, Carruth ends his discussion of Frost, naming him "the furthest evolution of the New England type we have had so far. . . ."

This opinion places Carruth in an opposite camp from Malcolm Cowley. Indeed, the polar opposition of their assessments of Frost's position in the New England tradition indicates the question's complexity. The Frost student might even use their essays as the outer boundaries of the debate, reading the other opinions in the light of these opposed points of view. The crucial factor remains the particular critic's definition of the New England tradition. Those, like Cowley, who see it as a matter of liberal politics and active social concerns will be forced either to exclude Frost or to lament his defection from the standards of Emerson and Hawthorne. But those who define the tradition as a matter of spiritual heritage—or even as a particular way of treating the New England locale in art—will probably affirm Frost's place in the long tradition, and then go on to show how he has assimilated the tradition's elements, shaping them to his own needs, and in so doing, giving them new direction. This latter interpretation seems more nearly correct.

References

Brower, Reuben A.
  1963. *The Poetry of Robert Frost: Constellations of Intention.* New York: Oxford Univ. Pr.
Carroll, Gladys Hasty
  1935. "New England Sees It Through," *Saturday Review of Literature* Nov. 9, pp. 3–4, 14, 17.
Carruth, Hayden
  1971. "The New England Tradition," *American Libraries* July–Aug., Oct., pp. 690–700, 938–48; reprinted in *Regional Perspectives: An Examination of America's Literary Heritage,* ed. John Gordon Burke, pp. 1–48. Chicago: American Library Assn., 1973.

Cestre, Charles
   1926. "Amy Lowell, Robert Frost, and Edwin Arlington Robinson," *Johns Hopkins Alumni Magazine*, Mar., pp. 363–88.
Chamberlain, William
   1969. "The Emersonianism of Robert Frost," *Emerson Society
Quarterly* Oct.-Dec., pp. 61–66.
Coffin, Robert P. Tristram
   1938. *New Poetry of New England: Frost and Robinson.* Bal-
timore: Johns Hopkins Pr.
Cook, Reginald L.
   1958. "Emerson and Frost: A Parallel of Seers," *New England
Quarterly* June, pp. 200–17.
   1964. "A Parallel of Parablists: Thoreau and Frost" in *The Thoreau Centennial*, ed. Walter Harding, pp. 65–79. Albany: State
Univ. Pr. of New York.
Cowley, Malcolm
   1944. "The Case against Mr. Frost," *New Republic* Sept. 11,
18, pp. 312–13, 345–47.
Cox, James M.
   1959. "Robert Frost and the Edge of the Clearing," *Virginia
Quarterly Review* Winter, pp. 73–88.
Cox, Sidney Hayes
   1934. "New England and Robert Frost," *New Mexico Quarterly* May, pp. 89–95.
Dougherty, James P.
   1966. "Robert Frost's 'Directive' to the Wilderness," *American Quarterly* Summer, pp. 208–19.
Duvall, S. P. C.
   1960. "Robert Frost's 'Directive' out of *Walden*," *American Literature* Jan., pp. 482–88.
Foster, Charles Howell
   1945. "Robert Frost and the New England Tradition" in *Elizabethan Studies and Other Essays*, Univ. of Colorado Studies,
series B, Oct., pp. 370–81.
Frost, Robert
   1954. "Thoreau's 'Walden': A Discussion between Robert Frost
and Reginald Cook," *Listener* Aug. 26, pp. 319–20.
   1959. "On Emerson," *Daedalus* Fall, pp. 712–18.
   1970. "A Tribute to Wordsworth," *Cornell Library Journal*
Spring, pp. 78–99.
Gerber, Philip L.
   1966. *Robert Frost.* New York: Twayne.
Hoffman, Daniel G.
   1960. "Thoreau's 'Old Settler' and Frost's Paul Bunyan," *Journal
of American Folklore* July–Sept., pp. 236–38.

Lynen, John F.
1960. *The Pastoral Art of Robert Frost*. New Haven: Yale Univ. Pr.; revised ed., 1964.

Monteiro, George
1968. "Redemption Through Nature: A Recurring Theme in Thoreau, Frost and Richard Wilbur," *American Quarterly* Winter, pp. 795–809.

Moore, Merrill
1937. "Poetic Agrarianism: Old Style," *Sewanee Review* Oct.-Dec., pp. 507–9.

O'Donnell, W. G.
1948. "Robert Frost and New England: A Revaluation," *Yale Review* Summer, pp. 698–712.

Parsons, Thornton H.
1963. "Thoreau, Frost, and the American Humanist Tradition," *Emerson Society Quarterly* Oct.-Dec., pp. 33–43.

Robbins, J. Albert
1965. "America and the Poet: Whitman, Hart Crane and Frost" in *American Poetry*, ed. Irvin Ehrenpreis, pp. 45–67. Stratford-Upon-Avon Studies 7, London: Edward Arnold.

Ryan, Alvan S.
1959. "Frost and Emerson: Voice and Vision," *Massachusetts Review* Oct., pp. 5–23.

St. Armand, Barton L.
1967. "The Power of Sympathy in the Poetry of Robinson and Frost: The 'Inside' vs. the 'Outside' Narrative," *American Quarterly* Fall, pp. 564–74.

Squires, Radcliffe
1963. *The Major Themes of Robert Frost*. Ann Arbor: Univ. of Michigan Pr.

Thompson, Lawrance
1940. *Emerson and Frost: Critics of Their Times*. Folcroft, Pa.: Folcroft Pr. for Philobiblon Club (250 copies originally published; reprinted 1969).
1942. *Fire and Ice: The Art and Thought of Robert Frost*. New York: Henry Holt.
1964. (editor) *Selected Letters of Robert Frost*. New York: Holt, Rinehart and Winston.
1966. *Robert Frost: The Early Years, 1874–1915*. New York: Holt, Rinehart and Winston.

Waggoner, Hyatt Howe
1941. "The Humanistic Idealism of Robert Frost," *American Literature* Nov., pp. 207–23.

Winters, Yvor
1957. "Robert Frost: or, the Spiritual Drifter as Poet," in *The*

Function of Criticism: Problems and Exercises. Denver: Alan
Swallow; also published in *Sewanee Review,* Aug. 1948, pp.
564–96.

Selected Additional Readings

Cook, Reginald L.
  1949. "Frost as a Parablist," *Accent* Aug., pp. 33–41.
Francis, Robert
  1953. "Robert Frost from His Green Mountain," *Dalhousie Review* 33:117–27.
Hoffman, Daniel G.
  1951. "Robert Frost's Paul Bunyan: A Frontier Hero in New
  England Exile," *Midwest Folklore,* pp. 13–18.
Moore, Virginia
  1931. "Robert Frost of New Hampshire," *Yale Review* May, pp.
  627–29.
Smith, Fred
  1932. "The Sound of a Yankee Voice," *Commonweal* Jan. 13, pp.
  297–98.
Stovall, Floyd
  1943. "Robinson and Frost" in *American Idealism,* pp. 167–86.
  Norman: Univ. of Oklahoma Pr.
Thompson, Lawrance
  1959. "A Native to the Grain of the American Idiom," *Saturday
  Review of Literature* Mar. 21, pp. 21, 55–56.
Van Doren, Mark
  1951. "Robert Frost's America," *Atlantic Monthly* June, pp.
  32–34.
Warren, Robert Penn
  1928. "Hawthorne, Anderson and Frost," *New Republic* May
  16, pp. 399–401.
Weygandt, Cornelius
  1934. *The White Hills.* New York: Henry Holt, pp. 231–54.
Yates, Norris
  1957. "An Instance of Parallel Imagery in Hawthorne, Melville,
  and Frost," *Philological Quarterly* Apr., pp. 276–80.

CHAPTER 5

Robert Frost as Nature Poet

O ne problem related to the discussion of Frost's literary heritage is definition of the poet's concept of nature. What does it mean to label Frost a nature poet? No one seems to agree. And yet nearly every student of modern American poetry will name Frost when asked if any significant nature poetry has been published since 1900. The reasons for this answer are obvious: Frost writes about birch trees and rose pogonias, mending walls, mowing, and going for water; his protagonists are nearly always isolated farmers, country laborers, or the poet-figure himself on a rural excursion; and his situations consistently revolve around country problems in a manner which provides an implied contrast with urban life. Serious readers know that these characteristics are only the surface qualities of nature poetry. An analysis of Frost's uses of nature must probe deeper. More intriguing —and more difficult—questions must be asked. What is Frost's concept of nature? Is he a leftover Romantic, a poet who was unwillingly pulled into the twentieth century? How does he handle post-Darwinian ideas of nature? Does he believe in communication with nature, or does he define it as nonhuman otherness? The variety of opinions discussed in this chapter illustrates the extent of critical disagreement. Very few can agree upon a reading of a sixteen line "nature" poem like "Stopping by Woods on a Snowy Evening," much less rally around a definition of the implications in his nature poetry. One of the more crucial questions for the reader to note is whether or not Frost's disavowal of philosophical poetry denies him the name nature poet. Just as difficult to determine, however, is what he means by woods, or stars, or roads. For this reason, the essays which discuss his specific natural images will be evaluated as well as those which analyze his status in the long tradition of nature poetry. Because chapter 2 is devoted to the early criticism of Frost, this chapter will begin with articles published after 1925.

Although not strictly concerned with Frost as a nature poet,

John Farrar's "Robert Frost and Other Green Mountain Writers" (*English Journal*, Oct. 1927) makes a good point of departure. For Farrar explores the apparent paradox in the fact that while authors sell their art in urban centers like New York, they nevertheless retreat to rural settings when they write. As he explains, country noises are occasionally loud, perhaps, but they are also less insistent—the noise seems only part of the scene. Mentioning Willa Cather, Edna Ferber, Edwin Arlington Robinson, and others, Farrar remarks that so many writers choose rural New England, especially Vermont, to write in even though they are not natives of the state. This observation is especially true of Frost, who, though born in California, established New England farms as if they were ancestral homes. The interesting point in this otherwise very minor article is that Farrar sees through Frost's mask of the farmer as artist.

There is no malice in Farrar's picture of the poet, no hint of exposé, no effort to find the "true" Robert Frost. He simply dismisses the poet's public image which was so popular in the 1920s: that of a farmer-poet who tramps mountains and who sweats with the mowing, the apple-picking, and the putting in of seed. According to Farrar, Frost has farmed, but is no farmer, just as he loves Vermont's mountains, but is no mountaineer. Yet, says Farrar, he has written the "best bucolic poetry ever produced in America." Although Farrar does not drive home the point, he is one of the first to challenge the Frost myth when he shows that the poet need not be a man of the soil in order to write superior nature poetry. Everyone accepts this generality, of course, but Frost in particular liked to nurture the image of himself as rustic man writing bucolic poetry. Better say that he, like so many authors, retreats to the country in order to find the calm necessary to write the poems he will sell in the city. Farrar goes astray on two points: first, that Frost sees, "for the most part, gentleness in nature," and second, that he is more the philosopher than poet. Both of these observations are wrong, but neither is developed enough to undercut the interest today's reader will find in this otherwise negligible essay.

A more significant study, as well as one of the earliest to focus on the meaning of the recurring dark woods imagery in Frost's poetry, is J. McBride Dabbs' "Robert Frost and the Dark Woods" (*Yale Review*, Mar. 1934). Dabbs' thesis is clearly stated: that whereas Frost's poems are immediately notable for the living quality of their realism, they are memorable for the "after-images" which linger. He finds Frost a true symbolist because the poet chooses the particular to represent the general as part of, in Goethe's words, the "living and instantaneous revelation of the inscrutable." For our purposes, the key to Dabbs' essay is his comment that the majority of Frost's symbolic poems focuses on man's relationship with nature. "Yet, though nature threatens man with destruction, its very challenge creates courage, and so life, within him. Nature exists—so far as man is concerned—to be fought against; but not to be destroyed, even were that possible, for that would be the destruction of man himself" (1934, p. 516). This statement may seem obvious to today's students of Frost, but it represents a significant step in 1934. Farrar's article, with its mention of Frost's faith in gentle nature, illustrates the popular view of the time—one which unfortunately persists even today—but Dabbs' suggestion of a more threatening nature is correct.

An equally important observation about Frost as nature poet is Dabbs' realization that Frost uses nature for more than the isolated backdrop of man's actions. Again and again in the earlier criticism, we read of the praise accorded Frost's accurate portraits of natural processes as if his main goal were photographs-in-words. Closer to the truth is the argument that Frost's primary concern is social man *in* nature. A close reading of the poems will reveal the poet's consistent interest in the interaction between the human figure and the natural scene. One of the most important symbols of this meeting, one Dabbs believes has a personal value to Frost, is the woods. He defines the woods as symbolizing "nature itself with its challenge and its fascination." The strength of this article is that Dabbs refuses to wrench the woods imagery into one meaning. Reading some of the earlier "woods" poems—"Into My Own," "Now Close the Windows," "The Sound of Trees"—he admits the difficulty of determining whether or not Frost's fascination with woods ever evolves into distinct fear. And it is here that Dabbs makes his key point for readers in 1934: that despite fear of the woods in one poem and love in the next, the most consistent characteristic is fascination. The woods play an ambiguous role in the scope of Frost's poetry, even though their meaning may be clear in an individual poem. The poet-figure pulls back from the woods as many times as he glances longingly toward them, and it is this "hesitancy," writes Dabbs, that makes Frost modern instead of a nineteenth-century Romantic poet. To the secluded nook in the woods Frost has added the modern shadow of doubt: should he plunge into the uncharted trees, or should he remain in the clearing?

The poet's classic use of the woods image is "Stopping by Woods on a Snowy Evening," a poem in which Dabbs hears the "insistent whisper of death at the heart of life." One might quarrel with his reading of this particular poem, but credit must be given to the general thrust of his essay—one of the first articles to challenge the misconception about Frost's use of nature.

Joseph Warren Beach's discussion of Frost in *The Concept of Nature in Nineteenth-Century English Poetry* (1936) is less specialized than Dabbs', though not necessarily less penetrating, because he analyzes Frost's place in the whole scope of English nature poetry. His fullest discussion of Frost can be found in the chapter "The Vanishing Point," where he argues that the "philosophical concept of nature has virtually disappeared altogether" from contemporary English and American poetry. Explaining his thesis, Beach insists that the modern literary mind is no longer willing to grapple with the traditional question of man's place in nature. Descriptions of natural beauty have been divorced from concepts of universal nature with the result that the earth and stars are either regarded as scenery or studied as objects. In addition, today's poets refuse to laud nature's inherent order or to point to it as evidence that man's fate will evolve rationally. Beach suggests other causes for the vanishing of nature poetry, but the heart of his argument is always that the philosophical concepts of nature, so prevalent in the last two centuries, have gone out of style. Contemporary poets have switched their allegiance from philosophical abstractions to a concern with man and his daily dramas.

To illustrate his thesis, Beach begins with the English Georgians. This discussion need not concern us, although it should be noted that he uses these writers to show what he terms "the unimportance of 'nature' " to twentieth-century poets. An evaluation of the Georgians is clearly an acceptable transition to Frost because of his close association with them during his sojourn in England from 1912 to 1915. In each case, Georgians and Frost, Beach denies the name "nature poet" because of the absence of philosophy in their poetry. What we have in this book is not a study of how various poets put different elements of nature poetry to work, but, rather, the establishment of a definition of nature poetry which is then applied to the writer. If his art fits the definition, he will earn the title of nature poet. But what if the definition clashes with the poems? The outcome of this aesthetic fracas is preordained, for Beach refuses to adjust his concept of nature poetry. And since it is based on nineteenth-century writing, it necessarily finds itself unable to accommodate twentieth-century poets. Poems lacking in philosophical character, no matter the intensity of their concern with nature, cannot qualify as nature poetry.

Frost's poems provide Beach with a brilliant illustration: *A Boy's Will* pays homage to "the ritualism of nature"; Frost, of all American poets, is the one most "feelingly" attached to earth; and his poems generally reveal an acute awareness of man's metaphysical dilemmas. But Frost is not a nature poet because "none of our poets has more steadily declined to formulate his thought in philosophical terms" (1936, p. 552). The closest Frost comes to meeting the test is in "West-Running Brook." Yet, writes Beach, Frost's invocation of nature in this poem is so modest as to pale before the "Power so awesomely regarded by Shelley and Emerson." Given Beach's definition, one cannot quarrel with his conclusions. His massive book remains a valuable source for those with questions about the development of English-language poetry during the past two centuries. But the suspicion lingers that Beach would have been happier if Frost, as well as others, had followed Wordsworth's lead, or Shelley's, or Emerson's, or anyone else's which might have persuaded him to continue the tradition of philosophical nature poetry. Rather than evaluate why and how the change has occurred, or discuss the ways new concepts of nature are revealed in contemporary poetry, Beach looks about him and laments what he reads.

Twenty years later Robert Langbaum published what amounts to a companion piece to Beach's book. In "The New Nature Poetry" (*American Scholar*, Summer 1959), he picks up the subject from where Beach laid it down—the emergence of twentieth-century poetry. Indeed, Beach's thesis is the subject of Professor Langbaum's opening paragraphs. Noting that Beach has the philosophical and protoreligious idea of nature in mind when he argues that the concept of nature has disappeared from contemporary poetry, Langbaum points out that, to the contrary, nature poetry is very much alive. Far from being extinct, it enjoys a revival of such high quality that Langbaum believes it is better than it has been in a long time. The key to his disagreement with Beach depends, of course, on the definition of nature poetry. Within the limits of his definition, Beach is correct when he laments the extinction of nature poetry. But, as Langbaum notes, notions of nature have been radically altered since the heyday of eighteenth- and nineteenth-century poetry. Today's concepts of nature depend upon "the mind-lessness of nature, its nonhuman otherness: a concept having nothing to do with optimism or pessimism" (1959, p. 324). The result is that the term "nature poetry" has fallen into dis-repute among readers who insist on looking for the traditional concept of nature in contemporary writing. If these readers will but acknowledge a different definition of nature as it re-lates to twentieth-century life, they will find remarkable ex-amples of the new nature poetry.

Accordingly, Professor Langbaum examines the poetry of Wallace Stevens, Marianne Moore, Frost, W. S. Merwin, Rich-ard Wilbur, and Richard Eberhart. Only his remarks about Frost need concern us here, but it should be noted that he con-siders the best contemporary nature poetry to be in opposition to the pathetic fallacy. Stevens' "The Snow Man" and Frost's "The Need of Being Versed in Country Things" are prime examples. Yet Langbaum believes that Frost is "less radically twentieth-century in his sense of nature" because the differ-ence between man and nature in his work is not as wide or as dangerous as it is in the poems of Stevens or Miss Moore. Man's life "weaves so inextricably in and out of nature" that the dif-ference "poses no real threat." Frost's momentary insights into the nonhuman otherness of nature, as in "Come In," are merely salutary. This does not mean, writes Langbaum, that Frost re-fuses to write of nature's destructiveness. He does, in poems like "Storm Fear" and "An Old Man's Winter Night," but his ex-amples of it are "seldom very frightening." Langbaum does not quarrel with these poems when he calls them idyls, but he nevertheless believes that they show only the slightest dishar-mony between man and nature. Unlike most contemporary na-ture poems, Frost's leave out what Langbaum terms the "agony of dying." The dangers in his poems are so slight that the ac-ceptances are gained without anguish, even in "Desert Places," which Langbaum reads as Frost's darkest nature poem.

This discussion may be strongly argued, but I, for one, disagree with his interpretations of individual poems which he cites for support and illustration. This is not to say that he is wrong, but only to suggest another point of view. Noting that Frost sees nature as a void in "Desert Places," Langbaum argues that the poet "turns into a kind of consolation that perception of an internal void which would be for another poet the most terrifying perception of all" (1959, p. 329). Perhaps so, but it seems to me that the poem's last stanza, beginning "They cannot scare me with their empty spaces," communicates bravado. The poet-figure's terror is so great that he tries to bluff his way out of it by balancing nature's emptiness with his own internal void. He questions why he should be scared of nature's empty spaces when his personal void terrifies him even more. Terror is terror if it is genuine—it makes little difference what causes it. Rather than consolation, he finds the fear magnified by his perception of two levels of emptiness.

Professor Langbaum's primary quarrel with Frost derives from what he considers to be the poet's refusal to stand at the forefront of contemporary ideas. Frost is thus a lesser poet than Yeats or Pound because his work puts us in contact with a "survival-making eternal folk wisdom. We can live by Frost's poetry as we could not by Yeats's or Pound's" (1959, p. 330). When it comes to the genius to render nature, Frost may be the best poet since Wordsworth. But, says Langbaum, he does not play a key role in our lives because he lacks the wilder sense of nature as defined by Darwin, Freud, and Frazer. Thus, his understanding of nature can never convey the sense of his own times. This essay is pivotal in the study of nature poetry. Of all the articles to be discussed in this chapter, Professor Langbaum's is one of the two or three which every student of modern poetry should read. Yet in the history of Frost criticism, it represents a traditional point of view. Published in 1959, nearly five decades after *North of Boston*, it nevertheless accepts the standard critical opinion of the previous forty-five years: Frost's poems of nature are generally benign and nearly always consoling. Many of today's readers would surely quarrel with this evaluation, for Frost's lyrics, including those discussed by Langbaum, are now often read as fearful expressions of darkness, alienation, and uncertainty. It would be difficult to specify a date when critical readings of Frost's nature poetry began to shift, but undoubtedly Lionel Trilling's assessment of him as a "terrifying poet" prompted a good many doubters to take another look. The irony is that Professor Trilling's speech was also published in 1959 (*Partisan Review*). It is not specifically concerned with Frost's nature poetry, and is, thus, beyond the scope of this chapter. But readers of Langbaum's essay might want to consult it as an alternative point of view.

One of the critics who does not write about the consolation found in Frost's nature poetry is W. H. Auden. His 1936 "Preface" to an English edition of Frost's poems (mentioned in chapter 2) is more a short introduction than an analytical essay, but it is interesting because of Auden's comment that nature poetry is "a sign of social specialization and social strain." His point is that the term "nature poetry" had no meaning before city life and country life began to seem separate fields of experience. Defining Frost as the kind of nature poet who lives in the country because he works there, Auden sees him as "almost the only representative" today of a poet who also tills his own land. Today we know that Frost worked the land more as a hobby than as a livelihood, but Auden is nevertheless correct when he comments on the slow pace of Frost's nature poems, the absence of mystical meditation traditionally associated with that subgenre, and the focus of the poems on the daily business of farming. According to Auden, Frost's nature poems are not written for "townees." The poet's tone is "melancholy and stoical," free from self-pity and void of personal commentary. Joining Auden in writing a preface to Frost's poems, C. Day Lewis (both articles are collected in *Recognition of Robert Frost*, ed. Richard Thornton, 1937) comments on the importance of the poet's ironic detachment. Frost may feel nature deeply, but his irony saves him from "the savage intensity of vision and the naive magniloquence which we find in Clare." Lewis finds a kinship between Frost's nature poems and Wordsworth's because both poets reveal a fundamental seriousness, detachment, and an even tempo. These short evaluations are not for the initiated reader of Frost, but they seem to me the perfect starting point for the student who is seriously approaching the poet's nature poems for the first time.

Robert Penn Warren's "The Themes of Robert Frost" (in *The Writer and His Craft: The Hopwood Lectures, 1932–1952*, 1954) is often considered one of the best general evaluations of Frost's art yet published. It is not specifically concerned with nature poetry, for as Warren explains, his primary interest is to examine some poems "to see how their particular truths are operative within the poems themselves." Yet his sensitive readings of the poems touch on the question of Frost's nature poetry in such a way as to contribute to the wide ranging critical views on this thorny subject. Warren begins with a close reading of "Stopping by Woods on a Snowy Evening." Although the details of his interpretation do not concern us, the conclusion is of interest: "So, our poem, which is supposed to celebrate nature, may really be a poem about man defining himself by resisting the pull into nature" (1954, p. 223). Suggesting that

Frost's dark woods house a "lethal" beauty, Warren notes what all close readers of Frost know: that the struggle to resist the lure of nature is a consistent theme in the Frost canon.

Warren is not interested in the developing controversy over the extent to which Frost may assume the name "nature poet." As he states in his opening paragraphs, labels do not concern him. Wordsworth and Emerson are not mentioned, nor are traditional philosophical concepts. Rather than experience a letdown, the reader of the essay feels a sense of relief, for here is an article which focuses on the poems themselves. Philosophical contexts and concepts of world view are important, to be sure, but occasionally the reader needs an essay which treats Frost's nature poetry for what it is—poems to be read. Warren's is this essay, and it is for this reason that he does not discuss the intellectual background to the idea of the nonhuman otherness of nature when he comments that "Come In" illustrates the difference between man's world and nature's: the bird "can only speak in terms of its own world, the world of nature and the dark woods, and not in terms of the man who is waiting for the darkness to define the brilliance of the stars" (1954, pp. 225–26). The contrast is always between two kinds of beauty, but man's reward comes not from contemplation of the scene but from action within it. Although Warren does not say so, Frost's celebration of action over contemplation when in the presence of nature would seem to suggest a prime difference between his poetry and nineteenth-century nature poetry.

An excellent reading of "After Apple-Picking" follows, and at the end of the article, Warren paraphrases the themes of Frost's nature poems. Man's ability to dream sets him apart from nature, but man is also in nature: "his best dream is the dream of the fact, and the fact is his position of labor and fate in nature though not of her" (1954, p. 233). With five or six decades of Frost criticism to consult, today's reader may complain that Warren's comments about the poet's nature poetry are too general. Perhaps so, but we must remember that Warren is not interested in the various categories or divisions of Frost's achievement. His readings are so sensitive that he enjoys the critic's highest level of success—he sends us back to the art itself, his comments in hand, to experience once again the beauties of the poems.

Carlos Baker's "Frost on the Pumpkin" (*Georgia Review*, Summer 1957) is more an appreciation of Frost, or a written portrait of the poet in his eighties, than a critical essay, but

Professor Baker's comments on nature poetry are relevant to this chapter. Remarking on Frost's "non-systematic system," he points out that the poet conceives of nature, man, and God as separate entities. Frost admires Wordsworth and Emerson, but he stops short of their belief in natural facts as emblems of supernatural truth. Baker's general conclusion comes to this: that although Frost "often deals in his poetry with natural objects, he is very far from being what is ordinarily thought of as a 'nature poet' " (1957, p. 125). This "ordinary" idea of the nature poet is never specifically defined, but it seems clear that Baker has in mind the philosophical concept of nature which Joseph Warren Beach believes to be the primary characteristic of nature poetry. Rather than decry the demise of traditional nature poetry, as Beach seems to do, Baker discusses the kind of poetry Frost writes in such a way that he also shows how the poems differ from Wordsworth's or Emerson's.

To begin, Professor Baker notes how often nature is separated from man in Frost's poems. Clearly his argument is at odds with Robert Langbaum's, and it is interesting that both critics use "The Need of Being Versed in Country Things" to make their points. But whereas Langbaum sees the poem suggesting how man's life weaves in and out of nature, Baker reads it as an illustration of the distance between the two. To support his reading, he discusses the poem's similes, remarking that the poet uses similes instead of metaphors because the former emphasize "an essential disunity." The chief lesson which man learns from nature is differentiation. Yet, says Baker, nature is also an "unwitting catalyst" for the poet. It promotes notions and suggestions in the ready mind, but man must supply the wits himself—nature will "say" nothing to him. This is because Frost shows nature to be a "kind of rough mechanism which operates and exists." According to Baker, Frost finds two primary qualities in nature: it endures, and it is often sinister. Neither Baker nor Frost denies the pleasures of natural beauty. Yet it is clear that Baker does not join those who interpret the poet's nature poems as benign or consoling. Nature's durability, that essence which dooms man to pass by unnoticed, and its destructive force, that power which can flick him aside like a leaf, are illustrated in poem after poem: "On Going Unnoticed," "Once by the Pacific," "The Most of It." It is in this sense, writes Professor Baker, that Frost underscores the nonhuman otherness of nature which Langbaum argues the poet ignores. Frost may hint that man exists beneath the "respective sovereignties" of nature and God, but he never suggests that they are one with man. Read along with the essays of Dabbs, Beach, and Langbaum, Baker's article adds to the dispute about Frost's nature poetry while it helps to clarify the lines of disagreement: is Frost's view of nature benign or fearful; is he too close to nineteenth-century concepts of nature to be considered a modern nature poet; and does he acknowledge or ignore the nonhuman otherness of nature?

In "Robert Frost and His Use of Barriers: Man vs. Nature Toward God" (*South Atlantic Quarterly*, Summer 1958), Marion Montgomery joins the debate. Noting what by now should be clear to readers of this chapter, that some critics often think of Frost as a nature poet in the Wordsworthian tradition, Montgomery begins by differentiating the two poets. Simply stated, Wordsworth is at his best displaying nature's panorama, whereas Frost focuses on the drama of man in nature. This essay hopes to answer two related questions: what is Frost's idea of the natural world, and what is man's relation to it? Montgomery clearly sides with those who believe that Frost insists upon barriers between man and nature. Defining the poet's attitude toward nature as "one of armed and amicable truce and mutual respect interspersed with crossings of the boundaries separating the two principles," Montgomery points to the roles which fences, windowpanes, and walls play in establishing man's difference from nonhuman otherness. Wordsworth would appreciate the experience described in Frost's "Two Look at Two," but he would not have insisted upon the significance of the fence which forever separates one world from another.

Unlike Wordsworth, Frost is never sure that nature will return his love. His poet-figure must maintain his guard, for he realizes that the natural world can destroy him. And if he happens to speak directly to objects in nature, as in "Good-by and Keep Cold," his tone is nearly always fanciful or humorous, as opposed to the high seriousness of nineteenth-century poetic addresses to nature. The natural world is at best impersonal and unfeeling, unable to express kinship and unwilling to return love. Montgomery adds an extra dimension to his essay when he discusses Frost's view of God. While this chapter is not the place to begin an evaluation of Frost's religious beliefs, we should take note of Montgomery's suggestion that both nature and God represent a nonhuman world to Frost. The barriers which cut off man from nature are not breached when man approaches God. There is no sense of "nearer, my God, to

thee." Man is invited to explore and to venture, to engage in
the breathless swing between the ideal and the real, but the
boundaries stand firm forever. This does not mean, of course,
that man should bow pessimistically before nature or God.
Montgomery correctly notes the poet's suggestion that it is
man's duty to bring order to his world. Frost's word for this
ordering process is "form," a term Montgomery does not use.
But the critic does show how Frost depicts the action of the
mind and hands as man's means to fashion a sense of order out
of his alienation in the natural world.

Although Montgomery writes of "the war between man
and the natural world," he does not picture Frost assuming
a militant stance when faced with nature's impersonal otherness. Nor does he discuss what Frost's nature poetry might mean
to a twentieth-century world. Rather, he defines the various
kinds of barriers found in Frost's poetry (between man and
man, man and God, man and nature) before turning to a summation of Frost's view of nature. Although some readers will
disagree, he is probably correct when he writes that Frost rarely
alters his idea of man's relationship with nature. From *A Boy's
Will* on through the later books, Frost has pictured his poet-
figure as a stranger who must acknowledge the natural barriers
before he can act. Once he understands his alienation, he will
be able to accept the chaos and the conflict as raw materials
for the manufacture of order. Nature is not orderly, nor is
God, at least as far as man can tell. Montgomery's best point
is his suggestion that the Frostian character who wants order
must fashion it himself, even at the risk of watching nature destroy it in the next moment.

Rather than contribute to the debate about the type of nature
poetry Frost writes, John T. Ogilvie follows the lead of J. Mc-
Bride Dabbs and concentrates upon a particular pattern in the
poems. Dabbs, we recall, hears the "insistent whisper of death"
in "Stopping by Woods," as well as points out the threat which
nature represents in many of the poems. In "From Woods to
Stars: A Pattern of Imagery in Robert Frost's Poetry" (*South
Atlantic Quarterly*, Winter 1959), Ogilvie demurs, suggesting
that the interpretation of death in "Stopping by Woods" may
impose too heavy a burden on the poem. Similarly, rather than
see the possibility of threat in Frost's dark woods, he writes
of the "perfect quiet and solitude" which exist side by side
with the world of social obligations. According to his reading
of "Stopping by Woods," the poem communicates the "di-

chotomy of the poet's obligations" both to the woods and to the social world.

Ogilvie's primary interest, however, is not in the interpretation of "Stopping by Woods" but in the role which the woods and stars play in Frost's poems. He correctly notes that the dark woods have been used repeatedly since *A Boy's Will*. More importantly, he suggests that the trees themselves are not just descriptive background but part of the drama. In "Going for Water" and "A Dream Pang," for example, the act of withdrawal into the woods is a subject which Frost endows with "almost ritualistic significance." The overtones in these early poems may be what Ogilvie calls "too romantic" for today's readers, "but the psychological pattern symbolized is of considerable interest in a total view of Frost's poetry" (1959, p. 66). For the poet shows that final escape into the trees must remain a dream. In reality, the poet-figure knows that his obligations to the world of men counter his emotional drift toward the woods, as in "The Vantage Point." As Ogilvie notes, the poet-figure should participate in both worlds, and this necessity "sets up a rhythm of continual advance and retreat which informs Frost's entire poetic expression" (1959, p. 67.) "Birches" illustrates this flexible policy of periodic, but not permanent withdrawal. The problem, as Ogilvie sees it, is that most readers know only the "neighborly" Frost even though the Frost of the dark trees, the poet who is "acquainted with the night," is the essential Frost. Even the creative impulse itself is identified with the woods in early poems like "Pan with Us" and "The Demiurge's Laugh." But this mood of youthful longing darkens perceptively following the lyrics in *A Boy's Will*. Rather than peaceful isolation or the place of healing retreats, the dark woods suggest thwarted desire or even painful alienation in later poems like "The Sound of Trees" and "A Leaf Treader." The poet continues to cherish the woods as his own, but he now realizes that they represent a place where he can lose himself as well as find his bearings—thus the ambiguity of poems like "Stopping by Woods." Lurking terror balances quiet satisfaction until in "Leaves Compared with Flowers" he cannot be "enticed into the dark woods at all."

Ogilvie does not explicitly say that Frost reached an impasse with his woods metaphor, but he does suggest that the poet's awareness of the changing role which the dark trees play caused him to shift his orientation. This suggestion may or may not be valid—it seems a little too neat to me—but Ogilvie is certainly correct in pointing out that somewhere around *West-Running Brook* (1928) and *A Further Range* (1936), Frost became less the "self-exploring lyricist of the earlier books." These later poems show him to be more neighborly, more likely to chat about contemporary issues, more outspoken. Even the manner of voice changes. Metaphor gives way to generalizations, and satire is used to convey opinion. Ogilvie overstates his case here, for all readers of Frost know that the poet relies on metaphorical indirection throughout his canon. But the critic's interesting suggestion that Frost's shift toward didacticism parallels an increasing use of star imagery is worth noting: "As loneliness and grief more and more fill those woods where youth and love once delighted, the poet turns his attention upward toward the abstract questions framed by the stars" (1959, p. 74). This is perhaps too dramatically stated, for it is doubtful that Frost's image patterns undergo such an abrupt aboutface. Although unavailable to Ogilvie, the final poem in Frost's last book ("In Winter in the Woods Alone," *In the Clearing,* 1962) echoes the themes and images of the earlier woods poems. Thus, the critic errs when he writes that the poet refuses to reenter the dark trees following the increased use of star imagery. On the contrary, "The Rabbit-Hunter," "The Draft Horse," and others show an older Frost still engaged in exploring the various meanings of the mysterious trees which intrigued him throughout his career. This essay is nevertheless recommended because of its comprehensive overview of a consistent image pattern in Frost's work.

Ogilvie's interest in Frost's woods imagery is paralleled by Paul F. Jamieson's investigations of Frost's use of mountains. No one, Jamieson included, would argue that mountain imagery forms the significant pattern that woods do, but as Jamieson notes in "Robert Frost: Poet of Mountain Land" (*Appalachia,* 1959), Frost thought enough about mountains to name two of his collections *Mountain Interval* (1916) and *A Further Range* (1936). This essay is not what is known as a scholarly article, nor even as an incisive investigation of mountain imagery. It is, rather, an informal discussion about a poet who often describes the mountains he lives among. Jamieson observes that Frost pictures nature to be "infinitely diverse. He does not try to cancel out differences by assuming, with the pantheist, that a spirit of love unites all things" (1959, p. 473). Joining those who argue—correctly in my opinion—that Frost pictures nature as an essential otherness forever separated from man, Jamieson discusses "Two

Look at Two" and "The Most of It" to illustrate the manner in which the poet shows nature to have its existence independent of man's needs or hopes.

Jamieson does not subscribe to Robert Langbaum's argument that Frost's poems posit only a slight disharmony between man and nature, for he insists that Frost's love of the natural world is impartial enough not to expect "counter-love" or special favors. But he probably would agree with Langbaum that the poet does not show the separation to be terrifying. The difference, of course, is that Langbaum considers Frost's stance to be a short-coming for a twentieth-century nature poet, whereas Jamieson, without getting into literary history, seems to approve of Frost's less fearful lover's quarrel with the world. As Jamieson notes, this less-than-terrifying attitude does not mean that the poet dodges the implications of diversity and risk. Confusion challenges him, and the wildness of the mountains offers him the opportunity to assert his presence: "His characteristic image of the human condition is the isolated farm nudged up against woods on a mountainside" (1959, p. 474). The rest of the essay presents short discussions of "The Mountain," "Build Soil," and "A Fountain, a Bottle, a Donkey's Ears and Some Books." Jamieson's point is best summarized by noting that he sees the mountains in Frost's poems as offering a challenge, a refuge, or an object of study. More advanced readers will demand fuller analysis, but many will find that this article can serve as a starting point for their own deeper readings.

George W. Nitchie's book *Human Values in the Poetry of Robert Frost: A Study of a Poet's Convictions* (1960) has already been discussed in chapter 3 as one of a substantial gathering of critical analyses which view Frost's achievement negatively. The first chapter, "The World of Nature," should be evaluated here because of its comprehensive definition of what Nitchie suggests is Frost's Edenic myth. Noting that Frost's values and his view of nature are "intimately related," Nitchie defines two kinds of nature poets: the ingenuous nature lover like W. H. Davies who reports his observations in verse, and the poet like Lucretius, Wordsworth, or Hardy "for whom external nature has a philosophically serious significance, either deliberately worked out or revealed by its implicit presence in a substantial body of work" (1960, p. 5). Frost's poems may occasionally recall Davies (Nitchie names "The Pasture" and "A Young Birch"), but most possess the ethical or metaphysical dimension which elevates them to the level of true importance.

Nitchie readily grants the worth of the poems, but he believes that Frost's achievement may be less than that of Wordsworth, Emerson, Thoreau, Hardy, or even Robinson Jeffers because Frost projects a mask of "skeptical or whimsical equivocation" instead of offering a "clear statement of principles." Apparently asking for a logical consistency in a poet's work, Nitchie points first to those poems which show man violating natural processes at his own peril ("A Brook in the City" and "There Are Roughly Zones") before he then discusses poems which depict man in trouble even though he seems in harmony with nature ("Blueberries" and "A Lone Striker"). Nitchie concludes with justification that nature is a "fairly protean term" for Frost and that its meaning changes from poem to poem in a way which prohibits the clear moral that men should follow nature's example. Frost so often depicts nature as incomprehensible that man's safest attitude seems to be a "prudential, non-utilitarian respect" toward a force he cannot understand.

Nitchie's point should recall Joseph Warren Beach's remarks, for he observes that Frost is uninterested either in developing a "philosophically consistent concept of nature" or in writing about nature as an object of philosophical speculation. What really interests the poet, says Nitchie, is "not definitions but attitudes," not investigations of what nature itself is but observations of how man responds to it. Nitchie does not damn Frost for this unphilosophical treatment of natural processes, but he is subtly critical. For according to Nitchie, Frost's elimination of complex intellectual formulations enables him to portray simple situations and clear attitudes: "it seems justifiable to say that Frost's 'nature' is important less as a concept than as a kind of withdrawal according to plan, a strategic evasion by means of which things are simplified, rendered graspable" (1960, p. 14). The word "evasion" characterizes Nitchie's definition of Frost's poetry throughout the remainder of the book. If the poet pictures nature as a strategic evasion, he is relieved from the burden of defining what nature means, and, at the same time, he is free to investigate how it functions. The reader must understand, however, that Nitchie never describes Frost's bucolic world as an "automatic problem solver." The poet has written too many poems like "Home Burial" and "The Fear" which chronicle alienation and loss of love within the rural retreat. But Nitchie does believe that Frost's world is a place in which ethically complicated choices are reduced to simplicity. Writing of "The Road Not Taken," he echoes Yvor Winters (discussed in chapter 3) when he accuses Frost of describing the choice of roads in a way which is "wholly arbitrary, whimsical, undetermined." The interpretation seems off the mark, for it misses the poet's amused description of a narrator who worries about where the other alternative might have led him, not to mention the biographical frame to the poem which suggests that Frost is making fun of his friend Edward Thomas.

Similarly, one wonders at Nitchie's disapproval of "Storm Fear" for expressing what he considers to be the oversimplified choice of surviving or not surviving. It is my belief that the question of survival in "Storm Fear" is basic, an ultimate query in a terrifying situation, but Nitchie feels that the question is too simply presented, that it avoids "a certain kind of psychic effort." The point here is not the relative soundness of my, or Nitchie's, reading of these two poems but rather, the definitions of meaningful choice and of Frost's rural world which Nitchie finds in the poems. The reader must have these definitions well in hand before he decides whether to accept or reject Nitchie's interpretations of individual poems. The critic willingly admits Frost's success with detailing the physical problems involved in "Storm Fear" or in "A Leaf Treader," but he believes the choices to be too clear-cut, too free of psychic, emotional, and philosophical complications because they are normally made within the context of the simplified rural world. Nitchie's summation is worth quoting: "Frost's nature, then, is primarily an evasion according to plan, a condition of strategic withdrawal, and the reason it is so satisfactory a refuge is that, simpler than man, it reduces the problem of choice to a kind of elemental either-or" (1960, p. 22).

Like most longer discussions of Frost's nature poems, Nitchie's turns to an examination of Frost and Wordsworth. He suggests that resemblances between them are largely superficial, the crucial point being the distinction that Wordsworth perceives an organic relationship between man and nature, whereas Frost does not. The result, of course, is that Frost rarely allows himself the rapture which Wordsworth feels when in the presence of nature, for he prefers to define nature as "other." This distinction may be obvious to the experienced reader of Frost, but Nitchie adds an extra level to the evaluation of Frost's nature poetry when he shows that the ideas of a discontinuous universe and of an impersonal nature are as old as Lucretius and, thus, hardly a twentieth-century concept. He understands that Lucretius' ideas are unacceptable in a Darwinian, Planckian,

Einsteinian world, but he nevertheless finds elements of Lucretian thought in Frost's portrayal of an indifferent nature. For
all this, Nitchie remains uneasy with Frost's ambiguity. He seems
to prefer Lucretius' (or any poet's) clear position to what he
calls Frost's "wistfulness, ambivalence, and teleological uncertainty." Frost's refusal to assert or deny teleology, as in "The
Strong Are Saying Nothing," bothers him, as do such famous
poems as "Design" and "For Once, Then, Something." Nitchie's
analysis of Frost's nature poetry is a well-reasoned minority report. Yet it is difficult to accept his censure of Frost when the
poet is less consistent than the critic thinks he should be. The
word which leaps at the reader from this chapter is "equivocal"
—for Nitchie it summarizes Frost's portrayal of nature.

Although not primarily concerned with Frost's nature poetry, Arthur M. Sampley's "The Myth and the Quest: The
Stature of Robert Frost" (*South Atlantic Quarterly*, Summer
1971) is relevant because it challenges Nitchie's thesis. Sampley
briefly summarizes Nitchie's argument in order to establish a
frame for his own suggestion that Frost does indeed have a
"logical view for interpreting life." This critical debate about
whether Frost does or does not have a consistent view of man's
relationship with nature seems to me beside the point—the
poems are all that matter. But because the debate apparently
affects critical acceptance of the poems, both sides should be
understood. According to Sampley, Frost's philosophical system
develops from the first principle that man's relationship with
nature and the universe is uncertain. As a result, man must admit his ignorance and then make the best adjustment he can.
The universe has direction and purpose, but man never dis-
covers the significance of the direction or the value of the purpose. Sampley admits Frost's ambiguity, and he continues, "The
fact that Frost reveals his view indirectly and symbolically does
not invalidate the philosophical position" (1971, p. 289). God
may seem to be interested in man's fate in one poem (for example, the early "The Trial by Existence") and uninterested in another (the late *A Masque of Reason*). But this dual view is
more an illustration of Frost's uncertainty than proof of his
inconsistency. Frost's system, then, can be defined as the problem of survival in a universe man cannot predict. Even the man
who believes in the reality of unknown purpose finds that he
must rely primarily on himself. Although he may periodically
retreat, he never cowers, for independence and courage strength-
en his ability to survive. Nitchie, we recall, argues that Frost

prefers to show man constructing his own designs and moral imperatives rather than picture him cooperating with nature or waiting for divine intervention. Sampley agrees. But whereas Nitchie is bothered by the poet's stance, Sampley celebrates it. He concludes that Frost's poems testify to the poet's understanding of twentieth-century man's courage when faced with an unpredictable universe.

The most complete analysis of Frost's world view as a nature poet is John F. Lynen's *The Pastoral Art of Robert Frost* (1960). In the preface to the 1964 revised edition, Lynen explains that his book is a study of poetic form. Believing Frost's content to be indistinguishable from his form, Lynen offers this book more as a study of a poetic mode than as a series of explicit interpretations. This does not mean that individual poems are not discussed—they are, but the purpose is always to "illustrate a kind of meaning rather than to offer a statement of what is meant" (1964, p. ix). Accordingly, he devotes the opening chapter, "The Pastoral Mode: Symbolism and Perspective," to the business of defining what he means by pastoral art. He begins by acknowledging a common complaint: Frost's poems demand less erudition in the reader because they seem to lack the complexity one normally associates with twentieth-century poetry. This argument is not valid, of course, for as Lynen points out, mastery of the deceptively simple surface of a Frost poem still leaves the reader with the task of deciphering meaning. An understanding of "what happens" in "Stopping by Woods" does not negate the persistent suspicion that "more" is at stake. Lynen's point is that the reader must interpret the poem symbolically, even though "Stopping by Woods" lacks overt symbolism. The difficulty of determining how the poem's elements encourage a deeper reading beyond that of the literal experience urges the reader to look elsewhere for an approach to the poem's meaning, specifically to the rural context. And it is here that Lynen sets down what might be considered the formative idea of his book, for he argues that too many commentators have viewed Frost's "ruralism" simply as a source of subject matter. It would be more correct to say that the rural world supplies Frost with his framework, with his point of view: "The rural world, however, is not only the area in which Frost finds his most congenial subjects; it provides the framework in terms of which he can most effectively picture reality. In other words, the rural world supplies not only the objects, the events, the characters he writes about, but also the point of view from which they are seen" (1960, pp. 6–7). Thus, Frost's mode of symbolic reference is different. It works not through allusion or metaphor or allegory, but, rather, through this special perspective which is essentially pastoral. This is not to say that most of Frost's poems are traditional pastorals, but only to remark that pastoralism most effectively defines the "characteristic design" at the center of his work.

Lynen points to a significant early review by Lascelles Abercrombie (discussed in chapter 2) as one of the first statements on Frost's pastoralism, and he correctly notes that no one followed Abercrombie's perceptive observation. For his own purposes, he defines the pastoral genre as "a particular synthesis of attitudes toward the rural world" (1960, p. 9). The rural countryside may be the subject of pastoral, but in true pastoral poetry, the subject is not exploited for itself. Rather, the poet is always conscious of the contrast between the rural world and a more sophisticated life-style, so that the pastoral poem is a means of commenting on urban problems. Pastoral pits the two sets of values against each other, exploiting the tensions to elaborate ambiguities and to draw attention to "the resemblances beneath the obvious differences." It may assume that the country man is closer to reality, that the humble life is purer than the high, and that the swain has a better understanding of himself and his world. Behind these assumptions lies the belief in an innocence which is at once desirable and attainable. But such idealization is only one quality of pastoral, for the best pastoral art never praises the rural world "at the expense of the great world beyond." Unlike those who sponsored the efforts of some of the more shallow pastoral poets of the eighteenth century, Lynen believes that the pastoralist must "of necessity" be a sophisticated artist writing for an intellectual audience. The pastoral poet's true power comes from his skill at maintaining the equilibrium of the rural and urban worlds, for he realizes that one must know city life before he can yearn for the supposed innocence of the country.

At first glance, Frost's claim to pastoralism may seem doubtful because he does not use the conventions which are popularly misconceived to be characteristic of the genre: lonely shepherds, lovely shepherdesses, the flock, flowers, and the dance. Lynen shows that these conventions are not at the center of the pastoral genre. Instead, they grew out of the myth of Arcadia which is only one imaginative version of rural life. It is possible for a poet to write pastorals while developing the context of other mythic rural worlds. Lynen follows this observation with a discussion of how the Arcadian myth decayed, suggesting that "Lycidas" is the "last great traditional eclogue in our language. . . ." Today's reader must understand that Frost could never have written pastorals in the context of the Arcadian myth, and that his achievement as a pastoralist, like that of Burns and Wordsworth, is individual rather than traditional. With justification, Lynen argues that Frost came into his own as an artist only when he adopted "the perspective of pastoral and wrote from the point of view of an actual New England farmer" (1960, p. 19). One reason for his success as a poet is his ability to convince us that the rural world represents human life in general. By making the rural world remote, Frost elevates it to a symbolic level, always aware of the definite contrast between rural and urban. Lynen writes, "His method is paradoxical in that his intent is to portray universal experience by revealing the basic realities common to both worlds, yet he achieves this by insisting upon their dissimilarity" (1960, p. 20).

What makes this argument so persuasive, what lifts it beyond an updated definition of pastoralism, is Lynen's consistent attention to how Frost's pastoral mode creates what he calls a "remarkable depth of reference" in the poems. Lynen is aware of the strong sense of symbolism at work in a Frost poem, and he admits the difficulty of trying to specify why the images are so suggestive. The solution, he feels, is found in an understanding of Frost's adaptation of pastoralism. The poet's rustic scene is rendered symbolic by its remoteness, and, thus, the familiar objects which belong to it take on symbolic suggestions. Lynen uses "The Pasture" to illustrate his argument that Frost unifies the object observed with the way it is seen. This particular poem is clearly an invitation to a specific place, but more importantly it invites the reader to accept a special point of view: "The pasture, then, is both the subject of the vision and its perspective; the mode of perception is embodied in the images themselves" (1960, p. 22).

A specific symbolic content is unnecessary because the objects are always described in a "framework of contrast" which suggests their universal properties. For this reason the symbolism of pastoral is usually broad and implied rather than particularized and stated. Lacking specific definition, the images in Frost's poems invite many levels of meaning, thus explaining why his symbolism is so difficult to interpret. The general area of meaning can be defined, but that area normally contains indefinite references, none of which can be designated the right one. Lynen is very likely correct when he suggests that Frost's refusal to create symbols with precise referents accounts for some of the dissatisfaction which today's symbol-oriented readers feel when reading his poetry. Their inability to draw a message or statement from, say, "Mending Wall" leads them to brand the poem imprecise, not realizing that the pastoral mode invites implication rather than precision. Frost does not write so that the wall in "Mending Wall" can be explicitly defined, but this does not mean that the symbolism is equivocal. Rather, following the pastoral mode, it is general, avoiding the specific kind of reference one is used to in the work of a poet like T. S. Eliot. Unfortunately Frost's method of symbolism has led some readers to deny that his poems have any symbolic allusion. Lynen's discussion of how pastoral affects Frost's art goes a long way toward correcting such wrongheaded opinions, and the following statement seems a good summation of his first chapter: "By thinking of Frost's symbolic reference as a vista rather than an arrow moving from image to referent, one can recognize specific references and yet see them in their proper perspective as particular meanings within the scope of a more general meaning" (1960, p. 31).

Lynen's second chapter, "New Hampshire and Arcadia: The Regional Myth," deals more directly with Frost's art. After setting up the definition and context of pastoralism in the opening chapter, Lynen shows how Frost uses local New England to reveal universals. This chapter is one of the most persuasive there is in dispelling the notion that Frost is a regional poet. As Lynen points out, one need have no direct knowledge of New Hampshire to understand the artistry of "After Apple-Picking." Lynen also counters those who insist that Frost fails to describe the whole of New England. Noting that the poet selects not what is there but what to his mind is representative, Lynen shows that Frost's process of "representing the locality as a whole through a limited set of visual images" is in fact a mode of symbolism. The proper way, then, to understand Frost's New England is in terms of a pastoral myth, for his New England is a modern substitution for the role once played by concepts of Arcadia. In other words, the New England of Frost's poems should not be read as local color portraits, nor as snatches of the real thing, but as myth. As he depicts it, the Northeast Corner is not just a geographical place; it has unity and stability, and it is a complete world within itself. If today's readers

have trouble accepting this New England as myth, it is because belief in the reality of it is still very much alive. Lynen
notes that the more Frost "emphasizes local differences, the more
he isolates New England, sets it apart, as it were, from the rest
of the universe. Yet it is this isolation which makes his New
England symbolic" (1960, p. 59). In the most complete discussion of "New Hampshire" that I have yet read, Lynen
analyzes the long poem to illustrate his argument.

The next three chapters are every bit as informative as the
first two, but the concerns of these three chapters will only be
mentioned here. In "The Yankee Manner: Style as Symbol,"
Lynen observes that although the expressiveness of Frost's language is deservedly praised as an example of his technical
achievement, expressiveness is not the only value of the poet's
idiom. More important may be his ability to make the language
itself "function as an image." In other words, the Yankee way
of speaking symbolizes a mode of thought. Thus, Lynen analyzes
the character who speaks Frost's lines because he believes the
speaker to be the link between style and meaning. In "Pastoralism and the Dramatic," he discusses the extent to which pastoralism affects the structure of Frost's nonpastoral poetry. This
chapter is especially concerned with defining Frost's dramatic
poetry and its relation to the modern adaptation of pastoral.
And in "Nature and Pastoralism," discussed at greater length in
chapter 4, Lynen defines the difference between nature poetry
and pastoralism, showing how many of Frost's poems combine
both genres. The same perspective which informs the pastorals
fashions Frost's vision of nature.

Professor Lynen admits that his concluding chapter, "Frost
as Modern Poet," is "frankly speculative," for it is here that he
muses over what the earlier chapters mean to an evaluation of
Frost's art in relation to twentieth-century poetry in general.
His objective is to point out Frost's modernity, and he begins
by defining the poet's concept of nature as "an image of the
whole world of circumstances within which man finds himself"
(1960, p. 162). Frost's nature poetry, writes Lynen, is surely
modern, for it illustrates today's rejection of the Romantic belief in the unity of man and nature, and it acknowledges the
increasing authority of science. Following a discussion of how
Frost's nature poetry bears a structural resemblance to more
characteristic modern poetry, Lynen specifies one of the key
ideas of his chapter: Frost's "method is to unify scientific nature
and the realm of human experience, not by blending them, but

by viewing reality as a vista of distinct but parallel planes"
(1960, p. 167). His expanded discussion of this idea will benefit
all those who are hard pressed to explain how Frost is a modern poet even though he does not write like Yeats, Eliot, or
Stevens. In both his nature poems and his pastorals, Frost emphasizes the value of the individual caught up in the fragmented
experience caused by technology. Nearly all major modern
poets have had to face this problem, but Frost seems different
to some readers because of his use of the rural world where
technology has yet to fragment life. These readers both accuse
him of dodging the issue and deny him status as a modern artist.
Lynen's book effectively counters this argument, for it shows
that Frost's retreat to a less-complex rural world is neither escap-
ism nor agrarianism, but, rather, an effort to gain the perspective needed to comment on contemporary life.

   An analysis of Dylan Thomas' "When all my five and country senses see" and Frost's "Beech" illustrates Lynen's point. Although Thomas' sonnet is stylistically complex in a "modern"
sense, its subject is a traditional theme restated in a new
way. But Frost's poem has a distinctively modern theme even
though its form is traditional. Neither poem is more or less
"contemporary" than the other, but Thomas' stylistic complexities often convince readers to name it the more modern
poem. Lynen's discussion is persuasive enough to balance some
of the negative criticism which brands Frost a twentieth-century poet who avoids contemporary ideas and crises. The primary weakness of *The Pastoral Art of Robert Frost* is that
Lynen overstates his argument by overdeveloping his thesis. He
also errs when he suggests that the poems of *North of Boston*
show an abrupt change from the lyrics of *A Boy's Will* since
Frost had by then discovered pastoralism. The facts show that
many of the poems in *North of Boston* were written during
the time that he was also working on the lyrics which eventually comprised *A Boy's Will*. But Lynen's new perspective
and exciting interpretations of individual poems override the
importance of these minor flaws. The book has a full index,
and a most useful checklist accompanies the paperback edition.

   Although Laurence Lerner's "An Essay on Pastoral" (*Essays
in Criticism,* July 1970) is more concerned with the literary
development of pastoral than with the specific poems of Frost,
the remarks on Frost are worth noting following a discussion
of Lynen's book. The essay, indeed, begins with Frost. Quoting "The Wood-Pile," Lerner points out how nearly every

detail in the poem assures us that we are listening to a country-man: the narrator can judge the age of the cord of maple; he looks for landmarks; he notes matter-of-fact details. Lerner writes, "We are going for a walk with an expert; he is good company in the woods, and knows it" (1970, p. 277). The remainder of this learned essay is a discussion of more traditional pastoral poetry. Lerner quotes, for example, poems by Sidney and Shakespeare to show how Elizabethan pastorals are generally uninterested in describing the countryside in terms of precise detail. Passages from Sidney's *Arcadia* show that the author delights more in describing the court than the country scene, whereas Frost's poem gains its strength from the accurate description of a walk in the woods. Shakespeare, Andrew Marvell, and other traditional pastoral poets clearly subordinate country life and natural detail to their desire to turn a startling analogy or to make a point about the present by creating a make-believe world. Their view of nature is not false but illusory. This essay, the greater part of which is beyond the scope of this chapter, should be read along with Lynen's *The Pastoral Art of Robert Frost*, for it summarizes the historical context of the pastoral tradition as it is defined in Renaissance literature.

In "Diminished Nature" (*Massachusetts Review*, Spring 1960), William H. Pritchard discusses the ways in which Frost's nature poetry differs from nineteenth-century Romantic nature poetry. As he correctly notes, both Frost and Wordsworth or Shelley explore the contradiction between the experience in nature as it is "imagined, remembered or longed for—full, exhilarating, unbounded—and experience as it is felt—partial, painful, limited" (1960, p. 477). Yet while Frost uses some standard characteristics of nineteenth-century nature poetry, he takes this traditional contradiction seriously enough to create new ways of dealing with it. Accordingly, Pritchard analyzes "The Oven Bird," "Hyla Brook," and "The Need of Being Versed in Country Things" as three poems which define a "central attitude" toward experience found in Frost's poetry.

"The Oven Bird" illustrates what Pritchard means by "diminished nature." The bird, for example, is not the speaker's special discovery—everyone has heard it. Nor is it the product of a particular time or place. The speaker, indeed, describes the bird like the good naturalist who relies on his "reportorial accuracy" for communication. This close correspondence which Frost establishes among a diminished natural scene, the appropriate bird's song, and the speaker's "decorous rendering of

both, is Frost's way of inverting the romantic relationship between a poet beset by tribulations and an object (frequently
a bird) whose condition is seen as admirably opposite to his
own" (1960, pp. 478–79). Comparison with Shelley's skylark
or even Hardy's "The Darkling Thrush" illustrates Pritchard's
point. These two nineteenth-century poems communicate a
dramatic moment of recognition which is absent in "The Oven
Bird" primarily because Frost's speaker does not direct our interest to his situation. Unlike Shelley's or Hardy's, Frost's celebration of experience in nature is "unextravagant." Pritchard is
surely correct when he chides those readers who find Edenic
overtones in the line, "And comes that other fall we name the
fall," for the speaker's obvious amusement undercuts a solemn
symbolic reading. As Pritchard explains, Frost "restylizes" a
typical Romantic situation by humanizing the bird, "giving
it that ability to look before and after which Shelley had la-
mented as the unfortunate burden of mankind" (1960, p. 482).

"Hyla Brook" works the same way as a poem in which a
stock situation evolves differently under Frost's guidance. Unlike the oven bird, however, the brook cannot keep up appearances—only the speaker can determine its worth. The poem's
opening lines establish the possibility of an elegiac tone, for we
learn that the brook has dried up. But Frost's nature is often
diminished. He finds nothing to lament in the scene, and, thus,
he surprises the reader with a celebration of the way the brook
is now: "This final line ["We love the things we love for what
they are"] substitutes a loving contemplation of the diminished
thing for the earlier appeal to memory." Things which are take
precedence over past glories, and the initiated reader will catch
the implied contrast to Romantic attitudes like that expressed
in Tennyson's line about the brook: "For men may come and
men may go/But I go on forever." These poems define a general attitude in Frost's nature poems. Faced with an experience
which has traditionally ended in elegy or prayer, Frost turns
it into an opportunity for knowledge. Pritchard's position is a
long way indeed from those who argue that Frost's nature poems
constitute a poetry of evasion.

Radcliffe Squires (*The Major Themes of Robert Frost*,
1963) also puts Frost squarely on the side of twentieth-century nature poets. In the chapter "The Poet as Naturalist," he
points to Frost's efforts to confront "the most basic distress of
modern life"—man's efforts to escape nature. Escape is necessary
because, since Darwin, man has realized that an unsentimental

look at nature confirms knowledge of decay and death. Squires readily admits that poets have traditionally accepted change as the "presumed necessity of nature," but he also shows that past poets have nearly always found a way to rescue man from the terrors of mutability. In a poem like "The Wood-Pile," however, Frost links all humanity to "the slow smokeless burning of decay." As Squires explains, "This pattern of birth and decay in nature, once established as a permanent recurrence, is contrasted with decay itself in such a way as to imbue with greater poignancy the transience of phenomena—including man" (1963, p. 40).

Poets have traditionally found solace in the permanence of the natural cycle even though it is composed of impermanence—Frost, however, often communicates what Squires terms "an emotional rejection of transience." A philosopher would have to take one side or the other, but the poet remains free to play with the contradiction of permanent inpermanence as a kind of truth. In "The Times Table," for all of what Squires amusingly calls its "slovenly logic," Frost shows us the truth that death is the rhythm of life. And yet, the poet protests that it is wrong to say so. To insist on a death rhythm is to bring "back nature in people's place." Frost, of course, expresses other moods ("Our Hold on the Planet"), but his primary mood is this "true-but-wrong" idea. A line from "The Census-Taker" is relevant here: "It must be I want life to go on living." Nature constantly reclaims the clearing which man has forged. Willing to admit this truth, Frost nevertheless insists that it is wrong. According to Squires, Frost's desire for life to continue, rather than the certainty that it will, saves the poet from typical twentieth-century despair. Squires' evaluation of Frost's nature poetry is clearly an "answer" to those who accuse the poet of equivocation. For as he reads the poems, he finds Frost's simultaneous acceptance and rejection of doom as a means of avoiding Romantic excess. Poems like "The Exposed Nest" and the even better "Out, Out—" show the human watchers experiencing normal griefs and yet convinced that life's more important task is to continue living—they grieve for the death and then turn to "their affairs." Squires is especially persuasive at the end of this nicely written chapter when he suggests that Frost sees life as the "great duty. Life triumphs by being as stubborn as nature, not more so" (1963, p. 46).

In a later chapter, "The Literate Farmer," Squires again indirectly challenges those who label Frost equivocal in his nature poems. The poet consistently probes the dissociation between man and nature, declining to choose one over the other. Suggesting that man must continually "enlarge" himself by challenging nature, Frost shows that motion, not ripeness, is all. Man's actions may be foolish as in "A Roadside Stand," but with action he makes a brave gesture. Squires correctly notes that human effort is more important to Frost than success or failure, an attitude which allows the poet to scorn a goal but admire the effort. This dual attitude is not equivocation but a means by which Frost can simultaneously admire and deplore man's action when faced with nature's continuous cycle of decay. Man can never claim a clear victory from his confrontation with nature, but the struggle both liberates him and clarifies his mind. Squires' approach is generally appreciative, as opposed to scholarly. He ranges among the poems with ease and knowledge, suggesting interesting interpretations in a prose style free from the dullness often associated with scholarship.

In "Frost and the Deeper Vision" (*Midwest Quarterly*, Autumn 1963), Barry D. Bort bluntly states that Frost is the only major contemporary poet who writes "convincingly" about nature. Bort must mean the nineteenth-century concept of nature when he uses the term "nature poetry," for he discusses the tradition of Wordsworth's "ennobling interchange" as an idea which was challenged by Thomas Hardy but which persists in the twentieth century. For some reason he writes that Frost's relationship with the great poets of the previous century has gone unexamined. His statement, of course, is wrong, as both this and the preceding chapters show, but he nevertheless believes that Frost's poetry needs to be placed in the context of those nineteenth-century giants who "understood nature as the basic referent"—Wordsworth, Emerson and Thoreau.

Bort begins by selecting those Frost poems which reveal the poet's complex attitude toward nature. Accordingly, he plans not to discuss poems in which nature plays the role of teacher ("On a Tree Fallen Across the Road") or those in which nature accidentally seems to benefit man ("Dust of Snow"). Instead he analyzes the poems in which one finds "a kind of testing, a wary and circumscribed insistence of the need not to make too much of nature and not to claim a reciprocity that nature may be unwilling or unable to give" (1963, p. 60). As Bort correctly notes, Frost's poetry has very little of Wordsworthian rapture or of the last century's faith in communion between man and nature, and it "skirts the question" of whether or not a deeper power is immanent in nature. Although Bort does not insist upon it, he is sketching the central difference between Wordsworth's pre-Darwinian and Frost's post-Darwinian world. He nominates "For Once, Then, Something" as a key poem in Frost's nature poetry, but, mistakenly, he specifically identifies the ambiguous "others" who chide the poet-figure as those who criticize the speaker for not "writing in the older tradition of nature poetry." Readers who recall this poem know that it is about perception and that Frost includes a series of intriguing religious images. Nowhere in the poem does he hint that it should be read as an oblique statement about his relationship with Romantic writers. Yet Bort takes the speaker's refusal to affirm or deny what he sees as an example of the poet's discrimination which permits him to "continue to write meaningfully in the all but dead tradition of nature poetry. By the strategy of not claiming too much, he suggests that the older tradition is not entirely dead" (1963, p. 61). Comparing this statement with "For Once, Then, Something," the reader can only conclude that the poem says no such thing.

On the other hand, Bort is correct when he writes that Frost's refusal to claim too much from nature separates him from Wordsworth. This difference is illustrated by noting how each poet sketches the people who live in nature. Wordsworth's "Resolution and Independence" suggests the leech gatherer's spiritual health, whereas Frost's "An Old Man's Winter Night" pictures the terror of the aged man's loneliness. Because Frost refuses to accept the Romantic faith in nature's willingness to answer man's needs, he avoids Wordsworth's or Coleridge's or Shelley's disappointment when the communion between man and nature fails. In the rest of the essay Bort discusses a series of poems, such as "The Most of It" and "A Passing Glimpse," which illustrates Frost's hesitancy about the reality of communion. The communion may be there—thus Frost keeps the Romantic tradition alive—but then again it may not be—thus he accepts the modern concept of nature.

Much more valuable is Nina Baym's "An Approach to Robert Frost's Nature Poetry" (*American Quarterly*, Winter 1965) in which she scolds readers who discuss Frost's poetry as if there were only one way to write about nature, the Romantic way. Even Frost's defenders, as she correctly observes, perpetuate the image of the poet as an "inspired plowman" when they accept the premises of the more negative critics. Professor Baym also challenges those who believe that Frost must have transcendental doctrine in mind, or that he implies a rebirth theme, just because he writes about nature and its cycles. "The way out of this dilemma," she writes, "is to abandon the approach to Frost through ideological preconceptions, and to put the poet not in a tradition of thought, but in a specifically 'poetic' tradition" (1965, p. 714). That tradition is mutability. The longer dialogue poems deal with the mutability of human relations, and the shorter lyrics show the speaker forced to respond to the natural scene by the pressure of mutability. Frost may call it "flux" or "alternation," but his "age-long" theme is mutability.

Nowhere, says Miss Baym, does Frost follow Emerson and insist that nature's laws correspond to the laws of the inner mind. Considering "correspondences" and the pathetic fallacy to be invalid approaches to nature, he finds that the New England landscape reveals only nature's physical laws, especially "the grim laws of change and decay." For all of the "teasing transcendental title" of "A Boundless Moment," this poem rejects the transcendental ideal, replaces images of spring with those of autumn and death, and shows the seasonal cycle to be an occasion for near disillusion. Man cannot base his hope on the assumption that the natural cycle tends toward rebirth. As Miss Baym realizes, the great bulk of Frost's nature poems describes autumn and winter. These poems convey mutability not only by their seasonal settings but also by their details which emphasize "the inevitable and ceaseless movement toward death—night fall, leaf fall, snow fall" (1965, p. 717). The seasons of rain and death are so dominant in his nature poetry that he seems hesitant to affirm spring's return from the onslaught of winter. Even in "The Onset," he cannot commit himself to an affirmation based on winter's "failure."

This article introduces a new element into the criticism of Frost's nature poetry with its analysis of how the poet uses scientific truths. Discussing "The Wood-Pile" and "West-Running Brook," Professor Baym argues that Frost is the one contemporary poet for whom scientific truth is not always at odds with poetry. These two poems, for example, combine traditional nature imagery with ideas based on the second law of thermodynamics in order to illustrate what Frost terms "the slow, smokeless burning of decay." This argument places Miss Baym on the side of the more recent critics of Frost's poetry, for she completely dismisses the popular image of the poet as beneficent nature poet to insist that his poems illustrate the entropic state of the world, wasted and running down. Caught in this predicament, man's only meaningful action is resistance. The power which enables him to resist the inevitable movement toward death is "mind" (see "Sand Dunes" and "All Revelation"). Frost may remain uncommitted to questions about the relation of man's mind to divine mind; indeed, he regards all teleological questions with suspicion. But if Frost has decided that speculations about ultimate purpose cannot be answered, he nevertheless refuses to embrace pessimism. Miss Baym writes that the "poems are full of such gestures of stay, transient but affirmative within realistic limits" (1965, p. 721). She refers, of course, to Frost's phrase "a momentary stay against confusion." His affirmation is always within the acceptable limits of nature's laws, and he consistently insists that all order is temporary. Mending a wall or stacking a woodpile is an act of ordering by which man expresses his need to resist. Death is not defeated, nor mutability sidetracked by these acts of resistance, but man's small gestures are finally more meaningful than grandiose theories about universal purpose which serve only to deceive. This article continues to be one of the best discussions yet available of the nonhuman world in Frost's nature poetry, especially the section devoted to the poet's non-Romantic treatment of mutability.

While I hesitate to mention my own work on Frost, the essay "Confusion and Form: Robert Frost as Nature Poet" (*Discourse: A Review of the Liberal Arts*, Summer 1968) also comments on his uses of the "momentary stay." Recalling Frost's statement that he "has only three or four pure nature poems. The rest were human portraits with a nature setting," I suggest that Frost generally uses nature in its broadest sense to mean milieu or the setting of human action. So many of his poems describe the interaction between man and nature in situations which reveal a correct or incorrect relationship between them. The correct relationship is based on man's awareness that he cannot expect direct responses from nature and that he must not interpret nature according to personal longings. Confusion results when man tries to see "more in the natural setting than the facts allow." Time and again Frost explores the ways by which man tries to clarify a particular moment, and he usually suggests that the conscious creation of form brings clarity to most situations. As the article points out, the opposition of confusion and form creates a tension which Frost discusses in his letters and describes in his poetry. "Because form is resistance to confusion, he insists that confusion can often serve as a stimulus for creativity and is thus no cause for pessimism" (1968, p. 391).

"Two Look at Two" is one of Frost's best descriptions of man's ability not only to recognize but also to accept his correct relationship with nature. The poem's main image, the wall, suggests the insurmountable barriers between humanity and non-human otherness. Refusing to see an impersonal event in personal terms, the lovers avoid the "unreasonable hope or despair that often results when too much is expected from nature." The deer's presence seems to be a sign from nature, but, as every reader knows, Frost qualifies the suggestion with the phrase "as if." In opposition to "Two Look at Two" is "The Most of It," a poem in which man confuses himself because he demands too much from nature. Frost frequently portrays his characters caught in situations trying to see something in nature which is not there. In "The Most of It," the man fails to realize his error, but in "Come In" and in "A Boundless Moment" the human figures reject the desire for a possible affinity between them and nature, thus avoiding confusion.

In addition to the trap of subjective interpretation, Frost's poems also describe man's mistaken belief that nature's power personally works against him. "Storm Fear" is a "compact picture of horror and fear," and "In Time of Cloudburst" mixes humor and depression. But while both poems acknowledge the ferocity of the storms, they suggest that man errs if he believes the storm to be striking against him personally. Frost, however, rarely gives way to pessimism. Limitation, loss, and pain are realities which encourage man to find meaning in life by reacting against them. The qualified affirmation we feel in his poetry comes from his belief that "the promise of man lies in his ability to endure within his limitations and to clarify his life by creating form" (Greiner, 1968, p. 396). Quoting from his letters, I suggest that Frost considers form to be not a remedy to chaos but a clarification of the moment. A balance, however, must be struck between too much resistance to confusion and too little. The staying power of form is only momentary, and those, like his sister Jeanie, who try for more permanent stays will find themselves broken under the pressure of confusion. The woman in "A Servant to Servants," on the other hand, falls to confusion because she does not resist enough. Poems like "West-Running Brook" and "All Revelation" describe how giving shape to experience can clarify life.

In the last section of the essay, I show how Frost's concern

with the "momentary stay against confusion" also informs his
ideas about writing poetry, thereby accounting for the organic
unity between his best poems and his method of writing. Letters to R.P.T. Coffin and Sidney Cox are quoted in which
Frost insists on his need for crudity and rawness as materials
which he can "shape up, unify however roughly." The point
to remember is that the stay which the creation of form encourages is always momentary, thus forcing man to create again
and again, be it a garden, a smoke ring, or a poem. In the well-
known words from "West-Running Brook," everything sweeps
away to the "Universal cataract of death." Man's greatness is
his momentary resistance to the current. Both this essay and
Miss Baym's explore the ways in which Frost treats the ever-
present threat of natural, overwhelming chaos.

In Lloyd N. Dendinger's "The Irrational Appeal of Frost's
Dark Deep Woods" (*Southern Review*, Oct. 1966), the discussion of Frost's nature poetry changes once again from exploration of what it means to say that Frost is a nature poet to
analysis of one specific natural image. Insisting that we allow
Frost's woods to remain woods, Dendinger suggests that we
label their attractiveness "the force of irrational impulse." He
then reads poems like "Stopping by Woods on a Snowy Evening" in the context of American literature's preoccupation
with the myth of the wilderness. As Dendinger notes, man's
fascination with the big woods is much older than America, but
the American wilderness has provided modern man with a sense
of scope, beauty, and potentiality. "Stopping by Woods" is
one more evocation of the lure of the woods which stretches
back in American literature from "The Bear" and "Big Two-
Hearted River" to *Huckleberry Finn, Walden*, and the Leather-
stocking saga. Deerslayer, Hester Prynne, and Huck Finn all
look to the woods as a possibility for starting fresh in a pure
land.

They dream about the possibility, but they find that reality
seldom meets the demands of their dreams. For according to
Dendinger, the "rational, mature judgment on an attempt to
escape to the wilderness is that it is wrong for practical reasons,
because it simply does not work; and for moral reasons, because it is an attempt to deny the human condition by returning to Eden" (1966, p. 823). Those readers familiar with the
scope of critical opinion concerning Frost's nature poetry will
realize that Dendinger's observation opposes those who believe
that Frost advocates a retreat to the woods because the rural

world offers a refuge of Edenic simplification. Dendinger admits that the lure of the wilderness is real, but he suggests that Frost's traveler, like Thoreau or Nick Adams, rejects irrational impulse "to return to a normal 'human' pattern of conduct, with its prescribed miles to be traveled and its promises to be kept." Thus, Frost's woods should be read primarily as woods, secondarily as death, and thirdly as that which entices man to respond to the dark and deep within himself. Dendinger disagrees with Robert Langbaum's argument that Frost's sense of nature is too much like Wordsworth's for him to play a major role in our time, and he points to "Desert Places," "Bereft," "Once by the Pacific," and "Out, Out—" as poems in which Frost, unlike Wordsworth, describes the "brutal savageness of the non-human world." I disagree with Dendinger's reading of "Desert Places," for the speaker's final tone of acceptance seems to me to be ironic, an act of bravado manufactured to counter his great fear. But I share Mr. Dendinger's general analysis of Frost's woods metaphor, and recommend his essay to those interested in how Frost handles a traditional theme in American literature.

Clark Griffith is also concerned with Frost's place in the tradition of American literature, but he investigates the topic in much greater depth. In "Frost and the American View of Nature" (*American Quarterly*, Spring 1968), he notes that with a casual reading of Frost, one is often less impressed by his modernity than by the way he seems to perpetuate the nineteenth-century attitude toward nature. Defining this attitude, Griffith specifies a tendency to see men and nature as the "two prime realities" and a fondness for joining the two in a dramatic encounter which teaches the human observer about himself and his world. This situation clearly applies, says Griffith, to the poems of homespun philosophy like "Mending Wall" and to the more introspective pieces like "Stopping by Woods." Even in the very darkest poems like "Design" the speaker gains insight from his observations of nature. But Griffith does not join those critics who describe Frost as a leftover Wordsworth. Insisting on Frost's "fundamentally romantic position," he nevertheless argues that Frost "strangely" modifies the tradition: the poet is "less sure" of nature's teachings, convinced only of the contradictions, mystery, and ambiguity which exist in man's relationship with the natural world. Frost's nature has value—that is, it is not a meaningless force—but it is at best bewildering. Griffith believes that Frost's interest in nature as an am-

biguous teacher both defines him as modern and relates him to
the American tradition. Thus, he examines Frost first in terms
of a concept of nature which was standard in America for decades; next in terms of the later nineteenth century; and finally
in terms of Frost's own time.

Griffith argues convincingly that, unlike late eighteenth-cen-
tury and early nineteenth-century Europeans, Americans never
sensed a cleavage between nature and man. Americans were far
too dependent upon the new land to doubt its meaning in their
lives. Nature was so "overpoweringly real" to the Puritans
that they had to regard it as more than a force to be con-
quered. Accepting nature as a kind of divine teacher, they believed its lessons to be messages sent by God. Nature may have
been a "bare figure" in Europe, but in America it was a "solid
fact." Griffith contrasts the ideas of John Locke and Jonathan
Edwards to illustrate the thinking which directly prefigured
American Romanticism. Years later, Emerson rejected Puritan
theology as the "mumps and measles of the soul," but he picked
up the Puritan belief in nature as divine teacher and remade it to
fit his transcendental ideas. Griffith's point is that the American
experience fostered a single attitude toward nature which endured for over two centuries, from the earliest Puritans to the
generation of Emerson and Whitman.

With the appearance of Melville and Dickinson, the birth of
modern American literature "may be said to have occurred."
Nature continues to be "swollen with significance," but "the
hitherto willing teacher now imparts nothing. She had ceased
to accommodate herself to man's desire to say exactly what she
signifies" (1968, p. 27). Griffith's understanding of nineteenth-
century American literature seems balanced and fair, and his
conclusion that Melville and Dickinson write in a world where
Emersonian hopes clash with disappointing realities seems correct. Melville's Ahab and Dickinson's poet-figure often turn
to nature for lessons, but they usually come away empty-hand-
ed. For the modern American writer, the traditional concept
of nature has weakened considerably. Aware that most readers
know why this change has occurred, Griffith only lists the prime
causes: Darwin, Freud, urbanization. Yet, he writes, despite the
fact that nature seems a good deal less friendly today, American contemporary writers continue both to approach nature in a
special way and to assign it a unique set of values. Although
such diverse authors as Faulkner, Steinbeck, Stevens, and Rob-

inson share a modern American view of nature, Frost, more than any other, illustrates how the post-Emersonian concept of nature has remained a powerful theme.

Griffith calls Frost "a twentieth-century exemplar of the American tradition of interpreting Nature." In his view, the poet has held onto the attitudes of the later Romantic movement while simultaneously adapting his art to the darker vision of the twentieth century. Thus, Frost would like to believe that man can learn by hearkening to nature's message, but he knows, to his regret, that nature is impersonal and opaque. This dual attitude accounts for the poignancy which pervades his lyric poems. To illustrate this argument, Griffith discusses three of Frost's darker poems: "Neither Out Far Nor In Deep," "Bereft," and "Once by the Pacific." Both man and nature are the "actors," for example in "Neither Out Far Nor In Deep," but man seeks order or truth while nature remains silent: "Nature rejects every human overture." Griffith points out that while Frost praises man for maintaining the watch despite his failure to learn anything, the poet also makes fun of human rigidity.

His reading of this especially fearful poem corresponds nicely with his general discussion about the roles of man and nature in American literature, and his interpretations of "Bereft" and "Once by the Pacific" are just as interesting. One of his most important conclusions is that the uncertainty of Frost's speaker in these poems ironically relates him to the speaker in Emerson's essays. Emerson's persona has been called "Man Seeing," and Griffith describes Frost's speakers as "Men Seeing, with a shrunken insight." Like Emerson's persona, Frost's poet-figures turn to nature, believing or hoping that nature has something to show them. But the resemblance ends here, for Frost's speakers have no assurance about what they see and no understanding of their often baffling experiences. This is an important observation, one which should renew interest in the relationship between Emerson and Frost. Griffith's "Frost and the American View of Nature" remains the best essay yet published on the place of Frost's poetry in the entire scope of the preoccupation of American literature with nature.

In "A Stay against Confusion" (*Science and Society*, Winter 1969), Annette T. Rubinstein once again turns to the problem of differentiating between Frost's view of nature and that of the nineteenth century. Repeating the well-worn observation that Frost is not a local colorist or a regional poet, she summarizes the past century's concept of nature by drawing on

Wordsworth, Emerson, and Dickinson. The argument is by now, of course, familiar to initiated readers: Wordsworth believes that spirit is immanent in nature and that man is at his best when he can communicate effortlessly with nature; Emerson more directly asserts the identity of God and nature; and Dickinson, although prudently maintaining her distance, nevertheless accepts nature as the place in which God and the soul can meet.

The discussion of Frost's concept of nature is just as familiar. Miss Rubinstein argues more strongly than other critics, Griffith for example, that Frost keeps "clear the channel of communication between himself and nature," and she suggests that the poet even occasionally experiences the rapture which Wordsworth feels in the presence of natural phenomena. Yet she quickly points out that any communication or sudden joy is mere good luck because Frost appreciates the gulf between human and nonhuman nature. Discussing "One Step Backward Taken," she writes, "There is no more malice or love in nature here than before, and the organizing intelligence, the perceiving mind, the informing spirit, is man's alone" (1969, pp. 32–33). Miss Rubinstein joins most recent critics of Frost's nature poetry when she insists upon the poet's refusal to accept the comforting idea of nature's divinity. Instead, she describes him as the first serious nature poet since Lucretius to write of nature with an "utterly matter-of-fact atheism. . . ." Quoting "The Most of It" and "The Need of Being Versed in Country Things," she discusses how Frost clearly shows the significance of a natural scene to depend upon the subjective interpretation of the human observer. Nature never communicates its meaning to man.

Theodore Morrison ("Frost: Country Poet and Cosmopolitan Poet," *Yale Review,* Winter 1969) offers a new twist to the debate when he declares that Frost is not a nature poet but a country poet. The difference, writes Morrison, is considerable. The poet who garners images from nature and who offers a philosophy of nature is not necessarily a countryman. Defining his term, Morrison reminds us that Frost was never seriously a farmer. Nor was he antimetropolitan. He was a citizen of the world who also cultivated his inclination toward country things. This inclination means, in part, that Frost knew how to raise a garden, cut down a tree, or milk a cow—in short, he was at home with the labor of farming even though he never made his living from the land. But as Morrison notes, being a countryman means more than indulging a tendency toward rural oc-

cupations. More went into his poems than New England landscapes, climate, and activities. "He was deeply and truly pene-
trated by the mores, the institutions, the economy, the people,
the mental horizon of the rural New England he memorialized in
his work" (1969, p. 180). Morrison is surely correct when he
suggests that to subtract the birches, rose pogonias, and brooks
from Frost's poetry would be to deprive him of more than locale.
The subtraction would deny Frost the "defining, tangible, physical conditions" which make his art distinctive. Still, Morrison
is unsure whether the rural trappings help or hinder Frost's reputation as a major poet. Most Americans are today so thoroughly
urbanized that they have difficulty identifying hyla brooks and
minor birds. This observation parallels that of some of the negative critics who argue that Frost is out of touch with modern
experience not because he fails to speak our language but because we cannot speak his. Unlike the negative critics, Morrison
suggests that the rural trappings will finally enhance the poet's
reputation because they have a way of helping Frost create a
world in which the reader can, with careful perusal, feel at
home. Details and fine shadings will be lost as the gap increases
between the country world and the urban reader's experience,
but this distance will also remove the temptation to view rural
life with a nostalgia which obscures the importance of the poem.

    "Stopping by Woods on a Snowy Evening" remains the
test case, writes Morrison. Today's reader may find horse and
sleigh travel a laughable simplicity from a vanished time, but he
nevertheless knows the experience of leaving and returning from
a journey. No matter the mode of travel, the poem invites the
reader to "share a solitary homeward journey under particular
circumstances." All he needs to do is adjust to the poem's situation. Morrison goes on to show that this poem does not describe a death wish but rather the "thought of life" against a
sober backdrop. The words "journey" and "sleep" should remind
us of life just as readily as they suggest death. He urges the
reader to examine "Stopping by Woods" in conjunction with
other Frost poems—"A Leaf Treader" and "Come In"—which
simultaneously illustrate the separation between man and nature
and show the poet's character as a true countryman. In these and
other lyrics, Frost expresses his reponsiveness to nature and yet
denies its authority in the same breath. The poet who is also
a countryman knows rural life too well to be taken in by nature's
apparent communication with him.

    The difference in Frost between the country poet and the

cosmopolitan poet depends chiefly upon locale. As Morrison notes, localization is less important in the more cosmopolitan poems like the *Masques* and "The Lesson for Today." Any "focus of experience" will do, for the country horizon expands into the human horizon. This part of the essay need not concern us, although it should be noted that Morrison underplays the fear in "Desert Places" and that he offers an exciting interpretation of the remarkable lyric "All Revelation." This nicely written article is not likely to dissuade future readers from calling Frost a nature poet, but it does add a different perspective to the debate about the kind of nature poetry he writes.

Like John Ogilvie and J. McBride Dabbs before him, Robert S. Vinson examines Frost's nature poetry in terms of a specific recurring image; but unlike them he chooses the road or path instead of the woods and stars. In "The Roads of Robert Frost" (*Connecticut Review*, Apr. 1970), Vinson suggests that among other facts about the roads in the poems, such as their ability to connect man with both other men and the past, is their illustration of the interaction of man with nature as well as the imposition of man upon nature. Vinson carefully distinguishes the metaphorical importance between paths and roads, for he observes that the path is normally a more personal byway than a road, and, thus, it suggests an intimate relation with nature. Because the significance of roads and paths varies from poem to poem, he discusses Frost's development of the image under three separate headings: "Leaving the Road," "Return to the Road," and "The Road Out."

Some of Vinson's conclusions are questionable. He argues, for example, that those who follow well-traveled roads are also expected to conform to "established social patterns and modes of thought." Yet I wonder if Frost applauds all those who leave the road. In "Into My Own" the poet-figure spurns the "highway where the slow wheel pours the sand," but Frost seems amused by the young narrator's immaturity. As Vinson shows, those who leave the road to investigate nature often find that a too-intimate relationship with natural forces results in confusion. When nature resists attempts to discover meaning, the poet-figure, often frustrated and weary as in "An Encounter," tries to save face by claiming that he is only "Half looking for the orchid Calypso." The personally forged path does not necessarily foster a better relationship with nature. But in "A Late Walk," the path permits a closer look at nature or even an invitation to meditation: "To one who, in the manner of a poet, sees symbolic meaning in what chances to happen, the invitation of Nature to stop what we are doing and think about ourselves may take a preemptory form. . ." (1970, p. 105). This article does not carry the weight that the discussions of woods and stars have, but Vinson is not at fault. The road image is not as ambiguous or as intriguing as woods and stars and, thus, it does not offer a substantial enough insight into Frost's ideas about nature.

The essays discussed in this chapter mark the areas of debate about Frost's nature poetry. Enjoying lyrics like "Two Look at Two," "Spring Pools," and "The Most of It," the careful reader invariably finds himself facing the same question which has initiated so much controversy: what does the term "nature" mean to Robert Frost? Clearly, the poet has no single definition in mind, but knowledge of the various feelings and ideas nature inspires in his poetry will help the reader appreciate the wide range of his lifelong interaction with nonhuman otherness. Just as important for any reader of Frost is his own definition of nature. For if the reader thinks of nature in nineteenth-century terms, as so many do, he will have to come to grips with the elements of fear and destruction which often characterize Frost's nature lyrics. If, on the other hand, he accepts Frost's status as a post-Darwinian nature poet, he will have to decide whether or not the poet's descriptions of nature's impersonality and incommunicability are forceful enough to speak to a twentieth-century world. In either case, the reader's gravest error would be to insist on a logical consistency.

References

Auden, W. H.
    1937. "Preface" to *Selected Poems of Robert Frost* (London 1936), in *Recognition of Robert Frost,* ed. Richard Thornton, pp. 293–98. New York: Holt.
Baker, Carlos
    1957. "Frost on the Pumpkin," *Georgia Review* Summer, pp. 117–31.
Baym, Nina
    1965. "An Approach to Robert Frost's Nature Poetry," *American Quarterly* Winter, pp. 713–23.
Beach, Joseph Warren
    1936. *The Concept of Nature in Nineteenth-Century English Poetry.* New York: Macmillan, pp. 547–59.

Bort, Barry D.
1963. "Frost and the Deeper Vision," *Midwest Quarterly* Autumn, pp. 59–67.

Dabbs, J. McBride
1934. "Robert Frost and the Dark Woods," *Yale Review* Mar., pp. 514–20.

Dendinger, Lloyd N.
1966. "The Irrational Appeal of Frost's Dark Deep Woods," *Southern Review*, n.s., Oct., pp. 822–29.

Farrar, John
1927. "Robert Frost and Other Green Mountain Writers," *English Journal* Oct., pp. 581–87.

Griffith, Clark
1968. "Frost and the American View of Nature," *American Quarterly* Spring, pp. 21–37.

Greiner, Donald J.
1968. "Confusion and Form: Robert Frost as Nature Poet," *Discourse: A Review of the Liberal Arts* Summer, pp. 390–402.

Jamieson, Paul F.
1959. "Robert Frost: Poet of Mountain Land," *Appalachia*, pp. 471–79.

Langbaum, Robert
1959. "The New Nature Poetry," *American Scholar* Summer, pp. 323–40.

Lewis, C. Day
1937. "Preface" to *Selected Poems of Robert Frost* (London 1936), in *Recognition of Robert Frost*, ed. Richard Thornton, pp. 298–302. New York: Holt.

Lerner, Laurence
1970. "An Essay on Pastoral," *Essays in Criticism* July, pp. 275–97.

Lynen, John F.
1960. *The Pastoral Art of Robert Frost*. New Haven: Yale Univ. Pr., revised ed., 1964.

Montgomery, Marion
1958. "Robert Frost and His Use of Barriers: Man vs. Nature Toward God," *South Atlantic Quarterly* Summer, pp. 339–53.

Morrison, Theodore
1969. "Frost: Country Poet and Cosmopolitan Poet," *Yale Review* Winter, pp. 179–96.

Nitchie, George W.
1960. *Human Values in the Poetry of Robert Frost: A Study of a Poet's Convictions*. Durham, N.C.: Duke Univ. Pr.

Ogilvie, John T.
1959. "From Woods to Stars: A Pattern of Imagery in Robert Frost's Poetry," *South Atlantic Quarterly* Winter, pp. 64–76.

Pritchard, William H.
1960. "Diminished Nature," *Massachusetts Review* Spring, pp. 475–92.

Rubinstein, Annette T.
1969. "A Stay against Confusion," *Science and Society* Winter, pp. 25–41.

Sampley, Arthur M.
1971. "The Myth and the Quest: The Stature of Robert Frost," *South Atlantic Quarterly* Summer, pp. 287–98.

Squires, Radcliffe
1963. *The Major Themes of Robert Frost*. Ann Arbor: Univ. of Michigan Pr.

Thornton, Richard
1937. (editor) *Recognition of Robert Frost*. New York: Holt.

Vinson, Robert S.
1970. "The Roads of Robert Frost," *Connecticut Review* Apr., pp. 102–7.

Warren, Robert Penn
1954. "The Themes of Robert Frost," in *The Writer and His Craft: The Hopwood Lectures, 1932-1952*, pp. 218–33. Ann Arbor: Univ. of Michigan Pr.

Selected Additional Readings

Brooks, Cleanth, and Robert Penn Warren
1951. *Understanding Poetry: An Anthology for College Students* (revised). New York: Holt.

Dabney, Lewis M.
1970. "Mortality and Nature: A Cycle of Frost's Lyrics," in *Private Dealings: Eight Modern American Writers*, eds. David J. Burrows, Lewis M. Dabney, Milne Holten, and Grosvenor E. Powell, pp. 11–31. Stockholm: Almqvist and Wiksell.

Monteiro, George
1971. "Robert Frost's Solitary Singer," *New England Quarterly* Mar., pp. 134–40.

Thompson, Lawrance
1960. "Nature's Bard Rediscovered," *Saturday Review* July 2, pp. 22–23.

Trilling, Lionel
1959. "A Speech on Robert Frost: A Cultural Episode," *Partisan Review* Summer, pp. 445–52.

Watts, Harold H.
1955. "Robert Frost and the Interrupted Dialogue," *American Literature* Mar., pp. 69–87 (discussed in chapter 3 herein).

CHAPTER 6

Frost as "Notable Craftsman"

U nlike so many poets who were his contemporaries during the renaissance which swept American literature in the 1910s and 1920s, Robert Frost never fashioned a formal theory of art. He did publish a few short essays and introductions in which he expressed his opinions about such matters as metaphor, form, and sentence sounds, but he refused to collect his prose or to increase the amount of his critical writing. Indeed, some of his most comprehensive statements concerning the art of poetry remain uncollected, scattered here and there among letters, interviews, and recorded talks. This does not mean, however, that Frost was unsophisticated about literary theory or uninterested in expressing his ideas. As a 1913 letter to John Bartlett shows, he was highly conscious of his own innovations with technique: "To be perfectly frank with you I am one of the most notable craftsmen of my time. That will transpire presently. I am possibly the only person going who works on any but a worn out theory (principle I had better say) of versification" (Selected Letters of Robert Frost, July 4, 1913). Some readers of this letter might accuse Frost of egotism, but his confidence was legitimate—recognition of his notable craftsmanship did indeed "transpire presently."

Yet because Frost declined to set down his principles in formal essays and critiques, he was often slighted as a nonintellectual poet. It was not until his death in 1963 that the general public had the opportunity to piece together his literary theory, for during his lifetime he refused to authorize publication of his letters or collection of his essays and interviews. Since his death, several collections of the pertinent material have been published with the result that today's reader has the opportunity to determine the scope of Frost's theory of poetry. This chapter will focus on his essays and recorded talks, exclusive of the letters and interviews (of which there are many), and of the essays on Wordsworth, Emerson, and Thoreau which are discussed in chapter 4. Significant articles by literary critics will also be discussed to illustrate how Frost's artistic principles have been accepted and interpreted over the years.

Frost's earliest known prose pieces are his editorials and articles published in the Lawrence (Massachusetts) *High School Bulletin,* especially the issues of September through December 1891, and his valedictory address, "A Monument to Afterthought Unveiled" (1892). This juvenilia is discussed in chapter 1—the present chapter is concerned with the poet's prose and recorded talks from his mature years. The primary source of his essays remains the collection edited by Hyde Cox and Edward Connery Lathem, *Selected Prose of Robert Frost* (1966). Fifteen of Frost's most important prose statements are gathered together in this volume, thus providing the student and fan of Frost with a representative sampling of the poet's thoughts about poetry; fellow artists like Amy Lowell, Edwin Arlington Robinson, and Emerson; and even baseball. The editors point out in their introduction that Frost's "other mood," as the poet referred to his prose, was usually the result of a necessity to compose a preface to his own work, or to acknowledge an honor, or to commemorate or help someone else. The subject and the occasion of each piece may vary, but in every preface and essay the voice "of the maker of great figures of speech" can be heard. Still, as the editors correctly note, Frost's prose is an "informality"—his formal statement will always be found in the collected poems. Perhaps Frost's willingness to stand on his poetry explains his reluctance to write more prose or to collect what he had already published. Cox and Lathem suggest other reasons: that his increased enjoyment in the role of the celebrity, especially in old age, blunted his enthusiasm for the time-consuming project of publishing a book of prose; and that he "was more interested in the growth of his metaphors than in bringing them to book" (1966, p. 9). This collection, therefore, is necessary reading for those with more than a cursory interest in the poet, for it includes the most important of Frost's relatively few prose pieces, most of which were published in obscure periodicals or books.

For some unstated reason, the editors have not arranged the selections chronologically. The first "essay," Frost's preface to his play *A Way Out,* was published in 1929, and its three paragraphs still remain a prime source for the poet's statements on the need for the dramatic element in poetry. Explaining what he calls "a dramatic necessity," the poet begins with three sentences well known to students of his poetry: "Everything written is as good as it is dramatic. It need not declare itself in form, but it is drama or nothing. A least lyric alone may have a hard time, but it can make a beginning, and lyric will be piled on lyric till all are easily heard as sung or spoken by a person in a scene—in character, in a setting" (1966, p. 13). Although not developed here, Frost's argument is based upon his theory of sentence sounds which he had promoted in letters and interviews between, especially, 1913 and 1920. Accordingly, he insists that sentences cannot hold the reader's or listener's attention unless they are dramatic, and that only the entanglement of the "speaking tone of voice" in the words can supply drama. Variation of sentence structure will not do. Without the dramatic element poetry degenerates into singsong. The editors comment that this essay could serve as an introduction to "all of the poet's beliefs about the art of writing" (1966, p. 13). This opinion may attach a bit too much importance to the three short paragraphs which make up the preface to *A Way Out,* for it implies that the preface is more significant than major essays like "The Figure a Poem Makes" and "Education by Poetry." Yet the preface is especially important to readers interested in Frost's use of sentence sounds, for the poet concludes: "I have always come as near the dramatic as I could this side of actually writing a play" (1966, p. 14). His poetry, including the "least lyrics," supports this statement.

One of the most important of Frost's essays, and surely the best known, is "The Figure a Poem Makes," a piece which originally served as the introduction to the 1939 and the 1949 editions of his collected poems. Although the essay is especially significant because of its outline of Frost's thoughts about organic creation, it is probably best remembered as the source of the poet's famous phrase "a momentary stay against confusion." This phrase relates to a question which Frost poses: how can a poem have wildness and still fulfill its subject? That is, how can a poem go its own way and still be controlled enough to express the poet's original mood? Arguing that the poetic process is organic, that the form and theme are not mechanically predetermined in the first line, he suggests that the figure of the completed poem constitutes a "stay" against the uncertainty attending the beginning of any artistic project. Thus "the figure a poem makes" is paradoxically "predestined" and "unforeseen" when the poet begins to write: it combines both the "stay" needed to control the poem's wildness and the freedom of wildness.

Frost also uses this essay to comment on sentence sounds. Calling sound the "gold in the ore," he suggests that "the object in writing poetry is to make all poems sound as different as possible from each other. . ." (1966, p. 17). Variation of vowels, consonants, syntax, and the like is not enough; the poet needs "the help of context—meaning—subject matter" (1966, p. 17). Metrical changes are also unlikely to alter sound because, as the poet points out in another well-known statement, the English language has but virtually two meters: "strict iambic and loose iambic." Many readers are likely to quarrel with Frost's narrow definitions of the ways to achieve variety in sound. Certainly, other poets will protest, for Frost typically dismisses alternative theories of verse, such as the use of sprung rhythm to avoid the monotony of the iambic meter. But Frost wants to use this essay to advance his definition of sentence sounds, and thus he declares that the best way to vary the sound of a poem is to include speaking tones: "The possibilities for tune from the dramatic tones of meaning struck across the rigidity of a limited meter are endless" (1966, p. 18).

These two major statements about the use of sentence sounds and about the necessity for organic creation support a larger generalization: that the figure a poem makes must develop naturally by what Frost calls a "straight crooked-ness." "The line will have the more charm for not being mechanically straight" (1966, p. 19). Although Frost does not name Edgar Allan Poe or the Imagists, he is apparently reacting against what he considers to be programmed methods of writing as defined in "The Philosophy of Composition" and in the preface to the 1915 annual *Some Imagist Poems.* For Frost insists that a poem's logic can be determined only "in retrospect, after the act. . . . It must be a revelation, or a series of revelations, as much for the poet as for the reader" (1966, p. 19). If a poet has the freedom of his material—that is, the freedom to use anything from his experience—he should permit the poem to run its own course from "delight to wisdom." Frost does not mean that the organic theory of art prohibits revision. He admits that a poem may be "worked over once it is in being, but may not be worried into being" (1966, p. 20). Calling for originality and initiative in his country, he asks for a similar kind of originality which will encourage him to fulfill the mood and form of the poem. This essay deserves its fame, for it includes some of Frost's most remarkable figures of speech.

"The Constant Symbol," originally published in *Atlantic Monthly* (Oct. 1946) and as the preface to the Modern Library edition of Frost's poems (1946), rephrases some of the ideas about organic creativity which first appear in "The Figure a Poem Makes." Frost begins by dismissing those critics who judge a poem's worth by its "hardness," by the amount of effort needed to understand it. More important, he suggests, are the metaphors used: "There are many other things I have found myself saying about poetry, but the chiefest of these is that it is metaphor, saying one thing and meaning another, saying one thing in terms of another, the pleasure of ulteriority. . . . Every poem is a new metaphor inside or it is nothing. And there is a sense in which all poems are the same old metaphor always" (1966, p. 24). This definition reflects ideas about metaphor which Frost develops more fully in "Education by Poetry," an essay published before "The Constant Symbol" but which follows the latter in the Cox-Lathem collection. His point here is that every poem is a great or small symbol of commitment: "a figure of the will braving alien entanglements (1966, p. 25). A poem should be judged not according to how "hard" it is but according to whether or not it fulfills its original intention. "The world," of course, cannot know the poet's intention, but as Frost writes rather sharply, "the world presumes to know."

As an example of commitment in his own art, Frost refers to "Stopping by Woods on a Snowy Evening." Smiling at what he calls "the recklessness of the unnecessary commitment" he made in the first line of the second stanza, he comments indirectly upon how the last word in that line all but committed him to a specific rhyme scheme. This particular poem should be evaluated on how it meets that commitment, and not especially on intention, for the intention is usually a special mood which only the poet knows. The poem cannot be forced into expression: "The only discipline to begin with is the inner mood that at worst may give the poet a false start or two. . ." (1966, p. 26). To illustrate, Frost selects Shakespeare's sonnet "When in disgrace with Fortune and men's eyes." The initial line, writes Frost, commits the bard to theme and form. Two lines more, and Shakespeare has the beginning of a rhyme scheme; three more, and "he has set himself a stanza." But as Frost notes, Shakespeare was probably going to write a sonnet when he began; thus the "only suspense he asks us to share with him is in the theme" (1966, p. 27). Will the poet "outlast or last out" the fourteen lines? Rigid commitments like these are why, says Frost, the sonnet is so suspect a form today. He then echoes "The Figure a Poem Makes," for he again insists that the poet's goal can be reached only by a "straight crookedness." He notes, for example, that he never would have committed himself to the well-known "treason-reason-season" rhyme of "Reluctance" had he realized in advance that the three words "about exhausted the possibilities." That particular rhyme is a constant symbol of his commitment to the poetic process.

A much better developed, less discursive essay is Frost's longest prose piece "Education by Poetry," originally published in the *Amherst Graduates' Quarterly* (Feb. 1931). Although little known except to Frost specialists, "Education by Poetry" is, in my opinion, the poet's most important single statement about his art. In the essay he both explains the relationship between poetry and experience and defines his ideas about metaphor. Frost's general concern here is to illustrate how poetry is essential to education, and he begins with a catalogue of the various ways by which teachers keep poetry out of the classroom. Some schools simply "bar" contemporary poetry. Others "let in" older poetry, but they destroy the art by teaching it as syntax or language—as anything but poetry. Still other schools permit the teaching of poetry, but no credit is given for the course. Although Frost expresses these opinions with tongue in cheek, he is clearly disturbed by what he considers to be the poor quality of college education. For he believes that students are being denied the opportunity to acquire "taste and judgment": "Why? Because they have not been educated enough to find their way around in contemporary literature. They don't know what they may safely like in the libraries and galleries. . . . They don't know when they are being fooled by a metaphor, an analogy, a parable. And metaphor is, of course, what we are talking about. Education by poetry is education by metaphor" (1966, p. 35).

Taste and judgment are related to what Frost ironically terms other "dread" words: imagination, initiative, inspiration, originality, and enthusiasm. He, for one, is not afraid of enthusiasm, but he insists that only a person who is educated by poetry can distinguish between genuine enthusiasm and "sunset raving." Sunset raving is the crude enthusiasm which affects those who are uneducated by poetry and which produces unintelligible "ohs" and "ahs." But true enthusiasm is "taken through the prism of the intellect. . . ." With this observation, Frost turns to his most complete discussion of metaphor: "I would be willing to throw away everything else but that: enthusiasm tamed by metaphor. Let me rest the case there. Enthusiasm tamed to metaphor, tamed to that much of it. I do not think anybody ever knows the discreet use of metaphor, his own and other people's, the discreet handling of metaphor, unless he has been properly educated in poetry" (1966, p. 36). But Frost, characteristically, does not rest his case "there." He uses the rest of the essay to define and illustrate the importance of metaphorical expression.

Poetry, for example, encompasses both trivial metaphors and profound thinking because it "provides the one permissable way of saying one thing and meaning another" (1966, p. 36). Indeed, Frost insists that all thinking, except perhaps mathematical analysis, is metaphorical. Yet true to his belief in the "momentary stay against confusion," defined in "The Figure a Poem Makes," he never claims that metaphorical expression is permanent. Push the metaphor too far, and it will break. Frost does not believe that confusion and chaos can be permanently stayed, but he does argue that facility with metaphor contributes to the momentary insights which make up a successful life. To illustrate, he discusses the metaphor of evolution. Admitting the brilliance of this metaphor when applied to the growth of the universe, he nevertheless points to how the metaphor "breaks down" when it is used to explain things like "the evolution of candy" or "the evolution of elevators." The point is that no one can know how far a metaphor should be stretched unless he is educated by poetry: "What I am pointing out is that unless you are at home in the metaphor, unless you have had your proper poetical education in the metaphor, you are not safe anywhere. Because you are not at ease with figurative values: you don't know the metaphor in its strength and its weakness. You don't know how far you may expect to ride it and when it may break down with you. You are not safe in science; you are not safe in history" (1966, p. 39). The "beauty" of metaphor is that it will always break down somewhere, and the challenge is to recognize when metaphorical expression reaches the breaking point.

Frost defines the greatest extension of metaphor as the attempt to "make" the final unity, "to say matter in terms of spirit, or spirit in terms of matter. . . . That is the greatest attempt that ever failed. We stop just short there. But it is the height of poetry, the height of all thinking, the height of all poetic thinking. . ." (1966, p. 41). This definition recalls a phrase from his poem "Directive"—"the height of the adventure"— and it is clear from "Education by Poetry" that Frost considers the demands of metaphorical expression to be both a challenge and a reward for the poet as he initiates his adventure into words. This experience is open to anyone who "comes close" to poetry, either by writing poetry or by reading it, "not as linguistics, not as history, not as anything but poetry" (1966, p. 43). And the person who gets close to poetry will understand the word "belief," especially the beliefs which Frost regards as crucial: self-belief, love-belief, art-belief, and God-belief. (Frost later extracted the four or five paragraphs on belief and published them separately as "The Four Beliefs.") His well-known nationalism sneaks in here when he digresses a moment to comment on national-belief. Expressing his suspicion of internationalism, he argues that a man mixes his metaphors if he believes that nations are now outmoded simply because "a Frenchman and an American and an Englishman can all sit down on the same platform and receive honors together. . ." (1966, p. 45). These last two pages or so of "Education by Poetry" may be extraneous, but they in no way blunt the impact of the discussion of metaphor. Frost explains his understanding of figurative language from the point of view of a poet instead of a literary analyst, from the perspective of a man committed to saying one thing and meaning another. This stimulating essay deserves to be better known.

Frost evidently considered "Education by Poetry" to be a major statement of his aesthetics, for he continued to work on it after its initial publication in 1931. On July 3, 1966, Edward Connery Lathem published a limited edition of a facsimile of "An Uncompleted Revision of 'Education by Poetry' " as a keepsake for those attending a Robert Frost gathering held at Dartmouth College. Mr. Lathem explains in his editor's note that the revision was found in the poet's papers after his death. This revision marks at least the second time which Frost personally rewrote the essay. The first was a revision of the transcript which resulted when Frost's talk "Education by Poetry" was stenographically recorded. The poet began the second version on his own copy of a reprint of "Education by Poetry" after it had been published in the *Amherst Graduates' Quarterly*. Since he apparently never completed his second revision, the editors of *Selected Prose* have wisely included the version of the essay as it was published in 1931. Still, the facsimile of the uncompleted revision makes fascinating reading, once the poet's handwriting is deciphered. Serious students of Frost should try to find a copy for comparison.

After "Education by Poetry," the next two essays in *Selected Prose* seem a letdown. Neither "Maturity No Object" nor "The Hear-Say Ballad" illustrates the poet's efforts to express his own aesthetics, perhaps because with these pieces Frost is writing introductions to someone else's work. "Maturity No Object" was originally published in 1957 as an introduction to an anthology of younger poets, *New Poets of England and America*. Once again, Frost takes up the subject of poetry and education: "My excuse is that school and poetry come so near being one thing" (1966, p. 49). He rephrases what he expresses better in "Education by Poetry"—namely that familiarity with the metaphors of poetry permits the reader to be at ease with all thinking, including the scientific and the philosophical. Although clearly not referring to those literary critics whom he often accused of overreading poetry, Frost insists upon the affinity of the scholar and the poet, the chief distinction being that a scholar gets his knowledge a bit too consciously. But in neither case—scholar or poet—is maturity an object of concern: "all poets I have ever heard of struck their note long before forty, the deadline for contributions to this book" (1966, p. 50). Maturity may initiate changes in one's art, but the poetry in *New Poets in England and America* will always be representative of the individual poet's work. Thus, Frost's challenge is not to the authors in this book but to the reader of it, for the reader is "on trial." He is "given his chance to see if he can tell all by himself without critical instruction the difference between the poets who wrote because they thought it would be a good idea to write and those who couldn't help writing out of a strong weakness for the muse, as for an elopement with her" (1966, p. 51). Frost poses a real problem here, one which is especially interesting when we recall his own struggle to find publishers who could recognize his "weakness for the muse."

"The Hear-Say Ballad," originally published in *Ballads Migrant in New England* by Helen Hartness Flanders and Marguerite Olney (1953), is a charming short discussion of the ballad. Quoting Addison's statement that all readers should love ballads unless they are unqualified by affectation or ignorance, Frost says that this challenge remains relevant today. The reason is that the spirit of balladry is also the spirit of all poetry:

ballads belong to the "none too literate." "No patronage of
ours will smile them out of using 'fee' for a rhyme word, 'lily-
white hands' for beauty, and lords and ladies for goodness
knows what away off here three thousand miles across the
ocean and after three hundred years of democracy" (1966, p.
56). With insight Frost notes that a ballad stays "Half-lacking"
unless it is sung because the voice and ear cannot determine
how to read a ballad until supplied with the tune. Thus, he
praises Mrs. Flanders for listening to the ballads being sung before she transcribed them for her collection. What finally counts
in a ballad is not the apparent flaws in meter, syntax, logic, and
sense, but the positive breaking of the voice with emotion as it
reads. This short introduction illustrates Frost's understanding
of one phase of the historical development of poetry.

The next two essays in *Selected Prose*, "Introduction to *King
Jasper*" and "The Poetry of Amy Lowell," are indirect revelations of Frost's opinions about two of his famous contemporaries, Edwin Arlington Robinson and Amy Lowell. Indeed, the
"Introduction" to Robinson's last book *King Jasper* (1935) may
have been the most controversial of Frost's prose statements
when it was published. It can be profitably read in the context
of the second volume of Lawrance Thompson's official biography
in which Thompson reveals how Frost's jealousy strained the
relationship between the two poets (see *Robert Frost: The Years
of Triumph, 1915–1938*, pp. 419–22). According to Thompson,
the experience of writing a tribute to "friend-and-enemy Robinson" was an ordeal which grew out of the poet's inability to
praise the work of any writer who might be considered a rival.
Frost, for example, refused to acknowledge Robinson's gift of
The Man Against the Sky, although Robinson thanked Frost
for a copy of *Mountain Interval*. Similarly, Frost declined an
opportunity to join the celebration of Robinson's fiftieth birthday, made "slurring remarks" about the sonnet "New England,"
and was especially jealous of the success of *Tristram*. Understandably, Frost had mixed emotions when Robinson's publisher asked him to write an introduction for *King Jasper*. In
the original draft of the essay, Frost managed to convey his
own opinions about and prejudices against experimental poetry
without mentioning Robinson's poem. When he named Robinson at all, it was usually to claim that Robinson agreed with
some of his own ideas about religious matters and about the difference between grief and grievances. It was only after Macmillan, Robinson's publisher, complained that the essay was too

much Frost that Frost brought in Robinson by quoting from poems like "Miniver Cheevy," "Mr. Flood's Party," and "The Dark Hills." Later, when the American Academy of Poets invited Frost to write a tribute to Robinson, he refused on the grounds that he had done his best in the "Introduction to *King Jasper*."

Certainly one way to read the essay is with this biographical material in hand. Yet for all of the controversy surrounding it, the "Introduction" remains one of the best sources of Frost's ideas about poetry, regardless of his jealousy of Robinson, for it reveals as much about Frost the poet as it does about Frost the man. He may not pay fitting tribute to his contemporary, but he does take the occasion to strike out at an age which "ran wild in the quest of new ways to be new" (1966, p. 59). Writing in his best sarcastic tone, he lists the various styles in which the new poetry was written: without punctuation, capital letters, metric frame, coherence, consistency, and even ability. Frost praises Robinson for staying "content with the old-fashioned way to be new" (1966, p. 60). In this way Robinson avoids the "fear of Man—the fear that men won't understand us and we shall be cut off from them." This fear parallels the other great fear, "the fear of God," which results when one suspects that he is not worthy. Frost's point is that correspondence remains as important in art as recognition—poets lose correspondence with the reader when they manufacture new ways to be new.

Similarly, writes Frost, poetry should not be used "as a vehicle of grievances against the un-Utopian state. . . . A distinction must be made between griefs and grievances" (1966, p. 61). This opinion echoes Frost's well-known distaste for the poetry of propaganda, and the unsympathetic reader is likely to dismiss this section of the essay as one more tiresome example of the poet's rather unimaginative conservatism. If so, the reader would miss an interesting discussion, for Frost suggests that grievances be restricted to prose and that griefs (presumably emotions resulting from alienation, resignation, loss of love, etc.) be left to poetry. He praises Robinson for being "a prince of heartachers amid countless achers of another part" (1966, p. 62). Frost then puts words into Robinson's mouth, but in doing so he succinctly expresses one of his most important ideas about poetry. Dismissing the notion that poetry can be written according to plan, he insists that it must be created in spite of artistic theories and critical analyses: "And poems are all that matter. The utmost of ambition is to lodge a few poems where they will be hard to get rid of, to lodge a few irreducible bits where Robinson lodged more than his share" (1966, p. 63). Robinson was so successful because he avoided grievances in order to face "the spiritual realities." When reading this essay, it seems clear that Frost is also praising his own ability to write meaningfully about griefs and spiritual realities. Thus, he can celebrate his contemporary because Robinson, or so he claims, agreed with him about the function of poetry.

Turning to Robinson's poetry, Frost immediately lauds "Miniver Cheevy," especially for the way in which the fourth "thought" ("Miniver thought, and thought, and thought,/And thought about it.") "turns up by surprise round the corner." This word adds what Frost calls "the intolerable touch of poetry" (1966, p. 64). He preceptively points out that the tension between Robinson's unhappy themes and his humorous touches accounts for his greatness. This observation leads Frost to one of his best known statements about poetic technique: "The style is the man. Rather say the style is the way the man takes himself; and to be at all charming or even bearable, the way is almost rigidly prescribed. If it is with outer seriousness, it must be with inner humor. If it is with outer humor, it must be with inner seriousness. Neither one alone without the other under it will do" (1966, p. 65). The combination of humor and seriousness makes poetry "merciless," as in "Miniver Cheevy" or "Mr. Flood's Party." Professor Thompson's account of the mixed emotions which plagued Frost when he wrote this Introduction is surely relevant, but I, for one, wonder if his interpretation of the essay is appropriate. It is true that Frost never mentions *King Jasper* and that he claims Robinson's agreement with several of his own opinions about poetry. But the "Introduction to *King Jasper*" reveals nothing specific of his apparent jealousy. To one unfamiliar with Thompson's biography, the essay sounds like very high praise indeed of a fellow poet whose life was a "revel in the felicities of language."

Frost's dislike of Amy Lowell also colors his three paragraph memoir of her, "The Poetry of Amy Lowell," which was first published in *The Christian Science Monitor* (May 16, 1925). Several factors contributed to his disapproval of Miss Lowell. Perhaps foremost among them was his negative reaction to her essay about him in *Tendencies in Modern American Poetry* (see chapter 2 of the present study), but Frost also disapproved of her overbearing personality and of her Imagist poetry. He must have written this tribute to Amy Lowell with some discomfort. Professor Thompson notes that Frost had to strike a balance between his admiration for her lively spirit and his distaste for her poetry. The reader unfamiliar with Frost's veneration of sound in poetry or with his theory of sentence sounds might read this memoir as a statement of praise. For the initiated, however, what is omitted is just as important as what is said. For example, Frost begins by arguing that the so-called test of time is the wrong way to determine whether or not a poem will last: "The proof of a poem is not that we have never forgotten it, but that we knew at sight that we never could forget it." Establishing this standard, he then cleverly avoids applying it to Amy Lowell because he knows that her poetry will fail the test: "How often I have heard it in the voice and seen it in the eyes of this generation that Amy Lowell has lodged poetry with them to stay" (1966, p. 71).

The distinction here between this essay and the "Introduction to *King Jasper*" is crucial, for although Frost praises Robinson's permanence, he never once admits that Miss Lowell has "lodged" a few unforgettable poems. Rather, he attributes the opinion of her worth to the anonymous "voice" and "eyes" of "this generation." His only real compliment is that she "helped make it stirring times" for those interested in poetry. Concluding with a comment about her Imagism, he notes that her appeal "lay chiefly in images to the eye. . . . Her poetry was forever a clear and resonant calling off of things seen" (1966, p. 72). This observation sounds like praise to those unacquainted with Frost's belief that poetry is chiefly sound. By pointing out Miss Lowell's "calling off of things seen," he is implicitly criticizing her failure to write with an appeal to the ear. This short essay is skillfully conceived so that Frost need not falsely praise her or openly detail her shortcomings. Only those familiar with his own ideas about poetry will be able to read between the lines. The remarkable thing about these two essays on Robinson and Amy Lowell is that his opinions have proved to be correct: from today's perspective it seems clear that, unlike Lowell, Robinson lodged a few poems where "they will be hard to get rid of."

Perhaps the most unusual essay in *Selected Prose* is "A Romantic Chasm," the introduction to the English edition of *A Masque of Reason* (1948) and not widely known in the United States. The editors of *Selected Prose* describe it as "a curiously quirky, difficult piece of prose." It would seem that emphasis should be on "quirky" rather than "difficult." Although referring to his old friendships with Englishmen Edward Thomas and John Haines, Frost's primary concern is to celebrate the affinities between English and American English. The essay seems quirky because it lacks the successful development of idea and the eye-catching turns of phrase which characterize most of the other prose pieces. Frost claims that he should have learned from reading Kipling about the differences between the two uses of English, but that he did not heed the examples until he studied H. L. Mencken. Glad for the common source of English and American English, he nevertheless argues that the distinguishing qualities of each language should be maintained at least to the degree of preserving unusual words: "Anyway I might be tempted to enlist with the forlorn hope who would sacrifice all the words in both languages except a very limited few we could agree on as meaning the same in both; only with the proviso that I should be drawn on the committee for vocabulary where I could hold out for certain favourites for my own use, such as *quackery* for remedies too unorthodox, *boustrophedon* for a more scientific eye-reading, . . . *onery* for the old-fashioned colonial pronunciation of ordinary with only one accent" (1966, p. 76). Frost wants to maintain the national distinctions, but, as he writes with tongue in cheek, he hopes that American English never seems too strange to Englishmen for fear that his own poetry would have to be annotated, provided with a glossary, or worse, studied. The thrust of this essay is consistent with the poet's lifelong fascination with sound and with turns of phrase. He offers *A Masque of Reason* to the English as an example of his kinship with them by language, but he also holds firmly to his right to create poetry with "an average ingenuity with figures of speech." Both countries must therefore keep "in practice with each other's quips and figures."

The "Preface to *Memoirs of the Notorious Stephen Burroughs*" (1924) is the earliest of the prose pieces in *Selected Prose*. It and the following essay, "Perfect Day—A Day of Prowess," are the lightest in tone, both excellent examples of Frost's irony and humor. Burroughs was a rogue with a romantic appeal, the kind of ne'er-do-well who often finds himself a folk hero to those who do not suffer from his various capers. With cheerful irony, Frost insists that Burroughs was not simply a rascal, but a man whose "chief distinction was hypocrisy." And why, Frost wonders, should a man be hounded if his Sunday sermons were sound, even if the sermons were stolen and the preacher not ordained? Frost is so pleased with Burroughs' writing skill that he advises the reader to place the *Memoirs* on the same shelf with books by Benjamin Franklin and Jonathan Edwards: "Franklin will be a reminder of what we have been as a young nation in some respects, Edwards in others. Burroughs comes in reassuringly when there is question of our not unprincipled wickedness, whether we have had enough of it for salt. . . . But sophisticated wickedness, the kind that knows its grounds and can twinkle, could we be expected to have produced so fine a flower in a pioneer state? The answer is that we had it and had it early in Stephen Burroughs. . ." (1966, p. 84). This passage clearly has a touch of irony, but it is also clear that Frost admires Burroughs' rashness. Having little value to those who read Frost's prose only as a key to his poetic principles, this essay is nevertheless interesting because it furnishes additional evidence that the poet did not like holier-than-thou do-gooders. In all probability Frost is serious when he writes that we need a little evil "for salt."

The second light-hearted piece, "Perfect Day—A Day of Prowess," was first published in 1956 for *Sports Illustrated* when Frost covered the All-Star baseball game. The poet's passion for the sport, while perhaps not as well known as Marianne Moore's, has been thoroughly documented by Lawrance Thompson in the biography. Believing that the word "prowess" can be applied to both baseball and poetry, Frost implies that the two activities are connected by their mutual emphasis on grace, fluidity, valor, and skill. Ken Boyer making "two impossible catches" and Yogi Berra smarting from a foul tip in his ungloved hand illustrate the kind of heroism which Frost sees in writing poetry. He points to his friendship with Ed Lewis, a National League pitcher as well as president of the universities of New Hampshire and Massachusetts, as an example of the unity between baseball and supposedly more intellectual activities: "The nearest of kin to the artists in college where we all become bachelors of arts are their fellow performers in baseball, football and tennis" (1966, p. 91). Clearly, Frost sees more in baseball than just sport. To him it represents the United States itself with acts and myths of symbolic importance: Walter Johnson throwing a silver dollar across the Potomac, Gabby Street catching a baseball dropped from the top of the Washington Monument, Johnny Temple swinging two bats before stepping to the plate to show that we must do "something beforehand a good deal harder than what we are just going to do," and the umpire as an example of impartiality and fairness which Supreme Court justices could emulate. In the guise of praising baseball, Frost celebrates America with a characteristic mixture of seriousness and humor.

"The Prerequisites" originally appeared in the *New York Times Book Review* (Mar. 21, 1954) and as the preface to a collection of Frost's poems *Aforesaid* (1954). It is another valuable statement of Frost's aesthetics, but in this essay the poet is primarily concerned with how to read poetry rather than with the technique of writing it. Recalling the trouble he had understanding the final stanza of Emerson's "Brahma," Frost explains the great pleasure which reading poetry generates: "Success in taking figures of speech is as intoxicating as success in making figures of speech" (1966, p. 96). But what happens if, like Frost with "Brahma," the reader does not meet with immediate success? He must return to the poem "by stealth," says the poet, and he must take care that he protects his chance to "see for himself what the poem is all about." No prefaces, footnotes, or subsequent explanations for him: "Being taught poems reduces them to the rank of mere information." The prerequisite for reading difficult poetry is a familiarity with many poems so that the reader can "circulate" among all of them. Clarifying his idea, Frost sets down one of the most famous of his observations in prose: "A poem is best read in the light of all the other poems ever written. We may read A the better to read B (we have to start somewhere; we may get very little out of A). We read B the better to read C, C the better to read D, D the better to go back and get something more out of A. Progress is not the aim, but circulation. The thing is to get among the poems where they hold each other apart in their places as the stars do" (1966, p. 97). This statement requires no comment other than to note that in this essay Frost specifies the way in which his *Collected Poems* should be read: not as linear progress from poem to poem but as circulation among all the poems.

"Remarks Accepting the Gold Medal of the National Institute of Arts and Letters" (see *National Institute News Bulletin*, v, 1939) was written after Frost expressed essentially the same ideas at the awards ceremony. In four short paragraphs Frost acknowledges the importance of public acclaim to the artist. Although he never says so directly, he hints at the pain which so many years of neglect caused him. The healthy poet, he writes, straddles the line between self-approval and the approval of society, but what happens if public praise is withheld?

Too often the artist must rely solely on self-appraisal: "For twenty years the world neglected him; then for twenty years it entreated him kindly. He has to take the responsibility of deciding when the world was wrong" (1966, pp. 101–2). The scientist, says Frost, has the advantage because he receives acclaim if his predictions are correct. Still, all is not lost for the artist. If his work fits into "the nature of people," he will know that the test has been met successfully: "I should like to have it that your medal is a token of my having fitted, not into the nature of the Universe, but in some small way, at least, into the nature of Americans—into their affections, is perhaps what I mean" (1966, p. 102). What is remarkable about this statement is that it turned out to be true. This recorded talk was published in 1939, more than a decade before the public veneration of Frost emerged, particularly in the 1950s and early 1960s. True, by 1939 Frost had already been awarded three Pulitzer Prizes, but he had not become the national hero that he was in his last years. If Frost is sincere in his belief that what truly matters for the artist is the acceptance of his work by the people, then he received more genuine acclaim than any other American poet of this century.

The final prose piece in *Selected Prose* to be discussed (the volume's concluding essay, "On Emerson," is evaluated in chapter 4 of the present study) is in fact a letter first published in the *Amherst Student* (Mar. 25, 1935) and known today as the "Letter to the *Amherst Student*." Several reasons support the editors' decision to single out this one short letter for inclusion in a collection of Frost's prose. It is an important statement of the poet's philosophical position when faced with apparently ceaseless turmoil. It is one of his least known but most explicit comments upon the tension in both life and art between confusion and form. The document also succinctly expresses his belief in the need for qualified affirmation.

After acknowledging the birthday congratulations from the Amherst student body, Frost launches into an evaluation of "the age" in 1935. Although the world is depression-ridden and sliding toward a new world war, Frost declares his impatience with the kind of talk which laments that this age is particularly bad. He sends the students to history in the hope that they will note how artists and philosophers have always claimed their age to be the worst: "All ages of the world are bad—a great deal worse anyway than Heaven. If they weren't the world might just as well be Heaven at once and have it over with" (1966, pp. 105–6). This statement reflects two consistent ideas in Frost's philosophy: earth, not heaven, is the "right place for love"; and man's duty is not to complain about the world but to try to live creatively within it. As he explains, thousands of years of progress have not made "the world any easier a place in which to save your soul." Those who try to get outside of "anything as large as an age" in an attempt to judge it can only "gape in agony" or "write huge shapeless novels, huge gobs of raw sincerity bellowing with pain and that's all they can write" (1966, p. 160).

Fortunately, says Frost, no one needs to know how bad the age is because there is always something to be done—the creation of form. "When in doubt there is always form for us to go on with. Anyone who has achieved the least form to be sure of it, is lost to the larger excruciations" (1966, p. 106). His philosophy is especially relevant because he does not limit the creation of form to the artist. Any creation—a basket, a letter, a garden, a poem—can stay the confusion as long as the form is consciously created. Indeed, Frost concludes the letter with a remarkable celebration of the age's "badness" and of universal confusion because he believes that the chaos supplies man with the necessity to create. The background may be "hugeness and confusion shading away from where we stand into black and utter chaos," but man can cope if he asserts a small figure of "order and concentration." Thus, Frost insists that man should not only take advantage of the chaos but that he should also recognize the practical reasons for desiring it: "To me any little form I assert upon it is velvet, as the saying is, and to be considered for how much more it is than nothing" (1966, p. 107). The ideas in this letter should send the reader to Frost's "West-Running Brook," a poem in which he celebrates the momentary resistance of a wave in the brook as a metaphor for the assertion of form before both wave and stream rush to the "universal cataract of death" which "spends to nothingness." Similarly, the reader should also compare this letter with the essay "The Figure a Poem Makes" in order to note how the poet applies the famous phrase "a momentary stay against confusion" to both the difficult process of artistic creation and the struggle to make something of one's life.

Selected Prose of Robert Frost is, therefore, a valuable collection not only because it gathers together fifteen of the poet's most important prose statements, but also because most of these were originally published in obscure journals. Not many readers have access to the *Amherst Graduates' Quarterly*, for example, or to the *National Institute News Bulletin*. In addition the editors supply short explanatory notes detailing the circumstances of publication for each essay. The major shortcomings of the collection are the absence of an index and the nonchronological arrangement. An index would have made the book a more accessible source for scholarly work on Frost, and chronological arrangement would have provided the reader with an easier means to gauge the development and variation of some of the poet's ideas.

The fifteen essays in *Selected Prose* form the heart of Frost's achievement in prose, but the poet published many other statements which are little known and often difficult to locate. Two of these selections can be characterized by pertinent quotations. In "Poet—One of the Truest," in *Percy MacKaye: A Symposium on His Fiftieth Birthday* (1928), Frost expresses an ideal which he never explains and which seems at odds with his general pragmatism: "That is but an incident in the general campaign he is forever on, to hasten the day when our national life, the raw material of poetry, having become less and less raw, shall at last cease to be raw at all, and poetry shall almost write itself without the intervention of the artist" (1928, p. 21). To the best of my knowledge, Frost never made anything more of this idea. And in "A Sermon" (1947), the poet expresses one of his favorite definitions of religion. The passage quoted below recalls a major theme in *A Masque of Mercy:* "Now religion always seems to me to come round to something beyond wisdom. It's a straining of the spirit forward to a wisdom beyond wisdom. . . . And the fear of God always has meant the fear that one's wisdom, one's own wisdom, one's own human wisdom is not quite acceptable in His sight" (1947, no pages).

The remaining prose pieces to be discussed deserve further comment because they provide more complete statements about the poet's aesthetics and philosophy. The earliest is "Introduction" to *The Arts Anthology: Dartmouth Verse, 1925* (1925), an essay which looks forward to "Maturity No Object" because in it Frost comments upon the progress of young, unknown poets. He might have titled the introduction "growth by waterspout," for he pointedly dismisses the beansprout as a metaphor for the artist's development, choosing the less conventional figure of the waterspout. The waterspout is more appropriate, writes Frost, because it suggests the unity of heaven and earth, of spirit and matter. The new poet begins "as a cloud" of the poets he knows from his reading experiences: "And first the cloud reaches down toward the water from above and then the water reaches up toward the cloud from below and finally cloud and water join together to roll as one pillar between heaven and earth. The base of water he picks up from below is of course all the life he ever lived outside of books" (1925, p. vii). Poets who die young rarely get beyond the first step of the figure, that is, beyond "the cloud" of all the poets they have read. Bringing something "down" from the established writers, poets fated to die young can lift nothing up. Frost here characteristically slurs the Imagists when he writes that in the case of Imagism the young poet brings influences "often a long way down." He lists the poems in this anthology which he believes still to be caught in the "cloud"—that is, "frankly derivative." His highest praise is reserved for those poems which have begun to "lift something up." This essay concludes with a general condemnation of the way poetry is handled in school. Arguing that the writer must "strike his individual note sometime between the ages of fifteen and twenty-five," Frost complains that the schools too often consider mischief and the muse to be one. He does not want poetry to be regularized in courses, but he would like for the arts to be encouraged: "Just setting the expectation of poetry forward might be all that was needed to give us our proportioned number of poets to Congressmen" (1925, p. ix).

In "Remarks on the Dedication of the Wilfred Davison Memorial Library" (1930), Frost again expresses his concern for the way poetry is taught. Although a memorial to Wilfred Davison, his remarks go beyond an obituary to foreshadow ideas which are more fully developed in the later essays "Education by Poetry" and "Poetry and School." Frost praises Davison because the latter understood the importance of poetry in education—he gave the Bread Loaf school "the bent of poetry." Frost writes: "I don't think there is anything very important without poetry. I don't think mathematics, science, is important without poetry, or amounts to much" (1930, no pages). Those who are familiar with Frost's ideas about art will recognize that the poet is indirectly expressing his beliefs that the educated person must be at home with metaphor and that reading poetry is the best way to become confident with metaphorical expression. Thus, Wilfred Davison deserves praise because he understood the significance of figurative language: "He just had always with him this poetic fineness: I think he never would willingly have any teacher on the place who would give to literature a meaning that wasn't intended by the person who wrote it." To Frost's mind, Davison was the ideal director of a school because he stayed "above the perversions of poetry" by making "the whole thing unpedagogical and poetic."

Frost's "Introduction" to Sarah N. Cleghorn's *Threescore* (1936) seems at first glance to be out of character, for in it the poet praises a reformer. His dislike of reformers is well known, for he saw them as meddlers, do-gooders, and idealists who ignore the permanence of confusion. Readers who know his socially oriented poems in *A Further Range* and the "editorials" of the later books should study this introduction because the poet discusses his ideas in such a way as to alter the definition of reform which the reader gets from only the poems. Characterizing Sarah Cleghorn as "saint, poet—*and* reformer," Frost launches into the kind of disparaging remarks about reformers which recall *A Further Range* (also published in 1936 during the depression). He claims that Cleghorn's poem about child labor has "more high explosive for righteousness" than all the prose of "the radical boundboys" caught in the atmosphere of revolution. The scornful phrase "radical boundboys" typifies Frost's general attitude toward reformers, one which earned him negative reviews in the 1930s. But his contempt is surely tempered by a second definition of reform which is unfortunately not as well known. In the introduction to *Threescore*, he distinguishes between reformers like Sarah Cleghorn, who "all her life long pursued the even tenor of her aspiration," and those "radicals" who jump from cause to cause: "Some of us have developed a habit of saying we can't stand a reformer. But we don't mean it except where the reformer is at the same time a raw convert to the latest scheme for saving the soul or the state. The last we heard of him may have been two or three fashions ago as one of the ultra-arty insisting that we join him in his minor vices at his wild parties" (1936, p. x).

Frost's scorn is still evident, but in the context of this essay it now seems less the ranting of an extreme conservative and more the result of distinction between types of reform. His respect for Sarah Cleghorn is based upon appreciation of her need to speak out for everything from black people to the threatened egrets in the Everglades. She never "came to grief" from minding another's business because she was like the partisan for whom "the great importance is not to get hold of both ends, but of the right end" (1936, p. xii). More skeptical readers may pro-

test that this introduction does not clarify the other side of
Frost's opinion of reformers as much as it testifies to his polite-
ness toward a woman from Vermont who never caused too
much trouble with her various causes. For support they can
point to the sarcastic statement in the introduction: "The fact
remains that I do know one or two people who have done
measurable good" (1936, p. xi). I would have to disagree with
these potential detractors, for it is my belief that in this one
essay Frost attempts to differentiate between his dislike of
meddlers and his praise of the genuinely concerned.

Two interesting but almost entirely unknown essays appeared in *Biblia* (Feb. 1938) under the title "Two Lectures
by Robert Frost." The first, "Poverty and Poetry," was delivered at Haverford College on October 25, 1937; the second,
"The Poet's Next of Kin in a College," was given at Princeton
on October 26, 1937. The editors of *Selected Prose* understandably omit these essays from their collection, for the published versions result from shorthand notes of Frost's spoken
words which the poet did not examine before their appearance
in *Biblia*. The essays, however, are valuable if the reader keeps
in mind the facts of publication.

In "Poverty and Poetry," Frost returns again to ideas which
clearly intrigued him all of his life: the definitions of poverty
and radicalism, and their relationship with art. This essay reflects his more commonly known thoughts about poverty, and
thus it contrasts with the near genial opinions expressed in the
introduction to *Threescore*. The same man who praises Sarah
Cleghorn for her radicalism is quoted in "Poverty and Poetry" as claiming to "do" charitable acts "only once in a great
while." Frost eases into his topic from opening remarks in which
he defends "his people," "the ordinary folks" he "belongs to"
and whom he writes about in *North of Boston*. Upset at the
way his "book of people" has been interpreted by cultivated
students and artists, he insists that his people are just like everyone else, that poverty does not make them different. He recalls
a book (*A Proletarian Journey*) by Fred Beal, who, like himself, lived in Lawrence, Massachusetts, but he implies that Beal
exaggerates the conditions of poverty in that small town.
Claiming that he does not "know how to measure poverty,"
Frost criticizes Beal for misusing the words "radical" and, particularly, "proletarian." Beal, writes Frost, cannot be a proletarian because he has famous kin and because he never knew
the European peasant life. To be a proletarian, one must liter-

ally "come up from nowhere." This observation leads Frost to his topic, the relationship between poverty and poetry.

If read too quickly, his comments might seem unnecessarily harsh. He insists, for example, that he wants the rich to keep away from the poor. Similarly, he writes that the Bible does not say that "you always have the poor with you. That isn't what it says. It says, 'For Christ's sake, forget the poor some of the time'" (1938a, no pages). Yet these comments are not severe, for, as he notes, he does not know how to measure poverty. His point is that we should forget about the material wealth of people and begin to treat everyone as human beings. Answering the charge that he writes about the poor, Frost comments: "I never measured that; I wouldn't have done it if I knew anything was going to be made of it. I didn't do it to get rid of the poor because I need them in my business" (1938a, no pages). Unfortunately, this passage has been misinterpreted to mean that the poet hopes to keep the poor in their place. But Frost means nothing more than the fact that the poor, regardless of their bank accounts, are people pretty much like everyone else. He defends the characters in *North of Boston* as men with common problems, perhaps unable to spend a lot of money but certainly able to love and fear and dream: "I just bring up the little question of the relationship and make a few suggestions, because I run the risk of reading about people—I wouldn't dare say whether they were rich or poor people" (1938a, no pages). In the remainder of the essay, Frost comments upon a few of his poems, especially those from *A Further Range* which he describes as having "a good deal more of the times in it than anything I ever wrote before." Those interested only in the poetry will enjoy reading his brief comments, such as the distinction between a lone striker and a "collectivist striker" ("The Lone Striker"), and the defense of the troublesome last part of "Two Tramps in Mud Time" as stanzas which have "nothing to do with the times." In short, this essay is much less controversial than it might seem at first glance.

"The Poet's Next of Kin in a College" has a totally different subject. In a manner which looks forward to his essay on the All-Star baseball game, "Perfect Day — A Day of Prowess," Frost praises the relationship between poetry and athletics. He is in his best humor here, for he runs down the list of academic departments which could have an affinity with the arts, only to reject them all in favor of the athletic department. The English professors, for example, are always the kindest, but these teach-

ers love poets to such an extreme that they disarm the writer
so that he cannot deal with editors, who generally hate poets.
The primary drawback with the English department is that it
gathers "all kinds of teachers." Frost immediately dismisses the
bibliographer, "the keeper of texts," as a man who means "very
little to the writer." The professor who lectures on poetry as
representative of an age ("if it is a rotten age, then it should be
rotten poetry") "does not matter to the poet at all." And those
who "meddle with" criticism are not helpful, either. Still, the
English department is kinder than the "socio-economic" department which Frost blames for "the vitiation of much of our
poetry today." The science department is nearer to poetry because it encourages creativity, and the philosophy teachers are
helpful because they promote insights. But because poetry is
mainly performance, the poet finds his nearest kin in the athletic department.

Establishing this rather unusual opinion, Frost recalls his
friendship with Ed Lewis, a premier National League pitcher
who gave up baseball to become a university president. Lewis
is not mentioned by name, but it seems clear that he is the object
of Frost's admiration: a great athlete who "looked on poetry as
performance." Recalling his "Introduction" to *The Arts Anthology: Dartmouth Verse, 1925*, Frost again restates his belief
that the poet (like the athlete) must strike his note between the
ages of fifteen and twenty-five. Most of all, the kinship between
poetry and athletics depends upon the demands of both kinds
of performances to maintain form. This idea, of course, is crucial to Frost's aesthetics, from his dismissal of free verse as form-
less to his celebration of organic form.

When one looks back over his own poetry, his only criticism
is whether he had form or not. Did he worry it out or pour it
out? You can't go back to a tennis game and play it over — except
with alibis. You can go back over a poem and touch it up — but
never unless you are in the same form again. Yet the great pleasure
in writing poetry is in having been carried off. It is as if you
stood astride of the subject that lay on the ground, and they cut
the cord, and the subject gets up under you and you ride it. You
adjust yourself to the motion of the thing itself. That is the poem.
[1938b, no pages]

This reaffirmation of the necessity for clearly discernible form
in poetry makes this little known essay worth remembering.

In "The Doctrine of Excursions: A Preface," *Bread Loaf*

Anthology (1939), Frost rephrases some ideas which must have been very much on his mind in 1939, for he expresses the same thoughts in "Remarks Accepting the Gold Medal of the National Institute of Arts and Letters" (1939), discussed above. Indirectly recalling his own long struggle for recognition, Frost uses this short essay to stress the importance of public acclaim for an artist. He rejects as an illusion the suggestion that the ideal atmosphere for the poet is creativity in private which is recognized only after the writer's death: "All we know is that the crowning mercy for an author is publication in some form or other" (1939, p. xix). As he explains, an artist can write for himself for years, but sooner or later he must be read if he hopes to continue. Frost admits that in appealing to the public the poet adds to his responsibilities — the poet must now judge his judges as well as himself. How can he tell if the public is right to receive him now when it ignored him for years? (The autobiographical allusion here is unmistakable.) "Why, when the final authority is his, should he be bothered with any other? The answer is an article in the doctrine of excursions" (1939, p. xix).

Frost praises Bread Loaf because it is a secondary means of publication for the author who brings a manuscript. He describes it as a place where a writer can "try his effect on readers" and where he "must brave the rigors of specific criticism." He concludes with the same metaphor which he uses in the National Institute remarks: the scientist has a means of determining self-esteem which is enviable because he can use the mathematical precision of his experiments to prove that he fits into the nature of the universe: "I should like to believe the poet gets an equivalent assurance in the affections of the affectionate. He has fitted into the nature of mankind" (1939, p. xx). This essay may not be an important source of Frost's ideas about art, but it is a significant sidelight on the biographical information now available. Acknowledging the need for publication and for acceptance by the people, Frost indirectly but clearly suggests how badly hurt he was during the long years of neglect, and why he later worked so hard to develop his role as the beloved old poet of the nation.

"Poetry and School" (*Atlantic Monthly*, June 1951) is not an essay but a series of short prose passages which the editors describe as entries from Frost's notebooks. I am unaware of the existence of the poet's notebooks; the passages quoted in this article read like restatements of well-worn Frost comments which he expressed all of his life. Included, for example, are the usual complaints about how poetry is taught. He also argues that "Improvement will not be a progression but a widening circulation," an opinion which later forms the heart of his essay "The Prerequisites" — that the way to appreciate poetry is in the context of all the other poems one has read. Although he taught literature at various colleges, Frost seems strongly opposed to the addition of poetry to a course syllabus. His main concern is that students become better readers, but he repeats his insistence that "poems are not meant to be read in course any more than they are to be made a study of" (1951, p. 30). The danger of too much reading in college is that the student might degenerate into a specialist who is more at home with literary criticism than with literature. This observation enables Frost to strike out at "the language of criticism" and indirectly to attack poems whch do not reflect his own definition of poetry: "Too many recent poems have been actually done in the language of evaluation. They are too critical in spirit to admit of further criticism" (1951, p. 31).

This collection of Frostian commentaries also includes several statements reflecting the poet's belief that poetry should appeal to the ear instead of to the eye. Describing the eye reader as a "barbarian," Frost praises the ideal reader as one who goes "no faster than he can hear the lines and sentences in his mind's ear as if aloud" (1951, p. 31). In short, this article is more a grab bag of quotable quotes than a discussion of ideas. Its appeal is to readers who are unfamiliar with the scope of Frost's work. Specialists will find the quotations to be signposts in remembered territory — even the old saw about free verse and tennis is included: "For my pleasure I had as soon write free verse as play tennis with the net down."

A more interesting essay is the transcription of "The Commencement Address" which Frost delivered at Dartmouth in 1955 (Dartmouth Alumni Magazine, July 1955). Once again, he expresses his general disappointment with the system of college education, but this time he touches on his personal experiences at Dartmouth during his short career as a student in 1892. Romanticizing his decision to drop out during his freshman year, Frost tells the graduating seniors that he "ran away" because he "was more interested in education than anybody in the College at the time" (1955, p. 14). This is an amusing statement, one which adds to the Frost myth, but it portrays Frost as more of a rebel than he really was. The truth is that he left Dartmouth because of loneliness for his future wife Elinor and because his mother needed help with the undisciplined students in her school.

Frost's message to the graduates, however, is more general. He gets in his usual complaint about rapid reading, observing that college students read ten times as much in one year as he does in ten years. Describing that method of reading as scansion, he says that college permits students to scan books to see if they want to read them later. His major point in this address is his belief that four years of college should enhance a student's confidence to the extent that he can maintain his individuality. By the time a student graduates, he should be able to accept any premise, to "take it up" and to give it something of his own. No need to contradict or to be ill-tempered: "My object in life has been to hold my own *with* whatever's going — not *against*, but *with* — to hold my own. To come through college holding my own so that I won't be made over beyond recognition by my family and my home town, if I ever go back to it" (1955, p. 15). Frost hopes that the students have developed to the point where they can take care of themselves not in the conflicts of disagreement but in the stresses of thought.

Perhaps the most interesting parts of this talk are Frost's comments about several of his poems. Calling "Mending Wall" a "countrified" poem, for example, he says that it explores how "all life is cellular." Commenting on the famous line from "Stopping by Woods on a Snowy Evening" ("But I have promises to keep."), he declares ironically: "And they pursued me about that, and so I've decided to have a meaning for it . . . : 'Promises may be divided into two kinds: those I make for myself, and those my ancestors made for me known as the social contract.' See, that's a way out of that" (1955, p. 15). He characterizes "The Gift Outright" as a poem about the beginning of the end of colonialism; he defines "Birches" as a retreat, as opposed to an escape, poem; and he insists that "Departmental" is "*very objective*," that it has nothing to do with his having suffered from departmentalism. This talk is witty, anecdotal, and an excellent example of Frost's skill at captivating an audience.

Another published example of Frost's speeches at various colleges is "A Talk for Students" delivered June 7, 1956, at Sarah Lawrence College. The poet's topic is freedom, especially the freedom to speak out, and a quotation will illustrate his genius for coming up with definitions and explanations which nearly always persuaded his listeners to accept his point of view:

Now the freedom that I am asked to think about sometimes is

the freedom to speak — to speak out academic and in the press,
or from the platform like this. I say I have the right to tell anything — to talk about anything I am smart enough to find out
about. Second, I am free to talk about anything I am deep enough
to understand, and third, I am free to talk about anything I have
the ability to talk about. The limitations on my freedom, you see,
are more in myself than anywhere else. There is no time when I
talk or when you talk that we ought not to introduce ourselves
with the expression, "I make bold to say." And making bold to
say means leaving out what you don't want to say. [1956, no
pages]

This passage requires no comment other than the observation
that it illustrates Frost's uncanny ability to convince the listeners
of his point of view by persuading them that they are hearing a
bit of his highly personal, even private, philosophy.

Frost's little known "Remarks on the Occasion of the Tagore
Centenary" (*Poetry*, Nov. 1961) is in some ways a rehash of
many of the essays and recorded talks discussed above. These
"Remarks" are a transcription of a talk the poet gave on April
19, 1961, to celebrate the centennial of the great Indian poet
Rabindranath Tagore, but Frost seems to have a hard time
referring to Tagore. In a manner reminiscent of his introduction to Robinson's *King Jasper*, he darts here and there among
various opinions and definitions which he believes Tagore would
agree with, thus talking more about himself than the artist he
is supposed to celebrate. The transcription is full of statements
which are more fully developed in other essays and poems and
which the Frost specialist will recognize as having acquired the
status of ready-made topics for the poet. For example, Frost
notes that, like himself, Tagore was a great nationalist, a comparison which leads him to paraphrase the definition of nationalism made famous (and controversial) in "Build Soil": "I'm a
terrible nationalist myself — formidable. I can't see how one can
be international unless there are some nations to be *inter* with.
And the clearer and distincter the better" (1961, p. 106). He
also distinguishes between Western and Eastern cultures as the
difference between meditation and contemplation. This distinction recalls "The Prerequisites," and, indeed, a few pages later
Frost mentions the difficulty he had with Emerson's "Brahma."
Similarly, he echoes the introduction to *King Jasper* and his
famous differentiation between griefs and grievances when he
argues that the purpose of poetry is "to raise trouble and sorrow
to a higher level of regard, not to get rid of either the trouble

or sorrow" (1961, p. 110). And "A Romantic Chasm" is recalled, with its plea for the preservation of national languages,
when Frost expresses his hope that the "great Bengali language"
be kept alive. Thus, in this talk he rephrases a number of his
standard ideas which are better stated elsewhere.

More importantly, these remarks confirm my suspicion that
the poet maintained a kind of storehouse of interesting ideas
which he drew on when asked to give a talk or to write an
introduction. In his later life especially, he apparently dressed
up old themes and observations instead of creating new ones.
The appeal of this essay is that it gathers together so many of
the poet's opinions. Only occasionally does he mention Tagore.
He even seizes the opportunity to read just a minimal amount
from the Indian's work, excusing himself on the grounds that
the translations are in free verse and that he does not read un-
structured poetry very well. The reader cannot help but believe
that Frost does not know enough about Tagore to elaborate
upon the other poet's achievement. Instead he reads from his
own poetry, and he repeats a number of opinions which by 1961
had become overused material. These apparent shortcomings
are better understood when we remember that at this time Frost
was in his late eighties.

"Between Prose and Verse" (*Atlantic Monthly*, Jan. 1962)
is a stenographic transcription of Frost's comments at a Bread
Loaf Writers' Conference. The poet ranges among several
topics, including Emerson and readings of his own poems, but
in general he keeps in mind the distinction between prose and
poetry. Declaring that poetry is not prose because "it has to be
a passionate thought," he lists a few do's and don'ts as advice to
fledgling writers. Poets, for example, need not know how to
spell. They can be loose with their syntax, and they do not
have to know how to punctuate. They must know, however,
how to write in both free verse and regular verse as well as the
"borderline" between prose and verse. In addition they must
understand the various poetic forms and the differences between
"strict" and "loose" iambic. "You have got to know the difference between an idea that will do in prose or in talk and all
that, and one that is more poetical. . . . The way to know about
that is to read the beginnings of poems, see how they begin, how
they launch out. See how soon they launch you into feeling,
tone, air" (1962, p. 51). Clarifying his distinction, Frost returns
to ideas he verbalized nearly fifty years earlier. He argues that
poetry, unlike prose, must be tonal, and that the best way to

develop poetic tone is through meter and rhythm. Neither alone
will do, but the stress of one on the other will "lift a sound"
or a tone from the poem. Frost does not say so explicitly, but
it seems clear that his remarks are calculated to deny tone to
free verse, since free verse avoids regular meter. Successful
poetry "all comes down to . . . a dip for depth." The first thing
to look for in a book or manuscript is how the poems affect the
ear: what is the relation of rhythm and meter; are the rhymes
successful?

The final half of this article is a question and answer session
in which Frost admits, among other things, that prose can have
rhythm. A reader is moved by either prose or verse when he
comes upon the "association of two things" which he does not
expect to see linked. This statement recalls his definitions of
metaphor in "Education by Poetry," and Frost describes these
unexpected associations or metaphors as "surprise" and "inevi-
tability." "You can get that in prose. . . . When prose is the
way it ought to be, it has rhythm. The other kind of prose is
declare, declare, declare until you don't know what to do with
your voice when you are reading it" (1962, p. 52). The reader
familiar with the development of Frost's ideas about literature
and writing poetry will recognize how Frost has emphasized
the relationship between poetry and sound all of his life. This
particular article is full of proverbial statements and turns of
phrase which attest to his wit and to his fondness for the memorable remark: "Poetry gives your voice so many ways of
behaving — cutting up with your voice" (1962, p. 53). What
makes this article so charming is his realization that he is not
delivering earth-shattering pronouncements likely to change the
course of literature. He is aware that his audience is sophisticated
and knowledgeable and that he is playing the role of the sage,
of the established poet. Midway through his remarks he pauses
to comment: "The amusing part of my saying all this is that it
doesn't matter at all. You probably know all about it" (1962,
p. 52). One has to admire the old poet's bemused assessment of
his status at the Bread Loaf Conference.

This engaging sense of self-amusement seems toned down but
not omitted in "Playful Talk," another transcription of an
address which Frost gave to the American Academy of Arts
and Letters (*Proceedings of the American Academy of Arts
and Letters and the National Institute of Arts and Letters,*
1962). The title is appropriate, for Frost entertains with a number of personal anecdotes and funny stories. Yet the sense lingers
that he is speaking to his audience not so much as a fellow

member of the academy but as the official consultant at the Library of Congress who has decided to let the members in on the status of the arts in Washington: "I'd like to hear what the Institute and the Academy want, because I think I'm going to have some say about it" (1962, p. 180). Frost's sense of humor surfaces when he tells the academy that his ultimate design as an unofficial member of the government is to have a secretary of the arts in the president's cabinet who would prevent the post office from stamping "Education Materials" on packages of books and poems.

This talk is a source for several anecdotes which were well-publicized in Frost's later years. One is his "complaint" about the limited duties of his official position. With tongue in cheek, he claims that he thought the title "Consultant in Poetry" meant that he would be consulted, as a poet, about everything: "They said, 'You needn't be limited to poetry any more,' and they made me a consultant in the humanities" (1962, p. 182). Equally well known is his account of President Kennedy's playful request to change "would" to "will" in the final line of "The Gift Outright," implying that America would approach perfection in Kennedy's administration. Indeed, this article is probably one of the best sources for information about Frost's assessment of his relationship with President Kennedy. Until the final volume of the official biography is published, "Playful Talk" will remain valuable as an account of the poet's "nomination" of Kennedy as the next president, of his comment that Kennedy represented "a fresh wave of Puritanism," and of the exchange over "The Gift Outright." Unfortunately, Frost does not discuss how he reconciled his political conservatism with President Kennedy's liberalism, but he does hint that he chose Kennedy because of the late president's New England heritage. Frost ends the talk with a series of comments upon a few of his couplets, a discussion of Greek history, and an amusing story about an American sailor's visit to the czar, all of which have their interest. But from today's perspective, the article is interesting primarily because of the information it contains about the Frost-Kennedy relationship.

His last public lecture, given at Dartmouth on November 27, 1962, was recorded and transcribed for publication by Edward Connery Lathem, coeditor of *Selected Prose of Robert Frost*. In "Robert Frost on 'Extravagance' " (*Dartmouth Alumni Magazine*, Mar. 1963), the poet talks about topics, including the universe itself, which might be termed extravagant because there is no demonstrable need for them. Recognizing gradations of extravagance, Frost distinguishes between man, who is extravagant because he is so wasteful, and poetry, which is extravagant because it is so clearly an extra in life. His attempt to define the term suggests that his definitions of extravagance and metaphor are related:

This is a little extravaganza, this little poem; and to what extent is it excessive? And can you go with it? Some people can't. And sometimes it's a bitter extravagance, like that passage in Shakespeare that so many make their novels out of: life is "a tale told by an idiot . . . , signifying nothing." That's an extravagance, of course—of bitterness. [1963, p. 21]

This statement recalls his discussion of metaphor in "Education by Poetry" because he is concerned with "how far" an extravagance can be carried before it loses readers or listeners. When he says that "Some people are incapable of taking it" [extravagance in poetry], he apparently means that they have trouble "taking" metaphor as well: "Some people can't go with you. Let 'em drop; let 'em fall off. Let the wolves take 'em" (1963, p. 23).

As in most of the recorded lectures and short prose pieces of his old age, Frost draws on ideas which he first expressed years ago. Calling politics an extravagance, he returns to the distinction between griefs and grievances which he stated so eloquently in the "Introduction to *King Jasper*." Poetry is an extravagance about griefs, about that which is irremediable. In other words, poetry deals in universals. But politics is only an extravagance about grievances, about that which can be resolved. Frost names "The Most of It" and "Never Again Would Birds' Song Be the Same" as two examples from his own poetry which illustrate extravagance, but he unfortunately fails exactly to explain his point. The article ends with readings from *In the Clearing* and with Frost's now standard barb at the critics who persist in overreading "Stopping by Woods on a Snowy Evening." Still, he must not be totally repulsed by literary analysis, for he explains in one of his last public remarks: "So many of them [his poems] have literary criticism in them — *in* them. And yet I wouldn't admit it. I try to hide it" (1963, p. 24).

The Critical Response

By roughly 1935 the scope of the literary criticism of Frost began to catch up with his poetry. That is, critical commentary matured beyond essay-reviews of his books and debates about whether he wrote free verse or whether his dialogue poems would be better expressed as short stories. This is not to say that all of the early criticism is facile or irrelevant. As pointed out in chapter 2, many of the essay-reviews, especially those by Lascelles Abercrombie, Wilfred Gibson, and Edward Garnett, helped to introduce Frost to a public that was puzzled by the poet's "old ways to be new." We should also remember that during these first years of publication Frost granted numerous interviews in which he clarified and advertised his ideas about prosody and sentence sounds. But general evaluations of his achievement, or detailed analyses of the relationship between his artistic principles and his poetry were not possible until he had established his reputation with a significant number of superior poems. This possibility materialized in the late 1920s and in the 1930s. By 1937 Frost had published six volumes of verse and two volumes of selected or collected poems, and he had been awarded three of his four Pulitzer Prizes. Critical commentary seemed to multiply accordingly. Many of the essays published during the next forty years focused on explanations of his literary principles, on analyses of the relationships between theory and practice, and on investigations of techniques in specific poems. Some of the more important of these articles will be discussed in the remainder of this chapter.

Robert Newdick was one of the first literary critics to begin a comprehensive evaluation of Frost's theory of poetry as expressed in the scattered essays and recorded talks. At one time planning a biography of Frost, Newdick collected and published more reliable information about the poet than anyone until Lawrance Thompson made available the letters and official biography. Newdick writes so well and has researched the material so thoroughly that his articles stand as a kind of milestone in the development of Frost criticism. Today, of course, most of his analyses are dated because of the publication of Thompson's books, but his work can still be profitably read as concise statements about Frost's various pronouncements upon the art of poetry.

In "Robert Frost and the Dramatic" (*New England Quarterly*, June 1937), Newdick focuses on the then little-known preface to *A Way Out* to explain why Frost considers the dramatic as "the most essential quality in artistic literary production." Newdick provides a valuable service for readers at the time by quoting liberally from the preface, and he asks a per-

tinent question: does the poet's practice square with his stated
theory? To find an answer, he asks three subordinate questions:
has the dramatic "figured prominently" in Frost's teaching; has
it "led him to formally dramatic composition"; and has it affected his poetry? Today's readers know that these questions
should be answered affirmatively, but such was not the case in
the 1930s. Newdick's contribution (particularly valuable until
the appearance of the later biographies) is his citation of biographical material which supports the affirmative answers to the
three questions and which was generally unknown in 1937.

Accordingly, Newdick discusses Frost's years as a teacher
at Pinkerton Academy (Derry, New Hampshire), State Normal
School (Plymouth, New Hampshire), and Amherst College.
The poet "enlarged the academy's view of the drama" by
supervising student productions of drama other than the classics
and Shakespeare: Marlowe's *Dr. Faustus*, Milton's *Comus*, Sheridan's *The Rivals*, and Yeats' *The Land of Heart's Desire* and
Cathleen ni Houlihan. Perhaps the most astonishing fact about
these plays which Frost was "directing" in 1910 and 1911 is the
production of two dramas by Yeats, who at the time was a
"contemporary" writer and thus normally considered by the
academic establishment to be unsuitable for study. Newdick
also reports that Frost's teaching of Shakespeare was revolutionary: "the students spent the class period extemporaneously
acting one-hour versions of the plays which they themselves had
arranged" (1937a, p. 264).

Just as he shows how the dramatic affected Frost's teaching,
so Newdick reports the history of the publication of Frost's two
"plays," *The Cow's in the Corn* and *A Way Out*. Of particular
interest is the list of critical comments about *A Way Out* which
remain generally unknown even today. W. S. Braithwaite, for
example, praised the play's "rich, idiomatic country speech,"
while Percy Hutchinson and Walter Pritchard debated whether
or not *A Way Out* would be effective "on the boards." The
rest of the article is an informed discussion of how Frost incor-
porates the sense of the dramatic into his poetry. Newdick comments on the "dramatic" arrangement of several of Frost's books,
particularly *A Boy's Will* and *New Hampshire*, and he supplies
penetrating analyses of the element of drama in the "least" lyric
"Flower-Gathering" and in the dialogue poem "Snow." He
points out, for example, that in "Flower-Gathering" "only one
person speaks, the poet; yet the poem is twice dramatic, first in
the give and take in the speaker's own mind, again in the give

and take implied between the speaker and the silent but smiling figure standing welcomingly in the doorway" (1937a, p. 267). His conclusion that Frost has followed the principles stated in the preface to *A Way Out* is thus well-substantiated.

An equally fine essay is "Robert Frost and the Sound of Sense" (Newdick, *American Literature*, Nov. 1937). Commenting upon "the most striking phenomenon in the poetry of the day," the renaissance of poetic drama as urged by T. S. Eliot, Maxwell Anderson, and Archibald MacLeish, Newdick reminds his readers that for forty years Frost has been addressing himself to the problem of capturing in poetry the range of speech tones. As in the previous article, he again establishes his argument by citing biographical facts which were then unknown. Thus, he discusses the poet's youthful enthusiasm for Shakespeare, the publication of "My Butterfly," the poor advice from William Hayes Ward that Frost should emulate Sidney Lanier's theory of musical notation in verse, and the complaint by Rev. William A. Wolcott that Frost's verses sounded too much like talk. All of this information is common knowledge now, yet this article retains its relevancy. Aware that Frost's emphasis on the use of "living" speech in poetry can be properly regarded only against a background of principle, Newdick devotes the rest of his essay to a gathering of the poet's published opinions on the "sound of sense."

He argues correctly that Frost's theory "strikes more deeply and embraces much more than simply a conversational manner in verse" (1937b, p. 290). Unlike so many of the new "poetic" dramatists, Frost relies on speech tones to convey meaning. Newdick acknowledges the poet's refusal formally to enter "the lists of literary criticism by writing *in extenso* of his principles and practices," and he apologizes for pulling together a mosaic of phrases and opinions scattered throughout interviews, introductions, and recorded talks (1937b, p. 291). The apology is unnecessary, for Newdick provides a service by calling attention to more than two dozen sources for Frost's statements about the sound of sense — some of them well publicized (such as W. S. Braithwaite's interview in the *Boston Evening Transcript*, May 8, 1915), some of them relatively obscure (*Christian Science Monitor*, Oct. 17, 1924). The reader who tracks down all of the cited sources will find that they contain the material necessary for a comprehensive definition of Frost's theory of sound in poetry. And, after reading Newdick's useful essay, the reader will also discover both an illustration of how the sound of sense works in specific poems (for example, "Birches" and "Stopping by Woods on a Snowy Evening"), and a summary of the earlier critical opinion about Frost's poetry. This article is recommended to anyone who desires a short, well-documented analysis of what Frost means by the sound of sense.

Newdick's "Robert Frost's Other Harmony" (*Sewanee Review*, Summer 1940) is an account of the poet's various prose pieces which were published before 1940. Its value is self-evident, for until the publication of *Selected Prose of Robert Frost* in 1966, readers had to rely on this kind of article for a listing of and commentary upon Frost's other harmony. Newdick's approach is historical, for he begins with Frost's valedictory address and with an account of the poet's journalistic contributions to the *Lawrence Sentinel* (a weekly) and to the *Lawrence American* (a daily). He is certainly correct when he observes that Frost's essays are "less harmoniously balanced in style" than the poems. Yet the prose retains some of the qualities of the poetry: "Characteristically it is marked by simplicity in vocabulary and diction, by numerous short packed sentences, and by homely telling images and illustrations. In general it has the tone and manner, to borrow Hazlitt's phrasing of his own ideal style, 'of lively, sensible conversation' " (Newdick, 1940, p. 411). Like the poetry, the essays have a touch of Frost's humor and irony. Noting that Frost has an "Emersonian unconcern" for the traditional separation of introduction, body, and conclusion of an essay, Newdick suggests that economy is the true distinctive quality of the poet's prose. Rhetorical devices and divisions are exchanged for synecdoche so that the reader is challenged to follow hints and suggestions. The essay concludes with a list of eye-catching quotes from Frost's prose and with a call for a collection of the poet's articles which, as it turns out, was not answered for twenty-six years.

Cleanth Brooks' chapter on Frost in *Modern Poetry and the Tradition* (1939) is concerned with the kind of poetry Frost writes, and it is thus a more general assessment than Newdick's. Brooks is interested in technique, in how the poems are put together, but happily his remarks are directed at the general reader. Noting that in the popular mind Frost is sharply contrasted with "tortured intellectual obscurantists," Brooks shows that Frost is much less direct than the casual reader supposes. Many readers observe the characters, anecdotes, and dramatic incidents in the poems, but they fail to realize that the poet employs these devices for the purpose of indirection. The mannerisms of the New England character often limit the range of the poetry, but they do not prevent irony from appearing in the context of "licensed whimsy" or "dry understatement." Brooks' general description of "The Code" and of Frost's poetry might be challenged today:

Except for the idiomatic and flexible blank verse, Frost makes use of no resources in the poem not available to the accomplished short story writer. The poetry is diluted and diffuse: A significant symptom of the diffuseness is the absence of metaphor. The very minimum of imagery is used. In general, Frost's metaphors are few and tame; and the occasional bold metaphor is confined to his very lightest poems: for example, to such a sally of self-ironic whimsy as "Canis Major." [1939, p. 111]

This observation seems curious when we remember the lyric poems and the emphasis Frost places on metaphor in essays like "Education by Poetry" and "The Constant Symbol."

Yet Brooks seems more interested in the dramatic dialogues like "The Code" and the poems of social comment like "Two Tramps in Mud Time" than in the shorter lyrics. Once this qualification is understood, the reader can consider his comment that "Frost does not think through his images; he requires statements." An example is "Two Tramps in Mud Time," a poem in which the theme is overtly stated "outside the symbolical method." And in poems like "Birches" and "Mending Wall," Frost dilutes his art by applying the mode of prose rather than of symbol. This observation is questionable, one which has elicited a great deal of debate. More easily acceptable is Brooks' statement that Frost is at his best when he does not philosophize. In superior poems like "The Wood-Pile" and "After Apple-Picking," the poet's problem is to "develop depth of feeling without seeming to violate the realistic and matter-of-fact elements of the situation with which the poem deals" (1939, p. 114). Frost's best poems illustrate this successful handling of tone. Brooks' bias in favor of complex symbolic poetry shows through here, of course, for he praises those Frost poems in which the symbolism is extended to the point at which great intensity is achieved. To demonstrate this intensity in a poem like "After Apple-Picking" is to indicate that the poem is "in reality a symbolist poem." Thus, Brooks argues that Frost's best work illustrates "the structure of symbolist-metaphysical poetry." This critical stance remains just as unusual and challenging today as it did in 1939.

Perhaps the best general introduction to Frost's ideas about poetry and poetic theory is Lawrance Thompson's *Fire and Ice:*

The Art and Thought of Robert Frost (1942). From today's
perspective, a Frost specialist might consider Thompson's book
to be dated because of the availability of a great body of critical
opinion which has appeared since its publication. It is, after all,
the first critical book on Robert Frost. But for general readers,
particularly those interested in the development of American
poetry in this century, *Fire and Ice* remains a wide-ranging and
well-argued introduction to the various elements in Frost's aesthetic creed. Especially relevant to this chapter is Thompson's
analysis of Frost's theory of poetry.

Thompson begins with a chapter titled "A Background of
Poetic Theories" in which he introduces the nonspecialist to
the definitions and counterdefinitions of literary theory which
have appeared since Plato. The purpose of this survey of literary
history is to provide context for Frost's theory of poetry, for
Thompson believes that the poet has "enriched the main stream
without trying to modify the direction, because his poetry has
been content with the old ways to be new" (1942, p. 3). Following this general introduction is an essay entitled "Robert
Frost's Theory of Poetry" which Thompson divides into sections on Form, The Poetic Impulse, Meaning, and The Poem and
the Reader. Although, as he correctly notes, Frost has shown
a "fresh vitality without recourse to the fads and limitations of
modern experimental techniques," the poet has nevertheless carried on his own innovation (1942, p. 18). Frost's self-imposed
restrictions in his theory of poetry save him from the two extremes of "nothing of content" and "nothing except content."
In other words, the poet disagrees with those who advocate
poetry as pure art or poetry as preaching.

Thompson is surely on firm ground when he suggests that
form is one of the most important characteristics which Frost
finds in poetry. The term means more than simply stanza form
and regular meter, elements which free verse avoids. It refers
to the balance of organization and content: "To give form in
poetry is also to employ that intricate method of conveying
organization, shapeliness, fitness, to the matter or substance or
context or meaning of the poem. Before meaning finds its place
in a poem it must become subordinated to its proper balance
with structure" (1942, p. 22). The relationship between form
and content is best explained by examining Frost's definition of
the poetic impulse. Frost hints that he finds himself moving
through the creative act as if by faith — the poem must be
"believed" into existence. Fresh recognition provides a kind of

crisis which finds release in the creation of a poem. Thompson describes Frost's belief in two kinds of recognition. "The first way occurs when some experience in the present inspires an emotional recognition that is more a matter of sense impression than of clear mental perception" (1942, p. 24). This now well known emotion — the "lump in the throat" — moves the poet into the creative act of writing a poem, and the details of the immediate experience find expression in art. Thompson provides an excellent reading of "Stopping by Woods on a Snowy Evening" to illustrate this type of poetic impulse. The second kind of recognition "occurs when the emotional pleasure is derived from the sudden mental perception of a thought which comes into sharp focus through the discovery and recognition of a particularly apt correspondence or analogy" (1942, p. 27). "For Once, Then, Something" illustrates this level of poetic impulse. The difference between the two types is clear if the reader remembers that the first is an emotional response finding resolution through expression in metaphor, while the second begins with the perception of metaphor. "The first leads the poet to venture into the writing of the poem as an act of faith, without foreseeing the outcome; the second leads the poet to give shape and weight to a rational correspondence which has been perceived clearly before he begins the writing of the poem" (1942, p. 28).

At the risk of oversimplifying, Frost suggests that the real poet is one who can remain true to both the mood and the material at the same time. One of the pleasures of form is that it provides the "momentary stay" against the confusion created by either the emotional response or the perceived correspondence. The harmony of mood and material helps the poet achieve the desired balance of form and content. Thompson ends his outline of Frost's theory of poetry with short discussions of how the poet tries to subordinate meaning to its "proper balance in structure" and of how he insists that the poem is successful only if it establishes a "basic correspondence" between writer and reader. Given Frost's distaste for didactic or propaganda poetry (although he is occasionally guilty himself), the reader can appreciate his desire to tone down explicit meaning. Similarly, his well-published dismissal of esoteric poetry accounts for his insistence that the successful poem establishes a correspondence between author and reader. In the rest of *Fire and Ice*, Thompson investigates the sounds of sense, metaphor, and the various stanza forms in Frost's poetry, evaluations which are valuable particularly to the reader who is beginning a concentrated study of Robert Frost. The nonspecialist will be especially interested in the generous number of passages quoted from Frost's statements about his theory of poetry.

Reginald L. Cook has similarly helped the reader by preserving Frost's numerous off-the-cuff remarks about his art. "Robert Frost's Asides on His Poetry" (*American Literature*, Jan. 1948) and "Frost on Frost: The Making of Poems" (*American Literature*, Mar. 1956) make fascinating reading because Cook publishes statements and opinions by Frost which cannot be readily found elsewhere. My purpose here is to call attention to these articles rather than to evaluate them, for a series of quotations with commentary by Cook does not invite the kind of analysis accorded the other essays in this study. Emphasis can be placed, however, on the more eye-catching definitions and witticisms which Frost coins in his informal talks about the art of poetry.

In "Robert Frost's Asides on His Poetry," for example, Cook notes that Frost is not at all reserved about discussing technique and theory. The poet enjoys pointing out the parallels between art and sports, for both recognize the objectives of "performance" and "prowess." There is no mystery about how a poem takes shape: "There is but one place to begin a poem and that is when in the mood. It takes its origin inside a person and after a period of indefiniteness it casts about for something to take hold of" (1948, p. 353). Clearly, form gives direction to idea— in this way, art clarifies reality. Frost explains that his goal is to make his poems "sound different" even if they are written in the same meter. His primary tones are talking ("Mending Wall"), intoning ("Acquainted with the Night"), and a combination of talking and intoning ("The Mountain"). Readers of this article will find other witty remarks as Frost describes his own poems.

"Frost on Frost: The Making of Poems" focuses more directly upon poetic theory. For example, Cook has preserved several of Frost's definitions of poetry: "the renewal of words"; "the triumph of association"; "a thought-felt thing." Frost also describes poetry as hinting, and he insists that the reader learn how to handle indirection: "Poems like 'Mending Wall,' 'Closed for Good,' and 'A Winter Eden' contain hints, but there is no hinting in 'A Witch of Coös,' 'A Peck of Gold,' or 'Stopping by Woods' " (1956, p. 64). The reader familiar with the range of Frost's comments on poetry will note that the poet consistently returns to two topics: the way a poem begins, and the need for form. Claiming that he does not know what inspiration means, he speaks of the kind of "moment" which "spoils you for life. You keep waiting around for it to happen." Still, he is aware that the waiting can be dangerous: "I don't want to grant that spontaneity can be simulated. I've got to have a visitation, a moment. There's always a danger in waiting for the moment. Your pen dries up" (1956, p. 67). And referring to form, he points to "The Silken Tent" and to "Why Wait for Science?" as two lyrics which satisfy him. Just as valuable are his comments on the role of narrative ("I want to write stories. The great thing is the story.") and the use he makes of discarded poems ("fragments of remembered failures"). These two articles provide valuable source material for those who want to determine Frost's theory of poetry, especially if the reader exercises discretion when applying the poet's comments to the poems themselves.

William Mulder's nicely written "Freedom and Form: Robert Frost's Double Discipline" (*South Atlantic Quarterly*, July 1955) follows the same tack. Outlining what he calls a "double discipline"—that is, freedom of material and the demands of regular form—Mulder "cons the poems . . . looking for open confession" of Frost's artistic faith. He draws on the essays, talks, and poems to formulate an outline of the basic opinions Frost has expressed about poetry. Thus, the initiated reader will find that he is once again encountering quotations from "The Constant Symbol" about metaphor, ironic observations from the "Introduction to *King Jasper*" about new ways to be new, and statements from "The Figure a Poem Makes" about the course of the poetic impulse. For the casual reader, however, this essay will prove to be an introduction to the more essential of Frost's opinions about the art of poetry. The value of this kind of study is that it normally invites the reader to pursue the topic, in this case, to read the primary sources themselves. Unfortunately, Mulder does not provide this opportunity, for he neglects to cite the sources. The Frost specialist can easily determine that the phrase "enthusiasm tamed by metaphor" comes from "Education by Poetry," but the general reader cannot possibly know about this obscure essay unless it is named in the text. Mulder does name the poems which he quotes from, thereby providing some aid for those who wish further to investigate the topic of Frost's aesthetics.

This one shortcoming aside, Mulder's observations about freedom and form in particular and about Frost's artistic faith in
general are valid and informative. His essay is a good summation of Frost's opinions about poetry.

A more specialized and, happily, different approach to the
analysis of Frost's poetic process is Langdon Elsbree's "Frost
and the Isolation of Man" (*Claremont Quarterly*, 1960). Noting
—and rejoicing—that the public image of Frost as a "latter-day
Emerson" has finally been replaced by the more accurate assessment of Frost as skeptic, Elsbree proposes to examine the
narrative structure of those poems he feels best illustrate the
poet's "most compelling treatment of human isolation." He
names "The Self-Seeker," "The Fear," and "The Housekeeper"
as examples, but he reserves "A Servant to Servants," "Home
Burial," and "The Death of the Hired Man" for analysis. This
essay is primarily a close reading of the latter three poems in
terms of narrative structure, and little is to be gained by paraphrasing Elsbree's interpretations. But the reader might find
useful an account of the paradigm which Elsbree establishes.

Generally, these poems begin with a "concise declarative
sentence" which specifies speaker and location. Frost then creates
tension based on an immediately named event or condition
"which seems ominous because of the speaker's tone" (for example, "Silas is back."), but which remains ambiguous because of insufficient detail. Following this laconic but porten-
tous beginning, Frost supplies details from the past and present
to clarify why the event seems threatening. "These clarifying
details culminate in a generalization which comes usually about
a third or half way through the poem, predicts the poem's conclusion, and completes the particularizing of the kind of isolation experienced by the characters" (1960, p. 30). The poem's
emphasis then shifts from revelation of details to arguments
about the event which continue until a character proposes a
course of action that foreshadows the end of the poem, often
ironic, usually bleak.

After establishing this paradigm, Elsbree offers detailed readings of the three poems mentioned above to show how the or-
ganizations of the poems result in a "powerful demonstration
of the immitigable pain and loneliness in life" (1960, p. 30).
His conclusions are certainly worth considering, for he correctly notes that despite sustained praise for *North of Boston*
most readers have neglected the organization of poems like
"A Servant to Servants." Instead, Frost has been commended
for his handling of speech rhythms and for his insights into hu-

man behavior. But as Elsbree points out, insights and speech rhythms are part of the narrative structure: "To neglect the organization of the narrative is to ignore that which determines how and when the speech rhythms will move and which constitutes the unified insight into human experience" (1960, p. 40). The reader may quarrel with various parts of Elsbree's interpretations of the poems, but he will have to admit that this analysis of structure, though sometimes rigid, suggests a new and fruitful subject for Frost studies.

In "Formal Devices in Robert Frost's Short Poems" (*Georgia Review*, Fall 1961), Eckhart Willige also examines several poems in terms of technique and form. As the title indicates, Willige is interested in Frost's very short poems, poems like "November" which are shorter than a sonnet. Admitting that no one can determine whether or not Frost uses formal devices consciously in "November," Willige analyzes the poem to show how it illustrates the union of form and thought. Of particular interest is his evaluation of the "basically iambic" rhythm which is "best discernible" toward the end of the poem. Several of the opening lines have "the rhythmical irregularities" of anapests and feminine endings: "This throws some light on Frost's instinctive way of starting a poem. He does not sit down beating rhythms with the knuckles on the table and commanding the words to fit. He has his opening sentence; and if it happens not yet to show the rhythmical theme but rather a variation, what does it matter? Sooner or later it will come" (1961, p. 326). Willige is probably correct when he notes that the "prevailing" feminine endings of "November" suggest a sense of hesitation and uncertainty which contributes to the mood of "melancholy and pessimism of the declining year." The casual rhyme scheme, the overlapping of rhymes (that is, the rhymes are not grouped), and the repetition of syntax are also noted as examples of formal devices in "November." Willige comments on "The Rose Family," "Lodged," and "The Rabbit-Hunter" as poems which illustrate Frost's theory that a poet should not begin writing with the form in mind. This short article is far from definitive, and some of the observations are debatable (for example, that the rhymes in "The Rabbit-Hunter" are so unobtrusive as to go unnoticed on first reading). Yet the essays by Willige and Elsbree call attention to an area of Frost studies which has not been adequately investigated—the ways in which the poems are put together.

Like Willige and Elsbree, Herbert R. Coursen, Jr. focuses on the poet's technique. In "A Dramatic Necessity: The Poetry of

Robert Frost" (*Bucknell Review*, Dec. 1961), Coursen discusses how the voices in Frost's poems affect the dramatic quality. Most readers of Frost notice the tension between retreat and confrontation, but Coursen suggests that the poet neither accepts nor rejects the antithesis of withdrawal and involvement: he does both, "thus indicating that the blending of opposing views is for Frost a key to life" (1961, p. 138). Examining the movement from voice to voice in the poems, Coursen speculates that the balance between different voices often results in a "seeming balance between alternatives." This essay is an especially difficult one to comment upon in such a way as to give the reader an adequate idea of its contents because it is filled with so many quotations from the poems. Coursen does not argue his points—he illustrates them. Nevertheless the highlights can be noted.

In some poems, for example, Frost often uses a commonplace interjection of fact to neutralize the voice of "rising inspiration." In others the process is reversed, but the result in both cases is a balance of real fact and poetic inspiration. The first two lines of "After Apple-Picking" are a good example of how Frost uses the "dissenting voice of poetry" in line two to counter the "prose" voice of line one. When he reverses "the position of his voices," as in "Once by the Pacific," the movement from specific to poetic, noted in "After Apple-Picking," is also reversed. Common language, such as "was lucky" and "It looked as if," counters the ominous suggestions created by the poetic descriptions of the approaching storm. Coursen's observation is debatable, and the reader must decide whether Frost uses his "voices" in so conscious a manner. In any event, Coursen correctly notes one of the effects of this balance between poetic and colloquial voices: the poet either "pushes his poem a step closer to the sphere of the reader . . . or he guides his auditor expertly into the realm of suggestion" (1961, pp. 145–46). The result is that the reader moves with the poet between the worlds of imagination and reality, experiencing the poise which the balance of different voices establishes.

One of the best evaluations of Frost's technique is Herbert Howarth's "Frost in a Period Setting" (*Southern Review*, Oct. 1966). Although more a general statement than an analysis of specific poems, this essay is so knowledgeable and so persuasively written that it prompts the reader to further examination of the way Frost's poems are put together. Just as important is Howarth's argument that Frost's experiments parallel the more

obvious innovations of Hueffer, Pound, and Eliot. This is
what Howarth means by the phrase "Frost in a period setting"—
that Frost deserves recognition as a key member of the American and British group of writers which between 1905 and 1925
revolutionized literature. There is, as Howarth points out, the
"case of affinity in Frost's monosyllables." Many readers have
praised the strength of the poet's lines of single syllables, but
Howarth emphasizes how this technique joins Frost with his
contemporaries, Hueffer and Pound especially, who were trying
to get at the "strength of brevity" by freeing poetry from what
they considered to be the linguistic excesses of Victorian literature. Lines like "We love the things we love for what they
are" ("Hyla Brook") are modern in their shortness and plain-
ness, in their spare evocation and freedom from color. Howarth
calls this tendency toward brevity and common speech a "neo-
Wordsworthian revolution." He admits that the textbooks do
not treat the 1905–25 movement in these terms, but he is surely
correct when he points out that a century after *Lyrical Ballads*
"the blood transfusion had to be administered all over again."
As Frost's letters to John Bartlett show (see chapter 1), he was
aware of his affinity with Wordsworth's experimentation and
of his efforts to "drop" to a common level of diction that even
Wordsworth "kept above." The difference between Frost and
his more militantly innovative contemporaries is that the poet
"readopted Wordsworth's whole program"—the language, the
people, the setting, and "conditions of life" (1966, p. 791).

Howarth also compares Frost's "audile imagination" with
Eliot's "the auditory imagination," making a transition to a
short discussion of the two poets. Of particular interest is his
suggestion that Frost has ties with seventeenth-century poetry similar to the better-known affinities between Eliot and
Donne or Marvell. Without the example of Herrick, writes
Howarth, it might have been harder for Frost "to have come
to the close versifying, the quasi-oriental silken tent, the mod-
ulations, of the first 20 pages of *A Witness Tree*" (1966, p.
793). Poems like "A Star in a Stone-Boat" and "A Record
Stride" show traces of the conceits and puns which are often
the trademarks of seventeenth-century poetry. And in "The Gift
Outright" and other superior poems, "the work is done that
Eliot intended should come of the rereading of the seventeenth
century: intellect and feelings move together, the sensibility is
reassociated" (1966, p. 795). Howarth speculates that Frost's
forms, conservative when placed beside the "mind-stretching

pictorial effects" of Eliot and Pound, may have mistakenly persuaded some critics that Frost was neither innovative nor modern. But the poet's new runs for iambic pentameter, his ar-
rangements of lines so that blank verse seems to be rhymed,
and his uses of Latin meters show that he is as innovative with
prosody as Eliot and Pound are with page patterns. Howarth
protests with justification that Frost would have received earlier
recognition if he had framed his achievements in technique
with formal, sophisticated theorizing. Praising Frost's experimentation, he concludes that the "clean, firm, whittled shapes,
the well-restrained rhetoric" are the poet's legacy. This essay
does not analyze the technical characteristics of specific poems,
nor does it compare Frost's theory with practice. But it so convincingly reevaluates the whole question of Frost's contribution
to the poetic renaissance of 1905–25 that it prompts a rethink-
ing of the poet's accomplishments with technique and form.

Frost's concept of sentence sounds remains without question
the one part of his theory which critics consistently praise.
Howarth, for example, calls it "Frost's special contribution to
the theory of poetry." To date the most complete discussion of
sentence sounds is Tom Vander Ven's "Robert Frost's Dramatic
Principle of 'Oversound' " (*American Literature*, May 1973). The
Frost specialist may not find new insights in this essay, but any
reader interested in American poetry is sure to read this analysis with profit. To begin, Professor Vander Ven quotes all of
the relevant definitions and illustrations of the concept which
Frost scattered throughout fifty years of letters, published lectures, interviews, and recorded talks. The reader who is unacquainted with the range of these comments will find that this
article pulls together the most informative of the poet's many
illustrations, thus saving him the task of tracking down Frost's
"offhand and annotative" treatment of his poetic principles.

Professor Vander Ven's strategy is simple and effective. He
devotes the first part of his essay to a discussion of what the
sound of sense is not, and the second half to an illustration of what
it is. Little is to be gained by paraphrasing all of his examples.
Suffice it to say that his conclusion is correct: "the entity which
is Frost's sound of sense is not individual words, it is not word
patterns, it is not metrical rhythm, nor is it context, i.e., a situ-
ational reference. Neither is it thought, since there can be sense
without the sound" (1973, pp. 243–44). It is more difficult,
however, to define exactly what it is. Ideally the sound of
sense helps Frost express what he believes to be a crucial ele-

ment in poetry: feeling or emotion. But as Vander Ven points out, Frost is not interested in creating voice tones of feeling. Rather, the poet hopes to capture the speaking tones of life, to set down on the page sentence sounds which most poets (and many readers) would not usually regard as poetical but which are the common tones of everyday expression. "The printed word communicates, is credible and persuasive, only as it is charged with the sound of sense, the elemental, emotional energy of a human being who feels so intensely and completely what he has written, that it is *an act of faith, word become deed*" (1973, p. 249, Vander Ven's emphasis). Yet Frost must still resolve the apparent problem that the tones of the human voice cannot appear on the printed page. How, then, does the poet communicate them to the reader? As Frost himself explains, no one can read aloud what he has never heard. The reader must recognize the sentence sounds from the situation established in the poem. Vander Ven's definition is precise: "A poem is not a sound of sense itself but the context for one. Given a context of signals which indicate fear or doubt, the reader will experience the sound of fear or doubt in the poem only if he has actually heard those sounds carried on the human voice" (1973, p. 250). Thus, the reader's contribution is nearly as critical as the poet's. He must recognize the reference to voice tones which are not literally present on the page. Professor Vander Ven concludes that perhaps "oversound" is the best word for these tones, for it suggests the suspension of the tones "above" the page instead of on it.

It seems safe to say that, despite a significant number of essays on Frost's literary technique, comprehensive evaluations have only just begun. Still needed, of course, are additional studies of sentence sounds and of such matters as the poet's understanding and application of metaphor, form, rhyme, and meter, especially if these studies concentrate on how Frost varies his principles from poem to poem to satisfy the demands of each creative experience. But the time has also come for more inclusive investigations. A valuable beginning would be the collection and publication of all of the fugitive essays, introductions, recorded talks, and interviews. Only specialists have access to journals like the *Dartmouth Alumni Magazine* and *Biblia*. Next, the field of Frost studies needs evaluations of how the poet's concepts of prosody, metaphor, sentence sounds, and so on developed during his many years of creativity. We need to address ourselves to such questions as: does the concept of the sound of sense vary in the later books; does the poet's drift into satire and topical commentary affect his prosody; does his handling of his literary principles in the dialogue and longer poems differ from that in the lyrics? Finally, we need comprehensive studies of the entire scope of Frost's achievement with technique to determine whether or not he was, as he claimed to be in 1913, one of the most notable craftsmen of his time.

References

Brooks, Cleanth
    1939. "Frost, MacLeish, and Auden," in *Modern Poetry and the Tradition*, pp. 119–35. Chapel Hill: Univ. of North Carolina Pr.
Cook, Reginald L.
    1948. "Robert Frost's Asides on His Poetry," *American Literature* Jan., pp. 351–59.
    1956. "Frost on Frost: The Making of Poems," *American Literature* Mar., pp. 62–72.
Coursen, Herbert R., Jr.
    1961. "A Dramatic Necessity: The Poetry of Robert Frost," *Bucknell Review* Dec., pp. 138–47.
Cox, Hyde, and Edward Connery Lathem
    1966. (editors) *Selected Prose of Robert Frost*. New York: Holt, Rinehart and Winston. Includes "Preface to *A Way Out*," "The Figure a Poem Makes," "The Constant Symbol," "Education by Poetry," "Maturity No Object," "The Hear-Say Ballad," "Introduction to *King Jasper*," "The Poetry of Amy Lowell," "A Romantic Chasm," Preface to *Memoirs of the Notorious Stephen Burroughs*," "Perfect Day—A Day of Prowess," "The Prerequisites," "Remarks Accepting the Gold Medal of the National Institute of Arts and Letters," "Letter to the *Amherst Student*," "On Emerson."
Elsbree, Langdon
    1960. "Frost and the Isolation of Man," *Claremont Quarterly* pp. 29–40.
Frost, Robert
    1925. "Introduction to *The Arts Anthology: Darmouth Verse, 1925*," Portland, Maine: Mosher, 1925, pp. vii–ix.
    1928. "Poet—One of the Truest," in *Percy MacKaye: A Symposium on His Fiftieth Birthday*, p. 21. Hanover, N.H.: Dartmouth, 1928.
    1930. "Remarks on the Dedication of the Wilfred Davison Memorial Library," Bread Loaf, Vt., no pages.
    1936. "Introduction" to Sarah N. Cleghorn, *Threescore*, pp. ix–xii. New York: Smith and Hass.
    1938a. "Poverty and Poetry," *Biblia* Feb., no pages.

1938b. "The Poet's Next of Kin in a College," *Biblia* Feb., no pages.

1939. "The Doctrine of Excursions: A Preface," in *Bread Loaf Anthology*, pp. xix–xx. Middlebury, Vt. Middlebury College Pr.

1947. "A Sermon," New York: Spiral Pr., no pages.

1951. "Poetry and School," *Atlantic Monthly* June, pp. 30–31.

1955. "The Commencement Address," *Dartmouth Alumni Magazine* July, pp. 14–16.

1956. "A Talk for Students" (Sarah Lawrence College, June 7, 1956), New York: Fund for the Republic, no pages.

1961. "Remarks on the Occasion of the Tagore Centenary," *Poetry* Nov., pp. 106–19.

1962a. "Between Prose and Verse," *Atlantic Monthly* Jan., pp. 51–54.

1962b. "Playful Talk," *Proceedings of the American Academy of Arts and Letters and the National Institute of Arts and Letters*, second series, New York, pp. 180–89.

1963. "Robert Frost on 'Extravagance,'" *Dartmouth Alumni Magazine* Mar., pp. 21–24.

Howarth, Herbert

1966. "Frost in a Period Setting," *Southern Review* n. s. Oct., pp. 789–99.

Lathem, Edward Connery

1966. (editor) "An Uncompleted Revision of 'Education by Poetry,'" Hanover: Dartmouth Publications.

Mulder, William

1955. "Freedom and Form: Robert Frost's Double Discipline," *South Atlantic Quarterly* July, pp. 386–93.

Newdick, Robert S.

1937a. "Robert Frost and the Dramatic," *New England Quarterly* June, pp. 262–69.

1937b. "Robert Frost and the Sound of Sense," *American Literature* Nov., pp. 289–300.

1940. "Robert Frost's Other Harmony," *Sewanee Review* Summer, pp. 409–18.

Thompson, Lawrance

1942. *Fire and Ice: The Art and Thought of Robert Frost*. New York: Henry Holt.

1964. (editor) *Selected Letters of Robert Frost*. New York: Holt, Rinehart and Winston.

1970. *Robert Frost: The Years of Triumph, 1915–1938*. New York: Holt, Rinehart and Winston.

Vander Ven, Tom

1973. "Robert Frost's Dramatic Principle of 'Oversound,'" *American Literature* May, pp. 238–51.

Willige, Eckhart

1961. "Formal Devices in Robert Frost's Short Poems," *Georgia Review* Fall, pp. 324–30.

Selected Additional Readings

Barry, Elaine
   1973. (editor) *Robert Frost on Writing.* New Brunswick, N.J.:
   Rutgers Univ. Pr.
Borroff, Marie
   1971. "Robert Frost's New Testament: Language and Form,"
   Modern Philology Aug., pp. 36–56.
Carlson, Eric W.
   1962. "Robert Frost on 'Vocal Imagination, the Merger of Form
   and Content,'" *American Literature* Jan., pp. 519–22.
Ciardi, John
   1958. "Robert Frost: The Way to the Poem," *Saturday Review
   of Literature* Apr. 12, pp. 13–15, 65.
Cook, Reginald L.
   1947. "Poet in the Mountains," *Western Review* Spring, pp. 175–
   81.
   1959. *The Dimensions of Robert Frost.* New York: Rinehart.
Dowell, Peter W.
   1969. "Counter-Images and Their Function in the Poetry of
   Robert Frost," *Tennessee Studies in Literature*, pp. 15–30.
Frost, Robert
   1938. "What Became of New England?" (Commencement Address, Oberlin College, June 8, 1937), *Oberlin Alumni Magazine*
   May.
   1957. "Introduction" to *A Swinger of Birches: A Portrait of
   Robert Frost*, by Sidney Cox, pp. vii–viii. New York: New York
   Univ. Pr.
   1966. *Twilight: A Facsimile*, Charlottesville, Va.: Clifton Waller
   Barrett Library.
Geyer, C. W.
   1971. "A Poulterer's Pleasure: Robert Frost as Prose Humor-
   ist," *Studies in Short Fiction* Fall, pp. 589–99.
Greiner, Donald J.
   1969. *Guide to Robert Frost.* Columbus, Ohio: Charles E. Merrill.
   1970. "On Teaching Robert Frost's 'Sentence Sounds,'" *English
   Record* Oct., pp. 11–14.
   1973. "The Use of Irony in Robert Frost," *South Atlantic Bulletin* May, pp. 52–60.
   1974. "Robert Frost's Dark Woods and the Function of Metaphor," in *Frost: Centennial Essays*, pp. 373–88. Hattiesburg:
   Univ. and College Pr. of Mississippi.
Haynes, Donald T.
   1972. "The Narrative Unity of *A Boy's Will*," *PMLA* May, pp.
   452–64.

Isaacs, Emily Elizabeth
1962. *An Introduction to Robert Frost.* Denver: Alan Swallow.
Lathem, Edward Connery
1959. (editor) "Freshman Days," *Dartmouth Alumni Magazine* Mar., pp. 17–22.
1966. (editor) *Interviews with Robert Frost.* New York: Holt, Rinehart and Winston.
1971. *Concordance to the Poetry of Robert Frost.* New York: Holt, Rinehart and Winston.
Napier, John T.
1957. "A Momentary Stay against Confusion," *Virginia Quarterly Review* Summer, pp. 378–94.
Nelson, James
1958. (editor) "Robert Frost," an interview with Bela Kornitzer, in *Wisdom: Conversations with the Elder Wise Men of Our Day*, pp. 13–23. New York: Norton.
Perrine, Laurence
1971. "Frost's 'The Mountain': Concerning Poetry," *Concerning Poetry* Spring, pp. 5–11.
Sohn, David A., and Richard H. Tyre
1967. *Frost, the Poet and His Poetry.* New York: Holt, Rinehart and Winston.
Thompson, Lawrance
1959 (rev. 1967). *Robert Frost.* Minneapolis: Univ. of Minnesota Pr.

Additional Study Guides

Bibliographies and Checklists

Anonymous
1938. *An Exhibition of the Work of Robert Frost.* Meadville, Pa.: Allegheny College.
Anonymous
1963. *Robert Frost, His Poems, Portraits, and Printers, 1913–1963: A Comprehensive Exhibit.* Lake Forest, Ill.: Lake Forest Academy.
Anonymous
1966. *Robert Frost: 1874–1963:* An exhibition of books, manuscripts and memorabilia arranged in honor of the Poetry Society of Virginia on the occasion of their meeting in Charlottesville. Charlottesville, Va.: Barrett Library.
Boutell, H. S.
1930. "A Bibliography of Robert Frost," *Colophon* May.
Byers, Edna Hanley
1963. *Robert Frost at Agnes Scott College.* Decatur, Ga.: Mc-Cain Library.
Clymer, W. B. Shubrick, and Charles R. Green
1937. *Robert Frost: A Bibliography.* Amherst: Jones Library.
Cook, Reginald L.
1969. "Robert Frost," in *Sixteen Modern American Authors: A Survey of Research and Criticism,* ed. Jackson R. Bryer, pp. 239–73. Durham: Duke Univ. Pr.
Crane, Joan St. C.
1974. *A Descriptive Catalog of Books and Manuscripts in the Clifton Waller Barrett Library, University of Virginia.* Charlottesville: Univ. Pr. of Virginia.
Greiner, Donald J.
1969. *Checklist of Robert Frost.* Columbus, Ohio: Charles E. Merrill.
Melcher, F. S.
1930. "Robert Frost and His Books," *Colophon* May, pp. 1–7.
Mertins, Louis and Esther
1947. *The Intervals of Robert Frost: A Critical Bibliography.* Berkeley: Univ. of California Pr.

Nash, Roy
   1944. (editor) *Fifty Years of Robert Frost: A Catalogue of the
   Exhibition held in Baker Library in the Autumn of 1943.*
   Hanover: Dartmouth College Library.
Newdick, Robert
   1936. "Robert Frost, Teacher and Educator: An Annotated
   Bibliography," *Journal of Higher Education* June, pp. 342–44.
   1936. "Bibliographies and Exhibits of the Work of Robert Frost,"
   Amherst Graduates' Quarterly Nov., pp. 79–80.
   1937. "Foreign Response to Robert Frost," *Colophon* Winter,
   pp. 289–90.
Parameswaran, Uma
   1967. "Robert Frost, A Bibliography of Articles and Books,
   1958–64," *Bulletin of Bibliography* pp. 46–48, 58, 69, 72.
Thompson, Lawrance
   1936. *Robert Frost: A Chronological Survey:* Compiled in connection with exhibit of his work at the Olin Memorial Library,
   Wesleyan University, April 1936. Middletown, Conn.: Olin
   Memorial Library.
Untermeyer, Louis
   1964. *Robert Frost, A Backward Look.* Washington, D.C.: Library of Congress.
West, Herbert Faulkner
   1947. "My Robert Frost Collection," in *The Mind on the Wing:
   A Book for Readers and Collectors.* New York: Coward.

Collections of Essays and Criticism

Cox, James M.
   1962. (editor) *Robert Frost: A Collection of Critical Essays.*
   Englewood Cliffs, N.J.: Prentice-Hall.
Greenberg, Robert A., and James G. Hepburn
   1961. (editors) *Robert Frost: An Introduction.* New York: Holt,
   Rinehart and Winston.
Simpson, Lewis P.
   1971. (editor) *Profile of Robert Frost.* Columbus, Ohio: Charles
   E. Merrill.
Tharpe, Jac L., and Gordon Weaver
   1974. (editors) *Frost: Centennial Essays.* Hattiesburg: Univ.
   and College Pr. of Mississippi.
Thornton, Richard
   1937. (editor) *Recognition of Robert Frost: Twenty-fifth An-
   niversary.* New York: Holt.

Books and Articles

Anonymous
    1946. "The Heritage of the English-Speaking Peoples and Their
    Responsibility." Gambier, Ohio: Kenyon College.
Ball State University Forum
    1970. A Frost issue, Winter.
Doyle, John Robert
    1962. *The Poetry of Robert Frost: An Analysis.* New York:
    Hafner.
Ford, Caroline
    1935. *The Less Travelled Road.* Cambridge: Harvard Univ. Pr.
New Hampshire Troubadour
    1946. A Frost issue, Nov.
South Carolina Review
    1974. A Frost issue, Fall.
Southern Review
    1966. A Frost issue, n.s. Oct.

Index

Names, books, and essays listed only in the References at the conclusion of each chapter are not included in the Index.

Abbott, Margaret, 3, 4
Abercrombie, Lascelles, 13, 23, 37, 50, 70, 73–74, 75, 76, 77, 226, 281
Academy, 70, 71
Adams, Frederick B.: *To Russia with Frost*, 54
Addison, Joseph, 257
Akhmatova, Anna, 54
Alexandria, 74
Alexeiev, Michael, 54
Allen, Hervey, 16
Alyansky, S. M., 52
American Academy of Arts and Letters: 110, 278; *Proceedings* of, 278
American Academy of Poets, 259
American Libraries, 200
American Literature, 123, 157, 173, 283, 284, 294
American Poetry, 197
American Quarterly, 173, 199, 235, 240
American Review of Reviews, 84
American Scholar, 121, 211
Amherst College, 6, 24, 31, 41, 68, 110, 265–66, 282
Amherst Graduates' Quarterly, 254, 256, 267
Amherst Student, 13, 265–67
Anderson, Margaret Bartlett: 6; *Robert Frost and John Bartlett: The Record of a Friendship*, 3–6, 10, 12
Anderson, Maxwell, 283
Anderson, Sherwood, 98, 185
Appalachia, 220
Arnold, Matthew, 32–33
Arvin, Newton: 114–15, 116, 118,

165; "The House of Pain: Emerson and the Tragic Sense," 164
Athenaeum: "Notices of New Books," 71
Atlantic Monthly, 40, 77, 78, 84, 185, 253, 273, 277
Auden, W. H., 69, 119, 134, 213–14

Babbitt, Irving, 19, 20, 102, 177–79
Baker, Carlos: "Frost on the Pumpkin," 215–17
Bartlett, John: 3, 4–5, 8, 19, 20, 71, 249, 293; Frost's attempt to manipulate, 5, 72; "Notes on Conversations," 4
Bartlett, Margaret, 71
Baxter, Sylvester, 83–84
Baym, Nina: 239; "An Approach to Robert Frost's Nature Poetry," 235–37
Beach, Joseph Warren: 216, 217, 222; *The Concept of Nature in Nineteenth-Century English Poetry*, 210–11
Beal, Fred: *A Proletarian Journey*, 270
Bellamy, Edward: *Looking Backward*, 23
Benét, Stephen Vincent, 113, 114
Bergson, Henri, 39
Berra, Yogi, 263
Bible, 32, 155, 174, 271
Biblia, 270, 295
Blackmur, R. P., 114, 117–18, 123, 163
Blake, Harrison, 171
Bogan, Louise: 127; *Achievement in American Poetry: 1900–1950*, 122–23

Bookman, 75
Bort, Barry D.: "Frost and the Deeper Vision," 234–35
Boston Herald, 83
Boston Transcript, 68, 82, 84–85, 283
Bowdoin College, 43
Boyer, Ken, 263
Boynton, Percy H.: 69; *Some Contemporary Americans,* 87, 100–102
Braithwaite, W. S.: 7, 94, 282; "Poet of New England," 84–85, 283
Bread Loaf, 268, 272, 273, 277, 278
Bridges, Robert: 23; Frost's criticism of, 13
British Columbia, 4–5
Brooke, Rupert, 50
Brooks, Cleanth: *Modern Poetry and the Tradition,* 284–85
Brower, Reuben: 166, 168; *The Poetry of Robert Frost: Constellations of Intention,* 146–50
Brown, Alice, 83
Brown, Warren R., 13
Browne, George H., 91–92
Brownson, Orestes, 201
Bruce, Robert, 104
Bryant, William Cullen, 59, 186
Bucknell Review, 292

California: 30, 45, 208; San Francisco, 19, 37, 88, 103
California, University of, at Berkeley, 30
Cambridge University, 130
Camus, Albert, 130
Canada, 72, 179
Carpenter, Frederic I., 111, 112–13, 114, 117
Carroll, Gladys Hasty: "New England Sees It Through," 184–86
Carruth, Hayden: "The New England Tradition," 200–203
Cather, Willa, 208
Century Magazine, 99
Cestre, Charles: 184; "Amy Lowell, Robert Frost, and Edwin Arlington Robinson," 181–84
Chamberlain, William: "The Emersonianism of Robert Frost," 167–69
Christian Science Monitor, 260–61, 283
Civil War, 187

Claremont Quarterly, 290
Cleghorn, Sarah N.: *Threescore,* 269–70
Coffin, Robert P. Tristram: 239; *New Poetry of New England: Frost and Robinson,* 186–90
Coleridge, Samuel Taylor, 235
Colophon, 67
Colum, Padraic, 20, 79–80, 92
Columbia University, 110
Connecticut Review, 245
The Conquest of Mexico, 25
Cook, Reginald L.: 28, 163, 169, 173; "Emerson and Frost: A Parallel of Seers," 160–62; "Frost on Frost: The Making of Poems," 288–89; "A Parallel of Parablists: Thoreau and Frost," 170–73; "Robert Frost's Asides on His Poetry," 288
Coolidge, Calvin, 116
Cournos, John, 75
Coursen, Herbert R., Jr.: "A Dramatic Necessity: The Poetry of Robert Frost," 291–92
Cowley, Malcolm: 119, 122, 124, 125, 126, 130, 132, 142, 154, 159, 190, 192, 203; "The Case against Mr. Frost," 120–21, 159–60
Cox, Hyde: (co-ed.) *Selected Prose of Robert Frost,* 250–67, 270, 279, 284
Cox, James M.: "Robert Frost and the Edge of the Clearing," 195–97
Cox, Sidney: 13, 19, 20, 69, 86, 239; "New England and Robert Frost," 183–84; *Robert Frost: Original "Ordinary Man",* 44–46; *A Swinger of Birches: A Portrait of Robert Frost,* 44, 45, 46–49
Crane, Hart, 197–98
cummings, e. e., 189

Dabbs, J. McBride: 217, 218, 245; "Robert Frost and the Dark Woods," 208–10
Daedalus, 151
Dartmouth College: 26, 37, 38, 103, 256, 274, 279; *Dartmouth Alumni Magazine,* 274, 279, 295
Darwin, Charles: 122, 136, 207, 213, 223, 232, 235, 241, 246; *The Voyage of the Beagle,* 170
Davies, W. H., 221

Davison, Wilfred, 268–69
de la Mare, Walter, 30
Deerslayer, 239
Dendinger, Lloyd N.: "The Irra-
tional Appeal of Frost's Dark
Deep Woods," 239–40
Denmark, 19
Derry, N. H.: 5, 18, 20, 28, 29, 32–
34, 282
Derry News, 5
De Voto, Bernard, 118–19
Dial, 83
Dickinson, Emily, 166, 241, 243
Discourse: A Review of the Lib-
eral Arts, 237
Donne, John, 293
Donoghue, Denis: 134–36; Con-
noisseurs of Chaos, 135–36
Dos Passos, John, 189
Dougherty, James P.: "Robert
Frost's 'Directive' to the Wilder-
ness," 173, 174–76
Douglas, Norman: Experiments, 71
Dreiser, Theodore, 98, 185
Dudley, Dorothy, 100
Duvall, S. P. C.: 175, 176; "Robert
Frost's 'Directive' out of Wal-
den," 173–74

East Berlin, 53
Eastman, Blanche Rankin, 29
Eberhart, Richard, 212
Edwards, Jonathan, 241, 263
Einstein, Albert, 224
Eliot, T. S.: 14, 21, 58, 102, 109,
118, 119, 121, 130, 133, 134, 135,
136, 151, 189, 193, 194, 195, 228,
230, 283, 293, 294; "The Hollow
Men," 119; The Wasteland, 174,
175
Elizabethan Studies and Other Es-
says, 190
Elliott, G. R.: 69, 87, 93–95, 97, 99,
198; "The Neighborliness of
Robert Frost," 93–94, 155
Elsbree, Langdon: "Frost and the
Isolation of Man," 290–91
Emerson, Ralph Waldo: 39, 57, 59,
115, 120, 121, 124–26, 127, 250,
277, 284, 290; affinity with Frost,
see chapters 4 and 5; "Brahma,"
148, 151, 264, 276; "Days," 164;
"Experience," 164; "Fate," 158;
"Monadnock," 151, 156; "Na-
ture," 153, 161, 164, 179; "The
Poet," 157, 199; "The Rhodora,"

148, 149, 163; "Self-Reliance,"
154, 157; "Uriel," 148, 152;
"Woodnotes," 163
Emerson Society Quarterly, 168,
177
England: 12, 20, 23, 31, 34, 35, 39,
40, 59, 66, 68, 72, 73, 80, 81, 82,
84, 85, 86, 87, 88, 92, 98, 103, 109,
130; see also Frost, trip to En-
gland
Engle, Paul, 69
English Journal, 208
English Review, 71, 76
Essays in Criticism, 230
Eutushenko, Evgeny, 52, 53, 54

Farrar, John: "Robert Frost and
Other Green Mountain Writ-
ers," 208
Faulkner, William: 109, 143, 196,
241; "The Bear," 239
Ferber, Edna, 208
Feuillerat, Albert, 69
Firkins, O. W., 89–90, 91
Fitzgerald, F. Scott, 109
Flanders, Helen Hartness: Ballads
Migrant in New England, 257
Flint, F. S., 13, 71–72, 78
Florida, 17
Ford, Ford Madox (Hueffer), 23,
74–75, 76, 77, 293
Foster, Charles Howell: "Robert
Frost and the New England Tra-
dition," 190–92
France, 97, 99
Franconia, N. H., 42
Frank, Waldo: Our America, 97–
99, 102
Franklin, Benjamin, 175, 263
Frazer, J. G.: 213; The Golden
Bough, 119
Freeman, John, 80–81
Freud, Sigmund, 112, 120, 122, 241
Frost, Carol, 9, 16, 17, 27, 28, 42
Frost, Charles, 11, 19
Frost, Elinor (White): 9, 13, 14,
19, 22, 23, 24, 25, 27, 28, 32, 35,
36, 38–39, 41, 42–43, 45, 59, 71,
82, 274; Frost's contradictory
statements about, 9, 17, 89; let-
ters of, 16–17; valedictory address
of ("Conversation as a Force in
Life"), 24
Frost, Irma, 42
Frost, Isabelle Moodie: 27, 29, 36,
37, 151; "The Artist's Motive,"

37; *The Land of Crystal,* 37
Frost, Jeanie, 9, 27, 42, 238
Frost, Lesley (Mrs. Lesley Frost
Ballantine): 14, 16, 17, 18, 28, 38,
42; foreword to *Family Letters
of Robert and Elinor Frost,* 14;
(ed.) *New Hampshire's Child:
The Derry Journals of Robert
Frost,* 31–34
Frost, Lillian LaBatt, 17, 28, 42
Frost, Marjorie, 9, 27, 42
Frost, Robert: ancestors of, 19, 36,
38, 81–82, 84; as teacher, 15, 23–
24, 26, 32–33, 41–42, 48; biographies of, 18–44, 55; birthdate, 10,
59, 88; classicist, 20, 74, 102; comments on literature, 7–8, 16, 48,
56–57, *see* chapter 6; complains
about collection of his letters, 2;
criticism of other writers, 39, 43;
7 (Edgar Lee Masters, James Oppenheim, Amy Lowell, Wallace
Stevens, Carl Sandburg), 9 (Amy
Lowell), 13 (Ezra Pound, Robert
Bridges), 30 (Edgar Lee Masters), 47 (Henrik Ibsen, George
Bernard Shaw, Wilfred Gibson),
59 (Edwin Arlington Robinson);
difficulty in finding publication,
59, 66–67, 71, 72, 77–78, 79, 81,
86, 92, 101, 264–65, 273; early
criticism of, 66–108; friend and
family man, 4–6, 7, 9, 16–17,
32–34; humor of, 8, 42, 46–48, 49,
50, 73, 76, 78, 82, 83, 87, 89, 94–
95, 97, 100, 102, 187, 191; letters
of, 2–18, 35; literary heritage of,
141–206; memoirs of, 44–60; modernity of, 118–20, 126–30, 133–34,
136, 137, 138, 229–30; nature poet,
69, 83, 123–24, 126, 129, 133, 145–
47, 148–50, 158, 164, 165–66, 172–
73, 175, 207–48; negative criticism of, 105, 109–40; "new humanist," 19, 20, 102, 177–79; politics of, 8, 23, 53, 114–17, 120–21,
122, 124, 153–56, 160, 162, 191–
92, 269; public mask of, 1–3, 7,
11, 18, 34–36, 40, 41, 46, 49, 57–
58, 60, 84, 101, 135, 136, 193, 195,
208; reaction to criticism, 6, 7,
29–30, 36–37, 58, 59, 75, 86, 89;
religious beliefs of, 42, 43, 46, 47,
124–25, 160, 217; self-appraisals,
6, 12; sentence sounds, 4, 5, 13,
47, 73, 74, 75, 77, 80, 89, 91, 97,

99, 103, 104, 111, 130, 144, 156,
167, *see* chapter 6; tension in marriage, 23, 27, 34–35, 36, 38–39,
41, 42–43, 58, 89; trip to Dismal
Swamp, 22, 26, 38–39; 55; trip to
England, 12, 19–20, 23, 31, 34, 39,
40, 59, 68, 84, 85, 86, 87, 88, 92, 103,
109, *see* England; use of metaphor and analogy, 161–65, 170–
73, 174, 220, 225–28, *see* chapter
6; valedictory address of ("A Monument to After-Thought Unveiled"), 32, 250

BOOKS OF POETRY

Aforesaid, 264
A Boy's Will, 5, 10, 13, 28, 39, 59,
66, 67, 70, 71, 72, 80, 81, 82, 89,
91, 93, 96, 104, 105, 115, 141, 148,
185, 193, 194, 218, 219, 230, 282
Collected Poems (1930), 111, 112
Collected Poems (1949), 264
A Further Range, 28, 114–18, 186,
198, 220, 269, 271
In the Clearing, 105, 220, 280
A Masque of Mercy, 124, 128, 245,
267
A Masque of Reason, 124, 128, 224,
245, 261, 262
Mountain Interval, 66, 69, 79, 80,
88, 92, 95, 98, 103, 104, 123, 138,
220, 258
New Hampshire, 66, 95, 100, 104,
123, 158, 282
North of Boston, 21, 37, 66, 70, 72,
73, 74, 75, 76, 77, 79, 80, 82, 83,
85, 87, 88, 89, 90, 91, 93, 95, 98,
104, 111, 122, 123, 127, 130, 138,
185, 194–95, 213, 230, 270, 271,
290
Selected Poems, 69
Steeple Bush, 124, 128, 137, 198
Twilight, 38
West-Running Brook, 68, 123, 220
A Witness Tree, 124, 137, 194, 293

PLAYS

The Cow's in the Corn, 31, 282,
A Way Out, 250–51, 281, 282, 283

POEMS

"Acquainted with the Night," 122,
128, 135, 202, 288
"After Apple-Picking," 128, 135,
215, 228, 285, 292
"The Aim Was Song," 16

"All Revelation," 237, 238, 245
"At Woodward's Gardens," 158, 159
"Auspex," 23
"The Ax-Helve," 69, 179–80, 191
"The Bear," 124, 125
"The Bearer of Evil Tidings," 125
"Beech," 230
"Bereft," 129, 172, 240, 242
"Birches," 47, 79, 92, 128, 171, 172, 191, 195, 219, 275, 284, 285
"The Black Cottage," 34, 39
"Blueberries," 222
"A Boundless Moment," 150, 236, 238
"Bravado," 136
"A Brook in the City," 178, 222
"Brown's Descent," 102
"Build Soil," 94, 115, 117, 120, 125, 132, 155, 186, 195, 221, 276
"Canis Major," 285
"The Census-Taker," 95, 187, 233
"Christmas Trees," 7
"Class Hymn," 31
"Closed for Good," 288
"The Code," 76, 82, 88, 92, 103, 285
"Come In," 137, 149, 212, 215, 238, 244
"A Considerable Speck," 121, 122
"A Cow in Apple Time," 102
"The Death of the Hired Man," 73, 76, 78, 82, 85–86, 88, 96, 103, 128, 131, 138, 183, 290
"The Demiurge's Laugh," 39, 171, 219
"Departmental," 167, 275
"Desert Places," 117, 122, 172, 191, 212–13, 240, 245
"Design," 118, 129, 136, 224, 240
"Directive," 133, 137, 168, 169, 172, 173–76, 195, 197, 256
"The Draft Horse," 220
"A Dream Pang," 219
"Dust of Snow," 56, 132, 234
"The Egg and the Machine," 124
"An Encounter," 245
"The Exposed Nest," 155, 233
"The Fear," 50, 76, 96, 97, 135, 138, 222, 290
"Fire and Ice," 134, 135
"Flower-Gathering," 83, 92, 282
"For Once, Then, Something," 42, 181, 202, 224, 235, 287
"A Fountain, a Bottle, a Donkey's Ears and Some Books," 221

"Gathering Leaves," 132
"Genealogical," 11, 19
"The Generations of Men," 79, 102
"The Gift Outright," 110, 135, 137, 275, 279, 293
"Going for Water," 194, 219
"Good-By and Keep Cold," 217, 220
"Happiness Makes Up in Height for What It Lacks in Length," 194
"The Hill Wife," 80, 125, 136, 200, 202
"Home Burial," 39, 76, 77, 78, 80, 86, 131, 138, 183, 194, 195, 200, 222, 290
"The Housekeeper," 172, 290
"A Hundred Collars," 50, 76, 78, 80, 88, 102, 103
"Hyla Brook," 34, 231, 232, 293
"In Equal Sacrifice," 104
"In Neglect," 81
"In Time of Cloudburst," 238
"In Winter in the Woods Alone," 220
"Into My Own," 103, 209, 245
"John L. Sullivan Enters Heaven," 8, 50
"La Noche Triste," 22, 25, 31
"The Last Mowing," 197
"A Late Walk," 245
"A Leaf Treader," 219, 222, 244
"Leaves Compared with Flowers," 219
"The Lesson for Today," 245
"Lodged," 172, 291
"A Lone Striker," 115, 124, 178, 186, 222, 271
"Love and a Question," 155
"The Lure of the West," 4
"The Master Speed," 22, 116
"Mending Wall," 75, 78, 92, 94, 96, 103, 128, 129, 228, 240, 275, 285, 288
"The Most of It," 126, 127, 128, 129, 135, 136, 137, 146, 216, 221, 235, 238, 243, 246, 280
"The Mountain," 97, 103, 138, 150, 221, 288
"Mowing," 92, 93, 95, 149
"My Butterfly," 25, 69, 283
"The Need of Being Versed in Country Things," 149, 212, 216, 231, 243
"Neither Far Out Nor In Deep," 118, 132, 190, 202, 242

"Never Again Would Birds' Song Be the Same," 280
"New Hampshire," 27, 59, 105, 120, 128
"Nothing Gold Can Stay," 31
"November," 137, 291
"Now Close the Windows," 209
"An Old Man's Winter Night," 122, 129, 135, 136, 197, 212, 235
"On a Tree Fallen Across the Road," 234
"On Going Unnoticed," 126, 216
"Once by the Pacific," 129, 172, 216, 240, 242, 292
"One Step Backward Taken," 243
"The Onset," 137, 138, 236
"Our Hold on the Planet," 136, 233
"Out, Out," 135, 191, 233, 240
"The Oven Bird," 163, 231–32
"Pan with Us," 149, 219
"Parting," 31
"A Passing Glimpse," 235
"The Pasture," 56, 221, 227
"Paul's Wife," 95, 176–77
"A Peck of Gold," 288
"Pertinax," 136
"Plowmen," 16
"Provide, Provide," 116, 118, 135
"The Rabbit-Hunter," 33, 137, 220, 291
"Range-Finding," 25, 171
"A Record Stride," 293
"Reluctance," 83, 93, 254
"The Road Not Taken," 41, 79, 125, 129, 178, 222
"A Roadside Stand," 155, 195, 234
"The Rose Family," 291
"Rose Pogonias," 149
"The Runaway," 101
"Sand Dunes," 158, 237
"The Self-Seeker," 79, 290
"A Servant to Servants," 79, 131, 135, 138, 172, 183, 194, 195, 197, 238, 290
"The Seven Arts," 7
"The Silken Tent," 129, 131, 137, 162, 289
"Snow," 25, 92, 95, 138, 188, 282
"A Soldier," 25
"Song of the Wave," 31
"The Sound of Trees," 79, 103, 125, 209, 219
"Spring Pools," 195, 246
"A Star in a Stone-Boat," 293
"The Star-Splitter," 158
"Stopping by Woods on a Snowy Evening," 35, 56, 128, 149, 188, 195, 197, 207, 210, 214–15, 218-19, 225, 239, 240, 244, 253, 275, 280, 284, 287, 288
"Storm Fear," 33, 92, 212, 223, 238
"The Strong Are Saying Nothing," 202, 224
"The Subverted Flower," 133, 137
"Take Something Like a Star," 137
"There Are Roughly Zones," 222
"The Times Table," 233
"To a Thinker," 115, 125
"The Traitor," 31
"The Trial by Existence," 24, 71, 104, 224
"A Tuft of Flowers," 93, 171
"Two Look at Two," 217, 238, 246
"Two Tramps in Mud Time," 115, 121, 122, 178, 285
"The Vanishing Red," 202
"The Vantage Point," 93, 219
"Warning," 24
"West-Running Brook," 22, 47, 123, 124, 168, 191, 211, 236, 238, 239, 266
"The White-Tailed Hornet," 158
"Why Wait for Science?," 289
"A Winter Eden," 288
"The Witch of Coös," 95, 191, 288
"The Wood-Pile," 76, 77, 92, 145, 171, 230–31, 233, 236, 285
"A Young Birch," 221

PROSE

"Between Prose and Verse," 277–78
"The Commencement Address" (Dartmouth), 274–75
"The Constant Symbol," 253–54, 285, 289
"The Doctrine of Excursions: A Preface," 272–73
"Education by Poetry: A Meditative Monologue," 153, 161–62, 251, 253, 254–57, 268, 278, 280, 285, 289
"The Figure a Poem Makes," 168, 251–53, 254, 255, 266, 289
"The Hear-Say Ballad," 257–58
"Introduction" to The Arts Anthology: Dartmouth Verse, 1925, 267–68, 272
"Introduction" to Edwin Arlington Robinson, King Jasper, 154, 258–60, 261, 276, 280, 289
"Introduction" to Sarah N. Cleghorn, Threescore, 269–70

"Introduction" to Sidney Cox, *A Swinger of Birches: A Portrait of Robert Frost*, 45, 46
"Letter to the *Amherst Student*," 265–66
"Maturity No Object," 257, 267
"On Emerson," 151–52
"Perfect Day—A Day of Prowess," 262, 263–64, 271
"Playful Talk," 278–79
"Poet—One of the Truest," 267
"Poetry and School," 268, 273–74
"The Poetry of Amy Lowell," 258, 260–61
"The Poet's Next of Kin in a College," 270, 271–72
"Poverty and Poetry," 270–71
"Preface" to *Memoirs of the Notorious Stephen Burroughs*, 262–63
"Preface" to *A Way Out*, 250–51, 281
"The Prerequisites," 264, 274, 276
"Remarks Accepting the Gold Medal of the National Institute of Arts and Letters," 264–65, 273
"Remarks on the Dedication of the Wilfred Davison Memorial Library," 268–69
"Remarks on the Occasion of the Tagore Centenary," 276–77
"Robert Frost on 'Extravagance,' " 279–80
"A Romantic Chasm," 261–62, 271
Selected Prose of Robert Frost, 250 67
"A Sermon," 267
"A Talk for Students" (Sarah Lawrence), 275–76
"Thoreau's 'Walden': A Discussion between Robert Frost and Reginald Cook," 169–70
"A Tribute to Wordsworth," 142–43
Frost, William Prescott, 26, 29

Garland, Hamlin, 30
Garnett, Edward, 70, 77–78, 80, 87, 91, 281
George, Henry, 19, 23
Georgia Review, 215, 291
Georgian poets, 50, 58, 115, 131, 157, 210

Gerber, Philip: *Robert Frost*, 166–67
Gibson, Wilfred: 23, 50, 68, 93, 281; Frost's criticism of 47; "Simplicity and Sophistication," 75–76
Gloucester Journal, 68
Goethe, Johann Wolfgang von, 78, 208
Gould, Jean: 29, 38; *Robert Frost: The Aim Was Song*, 25–27
Grade, Arnold: 32–33; (ed.) *Family Letters of Robert and Elinor Frost*, 6, 14–18
Gregory, Horace, 114–16, 118
Greiner, Donald J.: "Confusion and Form: Robert Frost as Nature Poet," 237–39
Griffith, Clark: "Frost and the American View of Nature," 240–42
Guest, Edgar, 116

Haines, John W., 30, 68, 262
Harcourt, Alfred, 20, 40, 86
Harding, Walter: (ed.) *The Thoreau Centennial*, 170
Hardy, G. H., 57, 59
Hardy, Thomas: 143, 221, 222, 234; "The Darkling Thrush," 232
Harper's, 70, 90
Harvard Alumni Bulletin, 68
Harvard University: 24, 29, 37, 56, 68, 83, 103, 110, 157, 158; the Norton Lectures, 56, 68
Hawthorne, Nathaniel: 120, 142, 159, 160, 190–92, 202, 203; *American Notebooks*, 191; "The Old Apple Dealer," 191; *The Scarlet Letter*, 190, 239; "Snowflakes," 191
Haynes, Donald T.: "The Narrative Unity of *A Boy's Will*," 193
Hazlitt, William, 284
Hemingway, Ernest: 175; "Big Two-Hearted River," 239; Nick Adams, 240
Henderson, Alice C., 83, 87
Herrick, Robert, 293
Hicks, Granville: 127; "The World of Robert Frost," 111–12
Hillyer, Robert, 113–14
Hoffman, Daniel G.: *Paul Bunyan, Last of the Frontier Demigods*, 176; "Thoreau's 'Old Settler' and Frost's Paul Bunyan," 176–77

Holden, Raymond, 14, 41
Holmes, John, 68
Holmes, Oliver Wendell, 99, 185, 186, 201
Holt, Henry, 20, 86
Housman, A. E., 30
Howarth, Herbert: "Frost in a Period Setting," 292–94
Howe, Irving, 127-29
Howells, William Dean, 70, 90–91, 201
Hudson Review, 164
Hueffer, Ford Madox: see Ford, Ford Madox
Humphries, Rolfe: 114; "A Further Shrinking," 116–17
Hutchinson, Percy, 282

Ibsen, Henrik: Frost's criticism of, 47
Imagism: 21, 118, 252, 260, 261, 268; *Some Imagist Poets*, 252
Independent, 12, 22, 24, 69, 81, 91
Isaacs, J., 169
Ives, Charles, 201

Jackson, Andrew, 153, 154
James, Henry, 194, 195, 201, 202
James, William, 39, 157, 168, 169
Jamieson, Paul F.: "Robert Frost: Poet of Mountain Land," 220–21
Jarrell, Randall: 136; *Poetry and the Age*, 136; "To the Laodiceans," 109, 136
Jeffers, Robinson, 113, 222
Jefferson, Thomas, 152, 175
Jewett, Sarah Orne, 184–86
Job, 32
Johns Hopkins Alumni Magazine, 181
Johns Hopkins University, 186
Johnson, Samuel, 147
Johnson, Walter, 263
Jones, Llewellyn: *First Impressions*, 104–105
Joyce, James, 56, 189
Journal of American Folklore, 176

Kafka, Franz, 130
Kaskin, Ivan, 52
Keats, John, 6, 189
Kennedy, John F., 13, 110, 279
Kenyon Review, 126
Khrushchev, Nikita, 52, 53–54
Kilmer, Joyce: "Trees," 138
Kipling, Rudyard, 262

Landor, Walter Savage, 57

Langbaum, Robert: 216, 217, 221, 240; "The New Nature Poetry," 211–13
Lanier, Sidney, 81, 283
Lathem, Edward Connery: 256; (ed.) *Interviews with Robert Frost*, 84–85; (co-ed.) *Robert Frost and the Lawrence, Massachusetts, "High School Bulletin": The Beginning of a Literary Career*, 31–32, 250; (co-ed.) *Selected Prose of Robert Frost*, 250–67, 270, 279, 284
Lawrence, D. H., 129, 130
Lawrence (Mass.) *American*, 284
Lawrence (Mass.) *High School Bulletin*, 22, 31–32, 38, 250
Lawrence (Mass.) *Sentinel*, 29, 284
Lenin, Nikolai, 54
Leonard, William Ellery, 59
Lerner, Laurence: "An Essay on Pastoral," 230–31
Lewis, C. Day, 69, 119, 214
Lewis, Ed, 263, 272
Lewis, R. W. B., 175
Lewis, Sinclair, 185
Library of Congress, 51, 279
Lincoln, Abraham, 151
Lindsay, Vachel, 8, 49, 50
Listener, 169
Locke, John, 241
London: 66, 82, 84, 86, 130; see England and Frost, trip to England
London Mercury, 80
Longfellow, Henry Wadsworth, 59, 99, 156, 185, 186, 188, 197, 201
Lowell, Amy: 13, 25, 56, 59, 70, 83, 91, 92, 93, 98, 100, 102–3, 104, 105, 111, 181, 182, 250, 258, 260–61; Frost's criticism of, 7; *Tendencies in Modern American Poetry*, 9, 86–89, 103, 111, 260
Lowell, James Russell, 59, 87, 99, 111, 144, 185, 186, 192, 201
Lucretius, 148, 221, 223, 224, 243
Lynen, John: *The Pastoral Art of Robert Frost*, 143–46, 225-30, 231

MacKaye, Percy, 267
MacLeish, Archibald, 56, 283
MacVeagh, Lincoln, 20
Markham, Edwin, 69
Marlowe, Christopher: *Dr. Faustus*, 282

Marvell, Andrew, 231, 293
Masefield, John, 82, 83, 130
Massachusetts: 263; Boston, 83, 185, 201; Cambridge, 201; Concord, 170, 194, 201; Lawrence, 18, 38, 270
Massachusetts Review, 162, 231
Masses, 8
Masters, Edgar Lee: 59, 79–80, 91, 93, 98, 194; Frost's criticism of, 7, 30; *The Great Valley,* 92; *Spoon River Anthology,* 79, 194
Matthiessen, F. O.: *American Renaissance,* 164
Melcher, Frederic: "Robert Frost and His Books," 68
Melville, Herman: 175, 241; Ishmael, 176; Ahab, 241
Mencken, H. L., 262
Mertins, Louis: *The Intervals of Robert Frost,* 27; *Robert Frost: Life and Talks-Walking,* 27–31, 72
Merwin, W. S., 212
Michigan, 68
Michigan, University of, 24, 26, 41, 110
Midwest Quarterly, 234
Milton, John: *Comus,* 48, 282; "Lycidas," 227
Mitchell, Stewart, 113–14
Monro, Harold, 50, 77
Monteiro, George: "Redemption Through Nature: A Recurring Theme in Thoreau, Frost and Richard Wilbur," 179–81
Montgomery, Marion: "Robert Frost and His Use of Barriers: Man vs. Nature Toward God," 217–18
Moody, William Vaughn, 159
Moore, Marianne, 212, 263
Moore, Merrill: "Poetic Agrarianism: Old Style," 186
More, Paul Elmer, 20
Morrison, Theodore: "Frost: Country Poet and Cosmopolitan Poet," 243–45
Mulder, William: "Freedom and Form: Robert Frost's Double Discipline," 289–90
Munson, Gorham B.: 22, 38, 177; "The Classicism of Robert Frost," 19; "Robert Frost," 20, 102; *Robert Frost: A Study in Sensibility and Good Sense,* 19–

21, 22, 102; "Robert Frost and the Humanistic Temper," 19
Nation, 89, 93, 117
Nation (London), 73
National Institute of Arts and Letters: 110, 264; *Bulletin* of, 264, 267, 273
New Deal, 122, 125, 154
New England: 35, 67, 73, 74, 86, 87, 88, 89, 91, 92, 98, 99, 100, 102, 103, 104, 105, 111, 112, 114, 115, 116, 120, 121, 122, 123, 279, 284; *see* chapters 4 and 5
New England Quarterly, 112, 113, 160, 281
New Hampshire: 3, 5, 32–34, 42, 44, 68, 157, 160, 228, 263; *see* Derry, Franconia, and Plymouth
New Masses, 116
New Mexico Quarterly, 183
New Poets of England and America, 257
New Republic, 40, 69, 70, 79, 87, 111, 114, 120, 127, 159, 190
New York, 21, 208
New York Times Book Review, 85, 86, 264
New York University, 110
Newdick, Robert: "Robert Frost and the Dramatic," 281–83; "Robert Frost's Other Harmony," 284; "Robert Frost and the Sound of Sense," 283–84
Nitchie, George W.: 225; *Human Values in the Poetry of Robert Frost,* 132–34, 221–24
Nobel Prize, 110
North Carolina, 22
Nutt, David (and Company), 5, 21, 28

Occidental College, 30
O'Donnell, W. G.: 196; "Robert Frost and New England: A Revaluation," 192–95
Ogilvie, John T.: 245; "From Woods to Stars: A Pattern of Imagery in Robert Frost's Poetry," 218–20
Olney, Marguerite: *Ballads Migrant in New England,* 257
Oppenheim, James: Frost's criticism of, 7
Outlook, 74
Ovid, 82

Paige, D. D.: (ed.) *The Letters of Ezra Pound*, 82
Palgrave's *Golden Treasury*, 24
Parsons, Thornton H.: "Thoreau, Frost, and the American Humanist Tradition," 177–79
Partisan Review, 114, 164, 213
Patmore, Coventry, 80
Payne, William Morton, 82–83
Pearce, Roy Harvey, 126–27, 129, 130, 134, 137
Pennsylvania, 74
Phillips Andover Mirror, 31
Pilgrim's Progress, 32
Pinkerton Academy, 3, 4, 29, 282
Planck, Max Karl, 223
Platonism, 152, 153, 154, 192, 286
Plymouth, N.H.: 44; Plymouth High School, 44; Plymouth Normal School, 44, 282
PMLA, 193
Poe, Edgar Allan: 56, 252; "The Philosophy of Composition," 252
Poetry, 25, 70, 81, 82, 83, 92, 100, 276
Poetry and Drama, 5, 50, 72, 77
Poetry Society of America: 40, 85, 110; *Bulletin* of, 85
Pound, Ezra: 16, 21, 23, 30, 39, 56, 70, 71, 84, 95, 102, 118, 119, 213, 293, 294; Frost's quarrel with, 13, 82, 85; support of Frost, 72, 81–82, 84–85
Princeton University, 20, 270
Pritchard, Walter, 282
Pritchard, William H.: "Diminished Nature," 231–32
Publisher's Weekly, 59
Pulitzer Prize, 110, 265, 281

Reeve, F. D.: *Robert Frost in Russia*, 51–54
Revue des deux mondes, 69
Rittenhouse, Jessie B., 85
Robbins, J. Albert: "America and the Poet: Whitman, Hart Crane and Frost," 197-98
Robinson, Edwin Arlington: 13, 59, 87–88, 95, 101, 113, 114, 159, 166, 181, 182, 185, 186–90, 199–200, 201, 202, 208, 242, 250; "Captain Craig," 199; "The Dark Hills," 258; *King Jasper*, 154, 258–61, 276, 280, 289; *The Man Against the Sky*, 258; "Miniver Cheevy," 258, 259; "Mr. Flood's Party," 258, 259; "New England," 258; *Tristram*, 258
Robinson Crusoe, 170
Robson, W. W.: "The Achievement of Robert Frost," 130–32
Roosevelt, Eleanor, 23
Rubenstein, Annette T.: "A Stay Against Confusion," 242–43
Russia: 51–54, 58; Moscow, 54, 58
Ryan, Alvan S.: 166, 168; "Frost and Emerson: Voice and Vision," 162–165

St. Armand, Barton L.: "The Power of Sympathy in the Poetry of Robinson and Frost: The 'Inside' vs. the 'Outside' Narrative," 199–200
St. Elizabeth's Hospital, 13
Saint Lawrence College, 38
Salinger, J. D., 175
Sampley, Arthur M.: "The Myth and the Quest: The Stature of Robert Frost," 224-25
Sandburg, Carl: 20, 56, 59; Frost's criticism of, 7
Sarah Lawrence College, 275
Saturday Review, 102, 118, 184
Science and Society, 242
Sedgewick, Ellery, 83, 84, 86
Sergeant, Elizabeth Shepley: 19, 25, 26, 29, 38, 68–69, 167; "Robert Frost: A Good Greek Out of New England," 21, 69; *Robert Frost: The Trial by Existence*, 21–25
Seven Arts, 8
Sewanee Review, 186, 284
Shakespeare, William, 32, 47, 189, 192, 231, 253, 282, 283
Shaw, George Bernard: Frost's criticism of, 47
Shelley, Percy Bysshe, 211, 231, 232, 235
Sheridan, Richard: *The Rivals*, 282; *The School for Scandal*, 48
Sidney, Philip: 231; *Arcadia*, 231
Smith, Henry Nash, 175
Smythe, Daniel: *Robert Frost Speaks*, 54–57
Snow, C. P.: *Variety of Men*, 57–59
Snow, Wilbert: "The Frost I Knew," 59–60; "New England in the New Poetry of America," 59

South Atlantic Quarterly, 217, 218, 224, 289
Southern Review, 130, 239, 292
Southey, Robert, 142
Spender, Stephen, 119
Spenser, Edmund, 189
Sports Illustrated, 263
Squires, Radcliffe: *The Major Themes of Robert Frost*, 165–66, 232–34
Stalin, Joseph, 57
Stedman, Edmund Clarence: (ed.) *An American Anthology*, 95
Steinbeck, John, 189, 242
Stevens, Wallace: 14, 109, 119, 133, 134, 135, 136, 212, 230, 241; Frost's criticism of, 7; "The Snow Man," 212
Street, Gabby, 263
Sullivan, John L., 8, 49–50
Surkov, Alexei, 52
Swedenborg, 37, 192
Swinburne, Algernon Charles, 117, 182
Synge, John Millington, 96

Tagore, Rabindranath, 276–77
Teasdale, Sara, 49
Temple, Johnny, 263
Tennyson, Alfred, 156, 182, 232
Theocritus, 74
Thomas, Dylan: 129, 130; "When all my five and country senses see," 230
Thomas, Edward, 13, 25, 40, 41, 68, 70, 76–77, 80, 87, 130, 178, 223, 262
Thompson, Lawrance: 14, 15, 23, 27, 28, 33–34, 44, 45, 46, 49, 51, 56, 60, 84, 168, 260, 261, 263, 281; evaluation of *The Letters of Robert Frost to Louis Untermeyer*, 7; evaluation of *Robert Frost: The Aim Was Song*, 25; evaluation of *Robert Frost: The Trial by Existence*, 22; official biographer of Robert Frost, 2, 17, 19, 34–44, 51, 167, 188; *Emerson and Frost: Critics of Their Times*, 152–56, 157; *Fire and Ice: The Art and Thought of Robert Frost*, 156–57, 285–88; *Robert Frost: The Early Years, 1874–1915*, 22, 34–39, 70, 141; *Robert Frost: The Years of Triumph, 1915–1938*, 19, 30, 39–

44, 94, 258; (ed.) *Selected Letters of Robert Frost*, 4, 6, 10–14, 16, 19, 35, 70, 71, 72, 75, 79, 81, 86, 87, 89, 91, 94, 110, 198, 249; (co-ed.) *Robert Frost and the Lawrence, Massachusetts, "High School Bulletin": The Beginnings of a Literary Career*, 31–32, 250
Thompson, Maurice, 69
Thoreau, Henry David: 39, 99, 121, 126, 222, 250; affinity with Frost, *see* chapter 4; *Journals*, 171, 191; "Life Without Principle," 178; *Walden*, 239, *see* chapter 4; *A Week on the Concord and Merrimack Rivers*, 171
Thornton, Richard: (ed.) *Recognition of Robert Frost*, 67–70, 71, 118, 214
Times Literary Supplement, 71, 72–73, 76, 77
Tolstoy, Leo, 54
Touchstone, 24
Traschen, Isadore: 132, 134, 136, 137, 138; "Robert Frost: Some Divisions in a Whole Man," 129–30
Trilling, Lionel: 165, 213; "A Speech on Robert Frost: A Cultural Episode," 164
Tufts University, 40, 110
Turney, Ida Virginia: *Paul Bunyan Comes West*, 176
Tvardovsky, Alexander, 52
Twain, Mark: 159, 185, 196; *Huckleberry Finn*, 239; *Tom Sawyer*, 101
Twentieth Century, 134

Untermeyer, Jean Starr, 23
Untermeyer, Louis: 13, 17, 20, 41, 69, 87, 89, 93, 98, 99, 101–2, 104, 198; Frost's attempt to manipulate, 8; *From Another World*, 6, 49–51; (ed.) *The Letters of Robert Frost to Louis Untermeyer*, 2, 6–9, 10, 16, 58, 89, 97; *The New Era in American Poetry*, 95–97, 101; *Robert Frost: A Backward Look*, 51

Van Doren, Carl: "The Soil of the Puritans, Robert Frost," 99–100
Van Doren, Mark: "The Permanence of Robert Frost," 67

Vander Ven, Tom: "Robert Frost's Dramatic Principle of 'Oversound,' " 294-95
Vergil, 157
Vermont, 170, 208, 270
Vinson, Robert S.: "The Roads of Robert Frost," 245-46
Virginia, 22
Virginia Quarterly Review, 94, 195
Virginia, University of, 4

Waggoner, Hyatt Howe: 168; "The Humanistic Idealism of Robert Frost," 157-59
Ward, Susan Hayes, 11, 12, 81
Ward, William Hayes, 12, 69, 283
Warren, Robert Penn: "The Themes of Robert Frost," 214-15
Washington, George, 151
Watts, Harold H.: 130; "Robert Frost and the Interrupted Dialogue," 123-24
Wellesley, 16
Wesleyan University, 21, 34, 59
West Germany, 54
Wheelock, John Hall, 95
Whicher, George F., 121-22
Whitman, Walt, 11, 75, 82, 84, 85, 91, 95, 98, 101, 113, 115, 167, 181, 185, 197, 198, 241
Whittier, John Greenleaf: 59, 87, 95, 115, 185, 186, 192; "Snow-Bound," 188
Wigglesworth, Michael: Day of Doom, 202

Wilbur, Richard: 179-81, 212; "Digging for China," 181; "Junk," 180
Wilde, Oscar: The Importance of Being Earnest, 48
William and Mary, College of, 110
Willige, Eckhart: "Formal Devices in Robert Frost's Short Poems," 291
Wilson, James Southall, 69
Wolcott, William A., 283
Wood, Charles Erskine Scott, 95
Wood, Clement: Poets of America, 102-104
Wordsworth, William: 32, 78, 80, 122, 131, 250, 293; affinity with Frost, 77, see chapters 4 and 5; "The Daffodils," 148; Lyrical Ballads, 293; "Michael," 131, 143; "Ode to Duty," 143; "The Prelude," 147; "Resolution and Independence," 122, 131, 145, 235; "Tintern Abbey," 147; "To a Butterfly," 147; "To a Cuckoo," 149
World War I, 8, 25, 77, 97
World War II, 114

Yale Review, 129, 192, 208, 243
Yeats, William Butler: 23, 30, 58, 71, 117, 119, 130, 133, 134, 135, 193, 213, 230: Cathleen ni Houlihan, 282; The Land of Heart's Desire, 282

Zenkenvich, Mikhail, 52